BUDDHIST THEOLOGY

Critical Reflections by Contemporary Buddhist Scholars

CURZON CRITICAL STUDIES IN BUDDHISM

General Editors:

Charles S. Prebish and Damien Keown

The Curzon Critical Studies in Buddhism Series is a comprehensive study of the Buddhist tradition. The series explores this complex and extensive tradition from a variety of perspectives, using a range of different methodologies.

The Series is diverse in its focus, including historical studies, textual translations and commentaries, sociological investigations, bibliographic studies, and considerations of religious practice as an expression of Buddhism's integral religiosity. It also presents materials on modern intellectual historical studies, including the role of Buddhist thought and scholarship in a contemporary, critical context and in the light of current social issues. The series is expansive and imaginative in scope, spanning more than two and a half millennia of Buddhist history. It is receptive to all research works that inform and advance our knowledge and understanding of the Buddhist tradition. The series maintains the highest standards of scholarship and promotes the application of innovative methodologies and research methods.

THE REFLEXIVE NATURE OF AWARENESS
A Tibetan Madhyamaka Defence
Paul Williams

BUDDHISM AND HUMAN RIGHTS
Edited by Damien Keown, Charles Prebish, Wayne Husted

ALTRUISM AND REALITY
Studies in the Philosophy of the Bodhicaryāvatāra
Paul Williams

WOMEN IN THE FOOTSTEPS OF THE BUDDHA
Kathryn R. Blackstone

THE RESONANCE OF EMPTINESS
A Buddhist Inspiration for Contemporary Psychotherapy
Gay Watson

IMAGING WISDOM
Seeing and Knowing in the Art of Indian Buddhism
Jacob N. Kinnard

AMERICAN BUDDHISM
Methods and Findings in Recent Scholarship
Edited by Duncan Ryuken Williams and Christopher Queen

PAIN AND ITS ENDING
The Four Noble Truths in the Theravāda Buddhist Canon
Carol S. Anderson

THE SOUND OF LIBERATING TRUTH
Buddhist-Christian Dialogues in Honor of Frederick J. Streng
Edited by Sallie B. King and Paul O. Ingram

BUDDHIST THEOLOGY
Critical Reflections by Contemporary Buddhist Scholars
Edited by Roger R. Jackson and John J. Makransky

BUDDHIST THEOLOGY

Critical Reflections by Contemporary Buddhist Scholars

edited by

Roger R. Jackson
and
John J. Makransky

CURZON

First Published in 2000
by Curzon Press
15 The Quadrant, Richmond
Surrey, TW9 1BP

Printed and bound in Great Britain by
TJ International, Padstow, Cornwall

British Library Cataloguing in Publication Data
A catalogue record of this book is available from the British Library

Library of Congress in Publication Data
A catalogue record for this book has been requested

ISBN 0–7007–1080–9 (Hbk)
ISBN 0–7007–1203–8 (Pbk)

PART III. CRITICAL RESPONSES

Table Of Contents

Preface

This volume had its genesis in a panel on "Buddhist Theology" in which the two of us (along with Rita Gross, José Cabezón, John Dunne, and Anne Klein) participated at the 1996 American Academy of Religion conference. The high attendance and warm response to the panel convinced us that the time was now right for scholars formed by Buddhist tradition, but also trained in the critical methods of the academy, to begin to offer their own perspectives to the ongoing contribution of Buddhism to the modern world.

By and large, scholars trained in Religious Studies (including Buddhist Studies) critically analyze the data of a religion at a distance from tradition, to develop theories of interest to the Western academy. By contrast, contemporary theologians who have been trained by and stand within a religious tradition use the same tools for a different purpose: to draw critically upon the resources of tradition to help it communicate in a new and authentic voice to the contemporary world.

The contributors to this volume are both academically trained scholars of Buddhism and Buddhists who have learned to interpret their world "dharmically" from traditional teachers within diverse communities of practice. Their learning and experience cover a variety of Asian Buddhist cultures, while their methods range from the historical, to the philosophical, to the sociological. As diverse as the contributors and their interests are, they share the broadly theological concern above, which distinguishes their approach from much of what has been written within the Religious Studies academy. Speaking from within Buddhist traditions as contemporary scholars, they employ two kinds of reflection: critically analyzing some aspect of Buddhist thought toward a new understanding in our time, or analyzing some aspect of contemporary thought from the critical perspective of Buddhism.

A number of texts have appeared in which Buddhist practitioners or scholars have written normatively on some aspect of Buddhism's relation to the modern world. Such texts often do involve an informed critical perspective on Buddhist or modern attitudes and ideas, but they are generally restricted to a particular subject-area, and often do not seek to think through the most fundamental theological questions: How are contemporary critical methods and Buddhist tradition to be wedded in a contemporary Buddhist mode of critical reflection? What are to be its proper sources of authority? How can it be applied with sensitivity to both the modern situation and the claims of Buddhist traditions? What methods are legitimately employed in the process?

It is these kinds of basic questions that our essayists address. Thus, while the collection includes many attempts to apply Buddhist theology to one or another modern situation, this application is undertaken against the background of a fundamental engagement with the basic questions of authority and method, modernity and tradition. In this sense, this volume may be among the first exercises in contemporary Buddhist critical reflection to begin to build, quite self-consciously, from the ground up.

Although most of the contributors to this volume are Western or Asian-American Buddhists, our circle of discussion includes more Asian Buddhists whom we hope will be contributing to such projects in the future. And although we sought balance in geographical areas of expertise, there remain lacunae (such as the lack of a Chinese Buddhism specialist) that should be filled in any future work.

Besides the members of the AAR 1996 panel noted above, we would also like to acknowledge the sage advice of Alan Wallace, Jeffrey Hopkins, Roger Corless, and Luis Gómez in the formation of this project; and the great editorial and moral support we have received from everyone connected with Curzon Publications, especially Charles Prebish in America and Jonathan Price and Marie Lenstrup in England. David McCarthy of LaserScript proved a most patient and responsive guru of the mysteries of preparing camera-ready copy. We also received indispensible technical assistance from Eric Fanning and Harriet Irwin of Carleton College.

Roger R. Jackson, Northfield, Minnesota
John J. Makransky, Chestnut Hill, Massachusetts

Editors' Introduction

I. BUDDHIST THEOLOGY: ITS HISTORICAL CONTEXT
(Roger Jackson)

The term "theology" most often is understood as denoting critical and/or systematic "discourse about God" in theistic religious traditions, especially Christianity, but also, among others, Judaism, Islam, and some forms of Hinduism. In fact, however, neither Judaism, Islam, nor Hinduism has innate to it an exact terminological equivalent to Christianity's "theology."[1] Furthermore, as Yves Congar has noted, Christians themselves only began consistently to apply the term to their sacred theorizing during the high middle ages, with the establishment of university faculties of *theologia* – prior to that, they tended to prefer such phrases as *sacra scriptura* ("sacred scripture"), *sacra erudito* ("sacred knowledge"), *divina pagina* ("divine pages"), or *sacra doctrina* ("sacred doctrine") (455–456). Nor is the term originally Christian: its *locus classicus* is in Plato's *Republic* (379a5), where it refers to poetical narratives about the gods; Aristotle equates *theologia* with mythological explanations of the world or, alternatively, with the science of metaphysics; and the Hellenistic writer Panaetius of Rhodes sees "theology" as threefold: mythological, philosophical, and political (Congar: 455).

Therefore, although "theology" has in recent times been deeply interwoven with theistic traditions, originally it referred not to talk about the one God, but, rather, to discourse (*logia*) about the divine (*theo*), however that might be conceived. Thus, notes David Tracy, "to speak of 'theology' is a . . . useful way to indicate the more strictly intellectual interpretations of any religious tradition, whether that tradition is theistic or not [and] to use *theo logia* in the literal sense of 'talk or reflection on God or the gods' suggests that even nontheistic traditions (such as some Hindu, Confucian, Taoist, or archaic traditions) may be described as having theologies" (446). Furthermore, adds Tracy, "theology" need not even imply belief in gods of any sort: as long as a tradition conceives some notion of ultimate reality, by whatever name, and however provisionally, "[i]nsofar as . . . explicitly intellectual reflection occurs [with respect to that ultimate] within a religious tradition, one may speak of the presence of theology in the broad sense" (447). Because they have taken the term in its narrowest – albeit most common – usage, as referring to discourse about God, educated modern Buddhists understandably have been reluctant to apply the term "theology" to their own or earlier Buddhists' theorizing about the sacred. If, on the other hand, they were persuaded to define it in the broader – and more basic – sense suggested by Tracy, simply as "intellectual reflection within a religious tradition," they might then be willing to acknowledge that, right from its inception, Buddhism has been deeply involved in "theological" activity, which might fruitfully be related to theological activity that has occurred in other traditions, whether theistic or not.

A recalcitrant Buddhist might object, however, that even in its broad sense, theology connotes prior acceptance of certain religious axioms and ideas, which are the basis for "intellectual reflection," and that Buddhism needs to be distinguished from other traditions precisely by its fearless abjuration of all presuppositions, animated as it is by the open, inquiring spirit modeled by the Buddha himself. Thus, Buddhism is more properly compared to "philosophy" in the West, especially after its separation from theology in the early modern period. It would take us too far afield to debate this point in detail; suffice it to say that, for every Buddhist text that employs a rhetoric of unfettered inquiry, there are probably ten more that are frankly rooted in religious presuppositions and purposes, and that, furthermore, even texts that claim to eschew all presuppositions often invoke them unconsciously. Thus, theology probably is at work even where it appears to be absent. It must be added, however, that even if Buddhist intellectual reflection is inescapably tradition-based, it still may be seen as animated by a truly "philosophical" outlook – as long as it is understood that outlook (like the outlook of philosophy in the West) is inevitably in tension with the claims of one or another tradition. Far from being inimical to open inquiry, theology thrives at the crossroads where the claims of tradition and the claims of reason intersect.

The recalcitrant Buddhist might take a different tack, however, and argue that, for most Buddhists – from learned pandits, to disciplined contemplatives, to unlettered devotees – the claims of reason never have had much purchase, for the aim of most Buddhists is an experience of a reality that is far beyond – and perhaps impeded by – rationality. If theology is centrally concerned with intellectual discourse, and is used as a basic descriptive term for what Buddhists have said and written for 2500 years, then the tradition is distorted, for theology, even if it exists in Buddhism, is beside the point, a merely conventional and provisional exercise at best. It is important to recognize that Buddhists seldom have been willing to rest content *merely* with intellectual reflection on their tradition. Nevertheless, they have left the world a vast legacy of such reflection, which has – rhetorics of non-conceptuality aside – been a significant part of

Buddhist life wherever the Dharma has spread. Furthermore, Buddhism is not alone among religious traditions in recognizing the limits of rationality; indeed, it may be a hallmark of "religions," and at least one way of distinguishing them from "philosophies," that their adherents cannot rest content only with pondering the ultimate; somehow, they must gain access to it, either directly or indirectly. Thus, we may use the term "theology" to describe conceptual activity within and about a particular religious tradition, without thereby implying that such activity is itself an avenue to the ultimate; it is just as true, after all, that the God of Christian theology is ineffable as it is that *nirvāṇa* or buddhahood transcends the range of thought.

Finally, our recalcitrant Buddhist might object that there is not and never has been any such thing as "Buddhist theology" for the simple reason that the term is an imported one, with no precise equivalent in any Asian Buddhist language, and that in using it, therefore, we gloss over a variety of important distinctions that Buddhists themselves have made in reflecting intellectually on their tradition. If, for instance, we can find no Sanskrit term that could plausibly be translated as "theology," or "theologian," then perhaps we are simply confusing categories and cultures by attempting to see ancient Indians as Buddhist "theologians" practicing Buddhist "theology." Is "Buddhist theology" equivalent to *abhidharma*? Or *darśana*? Or *pramāṇa*? Is a Buddhist theologian an *ācārya*? A *dharmabhāṇaka*? A *kalyāṇamitra*? Probably not. And if not, then what terms or categories might we discover in the culture of Indian Buddhism that *would* indicate to us how Buddhists conceived of their own intellectual reflections on tradition? Might we not be truer to tradition if we simply utilized native distinctions, say, among *sūtra*, *vinaya*, and *abhidharma*; or between *sūtra* and *śāstra*, *ābhidharmika* and *yogin*, and *arhat*s who are *prajñāvimukta* and *ubhayatovimukta*? Certainly, we must accord some priority to terms intrinsic to a particular tradition. We must recognize, however, that what is "intrinsic" is not always so easy to recognize, for "traditions" are subject to constant influence from extrinsic forces, and that their identity and stability are only relative. Thus, the very notion of a "foreign" term is to some degree problematic. Furthermore, even if "theology" is admitted to have been foreign to Buddhism up till now, there is nothing dictating that Buddhists may not adopt it into the tradition in the future, if it seems useful to so. And, given the term's broad cross-traditional applicability, it would seem that, at the very least for purposes of conversing with members of other traditions, it would be useful for Buddhists to admit that "theology" (at least in Tracy's sense) is something that they do and have done.

The admission that there is, and has been, such a thing as

Buddhist theology raises as many questions as it answers. For example, just what sort of Buddhist "intellectual reflection" counts as "theology"? Is the content of texts attributed to the Buddha (*buddhavacana*, e.g., *sūtras* and *tantras*) as legitimate a source of theology as treatises and commentaries (e.g., *śāstra* and *vṛtti*?) that reflect on those primary sources? Are the behavioral prescriptions of the Vinaya, the epistemological theories of Dignāga, the countless ritual texts spawned by tantric practitioners, or the ecstatic songs of the *mahāsiddhas* theological in the way that reflections on *dharma*-theory, the two truths, or the nature of *buddha* clearly are? Are there Buddhist texts that we would want to exclude, a priori, from the category of "theology"? By whose criteria would we determine that a text does not involve "intellectual reflection" on the tradition? These are not questions that can be answered here, nor is this the place for an account of the content or structures of two thousand years or more of Buddhist theological activity, whatever its parameters. In order better to situate the essays in this volume, however, it may be of some value to analyze briefly the *contexts* in which Buddhists have reflected intellectually on their tradition, both in the pre-modern and modern periods. Without entering into a debate about the appropriateness of periodizing Buddhist theology along lines that are essentially Western, let us simply indicate that, for us, the pre-modern becomes modern roughly at the point where Western ideas and institutions begin significantly to affect Asian Buddhist societies – generally in the late nineteenth or early twentieth century. In either period, the contexts in which Buddhist theology was practiced have been complex and various; here, we will consider them primarily in terms of two variables: institutional and cultural.[2]

In pre-modern Asia, Buddhist theology was an activity carried on primarily by celibate males within a Buddhist monastery and/or temple. This blanket assertion must, of course, be qualified in various ways. Men have not been the only ones to shape Buddhist theology: there have been women, both lay and monastic, who have contributed significantly to the tradition, such as the Indian nuns who sang the *Therīgāthā* and the great Tibetan tantric systematizer Ma gcig lab sgron. Not all the males who have contributed to the tradition were monastics: such crucial figures as the Indian *mahāsiddha* Saraha, the Tibetan poet and yogi Mi la ras pa, and the Japanese Pure Land reformer Shinran were laymen. Not all monasteries, let alone temples, housed only celibate men: there were and are strong traditions of lay religious leadership in Buddhist institutions in Nepal, Tibet, and Japan. Indeed, the term "monastery" belies a considerable variety of institutions, which differed from culture to culture, and ranged from tiny mountain hermitages, to small-town *vihāras*, to great monastic universities. Despite these qualifications, it nevertheless remains true that most of the figures whom we would designate without hesitation as Buddhist "theologians" were monks, living in one or another kind of monastery. So far as we know, Nāgasena, Nāgārjuna, Saṃghabhadra, Vasubandhu, Asaṅga, Candrakīrti, Dharmakīrti, Śāntideva, Śāntarakṣita, Jñānaśrīmitra; sGam po pa, Sa skya paṇḍita, Dol po pa, Klong chen pa, Tsong kha pa, 'Jam mgon kong sprul; Hsüan-tsang, Chih I, Tsung-mi, Fa-tsang; Saicho, Kukai, Dōgen; and Chinul all were monks, as was, of course, the "original" Buddhist theologian, Śākyamuni.

As scholar-monks, the Buddhist theologians of pre-modern Asia were an élite within an élite, for they were among the very few people within their societies who were able to separate themselves from lay life to follow the monastic calling, and they were, unlike the majority of the populace (and probably the majority of monastics) literate. This tended to give them a rather ambiguous status within society and the Buddhist tradition. On the one hand, the theologians probably were unknown to most of their contemporaries, including their fellow monks, whose lives did not revolve around sustained intellectual reflection, but, rather, cultic observance and ritual service; this, at least, is the implication of much of the epigraphic and archeological evidence (and many of the texts) that tell us how Buddhism was practiced "on the ground" in India and elsewhere in Asia. On the other hand, the talents of Buddhist theologians, like those of religious élites anywhere, were appreciated both inside and outside their institutional settings. To their fellow monks, Buddhist theologians may not have been fully comprehensible, but their literate status and their role in preserving and transmitting the Dharma, and in providing rational defenses of tradition, must have been appreciated. And, to the powerful and wealthy members of the secular élite, such as rulers and merchants, the theologians were seen as worthy interlocutors, and as sources of spiritual power and temporal legitimation. For these reasons, Buddhist theologians gained a social prestige considerably out of proportion to their numbers or popular renown.

Although concerns with prestige were unbefitting of monks or nuns, and often unsought by them, Buddhist monastics and their enterprises received considerable – if fluctuating – patronage in India from the time of Aśoka until the Muslim invasions. With the internationalization of Indian culture during this same period, Buddhism was exported along land and sea trade routes, and the monastic tradition founded in India became a pan-Asian institution. Because the production of written texts came to be (if it was not originally) one of the major enterprises of monasteries, the words of Buddhist theologians were preserved, transported from country to country, and translated from one language to another. They became in this way a kind of currency within élite circles in the Buddhist world, redeemable in a variety of social and cultural settings, and helping to provide both a raison d'être for the monasteries and a source of national pride, especially in regions (e.g., Sri Lanka, Tibet, Burma, Japan) where the forging of statehood and a literate culture coincided with the rise of Buddhism. Thus, while the practice of theology may never have been quite as vital to Buddhism as the theologians and their patrons would have us believe, it was, nevertheless, a persistent and prestigious part of what Buddhists did, "on the ground," virtually everywhere in Asia that the monastic tradition spread, from the first Aśokan missions to the dawn of the modern era.

Post-classical Western incursions into the Asian Buddhist world began with the journeys of Marco Polo (13th century), accelerated with the voyages and settlements of the Age of Discovery (16th-18th centuries), and reached a climax in the nineteenth and twentieth centuries, when Europeans, then Americans, came to exercise either direct colonial control (India, Sri Lanka, Burma, Indochina) or powerful influence (Japan, China, Thailand, Mongolia) over much of Asia. The colonial era, which ended in the mid-twentieth century, was followed by an era in which nationalist regimes dedicated to one or another form of either communism or capitalism came to power. The colonial, then communist and capitalist, interruptions of Asian civilization altered it profoundly, exposing Buddhists and others to ideas, institutions, and technologies almost inconceivably different from anything they had known before. Sometimes by choice, but most often willy-nilly, one Asian culture after another was exposed to ideas like secularism, the nation-state, democracy, or the dictatorship of the proletariat; institutions like the multinational corporation, the commune, or representative government; and technologies like those of the steamship, railroad, or telegraph, and, later, cars and airplanes, cinemas and television, e-mail and the Internet. Though many Asians either resisted or tried to ignore the incursions of what has come to be called "modernity," its penetration of traditional cultures and its alteration of ancient institutions was inexorable. During the colonial era, changes could be implemented by fiat, or by steady pressure, from the governing authorities; in the post-colonial period, it has been the forces of communist ideology, international markets, or both, that have tended to drive the process. Irrespective of its source or mode of implementation, modernity had, by the end of the twentieth century left hardly an Asian hamlet, and hardly an Asian Buddhist, unaffected.

The cultural and social changes that shook Asian societies in the nineteenth and twentieth centuries had profound implications for Buddhism and its institutions. As Asian societies became increasingly modernized and secularized, often ruled by a Western-educated élite and dominated by rising commercial classes, traditional religious ideas and institutions lost their dominance of the cultural landscape. Nearly everywhere, the power of Buddhist monasteries and monks was curtailed, whether by colonial powers intent on promoting Christianity, communist regimes who regarded religion as an opiate of the masses, or capitalist entrepreneurs who felt that religion was as much the property of lay people as of monastics. Although Buddhist theological activity had been confined primarily to monasteries for two millennia, the ebbing of their power did not signal the decline of Asian Buddhist theology, so much as its partial relocation to the sphere of educated lay people – one of the by-products of modernity, of course, is the increasing literacy of the laity.

As a consequence, though there continued to be important Asian Buddhist thinkers who were monastics – e.g., the Fourteenth Dalai Lama, Thich Nhat Hanh, Walpola Rahula, Bhikku Buddhadasa, Hsu Yun, and Yasutani Roshi – an increasing number of lay people began to make contributions, from university-educated philosophers such as K. N. Jayatilleke and Nishitani Keiji; to social reformers such as B. R. Ambedkar and Sulak Sivaraksa; to revivalist leaders such as Anagarika Dharmapala and Ikeda Daisaku; to meditation masters such as S. N. Goenka and Chögyam Trungpa Rinpoche. Thus, if Asian Buddhist theology prior to the modern era was confined primarily to the monasteries, today it has become decentralized, issuing not just from the *wat*s and *vihāra*s, but also from university departments and lay-oriented practice centers. We hardly need add that Asian Buddhist theology – never unanimous in its monastic past – is also today multi-vocal, for the interests and values of its different institutional settings may vary considerably: a monk and a university philosopher, for instance, live and think by very different sorts of rules, and their theological outlooks will differ accordingly. Whether monastic or layperson, however, virtually all Asian Buddhist theologians of note have had somehow to work at the crossroads where tradition and modernity meet, reinterpreting Buddhism in the face of the perplexities and challenges of the brave new world in which they, and their audience, find themselves. To fail to do so is to overlook theology's unceasing task of reinterpreting authoritative tradition in changing circumstances – and perhaps never in its history has Buddhism faced circumstances as unstable as those that have ensued upon modernity.

Another significant development within modern Buddhism is its transformation from an exclusively Asian tradition to a truly global one: since the nineteenth century, increasing numbers of Westerners have begun to the study its doctrines and attempt to live out its practices, and they have had an ever greater voice in the definition of what Buddhism is and will be as it moves into the future. Sustained Western interest in Buddhism originally was a byproduct of the growth of Orientalist scholarship, itself an element of Colonialism. Buddhist ideas were circulating in European intellectual circles by the beginning of the nineteenth century; they were, for instance, noted by Hegel, and cited with considerable (if misguided) enthusiasm by Schopenhauer. From the mid-nineteenth century onward, pioneering scholars such as Eugène Burnouf, F. Max Müller, T. W.. Rhys Davids, and Henry Clarke Warren began to translate and write about classical Buddhist texts for audiences in Europe and America. Trained mainly in philology and philosophy, and affiliated with universities, these authors adhered to an ideal of scholarly objectivity, and sought primarily to present and describe, rather than promote, Buddhist texts – though they did, of course, bring cultural and philosophical presuppositions to their work, often unconscious or unacknowledged. As works of Buddhist scholarship began to trickle down to the Euro-American reading public, enthusiasm for the ideas and, to a lesser degree, the practices, of Buddhism began to take hold. Intellectuals such as the American philosopher Paul Carus, the theosophists H. P. Blavatsky and Henry Steele Olcott, and the poet and scholar Edwin Arnold began to publish articles and books that presented Buddhism in a frankly sympathetic and popularly accessible manner. These early Western Buddhist "theologians" also began the process of cultural interchange that would bring Westerners into contact not just with Buddhist texts, but with actual Buddhists: Blavatsky and Olcott, for instance, traveled to India and Sri Lanka, where they helped spark a Buddhist revival that was carried on by the likes of Anagarika Dharmapala, while Carus was instrumental in bringing to America a number of Japanese Zen teachers and scholars, including D. T. Suzuki.

Through the first half of the twentieth century, popular interest in Buddhism increased gradually, as Buddhist ideas were promoted in the West by such figures as D. T. Suzuki, author of numerous essays on Zen Buddhism; W. Y. Evans-Wentz, editor of a series of translations of Tibetan meditation texts; Dwight Goddard, compiler *A Buddhist Bible*; and Christmas Humphreys, head of the Buddhist Society of London and editor of the journal, *The Middle Way*. Yet even by mid-century, Buddhism was still largely unknown in the West outside small intellectual circles. The increase in academic Buddhist scholarship during this period was more impressive: Francophone scholars like Louis de la Vallée Poussin, Sylvain Levi, and Étienne Lamotte brought to light many important Indian and Chinese Mahāyāna texts, while the riches of Tibetan scholasticism were explored by Feodor Stcherbatsky and Giuseppe Tucci, and work on the Theravāda tradition was continued by, among others, Caroline Rhys Davids and I. B. Horner. Like their late-nineteenth-century predecessors, these scholars were not without their biases, but by and large they approached Buddhism from a descriptive rather than a normative standpoint – there may have been theological implications to their work, but they were not, in general, consciously attempting to articulate a Buddhist vision for the Western world.

With the Second World War, everything began to change. The global nature of the conflict brought Asian and Western peoples together in conflict and cooperation on a scale never imagined before, and the development of improved technologies of communication and transportation (in part occasioned by the war effort), helped to assure that, after the war, Asia and the West would never be far apart again. Indeed, two of the hottest fronts of the Cold War that followed World War II were in Asia: Korea and Vietnam. Thus, the Western gaze, and especially that of America, was drawn to Asia starting in the 1930's, and never has left it since, through three wars, the renaissance of Japan, and the rise of communist China to international prominence. In the post-World War II period, Westerners visited a post-colonial, increasingly assertive Asia in unprecedented numbers, and most – whether soldier, businessperson, or tourist – served as witting or unwitting agents of modernity on the continent; at the same time, increasing numbers of Asians were settling in Western countries, adding to the cultural and ethnic diversity of often homogeneous populations.

The period during which Asian-Western contact began to increase also was a time of growing cultural disaffection in some of the most affluent parts of the West. Many of the educated young, in response to the moral dilemmas posed by what they saw as their civilization's legacy of war, racism, environmental destruction, and rampant greed and hypocrisy, began to look to Asia for alternatives ways of thinking and living. In the late 1940's and 1950's, leading lights of what came to be known as the Beat movement, such as Jack Kerouac, Allen Ginsberg, Gary Snyder, and Philip Whalen, began to experiment with and write about Buddhism, often on the basis of reading such earlier authors as D. T. Suzuki and Dwight Goddard. At the time, the unconventionality of their writings and life-styles placed the Beats at the margins of a still-conservative postwar society, but those same attributes helped assure that, when a sense of cultural dislocation became more widespread in the 1960's, the Beats would be seen as trailblazers – and that their enthusiasm for Buddhism would give the tradition a countercultural cachet that would fascinate thousands.

The disaffected young of the 1960's first learned their Buddhism from the Beats, but the more curious among them turned also to the works of academic or semi-academic Buddhist scholars such as Suzuki and Evans-Wentz from an earlier generation, and, of more recent vintage, Alan Watts, Herbert Guenther, Lama Anagarika Govinda, Sangharakshita, and Philip Kapleau Roshi. All of these figures were conversant with both Asian and Western traditions, and produced pioneering works that helped to shape Western perceptions of what Buddhism was, is, and could be – indeed, if there is a common element in their work, it is the blurring of distinctions between exposition and advocacy; to one degree or another, all of them were Buddhist theologians. At the same time, more traditional "objective" Buddhist scholarship continued quietly to flourish, as figures like Heinz Bechert, J. W. de Jong, David Seyfort Ruegg, David Snellgrove, Richard Robinson, Stanley Weinstein, Masatoshi Nagatomi, Leon Hurvitz, André Bareau, Ernst Frauwallner, T. R. V. Murti, and Nagao Gadjin added greatly to our knowledge of classical Asian Buddhist texts and traditions – though they were for the most part unread outside the academy.

A number of trends and events in the late 1960's and early 1970's helped to push Buddhism ever closer to the forefront of Western awareness. The ever-present fascination with "Oriental mysticism" increased dramatically with the widespread consumption of psychedelic drugs, which were said by many to induce states of consciousness like those described in Asian religious texts. Asian music and spiritual disciplines were embraced by a number of popular cultural figures, most notably the Beatles. Economic prosperity and rapid, inexpensive modes of transportation made travel to Asia by Westerners possible on a scale never seen before. Those travelers, whether visiting newly prosperous Japan, strife-ridden Southeast Asia, or India and Nepal – where a hundred thousand Tibetans had settled after fleeing to exile in 1959 – began to encounter Asian Buddhist teachers in their own settings, to study with them, take refuge (and sometimes monastic vows) from them and, gradually, to bring them to the West to teach either temporarily or permanently, whether in universities or, more commonly, meditation centers that were founded for the practice of one of three main meditation traditions: Zen, Theravāda, and Tibetan. Initially, these meditation centers were usually guided by Asian monastics, but from the beginning, their clientele was overwhelmingly drawn from lay members of the cultural and economic élite – eventually, more and more and more centers would be lay-run, as well. A number of converted travelers chose, when they returned to the West, to pursue the academic study of Buddhism. This cohort of "baby-boom Buddhologists" received its training in fledgling programs at such universities as Wisconsin, Washington, California, Virginia, Columbia, and Harvard – or, outside the United States, Toronto, Oxford, Hamburg, Vienna, Paris, the Australian National University, and ISMEO, in Rome. In America, many received assistance from the U.S. government, which believed it in the national interest to support the study of Asian languages.

Especially in America, but also elsewhere, the members of this generation of Buddhist scholars were unlike any before them (and unlike their contemporaries in the fields of, say, Hindu or Islamic studies) in that they most of them began as Buddhists, and had, in fact, turned to academia to learn more about a tradition that they practiced – often at the lay meditation centers. In this regard, they were reminiscent of scholars of Christianity or Judaism, who usually were Christians or Jews. Christian or Jewish scholars could profess (as well as study and criticize) their traditions in theological seminaries, but the new Buddhist Buddhologists had no such settings into which to graduate.[3] Rather, they were trained in the tradition of classical "objective" philological, historical, and doctrinal scholarship, and found their homes primarily in departments of Asian studies, philosophy, or, most commonly, religious studies; the latter were quite distinct from departments of theology out of which they had evolved, in that they insisted that their members be committed, both in research and pedagogy, to description rather than prescription. Thus, whatever their degree of personal commitment to Buddhism, the baby-boom Buddhologists had to (and many, in any case, wished to) keep their personal and academic lives quite separate – for only that way were employment, then tenure, possible. As these scholars moved through the academic system, they began to produce works that pushed Buddhist studies beyond where their mentors had taken it, providing ever more finely tuned explorations of a variety of texts and traditions, continuing to explore the classical philosophical material that had been at the core of the field since the 19th century, but also gaining a new appreciation for the insights into Buddhism "on the ground" that might be derived from epigraphic, archeological, anthropological, and sociological study.

They did not, by and large, produce works of Buddhist theology. The field hardly was barren for their absence, however, for, in a variety of non-academic contexts, works by Asian and Western

Buddhists began to appear that did speak about Buddhism in a normative, prescriptive manner. Texts by Asian Buddhists published in the West were in many cases traditional presentations of systems of doctrine and praxis, not significantly different from what might be presented to an Asian audience. Through the skillfully edited discourses and writings of figures such as Shunryu Suzuki, the fourteenth Dalai Lama, and Ajahn Chaa, as well as through translations of classic texts published in accessible versions, the traditional teachings of Asian Buddhism were available as never before, providing a sort of baseline for theological reflection. At the same time, a number of Asian Buddhists went a considerable distance toward their modernized Western audiences, engaging them at the level of science (e.g., Tarthang Tulku), psychology (e.g., Chögyam Trungpa), and metaphysics (e.g., the Dalai Lama). The most sustained reflection on the intersection between Buddhist tradition and modernity, though, arose among the members (and leaders) of lay-oriented meditation centers, who had to reconcile the two currents on a daily basis. In a whole range of fields, practicing Buddhists outside the academy (and a few Buddhologists) began to produce the works that, intentionally or not, were the charter texts of Western Buddhist theology. They ranged from the existential demythologization of Stephen Batchelor, to the scientific musings of Jeremy Hayward and B. Alan Wallace, the cybernetic Madhyamaka of Peter Fenner, the tantric eschatology of Robert Thurman, the social and political engagement of Ken Jones and Bernard Glassman, the ecological vision of Joanna Macy and Gary Snyder, the feminist perspective of Rita Gross and Karma Lekshe Tsomo, the meditative prescriptions of Jack Kornfield and Surya Das, and the ethical inquiries of Robert Aitken, Roshi.

It was only somewhat tardily – in most cases after they received tenure – that Buddhist scholars in the academy began to contribute to the emerging Western Buddhist theology. Those contributions were no less important for their belatedness, however, for academics were able to bring to their theological work a profound appreciation for the historical dimensions of Buddhism, and for critical and creative currents in Western intellectual life. Thus, to supplement the works of such pioneering academic theologians as Thurman and Gross (themselves continuing in a tradition founded by D. T. Suzuki, Guenther and others), a number of others began to contribute their voices, e.g., Anne Klein in feminist thought, Damien Keown in ethics, Lambert Schmithausen in environmental matters, José Cabezón in sexuality, Sallie King in social activism, Roderick Bucknell and B. Alan Wallace in meditation theory, and, in ontology, epistemology, and comparative philosophy, Stephen Heine, Jeffrey Hopkins, C. W. Huntington, Jr., Richard Hayes, and many others. Because they remained within the academy, with its elevation of the descriptive over the normative, these academic Buddhist theologians sometimes still embedded their constructive reflections on Buddhism within academic works, and in academic prose. Nevertheless, their contributions to constructing a Buddhist theology have become more and more overt, and more and more important.

Academic Buddhist theologians may not, as Charles Prebish has suggested, become the Western Buddhist equivalents of the scholar-monks who were at the heart of the traditional Asian Buddhist theological tradition, but their voices will be an important part of what is proving – at the end of the century in which Buddhism celebrated its 2500th anniversary – to be an increasingly polyphonic tradition. In traditional Asia, Buddhist theology emerged almost exclusively from the monasteries; today, it still has a home there, but just as commonly arises from lay-oriented meditation centers and academic departments. The language of theology is no longer just that of the traditional Asian texts, but, in keeping with the Buddha's exhortation to preach the Dharma in the vernacular, it is all the languages spoken by Buddhists, though perhaps above all, the international lingua franca, English. And, as befits a technologically plural world, it is transmitted through many media: not just traditional texts, or books and hard-to-find journals, but popular magazines like *Tricycle* and *The Shambhala Sun*, major conferences on everything from Buddhism and other religions to Buddhism and the health sciences, lecture tours by important Asian and Western teachers, Internet discussion groups like Buddha-L, and electronic journals and archives like the *Journal of Buddhist Ethics*. As in so many contemporary theological traditions, this polyphony of Buddhist sources, contributors, languages, and media sometimes seems set to collapse into cacophony and confusion, particularly where the crucial questions of how tradition and modernity (or postmodernity) remain to be reconciled. Whether or not such a collapse occurs may, in the end, rest on the ability of scholar-theologians, like those represented in this volume, to keep the threads untangled, and the choir in tune, in the long and complex *sūtra* that is the Buddhist way.

II. CONTEMPORARY ACADEMIC BUDDHIST THEOLOGY: ITS EMERGENCE AND RATIONALE (John J. Makransky)

The "scientific study of religions" is a twentieth century phenomenon. It emerged in the Western academy as a child of the Western enlightenment through a methodology designed to distinguish it from Christian theological study. Central to it has been the method of "epoché:" bracketing judgments of normative truth and value so as to open a new space in the academy for the in-depth study of non-Christian religions, free from the presumption of their normative inferiority to Christianity. With its emergence, the study of religion in the academy became segregated into two separate institutional niches. In North America and Europe, religious studies (or "history of religions") departments were created in hundreds of colleges and universities, while university divinity schools and departments of theology remained the loci of Christian theological studies. The meteoric rise of religious studies in colleges and universities made many new things possible. It has given millions of students a much more intimate knowledge and appreciation of world religions than previously possible, and continues to educate the wider public through many new kinds of publication and media. Of special importance to the present discussion, religious studies departments have also created new opportunities for non-Christian graduate students to engage in the critical study of their own religious traditions within the Western academy.

The latter development, though broadly welcomed, has had unintended and largely unacknowledged consequences: it has released new forces of interest in the academy. Religious studies method, by withholding normative judgments, opened space in the academy for new kinds of study of non-Christian religions, but did not provide the space to apply such findings to the theological concerns of those religions. The training of non-Christian scholars in the contemporary study of religions (including their own) has triggered, in some, a natural impulse to apply such knowledge to the theological needs of their traditions. This is an interest not merely to describe their tradition at a distance (from the bracketed, "value neutral" position of religious studies) but precisely to clarify the truth and value of their tradition from a critical perspective located within it. Thus, the training of non-Christian scholars in the religious studies academy has generated a strong new interest in critical, constructive theology that fits neither within the established method of religious studies nor under the rubric of Christian theology, the previous main locus of such work in Western culture.

This has had further unintended consequences. The religious studies framework that permits non-Christian religions to be taken newly seriously in the West excludes their being taken seriously on their own terms. Under the rubric of religious studies, the functionally secular Western academy mines world religions for its use: to generate research findings, publications, conferences to explore whatever may be of current interest and benefit to the academy. The "value neutral" method of religious studies was of course never value neutral. Rather, it implicitly established a value in religions divorced from the normative interests of their own religious communities: a value found exclusively in their capacity to fulfill the intellectual, social, and economic interests of the Western academy.

This contributes to the current re-evaluation of the assumptions upon which the separation between theological studies and religious studies was originally constructed. As Francis Schussler Fiorenza has pointed out, the "science of religion" was constructed upon late nineteenth century presuppositions about the nature of disciplinary knowledge which late twentieth century criticism largely rejects, while the ahistorical presuppositions that previously conditioned theological study have been replaced by the methods of historical and cultural criticism. The domains of religious studies and theological studies are appearing less mutually exclusive than before.[4] The recent turn toward theology on behalf of their religious traditions by non-Christians in the academy who presently possess no clear niche for such work will further contribute to this re-evaluation. Despite the diverse origins of theological interest within the academic study of religions, it is, among other things, good news for Christian theology, which will be enriched by the wider conversation that continues to unfold around it and in dialogue with it. .

This renascent interest in theology manifests vividly in the Buddhist studies wing of the religious studies academy, because the increasing prominence of Buddhist studies in the academy has been driven by the contemporary culture's growing interest in Buddhism, and that cultural interest is driven in significant part by an implicit theological concern to tap Buddhism as a source of truth and value for persons' lives. People who seek truth and transformative power in Buddhism include not only those who identify themselves as contemporary Buddhists, but prominently also Christians, Jews and others for whom Buddhist teaching or practice sheds light upon truths of their own traditions or upon possibilities for integration of those truths into their lives.

The current ground-swell of normative Western interest in

Buddhism is by no means a passing fad, any more than previous such ground swells in China, Japan or Tibet. Like other cultures in their early stages of Buddhist encounter, the West has just begun to discern its own face in the Buddha's teaching. Some postmodern analysts have argued that this is merely an imaginative projection, and of course it is partly that (as it was in China, Japan, Tibet). But it is not merely that. The remarkable cultural absorption of Buddhist thought and practice we are now witnessing is rooted in an intuitive recognition of its potential power to beneficially transform many aspects of the culture it now touches. As for previous cultures, this is the start of a profound cultural recognition that energizes masses of people across diverse social strata to explore more and more dimensions of Buddhist image, thought and practice over the long term.

Can Buddhist teaching and practice reveal the nature of reality beyond the webs of dichotomous thought? Can it shed light upon holism in embodied experience, beyond dichotomies of mind and body? Can it open new ways to heal body and mind? Can it profoundly effect ways we currently think, write, make music, paint, form relationships, recreate, educate our children? Can it reveal previously unnoticed limitations of postmodern responses to modernism, of feminist responses to patriarchy, of intellectual responses to the environmental crisis? Can it shed new light upon the West's resurgent interest in previously marginalized sources of its own spirituality? Can it shed light on so much because it ultimately derives from a transcendent knowledge (Sanskrit: *lokottara-jñāna*) whose creative potential is limitlessly adaptable? These are questions that concern truth, value and transformative power. Religious studies, as previously practiced, brackets such questions. But to bracket them is to render the academy irrelevant to the ground swell of interest in Western culture that generates the increasing presence of Buddhist studies in its midst.

If the contemporary situation generates pressing cultural questions that the religious studies academy has been ill-equipped to address, it generates equally pressing questions for Buddhist tradition that traditional Buddhist teachers have been ill-equipped to address. Is there a systematic coherence to be found within or among the competing Buddhist cultural traditions now planting their roots in Western culture (cultural traditions that have often ignored or disparaged each other)? What contemporary meaning and relevance is to be found in these ancient cultural expressions? What are the possibilities of authentic adaptation?

Such pressing cultural concerns now contribute to an especially strong theological push in Buddhist studies, because a number of its current representatives were set on their course by the same kinds of concerns, which took expression in them both through years of traditional study and practice under Asian Buddhist teachers and through training in the critical methods of the contemporary Western academy. A number of such scholars now find themselves equipped with both sets of tools, and an emerging scholarly purpose defined both by the cultural forces operative in and around them and by the contemporary theological needs of the Buddhist traditions in which they have trained.

The contemporary need of Buddhist tradition for critical reflection is as great as that of Western culture. The two needs are, of course, connected. Buddhist traditions want to communicate themselves in ways accessible to new worlds of interest. But to do this requires not only a knowledge of new languages in which to translate the old ways, but a critical perspective upon the old ways that understands how much of them has been the product of socio-cultural and historical forces that are inapplicable to new socio-cultural settings. Lacking such critical understanding, religious traditions such as Buddhism do unintended harm to persons and to their own reputations in new settings, then repeatedly misdiagnose the sources of harm.[5]

Historical critical consciousness developed in the Western academy which has been the locus of Christian theological study. Christian theologians now routinely inquire into the effects of historical, cultural, political, economic, and social conditions upon previous theological understandings, seeking to contextualize and critique previous perspectives so as to recover or newly emphasize other resources of tradition in light of contemporary knowledge and experience, and thereby to constructively re-engage the truth and value of Christian tradition for fresh re-appropriation. Such theologians view at least some of the critical methods of the contemporary academy as powerful (even providential) tools on behalf of their tradition, to help Christians authentically re-engage and clarify the truth of Christianity for a new time.

Unlike the Christian situation, the new historical and cultural awareness of Buddhism that religious studies has made available in the Western academy has not yet been profoundly integrated with Buddhist religious culture in most of Asia or the West. Historico-cultural critical consciousness, by and large, has remained the province of the Western academy at a great distance from the Asian Buddhist cultures that it studies. Asian Buddhist teachers are not trained in Western critical methods, and frequently have little interest in exploring the implications of critical findings for their own traditions.[6] Such methods are irrelevant to what has previously mattered in

Buddhist cultures, where Buddhist teachers and meditation masters have become accomplished through traditional, not contemporary critical, methods. Now Buddhist thought and practice is increasingly introduced into the West by such Asian teachers, and by a number of their outstanding Western students recognized as teachers of Buddhism in their own right. But for the most part, the training of such Western Buddhist teachers in the study of Buddhism has been traditional. Very few have been trained in the critical methods of the academy.

Thus, in contrast to the integration of Christian theology with contemporary critical thought, the rise of Buddhist studies in the religious studies academy has opened a gap between those who transmit the living experience and traditional understanding of Buddhism and those who critically analyze Buddhism to understand the historical and cultural conditions of its development. As Christian theologians know well, the latter findings are crucial for a religious tradition to appropriate if it is to find the voice to speak its truth anew.

This situation contributes to a great irony, which has not gone unnoticed in the West: Buddhist traditions that take pride in their knowledge of all kinds of human conditioning that cause suffering (Second Noble Truth) still lack the critical tools to diagnose the effects of cultural conditioning upon their own previous understanding and current communication, and how that conditioning now contributes to confusion and suffering. Because of this, Asian Buddhist traditions continue to require contemporary persons to conform inappropriately to aspects of ancient cultures that do more harm than good for the very life of their own traditions. One common example of this is the Asian Buddhist transmission of ethnic prejudice to Westerners unawares. Upon introducing Westerners to the Dharma, Asian traditions often continue to claim for themselves the only "pure" transmission of the Buddha's teachings, subtly conforming naive Westerners to the implicit understanding that all other Asian Buddhist cultures or traditions are corrupt. Other such examples appear in some of the essays of this volume.

In recognition of these issues, scholars who were formed both by Buddhist tradition and by the contemporary academy increasingly seek ways to respond both to their own culture's normative interest in Buddhism and to the inner necessity of Buddhist tradition to reflect critically upon itself and find new ways to express itself. Their hope is that, as in the past, such new reflection rooted in long community experience may contribute to authentic new understanding: by critiquing past elements of tradition inappropriate to a new time, recovering or re-emphasizing other elements, critiquing Western models inadequate for a fuller understanding of Buddhism, and exploring the potential of Buddhist experience to shine new light upon a host of contemporary cultural and religious concerns. This is the broad project of contemporary "Buddhist theology."

The term "theology," then, in "Buddhist theology," is used in a broad sense. It includes critical reflection upon Buddhist experience in light of contemporary understanding and critical reflection upon contemporary understanding in light of Buddhist experience. Like that of Christian theologians, it is the work of scholars who stand normatively within their tradition, who look to traditional sources of authority (in sacred text and previous forms of social practice and experience), who re-evaluate prior Buddhist understandings in light of contemporary findings and who seek thereby to contribute to the continuing development of their tradition in its relevance to new times and places.

Although, for reasons noted, the institutional loci for Buddhist theology are still largely undeveloped, we would argue that the forces behind its emergence and continuing evolution are ineluctable. At present Buddhist theology finds expression mostly in the margins of academia: in religious studies conferences where "theology" is still too often viewed with suspicion, in theology conferences where the central focus is Christianity, in settings for inter-religious dialogue, in recent writings on Buddhist ethics and contemporary thought, and now in this volume.

One purpose of this volume, then, is to inspire further exploration of ways that the pressing needs of Western culture and Buddhist tradition for Buddhist critical reflection may be met through new forms of interchange, new cooperative projects, and new institutional settings East and West.

NOTES

1 Jews increasingly have adopted the term "theology," but only in relatively recent times, and at least partially under the influence of interactions with Christianity (see, e.g., Cohen). Muslims traditionally speak of two branches of religious reflection, *kalāma* and *falasafa*; the latter is philosophy, but the former does approximate what Christians mean by "theology," both functionally and etymologically, for it means "discourse" about ultimate things (see, e.g., Glassé: 216–219, 309–312). Hindus, like other Indians, speak of the articulation of philosophical "viewpoints," *darśanas*, and while a *darśana* may include theological reflection (see, e.g., Pereira), there is much in *darśana* literature that is not related to discourse about the ultimate,

and there exist whole schools of thought whose *darśanas* reflect a complete lack of interest in or deliberate rejection of ideas about the ultimate.

2 The summary that follows is indebted to more works than can possibly be listed. Readers interested in the trends described, however, may, for the pre-modern period, consult the overviews of, among many others, Robinson and Johnson, Bechert, Warder, Schopen, Swearer, Ch'en, Kitagawa, and Samuel; and, for the modern period, Dumoulin, Tweed, Fields, de Jong, and Batchelor.

3 In the U.S., there were conspicuous exceptions to this as early as the 1970's, such as the Pure Land-founded Institute of Buddhist of Studies in Berkeley, the Tibetan Vajrayāna-based Naropa Institute in Boulder, Colorado, and the unaffiliated California Institute of Integral Studies in San Francisco. In the 1980's and 1990's, a number of Buddhist organizations began to develop programs that focused on a traditional presentation of classical theology, but sought to supplement that presentation with the insights of academically-trained Buddhologists.

4 See Fiorenza for a seminal analysis of forces in late twentieth century Western thought that push for fundamental re-evaluation of the distinction between religious and theological studies that was erected on the basis of late nineteenth century thought.. The recent resurgence of theological interest instigated by non-Christian entry into the academic study of religion complements and makes more vivid the very issues that Fiorenza has raised.

5 A stunning recent example of this: some Tibetan monks who now introduce Westerners to practices centered on a native Tibetan deity, without informing them that one of its primary functions has been to assert hegemony over rival sects! The current Dalai Lama, seeking to combat the ancient, virulent sectarianisms operative in such quarters, has strongly discouraged the worship of the "protector" deity known as Dorje Shugden, because one of its functions has been to force conformity to the dGe lugs pa sect (with which the Dalai Lama himself is most closely associated) and to assert power over competing sects. Western followers of a few dGe lugs pa monks who worship that deity, lacking any critical awareness of its sectarian functions in Tibet, have recently followed the Dalai Lama to his speaking engagements to protest his strong stance (for non-sectarianism) in the name of their "religious freedom" to promulgate, now in the West, an embodiment of Tibetan sectarianism. If it were not so harmful to persons and traditions, this would surely be one of the funniest examples of the cross-cultural confusion that lack of critical reflection continues to create.

6 Japan is certainly a partial exception to this, but there, too, there remains a tendency to segregate within academic institutions what is viewed as the confessional study of Buddha-dharma from the contemporary critical study of Buddhism.

REFERENCES

Batchelor, Stephen (1994). *The Awakening of the West: The Encounter of Buddhism and Western Culture.* London: Aquarian.

Bechert, Heinz and R. Gombrich, eds. (1984). *The World of Buddhism.* New York: Facts on File.

Ch'en, Kenneth (1964). *Buddhism in China: A Historical Survey.* Princeton: Princeton University Press.

Cohen, Arthur A. (1987). "Theology." In Arthur A. Cohen and Paul Mendes-Flohr, eds., *Contemporary Jewish Religious Thought: Original Essays on Critical Concepts, Movements, and Beliefs.* New York: Charles Scribner's Sons.

Congar, Yves (1987). "Christian Theology." In Mircea Eliade, ed., *The Encyclopedia of Religion,* vol. 14: 455–464. New York: Macmillan.

Dumoulin, Heinrich (1976).*The Cultural, Political, and Religious Significance of Buddhism in the Modern World.* New York: Macmillan.

Fields, Rick (1992). *How the Swans Came to the Lake: A Narrative History of Buddhism in America.* 3rd ed. Boston & London: Shambhala.

Fiorenza, Francis S. (1993). "Theology in the University," *CSSR Bulletin* (22: 2).

Glassé, Cyril (1989). *The Concise Encyclopedia of Islam.* San Francisco: Harper & Row.

de Jong, J. W. (1987). *A Brief History of Buddhist Studies in Europe and North America.* 2nd ed. Delhi Sri Satguru Publications.

Kitagawa, Joseph (1966). *Religion in Japanese History.* New York: Columbia University Press.

Pereira, José (1976). *Hindu Theology: A Reader.* Garden City, NY: Anchor/Doubleday.

Robinson, Richard and Johnson, Willard (1997). *The Buddhist Religion: A Historical Introduction.* 4th ed. Belmont, CA: Wadsworth.

Samuel, Geoffrey (1994). *Civilized Shamans: Buddhism in Tibetan Societies.* Washington, DC: Smithsonian.

Schopen, Gregory (1997). *Bones, Stones, and Buddhist Monks: Collected Papers on the Archaeology, Epigraphy, and Texts of Monastic Buddhism in India.* Honolulu: University of Hawaii Press.

Swearer, Donald (1995). *The Buddhist World of Southeast Asia.* Albany: State University of New York Press.

Tracy, David (1987). "Comparative Theology." In Mircea Eliade, ed., *The Encyclopedia of Religion.* New York: Macmillan, vol. 14: 446–455.

Tweed, Thomas (1992). *The American Encounter with Buddhism, 1844-1912: Victorian Culture and the Limits of Dissent.* Bloomington: Indiana University Press.

Warder, A. K. (1980). *Indian Buddhism.* 2nd ed. Delhi: Motilal Banarsidass.

PART I

BUDDHIST THEOLOGY: WHAT, WHY, AND HOW?

One

Buddhist Theology in the Academy[1]

José Ignacio Cabezón

BUT *THEOLOGY*?

Anyone at all familiar with the tenets of Buddhism will undoubtedly find it strange that a group of specialists in the field, after many years of attempting to purge the study of Buddhism of Western theistic terminology and presuppositions, should now be claiming that the time is ripe for the emergence of Buddhist *theology* as a discipline. Theology connotes, at least etymologically, the study of the nature of God. Given that this is the most common sense of the word, it might be useful to begin by explaining why, in my usage, "Buddhist theology" is not an oxymoron. I will discuss in more detail below what I take theology to be: roughly, a form of normative discourse, self-avowedly rooted in tradition, with certain formal properties. But for now, suffice it to say that I take theology not to be restricted to discourse on God, nor to presuppose the notion of an omnipotent, creator God. I take "theology" not to be restricted to its etymological meaning. In that latter sense Buddhism is of course *a*theological, rejecting as it does the notion of God. Understood *rhetorically*, however, as a kind of discourse with certain formal properties, and *functionally*, as having certain applications and purposes in the context of culture, "theology" *can* be meaningfully modified by the adjective "Buddhist."[2]

If, as appears to be the case, the word "theology" is so heavily laden with classically theistic semantic implications, might it not be less hazardous and more straightforward simply to opt for a different term? There are three reasons for not doing so: one practical, one theoretical, and one "political." (1) I do not believe that there is a practical equivalent to the word "theology." A term like philosophy simply will not do, since it, unlike theology, is neutral in regard to the religious affiliation of the agent engaged in the enterprise. On the other hand, new nomenclature (like *dharmo/alogy* and *buddho/alogy*), besides being infelicitous, will become meaningful only through consensual use, which in any discipline is difficult to achieve. (2) Even if we were to find such a term and agree to it, there is a theoretical reason for rejecting it. What I here term "Buddhist theology" is functionally equivalent to much of what is termed Christian or Jewish or Islamic theology; which is to say that this type of discourse functions for Buddhists in a way similar to its counterparts in other religious contexts. (3) Finally, there is a political reason for not abandoning the term "theology." The present project has as one of its chief goals the promotion of Buddhist theological discourse within the academy. To situate Buddhist theology within the academy is to suggest, as a political move, that it deserves a place *within* the field of Buddhist Studies and *alongside* the field of, for example, academic Christian theology. The use of the word "theology" is strategically important in accomplishing both of these aims.

I have chosen to adopt such a term, therefore, principally for practical, functional and politically expedient reasons (upayically, to coin a Buddhist term). Critical discourse that unapologetically locates itself within the Buddhist tradition (i.e., Buddhist theology) should be considered on a par with Christian theology as far as the academy is concerned; Christian theology should not be privileged over Buddhist theology; and indeed all such forms of discourse, regardless of their religious affiliation, should be given a proportionately equal voice in the academy so long as they can subscribe to the norms of open, rational inquiry. So much for terminological questions, now to substance.

A VOID IN DISCOURSE

A vacuum in discourse yearns as much to be filled as a vacuum in space. First, I seek to identify a form of discourse related to Buddhism – a form of discourse to be situated in the academy, but one that is presently all but absent there. Second, I suggest how this vacuum should be filled by commencing the process of laying the groundwork for the field of academic Buddhist theology. Buddhist Studies as an academic discipline has come a long way since its inception in the early nineteenth century.[3] But despite the strides, both quantitative and qualitative, the field has been reluctant to allow for the development of theological discourse as a scholarly option.[4] The reasons are varied and complex, and beyond the scope of this essay. Suffice it to say that I believe that the banishment of Buddhist theology from the discipline of Buddhist Studies has its roots in a positivistic ideology that pervades the discipline even to this day.[5] Imbued with the secularist ethos of the Enlightenment, and entrenched, albeit subtly at times, in the now passé world-view that scholarship in the humanities is to be modeled on that of the natural sciences,[6] the discipline has too often been content to focus on the linguistic aspects of texts to the exclusion of seriously engaging their doctrinal and practical content. When it *has* taken doctrine and practice seriously as objects of study, it has too often sought to engage these at most descriptively, eschewing attempts to treat them normatively.[7] Based on the naive assumption that the natural sciences are objective, and on the further false presupposition that religious adherents are subject to prejudices that make objectivity impossible, the discipline has also been reticent to take seriously the scholarship of believers, even, *per imposibile*, were they to deal openly, critically and rigorously with their subject matter, especially with normative questions. Because of the way it considers the object of research (doctrinal, ethical and practice-related claims as historical or cultural artifacts, and not as candidates for truth), the method used to analyze that object (descriptively, and not for their normative value), and the subject *qua* analyst (the objective, neutral researcher vs. the religiously committed, and therefore "contaminated," believer), Buddhist Studies has, whether consciously or not, banished Buddhist theology to a nether-land beyond the boundaries of what it considers true scholarship.

Apart from the fact that this has made believers feel a bit timid in the academy,[8] even when engaged in classical buddhological discourse, all of this has had little effect on the Buddhist world. In other venues Buddhists continue to engage in the art of theology and its ancillary sub-disciplines like catechesis, exegesis and polemics. In Asia, and in recent decades in the West, Buddhists persist in the practice of explaining their religion, demonstrating the relevance of their doctrines and practices to the present age, and defending the tenets of their faith vis a vis the challenges of competitors (e.g., those of other religious views and of secular modernity). But in the West this form of theology has often been uncritical. With few exceptions, it has either recapitulated traditional Asian Buddhist views with little thought to analyzing their relevance or worth in their new historical and/or cultural milieu, or it has, in the name of making Buddhism acceptable to the widest possible audience, commodified it, in the process draining the religion of all (or most) meaningful content, making it just one more strategy for living a stress-free life.

It can now be gleaned that is how the vacuum has been created: in the void of a triangle formed by the positivism of the discipline of Buddhist Studies at one corner, the often anachronistic, expository mode of traditionalist scholarship at another, and the commodified discourse of much of the popularist literature at the third. My purpose here is not to suggest that each of these forms of discourse has no place in the understanding and appropriation of Buddhism,[9] but that they should not impede the development of a new form of discourse that is equally important: that of academic Buddhist theology. Put another way, my intention is not to dismiss these forms of discourse generally – indeed, I believe that each, in its own way, contributes to the academic Buddhist theological enterprise – but only to suggest (a) that none of the three are substitutes for the form of discourse I am calling for here, and (b) that each needs to be purged of the implicit ideologies that, reductionistically, assume their respective discourses to be uniquely valid, thereby impeding alternatives discursive options.

A detailed critique of the ideologies endemic to the reductionistic versions of these forms of discourse would take us too far afield from the present task. Suffice it, then, to offer these brief remarks by way of suggesting at least the direction of such a critique. To the positivist, the theologian should reply (a) that commitment to the tradition does not prevent a critical perspective any more than a lack of commitment guarantees it, and (b) that after the work of philology is done, there still remains the question of the truth of doctrine; to the traditionalist, that even when doctrine is understood, there is still the issue of relevance: what aspects of Buddhist doctrines and of its technologies of practice should be given priority, and how these are to be appropriated, both individually and communally, in the contemporary cultural milieu; and to the popularist, (a) that it will not suffice to focus arbitrarily on aspects of the tradition to the exclusion of others, or worse, to allow the consumerist demands of our culture to dictate our theological agenda, and (b) that even once that agenda has been rigorously circumscribed, there still remains the task of arguing for it using all of the scholarly tools at our disposal.

Of course, the reductionistic ideologies present in these three forms of discourse are problematic not only because they stand in the way of the emergence of academic Buddhist theology as a discipline, but for other independent reasons. Positivism lacks sufficient awareness of subjectivity. Being naive about the role of the subject in its own discourse, it portrays itself as an objective enterprise vis a vis the scholarship of the religiously committed, and thus to summarily dismiss the latter. Traditionalism, to the extent that it conflates exegesis and criticism, believes that the mere explanation of doctrine is all that is required of the theologian. Lacking, as it does, a nuanced notion of history, it fails to pay sufficient attention to the fact that doctrine and practice can be appropriated only in specific contexts. Popularism, to the extent that it succumbs to consumerist demands, at its best simply lacks intellectual rigor, while at its worst goes beyond mere sloppiness to a kind of anti-intellectualism that makes careful, critical scholarship superfluous, anathema or both. It shows little concern for the detailed scholarship that has been done on texts. It also lacks sufficient commitment to the tradition as a whole. Suffering from a pick-and-choose mentality that it justifies in the name of relevance, it is too ready to arbitrarily dismiss doctrines that are problematic or that on the surface appear anachronistic, thereby evincing as well a kind of intellectual defeatism.

But if these three modes of discourse themselves fail to be sufficiently academic, or Buddhist or theological, and if in their more extreme, reductionistic versions they actually impede the emergence of academic Buddhist theology, it should also be clear that each of the three suggests to theologians *positive* qualities that are crucial to their enterprise. Rigorous text-critical work that pays attention to historical and cultural context, as well as the commitment to free and open inquiry (both the legacy of Buddhology), are pivotal to the theological task; equally important is the critical spirit, the piety, the devotion to practice and the commitment to tradition that derives from the inspiration of traditional scholarship; finally, the popular literature reminds us that the theologian's task is a constructive one that seeks to make Buddhist doctrine relevant to contemporary circumstances. While the three modes of discourse described above create the vacuum that I suggest ought to be filled by academic Buddhist theology as an enterprise, they also inform that undertaking in positive ways.

PRECURSORS TO AN ACADEMIC BUDDHIST THEOLOGY

It is, of course, an overstatement to claim that academic Buddhist theology has been utterly nonexistent as a form of discourse. In the literature of each of the three areas just described we find some examples of work that approaches academic theological discourse, some, more limited, examples that exhibit many of the features of this form of discourse, though perhaps not recognizing themselves as theological per se, and even a very few that do.

As I have pointed out elsewhere (Cabezón 1995: 258n), even while depicting their work as descriptive and analytically objective, Buddhologists sometimes cross the line, tentatively and cautiously, into normative, quasi-theological discourse (see Schmithausen: 2, 56).[10] Other works in the field of Buddhist Studies, while perhaps not recognizing themselves as theological, are less reticent to engage in academic theological discourse. Fenner, for example, clearly situates his work as the result of his experience as a practicing Buddhist (xvii) and sees his task to be that of "producing an intelligible and relevant interpretation of Middle Path analysis" (xviii) using a system-cybernetics model. Similarly, Guenther and Thurman use Buddhist parallels to other strands in Western philosophy as a way of making Buddhist ideas both accessible and acceptable to a Western (particularly an intellectual) audience. Whether these various works succeed in their reading of Buddhism through their respective Western hermeneutical lenses may be questioned, as may be the need for such a reading to the task of Buddhist theology.[11] Be that as it may, each of these works has at the very least strong affinities to the enterprise of academic Buddhist theology, whether or not they recognize themselves as theological.

There is, moreover, some scholarly work that does recognize itself to be explicitly theological. In feminist scholarship in the field of Buddhist Studies, particularly in the work of Rita Gross, we find operative, from an early date, a self-avowedly theological agenda (see Gross 1984, 1986, 1987, 1993). No less theological, though arguably less explicitly so, is the work of Anne Klein.[12] More recently, John Makransky sees the impetus behind his work on the Mahayana doctrine(s) of buddhahood, which is primarily devoted to a careful study of the classical sources, to be in large part theological (xiii–xiv), at least in so far as it is for him motivated by overtly religious questioning.[13]

As is the case with literature that situates itself in the discipline of Buddhist Studies, there is also to be found, in the work of several eminent, contemporary, traditional scholars, literature that is paradigmatic of constructive theological inquiry, despite the fact that most of it does not rely upon a formal Western scholarly apparatus. Examples include much of the work of His Holiness, the Dalai Lama (1988, 1996a, 1996b, 1996c, forthcoming), Thich Nhat Hanh (1987, 1992a, 1992b, 1993), Sulak Sivaraksa (1985, 1986) and Ajahn Buddhadasa. While maintaining a strong commitment to their respective traditions, because of their willingness to reach beyond the historical horizons of the texts and the boundaries of their own cultures, each of these influential Buddhist teachers (and there are others as well) directly confront, in much of their writing, the issue of the relevance of Buddhist doctrine and practice to the modern world. In so doing, they avoid succumbing to the problematic form of traditionalism described above.

Several of these figures have themselves been concerned with the applicability of Buddhism to the social and political realms.[14] Among the more notable examples of work by Western scholars (often inspired, incidentally, by the religious leaders just mentioned) who concern themselves with the relevance of Buddhist principles to the social/political sphere we might mention that of Joanna Macy (1983, 1985) and Ken Jones. Both the traditional and Western work concerned with such issues can, at the very least, form the foundation for a more evolved and rigorous academic social/political theology, one that has yet to develop fully within the Buddhist tradition the way that German political theology or Latin American liberation theology has within the Christian tradition.

Mention must also be made of a burgeoning more general *popular* literature in the West that is also theological in character. Notable in this regard is the work of Sangharakshita (1979, 1984), Stephen Batchelor (1983, 1990, 1997), Subhuti, Martin Willson, and B. Alan Wallace (1989, 1993). Each of these authors in his own way grapples with the issue of the relevance of Buddhist doctrine to contemporary life and thought. Each bears witness to the critical spirit that is so important a part of the academic Buddhist theological task; and each is grounded in the sources of his respective tradition, even if the explicit voice of those traditions are often muted in their work. If the work of these authors is not *academically* theological it is because, being directed at a more popular audience, they do not feel the need to abide by the norms of scholarly discourse, especially as regards the Buddhist textual tradition.[15]

In concluding our discussion of Buddhist theological work to date, it behooves us to mention some of the more important periodical literature. There is of course in the Western Buddhist world a long tradition of the more popular press that begins with journals like *The Middle Way* and *The Buddhist Review*[16] and continues up to the present times with the magazine *Tricycle*. These publications, and other serials like the *Vajradhaṭu Sun* (now the *Shambhala Sun*), the *Snow Lion Newsletter*, *Insight* and some of the publications of the Institute for Buddhist Studies in Berkeley, have sometimes acted as informal venues for theological reflections and debate. They are important resources for the academic theologian: informing us of issues that are important to our communities, and acting as venues for the more popular dissemination of our scholarly findings.[17] One expects electronic venues, like chat lines, subscription lists and the world-wide-web generally to increasingly serve in this capacity as well.

To summarize, there already exists a limited, but growing, body of Buddhist work that can be characterized as theological (or proto-theological), even if only a small portion of this is scholarly in nature, and even if only a still smaller percentage recognizes itself as theological. But it is equally clear that until the recent attempts to motivate such discourse in the context of the American Academy of

Religion, there has been virtually no cognizance of the possibility of academic Buddhist theology *as a field unto itself.*

CONTEXT AND THE BOUNDARIES OF TRADITION

Like all religious traditions with a long history and a cultural breadth that is the result of geographical diffusion, Buddhism is a multifaceted thing. There is, as many scholars have pointed out, no single Buddhist tradition: there is no Buddhism, only Buddhisms. If Buddhist theological discourse must emerge, as I think all forms of theology must, from within a tradition, this implies that academic Buddhist theology too will be inevitably partial and of necessity perspectival. Buddhist theologians therefore have no choice but to associate themselves with one among the many Buddhist sub-traditions, and to speak from within that partial perspective. I do not mean for this to be read as implying a kind of relativism, however. When the positions of these various theological sub-traditions contradict each other, they will have to be adjudicated in the only court available to us, that of open, critical dialogue.

For many – perhaps for most – Western Buddhist theologians, the subtraction out of which we speak will be an already existing school of Asian Buddhism: the one in which we have been enculturated and to which we give our allegiance. In some cases, Western Buddhist theologians may choose consciously to affiliate with, and therefore to represent, more than one sub-tradition, but this, as I shall argue below, will be the exception rather than the rule. In any case, even when multiply situated, it seems to me that the contours of the composite tradition that form the site out of which these Western Buddhist theologians think/write/practice will be, at least for the time being, determined by the contours and boundaries of Asian forms of Buddhism.

But as Buddhism continues to take root in cultures outside of Asia, we should find non-Asian forms of Buddhism serving increasingly as the home traditions out of which Buddhists venture in their theological journeys. In some instances these may be coterminous with national Buddhisms (British, German, Cuban, South African), especially in the case where national boundaries also serve to give these traditions a distinctive cultural form. But in this increasingly global culture, I suspect that the boundaries of these new forms of Buddhism will not be determined by national identity, but by other factors, like language, socio-political world-view and especially lineage. Hence, Anglo-American Theravāda, or Austro-Germanic Rinzai Zen, or Euro-

American dGe lugs may be the more plausible units of tradition rather than, say, American or Zairian Buddhism. In addition, the importance of the role of charismatic teachers in most forms of Buddhism, and the distinctive imprint they have left and continue to leave on the traditions they have founded worldwide, may very well yield new arrangements of tradition that transcend national, linguistic and cultural boundaries. But my purpose here is not to speculate at any length about the units or the distribution the Buddhist tradition may take in the future. It is simply to make the point that, given the importance of tradition to theology, we cannot take the notion of tradition for granted. Not only will theologians have to identify their traditional affiliation – admitting, as it were, the partial and perspectival nature of their discourse – they will, at some point in time, have to turn their attention critically to the notion of tradition itself.

The boundaries of the Buddhist tradition outside Asia are, as I have stated, still in flux. Part of the reason for this, it seems to me, has to do with the fact that there has yet to emerge a full-fledged scholarly mode of Buddhist theological discourse in non-Asian cultures, one whose intellectual home is in the academy. The role of the academy in bringing legitimacy, stability and longevity to Buddhist traditions cannot be overestimated. Western Buddhist academic theologians, for the foreseeable future, will continue to seek their Buddhist inspiration principally from the Asian traditions that have nourished them, but their theology will also be pivotal to the emergence of new and distinctive traditions in the West. Rather than implying that the relationship between theology and tradition is one-sided, however, perhaps it is more accurate to say that Western Buddhist theology and Western Buddhist traditions will have to bootstrap themselves into existence, each depending on the other for support.

Western Buddhist academic theology, therefore, will emerge as a sectarian enterprise; and the configuration of its sectarian divisions will, for the foreseeable future, be homologous to those of Asian Buddhism. Of course, one might imagine a scenario in which an academic theologian will choose consciously to rely on the sources of more than one Asian tradition, but this will be rare. It will be rare, it seems to me, (a) because of the sociological pressures exerted by the logic of sectarianism – in which traditions see themselves as individual and unique, and in which these traditions often require the undivided loyalty of the adherent, (b) because of the difficulty of "mastering" more than one tradition, and (c) because of the difficulty of harmonizing disparate traditions.[18] That academic Buddhist theology will, for the foreseeable future, be divided according to Asian sectarian lines, is, however, a contingent, and not a necessary, characteristic of this form of theology in the West. It is quite conceivable that some distant form of this discourse will cross sectarian lines in ways that we would find unimaginable today.

That academic Buddhist theology is a sectarian undertaking is a fact that has implications not only to the first-order task of doing theology, but also to the second-order, theoretical task of characterizing theology. Theology will *look* quite different to a theologian grounded in the Zen tradition and to one grounded in the Indo-Tibetan sources.[19] Now an awareness and public declaration of the nature of one's subjectivity is an essential aspect of theology, and identifying the portion of the Buddhist tradition with which one is affiliated is a crucial part of this task. I myself turn to the sources of the Indo-Tibetan tradition, especially as they are studied, practiced and lived-out in the great monastic institutions (*gden sa*) of Tibet, for my theological grounding. My reasons for choosing to identify with this tradition are of course largely due to the contingent fact that this is where I received much of my religious formation. But I would like to think that there are reasons for my chosen affiliation other than those having to do with happenstance, that is, with the historical accidents and chance meetings that constitute my own individual spiritual journey. The vast and diverse resources of the Indo-Tibetan tradition, it seems to me, could provide *any* scholar with ample raw material for constructive theological work. Its commitment to systematic, open and rational inquiry is in accordance with the academic theologian's analogous methodological requirements. Additionally, its rich hermeneutical insights, and its generally skeptical attitude regarding the role scripture should play in theological discourse, give the theologian the kind of freedom necessary to make ancient doctrine relevant to contemporary circumstances. Finally, its attempt to balance theory and practice – the conceptual study of doctrine and its internalization in meditation – serves as a continual reminder that the Buddhist theological task must take both into account, and that it can be reduced to neither.[20]

WHY ACADEMIC?

I have been arguing in this essay for a form of Buddhist theology that is academic and scholarly, noting the fact that there is a void in discourse that yearns to be filled by such an undertaking. But not all voids, of course, deserve to be filled. So it behooves me at this juncture to say a few words concerning why I think that a form of

Buddhist theology that is academic is a desideratum. In so doing, I hope to supply motivations for the discipline that go beyond a mere "principle of plenitude" type of aesthetic argument that claims that in the continuum of discourse, the instantiation of all of its possible forms is preferable to the leaving of gaps.

What do I mean by *academic*? What makes a particular form of Buddhist theological discourse *academic*? In large part I mean simply that such discourse abides by the accepted norms of contemporary scholarly practice in the humanities.[21] But this of course substantially begs the question, for what precisely are these accepted norms? In addition, what warrants their acting as standards on which to base a form of religious discourse like Buddhist theology, and what is to guarantee that such norms, foreign as they are to both the theory and practice of Buddhist tradition, should serve the purpose of the Buddhist theologian?

The first of these latter three questions is enormous in its scope. It calls for nothing less than a full characterization of Western scholarship in the humanities, which, it should go without saying, is beyond the scope of this or any other essay. At the risk of banality, and, worse, of falling "into passionate generalities inherited from a past just about as unexamined in this regard as the present" (Geertz: 183), let me simply note some of the more important features of scholarly discourse that I see as especially important to Buddhist theology. Some of these I have already mentioned (by way of their absence) in my critique of popularism above, but I reiterate them here for the sake of completeness.

First is a commitment to breadth of analysis: to the examination of all relevant sources, and especially all of the textual sources of one's tradition relevant to the specific problem under investigation. This is of course an ideal that is never fully realized, but for the scholar, comprehensiveness is an ideal worth striving for. In particular, a commitment to breadth of analysis implies that no source will be dismissed in an ad hoc manner. I take such a commitment to imply a willingness to grapple with what, from a contemporary perspective, might be considered the most problematic and anachronistic portions of the tradition. I take it also to imply an obligation to consider both the primary sources (in the original languages where at all possible), and the secondary scholarly literature. Finally, I take it that breadth of analysis implies engaging those portions of other religious traditions, and of the secular intellectual tradition, that in some way illuminate (either by supporting *or* challenging) positions taken in the Buddhist sources.

Second, I take the chief method of theological scholarship – the *way* of engaging one's object – to be a *critical* one. An interdisciplinary history of the notion of criticism in the human sciences, and of its relationship to the Western academy, has yet to be written, as has a detailed philosophical treatment of the notion of the critical. Some of the more interesting contributions to this subject are to be found in the work of sociologists (Bourdieu), and literary critics (Bove; Culler: 3–56; Davis and Schleifer; Bizzell). A great deal of this work is relevant to the construction of the notion of the critical in theology: the distinction between modernist and traditional forms of criticism (Bourdieu), or that between historical/philological and interpretive (Culler), or between criticism and critique (Davis and Schleifer), or between institutionalized/academic and public/journalistic (several of the above scholars).

A detailed treatment of the notion of criticism, even as circumscribed by its role in theological discourse, is of course beyond the scope of the present discussion, but a few words at least are called for. On the one hand, criticism proceeds in the direction of making the less familiar more so. As Sontag states, it strives to show us both that things are what they are and how they are what they are (14).[22] Hence, for example, higher textual criticism attempts to determine the origins of texts and doctrines, and to contextualize these both in regard to other texts and in regard to the culture in which they emerged, shedding light on their meaning vis a vis the past. But in a countermovement, criticism should act to defamiliarize what is too familiar. In the words of Marshall McLuhan, "it is critical vision alone which can mitigate the unimpeded operation of the automatic" (87). In short, criticism is a double movement, and this is captured well in the words of Geertz, when he states the purpose of research to be the rendering of things "intelligible to those to whom they seem foreign (as well as, indeed, to those who have them, to whom they seem merely inevitable)" (155–156).

The critical spirit in academic Buddhist theology should evince this double-movement. It should make more familiar the texts and practices of Buddhist cultures that are distant from us in both space and time. In its countermovement, it should force us to step back and to question that which has become second nature by virtue of its proximity (both in Buddhism and in our own culture); it should force us to examine the very presuppositions of our religion, our world and even our discourse. What is more, such a critical spirit should be all-pervasive and all-penetrating. No portion of our enterprise should be exempt from its scrutiny, and there is never any a priori reason to limit the depth of such scrutiny. Both horizontally, across the tradition, and vertically, within any specific critical venture, freedom of inquiry should reign.

Third, academic scholarship requires a commitment to the use of a formal apparatus. This includes general features like systematicity in exposition,[23] and the explanation of lacunae in one's arguments or sources; and more formally stylistic ones like appropriate annotation and citation, completeness of bibliographical information, the indexing of book length works, and so forth.[24] Such observations would perhaps be trite were it not for the fact that most Buddhist theological work today lacks such an apparatus.

Why are these academic norms – breadth of analysis, a critical spirit, and the use of a formal apparatus – important? There are, I believe, two reasons for this. The first is to be found in the proven worth of such norms. History has, I believe, demonstrated the validity of a scholarly mode of discourse. Consider, for example, the enormous strides that have been made in the field of Buddhist Studies in the past century by those who have subscribed to such norms. That knowledge in this field, as in any other, is incremental, and requires access to ever-increasing numbers of sources (breadth), and their rigorous (orderly, formal) and critical treatment, is self-evident from even the most cursory perusal of the history of scholarship. That there exists in academic modes of discourse the danger of isolation and irrelevancy born from hyper-specialization, what Hannah Arendt calls "the famous knowing of more and more about less and less," or that it can lead "to the development of a pseudo-scholarship which actually destroys its object" (132), is of course no argument against scholarship generally. Breadth of analysis must go hand in hand with breadth of vision, and it must lead beyond itself to the accomplishment of worthwhile human goals. When originality or relevance is lacking in scholarship surely the fault lies elsewhere than in the use of scholarly norms. And to those who would accuse me of an outmoded evolutionism or progressivism in regard to scholarship, I reply simply, "Is it not indeed the case that, even in a subspecialty like *prajñāpāramitā* studies, we know more today than we did in the early decades of this century?" The norms of the academy have stood the test of time, and continue to this day to stand *us* in good stead.

There is, however, another reason for abiding by such norms, one to which I have already alluded. The rise of non-Asian forms of Buddhism as traditions in their own right largely depends upon their social legitimation. There is arguably no greater form of social legitimation than acceptance in the academy, and this requires the emergence of a mode of theological discourse that subscribes to its norms.

That such norms are not fixed, that they are contested, that they change across disciplines and with time, and that they change in conversation with the norms of other scholarly cultures is perhaps a truism. Important to note in this regard is the way these norms – and, indeed, the very characteristics of thought – are changing as a response to computerization, as in the works of Heim, Lanham, and Nunberg and Eco. As an aside, it is interesting to mention the work of Holtzman, who suggests not that Buddhist studies will change as a result of electronic media, but that Buddhism (and specifically the thought of Nāgārjuna) may be of use in helping us to conceptualize new forms of digital expressions! Be that as it may, and granted that academic norms and forms of expression are far from immutable, my point still stands.

Finally, what of the charge that these norms are foreign to the Buddhist tradition, that to abide by them is to capitulate to Euro-American modernist notions of what constitutes serious scholarship? Of course, each sub-tradition of Buddhism will have to answer this question in its own way. As for the response of my own tradition, there is little that seems foreign in the academic norms I have outlined above: related to content (breadth), to method (critical) and to style (formal).[25] Since I have dealt with this issue recently elsewhere (Cabezón forthcoming), I remain content to point out here that there is little variation between what constitutes good scholarship in the Indo-Tibetan sources and in the modernist West. True, traditional theologians have perhaps been less than meticulous about text-critical questions,[26] and occasionally less than careful about their use[27] and citation[28] of sources, and this is not a trivial point. However, the same can often be said about Western scholarship. Moreover, there is nothing in traditional Indo-Tibetan scholarship that stands in the way of the use of text-critical or formal Western academic apparati, and this, it seems to me, is the more important point.

Before proceeding to the last section of this essay, it is necessary to mention, even if briefly, the debate that has raged in the Religious Studies academy concerning the question of whether or not theology belongs there (see Ogden; Griffin and Hough). It has been Christian theologians who have been at the forefront of this discussion. The issues are of course complex: ranging from theoretical ones (what is the nature of theology?) to ostensibly pedagogical ones (should students be exposed to the religious aspects of their cultural heritage?) to legal and political ones (does the separation of church and state permit the teaching of theology in the public university?). Such issues must eventually be confronted by the academic Buddhist theologian as well. On the one hand, facing the issues, and learning from what Christian theologians have had to say about them, will enrich our understanding of our own enterprise and of its place vis à vis the various institutions that comprise the academy. On the other, Buddhists, by adding our own voice to these discussions, will, I believe, contribute significantly to it. Some observations by way of example might help to suggest how.

The case for situating Christian theology within the mainstream of the academy has sometimes been made either by granting victory to secular notions of what constitutes critical inquiry (by conceding, too early, that critical discourse belongs to the public realm of the secular and then arguing for a theology that conforms to such critical norms) or by weakening the notion of academy (for example, by arguing that the critical discourse of Religious Studies is no less dogmatic and subjective than is theological discourse). Both of these moves, I believe, are, at least for Buddhists, problematic.

To allow the notion of criticism to be dictated by secular, public norms is in a sense to surrender even before the battle. It is to concede to the fact that the classical theological tradition is *un*critical, lacking its own norms for rational inquiry. The secular, public realm comes then to take the place of tradition as the site out of which theological criticism operates. This results in a kind of theological homelessness, and with it both less cognizance of and less responsibility to one's historical antecedents. If this is the price to be paid for admission into the academy, then better to pass.

On the other hand, to weaken the notion of academy by suggesting that, as with theology, its discourse *too* is contextual and subjective, is a move that, though partially true, is fraught with peril. In some cases it has led to protectionist strategies, to a segregation of theological discourse that, though perhaps permitted a place alongside of, is now considered immune from the critique that is implied by, other forms of discourse, and, in turn, is impotent itself to critique them.[29] In other cases, such a move has resulted in out and out relativism.

My goal here, however, is not to argue for the place of theology generally in the academy. How other theological traditions apply for admission is their own business. Instead, I wish to make the case for my brand of Buddhist theology in particular. This is, I believe, the way such a discussion should proceed, that is, on a case by case basis. That Christian or Jewish theology has a rightful place among other forms of discourse in the Religious Studies academy is no guarantee of the fact that the same is true for Buddhism, or for all forms of Buddhism. Since theological traditions are as diverse as disciplines, each tradition will have to make the argument for itself, and those arguments will have to be judged on their own merits.

My claim here is that the nature of Buddhist theology (or at least my brand of Buddhist theology) is such that the case for its inclusion in the mainstream of academic discourse can be made without falling into either of the two extremes mentioned above: without abandoning a notion of the critical that is particularly religious and without falling into a separate-but-equal view of the religious and secular academic worlds. Both classical Buddhist theology and the contemporary academic variety that I envision as its heir, as I have claimed, already subscribe to critical principles that are consonant with those of the academy. Of course, the academy itself is not univocal on what constitutes free and open inquiry (consider post-structuralism!), but that is irrelevant to my point here. It suffices for my purposes that academic Buddhist theology that is responsible to tradition be committed to some set of such principles with a relatively large constituency in the academy. And this, it seems to me, is possible.

THE BUDDHIST SOURCES OF BUDDHIST THEOLOGY

If Buddhist theology is to be responsibly constructive, as I have stated above, this means that it must take tradition – and especially the textual sources of the tradition – seriously. This should be true as much of first order theological discourse as it is of the second order theoretical discourse of which this essay is an example. I am certain that it has not gone unnoticed that up to this point I have failed to mention in any substantive way what the Indo-Tibetan sources take the theological task to be. Let me do so now, even if briefly, by way of conclusion.

I could, at this point, explore what some of the great texts of Indo-Tibetan Mahāyāna Buddhism have to say about the goal of their discourse (self- and other-perfection), about its relationship to praxis (that theology is a necessary prerequisite to meditative practice but cannot take the place of it), about method (that it be comprehensive, formal, critical and rationalist), about the relationship of theological discourse to the scriptures (one of qualified dependence), about the rhetorical features of theological texts (many and varied), about their structure (that it is systematic) and about their intended audience (mostly, but not exclusively Buddhist, and certainly not the Buddhist masses). The texts have a great deal to say about each of these topics, and, more important, they have a great deal to say to academic Buddhist theologians about how they should engage these various theoretical issues. But I choose instead to focus on a single question: the classical Buddhist depiction of the theologian himself or herself.

No Buddhist text, of course, speaks directly of the subjectivity of the theologian. This is a modernist (or, perhaps more accurately, a postmodernist) concern. But the texts do offer us traces and glimmers that can be utilized by the contemporary theologian in the construction of such a notion, one that is relevant to our contemporary needs. Retrospectively, we can identify theologians in the Indian tradition as those who compose theological tracts (Sanskrit *śāstra*; Tibetan *bstan bcos*). There is considerable discussion in the Indian and Tibetan sources concerning the nature of such tracts. The Tibetan scholar Bu ston Rin chen grub (1290-1364), following the early Indian Mahāyāna text known as the *Uttaratantra*, defines a *śāstra* as "a work that explains the meaning of the Buddha's word, is in accordance with the path for the attainment of emancipation, and is composed by someone with an undistracted mind."[30] What does this imply about the author of such a text – the theologian? Bu ston's definition tells us that (a) a theologian is someone who has scholarly access to the scriptures (one cannot explain the meaning of words that one has not studied and understood), (b) that a theologian is motivated by the desire to lead others to emancipation, and manipulates the scriptures to this end, and (c) that he or she is not only a practitioner of Buddhism, but has reaped the fruits of such practice, at least to the point of having attained a certain degree of mental stability ("an undistracted mind"). This tells us a great deal about the subjectivity of the Buddhist theologian. A Buddhist theologian is, first of all, a Buddhist. This is not a banal observation, given that in today's theological climate there are many theologians who would claim that it is possible to engage in their task without allegiance to a religious tradition.[31] But more than that, theologians are scholars[32] who have mastered the scriptural tradition of Buddhism to the point of being able to explicate its meaning. Theologians must be skilled in the art of exegesis, sufficiently aware of the world around them to be able to unleash in their respective cultural milieus the liberative power of the texts that they manipulate, and sufficiently motivated by the welfare of others to have the will to do so. Finally, Buddhist theologians are individuals who have themselves tasted the emancipatory power of Buddhist doctrine, and who therefore speak out of experience. If we take all of these demands literally, it puts a tremendous burden on academic Buddhist theologians, for over and above religious commitment, an intellectual mastery of the tradition, and a mastery of the norms of traditional and contemporary scholarly discourse that are required to explicate it, it requires of them its (at least partial) internalization.

Most of all, I think, Bu ston's words put our work into perspective. They humble us. They force us to admit that for many, perhaps for most, of us, ours is at most a pseudo-theology, born perhaps from minimal competence and good intentions, but in any case not sufficiently immersed in the rich waters of transformative praxis. And this is good to know.

In another classic text of the Tibetan tradition, the early scholastic master Sa skya paṇḍita Kun dga' rgyal mtshan (1182-1251), explains the activity (*bya ba*) of scholars (*mkhas pa*) to be threefold: explanation (*'chad pa*), disputation (*rtsod pa*) and composition (*rtsom pa*) (Jackson: 5). As defined by their work, then, theologians (that is, *religious* scholars) are individuals who explain the doctrine, having mastered the subject matter (Jackson: 3), so that they are not ignorant of it (*shes bya rig pa'i gnas la ma rmongs pa*) (Krang dbyi sun et. al.: 304–305). Having done so, they defend the views of their tradition through the art of polemic. Finally, they are *authors*, sharing their views with others. For Sa skya paṇḍita these three activities are not only descriptive, they are *prescriptive*: they are activities that, in this case religious, scholars must undertake. The first point reiterates one already made by Bu ston – that theologians must be masters of the Buddhist sources. The third emphasizes the public nature of the theological task: it is incumbent upon theologians to make their views known, as authors.[33] The second further elucidates the nature of the public authorial task and of commitment to tradition: Buddhist theologians must be willing not only to subject their reflections on the tradition to public scrutiny, they must defend them (and implicitly their tradition) when faced with challenges. There emerges from the work of Sa skya paṇḍita, then, a picture of the Buddhist theologian, once again, as a committed master of his or her tradition. But in addition, theologians must be public scholars, who are obliged to communicate the views of their tradition, willing to subject them to public scrutiny, and duty-bound to defend them.

Some of my recent, and as yet unpublished, textual/historical research on the colophons of classical Buddhist theological texts in high scholastic Tibet indicates that the theological task was a more communal than an individual enterprise. Despite the fact that a single individual is usually identified as the "author" (literally, "creator": *mdzad pa po*) of a theological work, the colophons of these texts make it clear that the composition of such texts involved a variety of scholars of varying levels of expertise and competence. Hence, theological authorship is a more corporate and social undertaking than it is in the contemporary West. This fact should make us pause and ask ourselves the extent to which we, as contemporary theologians, rely on others in our scholarly work. It should also make us question the scholarly identity into which we have been enculturated: that of the lone, self-sufficient and solitary individual. Arguably, it should push us to full disclosure of the debt we owe to others even in the work we consider our own, to more corporate and communal scholarly work, and, most important, to the creation of a community of scholar/ theologians based on our common work.[34]

Of course, a great deal more could be said about how the theologian is depicted in the classical texts. We could, for example, plumb the hagiographical literature to glean what facets of subjectivity the tradition puts forward as essential to the theologian's identity. Or alternatively, we could look to theological tracts themselves to see how classical theologians construct a notion of their own subjectivity through a variety of rhetorical artifacts. Then, of course, there remains the task of applying these lessons to *our* discourse as contemporary academic Buddhist theologians. What role, for example, do literary expressions of piety play in the classical construction of theological subjectivity? What role do/should they play in our own work? Exploring these and similar issues would greatly enhance both our effectiveness and our self-awareness as theologians.

The viability of academic Buddhist theology as a discipline will be proven, like the proverbial pudding, only after it is done. I take it that it is largely the purpose of this volume to allow us a taste of this emerging field. A theory (from Greek *theōros*, spectator) of academic Buddhist theology, strictly speaking, requires an object, and so this essay is in a sense premature: more like looking into an empty theater and dreaming the possibilities of a work of drama than actually seeing one. But perhaps that is not such an odious position in which to find oneself: to have the opportunity to pause and dream.

NOTES

1 An earlier version of this paper was presented in the Theology and Religious Reflection Section at the annual meeting of the American Academy of Religion in Philadelphia in 1995. The author wishes to express his gratitude to the steering committee of that section for their openness to receiving proposals from non-Christian religious perspectives. This essay has profited from the substantive reading given to it by my three colleagues at Iliff, Delwin Brown, Sheila Davaney and William Dean, from the very helpful comments of the two editors of this volume, and of Paul Griffiths as well as from the editorial comments of Davis Powell.

2 In fact, there is already precedence for this more general usage of the word theology in the academy. See, for example, Ogden (4, passim). There is much that I find helpful in Ogden's essay, although there are,

I believe, problems as well. Especially problematic is his characterization of "philosophical theology" (7), which, though not completely clear, seems to amounts to nothing more than philosophical reflection related to human existential questions, and which therefore belongs more to the realm of philosophy than to that of theology.

3 For a brief and partial historical overview of the field see de Jong (1972: pts. I and II; and 1984); for more recent developments in the field see Gómez; and Cabezón (1995).

4 To date, it has been the Theology and Religious Reflection Section of the American Academy of Religion which has been most responsive to our overtures. The Buddhism Section, on the other hand, has been less hospitable as a venue for theological discourse.

5 The characterization of that positivism that follows is admittedly a caricature. My claim is not that Buddhologists operate consciously from within such a world-view, but rather that the warp and woof of the discipline is imbued with the perfume of such an ethos *vāsanā*-like.

6 For a critique of this view as it applies to theology see Griffin: 6–10.

7 To treat a claim doctrinally is as much to consider the possibility of its falsity as it is to consider the possibility of its truth. Not all forms of normative discourse are theological, though all theological discourse is normative. That greater emphasis needs to be placed on the normative assessment of doctrines is a point made most recently by Griffiths (1994) in his call for the "doctrinal study of doctrine," even if such a study is for him a philosophical rather than a theological endeavor..

8 Consider, for example, the observations of Eckel regarding the Buddhist believer in the academy. He states that while the sense of their conviction "is palpable, the discourse of conviction is furtive, embarrassed, naive, or, much of the time, entirely absent. When it does manifest itself . . . it is greeted with a strained combination of dismay and consternation – a sense that something has gone wrong (in method if not in substance), but one is not permitted in public to say how and why" (1099). Eckel is not totally clear on this point, and although he is reluctant to call it Buddhist theology, it seems to me as though much of his article could be read precisely as a call for the kind of Buddhist academic theological discourse I am advocating here.

9 Granted that, as portrayed here, each is in some sense lacking, even as regards its own unique task and goals; but this does not mean that in a modified form, each has contributions to make. These modifications would not only make each of the three forms of discourse more effective, it would also open up the space for the emergence of academic Buddhist theological discourse.

10 Schmithausen's work is not, strictly speaking, theological in character because he does not self–identify with the Buddhist tradition (see below concerning the conditions necessary to have full-blown

theological discourse). The fact that he demonstrates a committed passion for a normative position (albeit an ecological one) as well as a high degree of subjective awareness, both hallmarks of theological discourse, bespeak the at least quasi-theological nature of his work. The same might be said of the work of Reichenbach, though the latter work seems to be more sympathetic to a Hindu rather than a strictly Buddhist view.

11 Particularly questionable, it seems to me, is the notion – manifest more in a work like Kirtisinghe's than in those just mentioned – that Buddhist thought requires, for its legitimation, the establishment of parallels to the Western intellectual tradition, in Kirtisinghe's case, Western science. This is not to say that comparison of Buddhist to Western thought is inappropriate, but only that neither the validity nor the relevance of Buddhism is dependent on the existence of similarities to the Western intellectual tradition.

12 That it is feminists who should have been the first to self-consciously identify themselves as Buddhist theologians is, I believe, no accident. Normative critique is of course woven into the very warp and woof of feminist theory, as is a strong sense of subjectivity – including a kind of fearlessness in self-identifying as a believer – both of which are essential to theological thinking.

13 Makransky, though he does not explicitly work through the constructive theological implications of his research in that particular book, begins to do so in his essay for this volume. Put another way, *Buddhahood Embodied* might be seen as a historical theological exercise, while his work in this collection might be considered a more constructive theological one.

14 Queen and King offer a good overview of several of the movements inspired by these (and other) leaders. Despite the fact that much of that volume is descriptive of the views and the program of action of these various movements, it is a useful resource for those who would engage in the more normative enterprise of reflecting theologically on the relationship of the Buddhist tradition to culture, society and the real-political domain; see below.

15 This is perhaps more true of Wallace, Subhuti and Batchelor than it is of Willson. Wallace's *Choosing Reality* is quite rigorous when it comes to Western science and the philosophy of science, but less so when it comes to the Buddhist sources.

16 On the latter see "Allan Bennett: Theravada Monk and Pioneer Publisher," in *Tricycle: The Buddhist Review* (Winter, 1997) 25–27.

17 Also important in this regard are various conferences that are increasingly seen as venues for the shaping of "American Buddhism"; see Queen for a synopsis of one such conference.

18 To take just one example, consider the difficulty of harmonizing just two schools of Tibetan Buddhism – the rNying ma and the dGe lugs – which, *pace* the eclectics who see them as "amounting to the same thing," in point of fact hold several key contradictory doctrines as well

as contradictory methods of religious reflection/praxis. On this, see Williams (1998), which explores some of these various incompatibilities using the doctrine of *rang rig* (self-awareness) as a focus. Of course, it might be argued that the Western Buddhist theologian should learn to live, koan-like, with such contradictions in the name of "diversity, difference, plurality," but I believe that this flies in the face of our commitment to the norms of the academy.

19 This is not to say that there will be no overlaps, but there will also be differences, and these differences will have to be adjudicated, at some point in time, the way that all religious differences should be: through dialogue. I do not therefore mean to imply by the present discussion a kind of relativism.

20 In a recent article Griffiths (1998) sets forth various arguments for the relevance of scholasticism as a form of discourse, even (perhaps especially) in the contemporary intellectual climate. Many of these arguments could be applied, *mutatis mutandis*, to scholastic Buddhist theological discourse.

21 As I have already noted above, the Religious Studies academy in general, and Buddhist Studies in particular, has shown itself to be somewhat allergic to the idea of normative, especially theological, discourse. That I take this to be an irrational and unsupported bias – one in accordance to which academic theologians should not (indeed, by definition, cannot) abide – should be clear.

22 I disagree with Sontag, however, in her claim that this vitiates interpretation.

23 Although I am not prepared to make the stronger claim that would equate systematicity and truth, I must admit that the words of Pannenberg strike a chord with me when he states, "Systematic presentation is itself a test of the truth-claims of each of the specific assertions that enters into a comprehensive account. The reason is that truth itself is systematic, because coherence belongs to the nature of truth. Therefore, the attempt at systematic presentation is intimately related to the concern for the truth that is searched for in the investigation of traditional teaching" (84). See also the following note.

24 I am not unaware of the fact that much of my (admittedly scholastic) emphasis on orderliness and completeness might be considered by some problematic. For example, Rorty (365–372) believes that an emphasis on systematicity impedes the acceptance of non-standard forms of analysis ("the abnormal") and he goes on to counterpose systematic forms of analysis to those that edify. Whether or not this has been true of the Western tradition, whether systematicity impedes other forms of discourse and whether systematic/edifying is a valid distinction in the history of Western thought, it is perhaps enough to say that I believe this not to be true in general. Bourdieu, on the other hand (29), sees many of the formal criteria of academic scholarship that I list here as representing a kind of scientificity. To him, I would

reply simply that what makes his own work convincing is precisely his adoption of such norms.

25 Although couched in different terms, it seems to me that Paul Griffiths' claim that *abhidharma* is a form of denaturalized discourse can at the very least be read as supporting the claim I am making here. See Griffiths 1990.

26 It should be pointed out, however, that such questions are not unknown to traditional scholarship, especially when they impinge upon important issues of doctrine. Consider, to take just one example, the detailed discussions concerning the ascription of the *Akutobhayā* to Nāgārjuna in the Tibetan sources; see Cabezón 1992: 82–84, and 232n, 237–238n.

27 For example, on the dGe lugs tradition's questionable use of *Bodhicaryāvatāra* 9: 140, see Williams 1995.

28 Traditional theologians often cite scriptural material from memory, and this at times leads to errors. These errors are sometimes corrected by editors, but not always. Even when such material is cited accurately, there is no custom of making full reference to the source of the citation. In part, this can be explained by noting that many traditional theologians had, as it were, mental access to the sources, in so far as they had memorized the more important texts. But for the contemporary theologian, for whom the accuracy of the citation and its context vis à vis other portions of the text are pivotal, and who, more often than not, does not have the advantage of mental access, this less rigorous tradition of citation represents a limitation in traditional theological work.

29 Consider, for example, what Pannenberg states (90–91): "It actually represents a retreat from the arena of public critical discourse of truth claims of all sorts, a retreat into some sheltered corner of personal preference." See also Proudfoot.

30 For a fuller discussion of this passage, some later Tibetan responses, and full references to the Indian and Tibetan texts, see Cabezón 1994: 45.

31 In my view it is precisely the fact that theologians speak from a self-avowedly religious perspective that distinguishes them from philosophers, who remain rhetorically silent concerning their religious identity in their discourse. Theologians who claim that theology is possible without the theologian publicly situating himself or herself in a religious tradition have no way of distinguishing between theology and philosophy as disciplines, and this is itself a disadvantage of such a position. This, however, still leaves open the question of whether a religiously committed form of discourse (theology, in my view) is functionally different from one that is not so committed (say philosophy). The Buddhist sources of course claim that it is: that to situate oneself within the tradition, and to make this known rhetorically in one's work, does make a difference. But I realize that it is not sufficient simply to cite the texts on this point. That

difference – the difference that it makes to engage in religiously committed discourse (theology) – will have to be articulated and argued for in a public fashion, although that is the subject for another paper.

32 This being said, the Tibetan tradition is not unaware of the fact that it is possible to be a scholar (*mkhas pa*) without being either morally upright (*btsun pa*) or having goodness of heart (*bzang po*). That a true theologian must have all three qualities, however, is, at the very least, implied.

33 To whom these views are to be made known, that is, the audience of theological texts, is a complicated issue. It is a complicated question even in the traditional sources, and becomes more so when we consider the question of what the audience of contemporary Buddhist theology is and should be, given, for example, the much higher level of literacy and education of lay Buddhists today, especially in the West. Relevant to this issue is the literature on a series of question that have concerned Christian theologians in recent years: the extent to which theology should be a public enterprise, what precisely this means, and what it implies (see Tracy; Cady; Dean). I foresee the conversation between the Buddhist and the Christian theologian on this issue to yield interesting and useful insights for both parties.

34 On the role of work in community-building see Rupp.

REFERENCES

Arendt, Hannah (1972). "On Violence." In *Crises of the Republic.* San Diego: Harcourt, Brace & Co.

Backman, Mark (1987). "Introduction." In Richard McKeon, ed., *Rhetoric: Essays in Invention and Discovery.* Woodbridge, CT: Ox Bow Press.

Batchelor, Stephen (1983). *Alone with Others: An Existential Approach to Buddhism.* New York: Grove Press.

Batchelor, Stephen (1987). *The Faith to Doubt: Glimpses of Buddhist Uncertainty.* Berkeley: Parallax Press.

Batchelor, Stephen (1997). *Buddhism Without Beliefs.* New York: Riverhead Books.

Bourdieu, Pierre (1988). *Homo Academicus.* Trans. Peter Collier. Stanford: Stanford University Press.

Bové, Paul A. (1986). *Intellectuals in Power: A Genealogy of Critical Humanism.* New York: Columbia University Press.

Buddhadasa, Ajahn (1986). *Dhammic Socialism.* Ed. Donald K. Swearer. Bangkok: Thai Inter-religious Commission for Development.

Cabezón, José Ignacio (1992). *A Dose of Emptiness: An Annotated Translation of the sTong thun chen mo of mKhas grub dGe legs dpal bzang.* Albany: State University of New York Press.

Cabezón, José Ignacio (1994). *Buddhism and Language: A Study of Indo-*

Tibetan Scholasticism. Albany: State University of New York Press.

Cabezón, José Ignacio (1995). "Buddhist Studies as a Discipline and the Role of Theory." *Journal of the International Association of Buddhist Studies* (18: 2) 231–268.

Cabezón, José Ignacio (forthcoming). "Scholarship as Dialogue." *Buddhist/Christian Studies*.

Cady, Linell (1993). *Religion, Theology and American Public Life*. Albany: State University of New York Press.

Culler, Jonathan (1988). *Framing the Sign: Criticism and Its Institutions*. Norman and London: University of Oklahoma Press.

The Dalai Lama, H. H. (bsTan 'dzin rgya mtsho) (1988). *The Bodhgaya Interviews*. Ed. José Ignacio Cabezón. Ithaca: Snow Lion Publications.

The Dalai Lama, H. H. (1996a). *Beyond Dogma: Dialogues and Discourses*. Trans. Alison Anderson, ed. Marianne Dresser. Berkeley: North Atlantic Books.

The Dalai Lama, H. H. (1996b). *The Good Heart: A Buddhist Perspective on the Teachings of Jesus*. Introduction and Christian Context by Father Laurence Freeman. Trans. Geshe Thupten Jinpa, ed. Robert Kiely, Boston: Wisdom Publications.

The Dalai Lama, H. H. and Jean-Claude Carriere (1996c). *Violence and Compassion*. New York: Doubleday.

The Dalai Lama, H. H. (forthcoming). *An Ethics for the New Millennium*.

Davis, Con and Ronald Schleifer (1991). *Criticism and Culture: The Role of Critique in Modern Literary Theory*. Essex, England: Longman.

Dean, William D. (1994). *The Religious Critic in American Culture*. Albany: State University of New York Press.

Eckel, Malcolm David (1994). "The Ghost at the Table: On the Study of Buddhism and the Study of Religion." *Journal of the American Academy of Religion* (LXII: 4) 1085–1110.

Fenner, Peter (1995). *Reasoning into Reality: A System-Cybernetics Model and Therapeutic Interpretation of Buddhist Middle Path Analysis*. Boston: Wisdom Publications.

Geertz, Clifford (1983). "The Way We Think Now: Toward an Ethnography of Modern Thought." In *Local Knowledge*. New York: Basic Books.

Gómez, Luis O. (1995). "Unspoken Paradigms: Meanderings through the Metaphors of a Field." *Journal of the International Association of Buddhist Studies* (18: 2)183–230.

Griffin, David Ray (1991). "Professing Theology in the State University." In David Ray Griffin and Joseph C. Hough, Jr., eds., *Theology and The University: Essays in Honor of John B. Cobb, Jr.*, 3–34. Albany: State University of New York Press.

Griffin, David Ray and Joseph C. Hough, Jr., eds. (1991). *Theology and The University: Essays in Honor of John B. Cobb, Jr.* Albany: State University of New York Press.

Griffiths, Paul J. (1990). "Denaturalized Discourse: Abhidharmikas, Propositionalists, and the Comparative Philosophy of Religion." In Frank E. Reynolds and David Tracy, eds., *Myth and Philosophy*, 57–91.

Albany: State University of New York Press.
Griffiths, Paul J. (1994). *On Being Buddha: The Classical Doctrine of Buddhahood.* Albany: State University of New York Press.
Griffiths, Paul J. (1998). "Scholasticism: The Possible Recovery of an Intellectual Practice." In José Ignacio Cabezón, ed., *Scholasticism: Cross Cultural and Comparative Perspectives.* Albany: State University of new York Press.
Gross, Rita M. (1984). "The Feminine Principle in Tibetan Vajrayana Buddhism: Reflections of a Buddhist Feminist." *Journal of Transpersonal Psychology* (16: 2)179–192.
Gross, Rita M. (1986). "Suffering, Feminist Theory and Images of Goddess." *Anima* (13) 39–46.
Gross, Rita M. (1987). "I Will Never Forget To Visualize That Vajrayogini is My Body and Mind." *Journal of Feminist Studies in Religion* (3: 1) 77–89.
Gross, Rita M. (1993). *Buddhism After Patriarchy: A Feminist History, Analysis and Reconstruction of Buddhism.* Bibliotheca Indo-Buddhica Series, no. 148. Delhi: Sri Satguru Publications.
Guenther, Herbert V. (1984). *Matrix of Mystery: Scientific and Humanistic Aspects of rDzogs-chen Thought.* Boulder and London: Shambhala.
Hanh, Thich Nhat (1987). *Being Peace.* Berkeley: Parallax Press.
Hanh, Thich Nhat (1992a). *The Diamond that Cuts Through Illusion.* Berkeley: Parallax Press.
Hanh, Thich Nhat (1992b). *Touching Peace: Practicing the Art of Mindful Living.* Berkeley: Parallax Press.
Hanh, Thich Nhat (1993). *Love in Action: Writings on Non-violent Social Change.* Berkeley: Parallax Press.
Heim, Michael (1987). *Electric Language: A Philosophical Study of Word Processing.* New Haven and London: Yale University Press.
Hotzman, Steven R. (1994). *Virtual Mantras: The Languages of Abstract and Virtual Worlds.* Cambridge, MA: MIT Press.
Jackson, David P. (1987). *The Entrance Gate for the Wise (Section III): Sa skya Paṇḍita on Indian and Tibetan Traditions of Pramāṇa and Philosophical Debate.* Wien: Arbeitskreis für tibetische and buddhistische Studien Universität Wien.
Jones, Ken (1989). *The Social Face of Buddhism: An Approach to Political and Social Activism.* London: Wisdom Publications.
de Jong, J. W. (1974). "A Brief History of Buddhist Studies in Europe and America." *The Eastern Buddhist* (7: 1) 55–106; (7: 2) 49–82.
de Jong, J. W. (1984). "Recent Buddhist Studies in Europe and America, 1973-1983." *The Eastern Buddhist* (17: 1) 79–107.
Kirtisinghe, Buddhadasa P. (1984). *Buddhism and Science.* Delhi: Motilal Banarsidass.
Klein, Anne Carolyn (1995). *Meeting the Great Bliss Queen: Buddhists, Feminists and the Art of the Self.* Boston: Beacon Press.
Krang dbyi sun et. al. (1993). *Bod rgya tshig mdzod chen mo.* Mi rigs dpe skrun khang.

Lanham, Richard A. (1993). *The Electronic Word: Democracy, Technology and the Arts.* Chicago and London: The University of Chicago Press.
Macy, Joanna (1983). *Despair and Personal Power in the Nuclear Age.* Philadelphia: New Society Publishers.
Macy, Joanna (1985). *Dharma and Development: Religion as a Resource in the Sarvodaya Self-help Movement.* (Revised ed.) West Hartford, CN: Kumarian Press.
Makransky, John (1987). *Buddhahood Embodied: Sources of Controversy in India and Tibet.* Albany: State University of New York Press.
McLuhan, Marshall (1951). "Magic that Changes Mood." In *The Mechanical Bride: Folklore of Industrial Man.* New York: Vanguard Press.
Nunberg, Geoffrey, and Umberto Eco, eds. (1996). *The Future of the Book.* Berkeley: University of California Press.
Ogden, Schubert (1981). "Theology in the University." In Mark C. Taylor, ed., *Unfinished . . .: Essays in Honor of Ray L. Hart.* Journal of the American Academy of Religion Thematic issue, vol. 48, no. 1. Chico, CA, Scholars Press.
Pannenberg, Wolfhart (1991). "The Task of Systematic Theology in the Contemporary University." In David Ray Griffin and Joseph C. Hough, Jr., eds., *Theology and the University: Essays in Honor of John B. Cobb, Jr.*, 81–93. Albany: State University of New York Press.
Proudfoot, Wayne (1985). *Religious Experience.* Berkeley: University of California Press.
Queen, Christopher (1997). "Professing Buddhism: The Harvard Conference on Buddhism in America." *Society for Buddhist-Christian Studies Newsletter* (20) 4–5.
Queen, Christopher S., and Sallie B. King, eds. (1996). *Engaged Buddhism: Buddhist Liberation Movements in Asia.* Albany: State University of New York Press.
Reichenbach, Bruce R. (1991). *The Law of Karma: A Philosophical Study.* Honolulu: University of Hawaii Press.
Rupp, George (1991). "Communities of Collaboration: Shared Commitments/Common Tasks." In Sheila Greeve Davaney, ed., *Theology at the End of Modernity.* Philadelphia: Trinity Press International.
Sangharakshita, Mahasthavira (1979). *Peace is a Fire. . .: writings and sayings.* London: Windhorse.
Sangharakshita, Mahasthavira (1984). *Buddhism, World Peace and Nuclear War.* Glasgow: Windhorse.
Schmithausen, Lambert (1991). *Buddhism and Nature.* Studia Philologica Buddhica Occasional Papers Series VII. Tokyo: The International Institute of Buddhist Studies.
Sivaraksa, Sulak (1985). *Siamese Resurgence.* Bangkok: Asian Cultural Forum on Development.
Sivaraksa, Sulak (1986). *A Buddhist Vision for Renewing Society.* Bangkok: Tienwan.

Sontag, Susan (1964). "Against Interpretation." In *Against Interpretation.* New York: Dell Publishing Company.
Subhuti, Dharmachari (Alex Kennedy) (1988). *Buddhism for Today. A Portrait of a New Buddhist Movement.* (2nd ed.) Glasgow: Windhorse Publications.
Thurman, Robert A. F. (1984). *Tsong kha pa's Speech of Gold in the Essence of True Eloquence.* Princeton: Princeton University Press.
Tracy, David (1981). "Defending the Public Character of Theology." *The Christian Century* (April 1).
Wallace, B. Alan (1989). *Choosing Reality: A Contemplative View of Physics and the Mind.* Boston and Shaftesbury: Shambhala.
Wallace, B. Alan (1993). *Tibetan Buddhism from the Ground Up.* Boston: Wisdom Publications.
Williams, Paul (1995). "Identifying the Object of Negation: On *Bodhicaryāvatāra* 9:140 (Tib. 139)." *Asiatische Studien/Études Asiatiques* (49: 4) 969–985.
Williams, Paul (1998). *The Reflexive Nature of Awareness: A Tibetan Madhyamaka Defence.* Surrey: Curzon Press.
Willson, Martin (1987). *Rebirth and the Western Buddhist.* (2nd ed.) London: Wisdom Publications.

Two

Buddhist Theology?[1]

Rita M. Gross

Buddhist theology is at this point a hybrid Western enterprise; for the most part, it consists of the self-conscious reflections of recent Western converts to Buddhism who also have professional training and interest in the construction of religious thought. These Western Buddhist "theologians" represent one method for adapting Buddhism to its new Western home and for bringing the wisdom of the Buddhist tradition to Western religious and social thought. Because of its newness and hybrid form, Buddhist theology is subject to skeptical criticism from two directions. On the one hand, many Western academics, especially those trained to study Buddhism as outsiders, react quite negatively to their colleagues who engage in the construction of Buddhist discourse. On the other hand, some Buddhists, both Asian and Western, react negatively to Western Buddhists who actively construct Buddhist thought rather than merely absorbing traditional Buddhist outlooks without commentary or interpretation.

In this chapter, I will respond primarily to the academic critics of Buddhist theology, though I will also discuss more briefly the potential hostility of Buddhists who might claim that the construction of Western Buddhist theology is premature or unwarranted. In my view, the question of Buddhist academic theology is twofold at this point: should we do it? and what should we call it? "It," of course, is Buddhist theology. Of these two questions, the second is, in my view, far more difficult to resolve. The first question, I would contend, should be resolved once and for all with a resounding "yes," despite the views and opinions of some professional Buddhologists, who do not even consider the questions before us to be legitimate questions. Such judgments result in an unfortunate impasse. Some years ago when responding to a request for feedback on the effectiveness of the Buddhism section of the American Academy of Religion, the venue in which much Buddhological scholarship is presented, I wrote that "at present it is very difficult for Buddhists to participate in the Buddhism section, due to its narrow views of proper methodology and subject matter." It is truly ironic when Buddhists find it difficult to discuss

Buddhism in the Buddhism section, but that is not infrequent these days.

IS BUDDHIST "THEOLOGY" A LEGITIMATE TOPIC FOR SERIOUS SCHOLARLY DISCOURSE?

In this section of my comments, I will not be saying anything that I have not already said many times, especially in the appendices to *Buddhism After Patriarchy.* I have long suggested that the dividing line between normative-constructive studies in religion and descriptive scholarship is not as neat as many detractors of theology would like to contend. Rather, the rise of descriptive, historical scholarship about religion depends on certain philosophical developments and a specific world-view that became fashionable in the nineteenth century. One could say, using the term "theology" in a very broad sense, that the preference for descriptive over normative studies is a "theological" or normative position itself. I have also often discussed my methodological conversion to this heresy, which results from my painful and difficult battles as a young feminist scholar who was taught that the prevailing androcentric methodologies of thirty years ago were adequate descriptive tools for the study of religion, and, most decidedly *not* subjective, normative, or prescriptive categories lodged in the scholar's world-view (see Gross 1997). Feminists have demonstrated that androcentric methods were a normative not a descriptive position; ever after that, I have been quite skeptical of claims that one can do purely descriptive work. If it is impossible to do purely descriptive, "objective" work, why the fear and loathing of normative, constructive scholarly discourse, especially when it is methodologically self-conscious and up front about its agenda?

However, my main interest in this context is not to discuss the impossibility of purely descriptive scholarship, which somewhat puts the ball in the court of detractors of Buddhist theology. I have no quarrel with those who like to do more descriptive, linguistic, or historical scholarship about Buddhists from other times and other places. I only object to the claim that such scholarship is *the only legitimate way for Buddhism to be discussed in the academy* and the consequent difficulty of finding a hearing and a venue for those of us who like to do Buddhist theology. Thus the more important question concerns why it is important and legitimate to engage in Buddhist normative discussions.

Buddhism is a major intellectual and spiritual force in the messy contemporary world of political chaos, environmental degradation, and social-economic injustice, not merely a set of philosophical texts and artifacts from times past. Therefore, study of Buddhism need not be limited to historical and philological questions, as if Buddhism were irrelevant in the contemporary world and its confusion and pain, or did not participate in them. Given the profundity of the Buddhist tradition historically and its impact on world history as a whole and on major cultures, it is strange to imagine that exploring what that tradition might have to offer today is deemed to be "off limits" by some who make claims about what should and should not be discussed by contemporary Buddhist scholars.

As a Buddhist scholar-theologian, my agenda is to bring my experiential knowledge of Buddhist thought and practice into discussions of contemporary issues and problems, to work with the collective wisdom, compassion, and skillfulness of Buddhist traditions to suggest ways of alleviating the individual and collective suffering rampant in the world. To date, I have done this mainly in connection with the social justice issues brought up by feminism. More recently, I have been asked to contribute several essays on Buddhism and ecology. But since I use Buddhist concepts and categories to think about almost everything, these published works are only the tip of the iceberg.

Such an agenda, of course, *presupposes* that I have at least somewhat *accurate* knowledge of Buddhist thought and Buddhist practices. As is the case with theologians who speak for other religions discussed by academic professionals, Buddhist theologians who work within the academy also have significant allegiance to the standards of the academic study of religion. We do not throw our knowledge of history, language, or philosophy out the window because we use Buddhism as a resource *with which to think about* contemporary problems. We simply are quite interested in using Buddhist categories with which to think about our world, often because, as Buddhists, that is precisely what we do twenty-four hours a day. We have found Buddhism to be extremely useful in thinking about our lives and about major contemporary issues and problems. We want to discuss our findings in a collegial environment, as is commonly done by other scholars who order their lives by any other philosophical or religious system. That such an agenda should be troubling to other scholars or considered illegitimate scholarly discourse is incomprehensible to me.

Furthermore, I would argue that, as humanistic scholars who know a great deal about alternatives to Western thought, which has gotten us into some fairly urgent and distressing situations, we have responsibilities to use our knowledge to address those problems, rather than to leave troubling issues of social and environmental justice to those less knowledgeable, with less respect and good will for diverse and alternative world-views. Academic scholars and teachers, especially those of us who are paid to teach large undergraduate classes, have some impact on emerging attitudes and opinions. For us to teach and write about the alternative explanations of reality that we have spent our lives researching as if they are irrelevant to the world in which we live is to belittle those thought systems. It might also justifiably earn us the evaluation that what we do is "merely academic" in the worst sense of the term "academic"--not mattering. making no difference whatsoever. One could then ask how we will justify our academic positions to a skeptical public which resents our salaries and our tenure.

Finally, it is ironic to note that we scorned Buddhist theologians are now writing what will become primary texts for future generations of Buddhologists. Future scholars will want to know what twentieth century Western Buddhists, new to the tradition, thought and how their knowledge and practice of Buddhism affected their lives and the way they worked with the contemporary issues of their day. If, in the past Buddhist scholars had observed the guidelines for proper academic discourse set up by some current scholars, these same scholars might have nothing to study because previous scholars would not have written the normative texts that now are the basis for "legitimate" scholarly discourse.

WHAT SHOULD WE CALL "IT"?

What should contemporary Buddhists who use Buddhism as something *with which* to think, rather than only as something to think *about*, call their enterprise? Personally, I do not have the allergic reaction to the term "Buddhist theology" experienced by some of my colleagues, despite that fact that the phrase is something of an oxymoron. That may be because I have always enjoyed speculative thought more than historical and philological research and because I am quite familiar and comfortable with Western feminist theology, even having been a Jewish feminist theologian in a "former life (Gross 1979, 1983). I chose the study of religion over any other discipline because I wanted to spend my life working with and thinking about ultimate reality, which, in my view, is handled more directly by religion than by any other human enterprise. And I chose comparative religion over any other sub-field because it seemed silly to me, even in 1965 as a twenty-one year old graduate student, to confine one's searchings to what one's own culture had proposed about ultimate reality.

One could argue that the term "theology" is inappropriate for Buddhism, a non-theistic religion. But I do not believe that contemporary theology is any longer always about a personal anthropomorphic creator deity in the classical sense. Theologians of Jewish and Christian persuasion write and talk about an ultimate reality that is not always the classical anthropomorphic deity and I think it is quite well-known that Buddhist theologians would not be writing about such a deity. The term "theology" does have two distinct advantages in my view. The first is that it is well-known and at least reasonably well understood by the audiences to which we write and speak as professional academics who think about religion, which is important since I do not address myself only to other Buddhists or to Buddhologists. The second is that the term clearly connotes that we are thinking *within* the confines of a specific tradition, not as free agents, and we place ourselves under the authority of that tradition. Of course, this does not mean that we accept the received tradition lock, stock, and barrel without suggesting contemporary interpretations of that received tradition. That is why we are "theologians," not only historians or philologists. But, nevertheless, I work *within* the broad confines of the Buddhist system. For these reasons, I definitely would not want to call my work "philosophy," because I believe that the difference between philosophy and theology is not whether one thinks speculatively about the nature of ultimate reality but whether one considers one's self to be working within a given system and under its authority, or whether one considers one's self to be a free agent under no authority. Therefore, I actually regard the phrase "Buddhist philosophy" to be more of an oxymoron than "Buddhist theology," though I suspect many will disagree with me on that issue.

Nevertheless, the practice of working within a system rather than as a philosophical free agent brings up interesting issues for the Buddhist theologian, *qua* Buddhist. Theology, as commentary within a system, actually expands and develops that system. Therefore, in any age, contemporary theology can be at odds with the conservative status quo of the system, and Buddhist theology is no exception. For example, there is no question that I feel the usual feminist frustration with "institutional drag," that I feel there is no excuse for Western Buddhists to move so slowly on some very basic issues, like gender neutral language in English language chants and texts and more female imagery in the main meditation halls. But, more important, what of potential conflicts between myself as a Buddhist theologian and my Buddhist teachers? Because I work within the system as a Buddhist, I do present most of my Buddhist theology to my Buddhist teachers, though I am seeking to keep them informed of my work, rather than seeking their imprimatur. The question of what would happen if Buddhist authorities were to suggest that some of my Buddhist theology is inappropriate has not arisen for me in a strong fashion. I have endured several harrowing conflicts with other Western Buddhists who are formally higher in the teaching hierarchy than I am. These were mainly with white males who objected to certain feminist practices I advocate in Buddhism, though some Western Buddhist women have also rejected my Buddhist feminism. The most significant of these conflicts was negotiated through discussion when I refused to simply obey orders, and I am pleased to report that through non-aggressive and non-confrontational discourse, my suggestions prevailed. Were the situation to become more extreme, I feel fairly certain of what my stance would be. I am a loyal critic rather than a true believer and will continue do what I can to enlighten the establishment. I have the complex loyalty to a traditional religion that is common among feminist theologians who chose to write and think in continuity with one of the current major religions in spite of its flaws.

To return to the question of whether "theology" is the appropriate term for work we are discussing, despite its advantages, I am not so attached to the term "theology" that I would not willingly, even eagerly, give it up if we could find a more acceptable accurate alternative. But that is not easy. Clearly the term "buddhology" would not work, for it has come to mean historical and philological studies about Buddhism in other times and places. Furthermore, Buddhist theologians do not especially focus on the Buddha, which would be the connotation if we used that term to name constructive normative Buddhist thought.

Is there a more appropriate term for doing contemplative, speculative Buddhist thought? The term "theology" is clearly a Western term, as is the distinction between theology and philosophy that seems important to me. Is there a way to find or coin a more traditional Buddhist term? Clearly, if we look at traditional Buddhism, what we are doing as Buddhist theologians is studying and commenting on the Dharma, a time-honored practice in Buddhism. But what could one call the discipline and the practice of studying and commenting on the Dharma and coming up with dharmic solutions to twentieth century issues? Are we doing "dharmalogy"? Such a neologism is awkward and ugly-sounding. But, technically, it is more accurate than either "theology" or "buddhalogy." Neologisms have the disadvantage of being unfamiliar, needing constant explanation. And they often don't catch on, which renders them useless. On the other hand "androcentrism" was also a neologism when we began to use it twenty-five years ago, but, due to the great need for such a term in the language, it has caught on quite well and has become standard English. As more Western, English-speaking people become to study and comment on the Dharma, there will be more need for a word to name what we do. Perhaps "dharmalogy" would catch on.

Or perhaps we should avoid the Western tendency to turn every kind of study into an "ology" and avoid any term with that ending. As the more user-friendly term "god-talk" is replacing the term "theology" in some contexts, perhaps we could say that we do "dharma-discourse," a suggestion that I think may have some merit. We make suggestions as to the contemporary interpretations and applications of the classic formulations of *Buddhadharma*, and I think the term "Dharma-discourse" could come to mean precisely that.

Unfortunately, there is also a serious problem connected with this term. There is as yet no term for someone who engages in god-talk, other than "theologian." If we were to call our activity "Dharma-discourse" what would we call ourselves? The traditional term would be "Dharma teacher," the term I am called when I present my comments in a Buddhist context to a Buddhist audience. But the term is less appropriate in the academy, which does not presume that we share the same outlook or are one another's teachers. Nor does the term leave much room for the suggestive, speculative, and provisional nature of many of the ideas we Buddhist theologians are presenting. Our comments, in hindsight, may not turn out to very appropriate and may not be included among the ever-increasing canon of genuine Dharma. In my opinion, the term "Dharma teacher" should be reserved for traditional teachings contexts and the assumptions that go with that context, not used of the kinds of work done by academic theologians.

Are there any alternatives? Perhaps we should simply say that we are Buddhist scholars, and, as such, we engage in Dharma-discourse in addition to studying Buddhology. This is a very simple, clear solution. The only problem with that suggestion is making clear that we are *Buddhist* scholars, insiders, talking about Buddhist teachings normatively, not only *scholars* studying about Buddhism. Ambiguity and confusion between Buddhologists and Buddhist scholars could be rampant and widespread unless we can agree to make clear that a Buddhist scholar is different from a Buddhist studies scholar. A Buddhist scholar is an insider; a Buddhist studies scholar doing scholarship about Buddhism could be either an insider and an outsider. And, of course a Buddhist scholar could also sometimes manifest as a Buddhist studies scholar, though the reverse would not be possible. Given all that confusion and complexity, it may be best simply just to opt for the oxymoronic, but culturally appropriate (for Western Buddhists) term "Buddhist theology." To me, that compromise seems unproblematic, but I would be delighted with a better solution than any of which I have thought.

NOTES

1 This paper originally was presented in a session on Buddhist Theology at the 1995 annual meeting of the American Academy of Religion, in New Orleans, Louisiana.

REFERENCES

Gross, Rita M. (1979). "Female God Language in a Jewish Context." In *Womanspirit Rising: A Feminist Reader in Religion.* Carol Christ and Judith Plaskow, eds. San Francisco: Harper and Row.

Gross, Rita M. (1983). "Steps Toward Feminine Imagery of Deity in Jewish Theology." In Susannah Heschel, ed., *On Being a Jewish Feminist.* New York: Schocken Books.

Gross, Rita M. (1997). "Why Me?: Reflections of a Wisconsin Farm Girl Who Became a Buddhist Theologian When She Grew Up." *Journal of Feminist Studies in Religion.*

Three

Three Dimensions Of Buddhist Studies

B. Alan Wallace

THE QUESTION OF TERMINOLOGY

In these early discussions of the relation between purely academic approaches to the study of Buddhism and Buddhist approaches, we immediately confront the question: What do we call the Buddhist approach? Following the lead of confessional scholars in the religions of Judaism, Christianity, and Islam, we may call this approach *theological*, but this immediately raises qualms on the part of many Buddhist scholars who contend that the term *theological* is simply inappropriate within the context of Buddhist studies. One might defend the use of this term on the grounds that even Theravāda Buddhism acknowledges the existence of a host of gods, including Indra and Brahmā, regarding them as lofty beings within *saṃsāra*, while a Buddha is viewed as superior to all other humans and gods. Clearly, Theravāda Buddhism is not non-theistic in the sense of denying the existence of gods altogether, but it is not theistic in the sense of deifying the Buddha or anyone else in any way comparable to the God of Moses or of Jesus.

Within Mahāyāna Buddhism, on the other hand, many treatises assert the existence of the *dharmakāya* as an omnipresent, omniscient, omni-benevolent consciousness, which takes on a myriad of forms to which Mahāyāna Buddhists offer devotions, supplicatory prayers, and worship, much as in Near Eastern theistic religions. Further, proponents of Atiyoga and other Vajrayāna doctrines affirm the existence of the Primordial Buddha, Samantabhadra, as the ground and origin of the whole of *saṃsāra* and *nirvāṇa*; and they view all phenomena as creative expressions of Samantabhadra, whose nature is none other than the *dharmakāya*, which, in turn, is nondual from the primordial awareness of every sentient being.[1] Within these contexts, the term *theology* appears more and more applicable to Buddhism, despite the real and important differences between the theologies of the Near-Eastern religions and Buddhism.

Applying the term *Buddhist theology* to the Buddhist study of Buddhism may be more effectively criticized on the very different grounds that it is too narrow a term; for the Buddhist canon includes treatises on many topics that fall outside the scope of theology, including logic, epistemology, ontology, social and cognitive psychology, physiology, physics, cosmology, and medicine. This is not to say that the Buddhist tradition addresses these topics in the same ways that they are studied in the modern world, but it does raise many of the same issues commonly addressed in the corresponding contemporary fields of study.

This raises the larger question as to whether the very inclusion of the totality of Buddhism within the Euro-American category of *religion* is itself an act of ideological hegemony. To use a common analytical tool of Buddhist logic, I would suggest that there is in fact a "four-point relation" between Buddhism and religion, which entails the existence of instances of (1) both Buddhism and religion, (2) Buddhism but not religion, (3) religion but not Buddhism, and (4) neither.[2] The following are instances of those four categories:

1. The Buddhist abstention from killing on the grounds that such an act karmically leads to miserable rebirths and obstructs one's progress towards liberation is an instance of both Buddhism and religion. Buddhists commonly acknowledge that such abstention from killing on ethical grounds is an instance of Buddhist practice and therefore of Buddhism itself, so this is not contested. Moreover, few would deny that this is an instance of religious practice and therefore of religion. Van Harvey, for instance, observes that in deeming something religious we ordinarily mean a perspective expressing a dominating interest in certain universal and elemental features of human existence as those features bear on the human desire for liberation and authentic existence (Harvey: chap. 8). By that criterion, the Buddhist perspective on the virtue of non-violence may clearly be deemed religious.

2. The instructions on diagnosing physical disorders presented in the *Four Medical Tantras* (Tib., *rGyud bzhi*), which provide the textual basis for the whole of the Tibetan Buddhist medical tradition, may be cited as an instance of Buddhist teachings, for, according to Tibetan Buddhist tradition, they are attributed, to the Buddha himself (Clark: 10).[3] Insofar as health maintenance is viewed by Buddhists simply as a means to assist them in their pursuit of favorable rebirth and liberation, then even these teachings may be deemed religious. The same may be said of the many Buddhist writings on logic, epistemology and other topics that are not commonly deemed *religious*. To that extent, all Buddhist theories and practices may indeed be regarded as religious, in which case there is only a three-point relation between Buddhism and religion. But insofar as topics

such as Buddhist medicine, logic, epistemology, and psychology are viewed in their own right, irrespective of their relevance to favorable rebirth and liberation, they may be classified as instances of Buddhism, but not religion.

3. The ancient Hebrew practice of sacrificing animals to God is an instance of religious practice (according to the above criterion), but is not an instance of Buddhist practice.

4. Quantum mechanics is neither religion nor Buddhism. Generally speaking, quantum mechanics is concerned with the nature of the smallest units of mass and energy, which has no obvious bearing on the universal and elemental features of human existence as those features bear on the human desire for liberation and authentic existence. Moreover, the principles of quantum mechanics are nowhere found in any Buddhist texts, so that science would appear to be neither a religion nor a science. This is not to deny the fact that there are theoretical conclusions drawn by quantum physicists that bear resemblances to some assertions within Buddhist doctrine.[4]

On the other hand, in the recent past, there have been several writers, most notably physicist Fritjof Capra, who claim that the deepest truths of quantum mechanics are identical to the deepest truths of various mystical traditions, including Buddhism (see Capra). In a similar vein, physicist Paul Davies has written a number of popular books declaring that a new religion is emerging from modern physics (see Davies). This is not a late twentieth-century innovation. During the Scientific Revolution, many eminent scientists, such as Robert Boyle, regarded scientific inquiry as a form of worship performed by scientists in the temple of nature. Nor is this notion confined to natural scientists. In the late nineteenth century, Emile Durkheim claimed that science pursues the same end as religion, and it is better fitted to perform the task. In his view, scientific thought, which he maintained is "only a more perfect form of religious thought" (477), properly supplants the cognitive authority of religion altogether. Thus, for some people science in general and quantum mechanics in particular may indeed be instances of religion, but I would still maintain that quantum mechanics as such is not a religion, Buddhist or otherwise.

If there is in fact a four-point relation between Buddhism and religion, it is incorrect to classify Buddhism simply as a religion. If it were legitimate to deem it a religion since it bears much in common with other religions, it would be equally legitimate to classify it as a philosophy, a holistic medical system, and as a psychology. Buddhism is not simply a religion, so the Buddhist study of this tradition is not simply theological. It can quite rightly be claimed that medieval Christianity, prior to the Scientific Revolution and the secularization of institutions of higher learning, was also not simply a religion in the modern sense of the term; for it, too, incorporated many elements, particularly from non-Christian, Greek sources, that are not strictly religious in nature. However, a significant difference remains between Buddhism and medieval Christianity: while Buddhism includes many theories and methods of philosophy, psychology, and medicine, and so on within its accepted canons of teachings attributed to the Buddha, medieval Christianity added such theories from outside, non-Jewish and non-Christian sources. While the Bible is paradigmatically a religious treatise, the Buddhist canons do not lend themselves to such a straightforward classification.

Dharmology is another term that has been proposed to denote Buddhist approaches to studying the theories and practices of Buddhism. Buddhism, however, is not equivalent to Dharma, for Buddhist texts commonly refer to non-Buddhist Dharmas, or religious doctrines. Moreover, in a broader sense, *dharmas* include mundane concerns (*laukikadharma*) and most broadly speaking, all phenomena. Thus, *dharmalogy* is far too encompassing a term to use for a specific approach to Buddhist studies. And yet from another perspective, this use of *dharmology* is too limited, for it indicates the study of Dharma, as opposed to the study of the Buddha and the Saṅgha.

In this essay I would like to move away from the terms *Buddhist theology* and *dharmology* and propose that there are not only two but three approaches, or dimensions, to the study of Buddhism. These correspond to the orientations of the Buddhologist, the Buddhist theorist, and the Buddhist practitioner.

THE BUDDHOLOGIST

The modern scholarly study of Buddhism commonly known as Buddhology may be defined as the objective, scientific study of the various manifestations of the Buddhist tradition, including its texts, doctrines, uses of language, ways of reasoning, rituals, beliefs, practices, biographies, historical developments, and cultural contexts. Thus, the academic community of Buddhologists includes philosophers, historians, anthropologists, sociologists, and philologists who have chosen Buddhism as their field of study. In adopting the ideal of objectivity, Buddhologists align themselves with a central principle of the most dominant method of acquiring knowledge in the modern world, namely the "scientific method," which provides Buddhology with the same authority as the other social sciences within the academy.

One aspect of this principle of objectivity is that one's assertions must be epistemically objective, i.e., observer independent, implying that they are equally accessible to all "competent observers." In its most defensible guise, this ideal demands that researchers strive to be as free as possible of personal bias and prejudice in their collection and interpretation of information. In its least defensible form, it demands that objective knowledge must not involve any subjective aims or purposes, an ideal that has never been achieved by any of the sciences. We all have working assumptions and priorities that inevitably influence what we study and how we study it.

Within the scientific tradition, objectivism has a much deeper connotation than freedom from subjective bias. Scientific objectivism can be traced back to the attempt on the part of the pioneers of the Scientific Revolution to view reality from a vantage point that transcended the limitations of human subjectivity. From its inception, modern science was after a "God's-eye view" of the physical universe, entailing a total objectification of the natural world, and, implicitly, the exclusion of subjective contamination from the pursuit of scientific knowledge. This ideal has so captured the modern mind that scientific knowledge is now often simply equated with objective knowledge.

In the secularization of the modern world, there has been a shift in ideal from a God's-eye-view to the "view from nowhere" (Nagel) that is, a perspective that is totally free of subjective contamination, not localized in any particular time or place, but with no pretense of divine transcendence. Much modern Buddhological literature appears to adopt this ideal by studying Buddhism as if the researchers themselves were detached, disembodied, timeless, impartial observers of the phenomena of Buddhism. This ideal might be called the "Arhat's view" of Buddhism, that is, the disengaged view of someone who has already "crossed over to the other shore" and regards the raft of Buddhism from a distance. This actual accomplishment of this ideal, however, is highly suspect, for researchers in any field bring with them their own assumptions, questions, and goals that are invariably tied into their own culture. It is therefore misleading to suggest that a non-religious perspective is somehow intrinsically less biased or more objective than a religious one.

For modern Buddhologists, the culture in which we live is dominated by the metaphysical principles of scientific naturalism, including physicalism, reductionism, monism, and the "closure principle," which states that only physical processes act as causes in the physical universe. While modern science, guided by those principles, continues to make great strides in understanding the objective, physical world, its scientific inquiry into the nature of the human mind is a relatively new and primitive discipline. And when it comes to understanding the origins, nature, causal efficacy, and fate of consciousness, science has left us in total ignorance, concealed at times by a smoke screen of assumptions and speculations (Güzeldere). In short, scientific naturalism provides useful guidelines for studying a wide array of objective phenomena, but those very guidelines hamper the scientific study of subjective phenomena, which are not easily accessible to third-person observers. The reason for this is that the principle of objectivism, in the sense of the demand for observer independence, simply cannot accommodate the study of subjective phenomena, for it directs one's attention only to those objects that exist independently of one's own subjective awareness. This principle encourages scientists to pursue their research as if they, as human subjects, do not exist. It is no wonder then that science presents us with a view of a world in which our own subjective existence is not acknowledged, and the notion of the meaning of our existence cannot even be raised.[5]

Buddhologists who adopt this "objective" approach tend to focus only on the external "surfaces" of the Buddhist tradition – its texts, external rituals and so forth – without penetrating through to their underlying, subjective experiences of practicing Buddhists. Thus, even Buddhological texts purporting to study Buddhist meditation may deal only with Buddhist literature on meditation, without ever questioning whether or not Buddhists have ever actually had any of the experiences recounted in their texts. Much that goes under the rubric of *the scientific study of Buddhism* actually bears a closer parallel to medieval scholasticism than it does to any modern empirical science. For such scholars, the arrival of Buddhist texts in modern university libraries constitutes, for all practical purposes, the arrival of Buddhism in the West (Almond).

The secular, academic discipline of religious studies may insist on purely naturalistic causes of religion, whereas theology acknowledges divine influences on the origination and development of a religious tradition. But this distinction between natural and supernatural origins of religion does not readily pertain to Buddhism, for even paranormal abilities and extrasensory perception are considered by Buddhists to be *natural.* Moreover, the notion that religion as such deals with the sacred, while science deals with the profane also does not hold for Buddhism; for Buddhist theories and practices are concerned with both ultimate and relative, sacred and profane, truths. Buddhologists may simply not comment on whether or not there are culturally transcendent influences on the origins and development of the Buddhist tradition. However, by ignoring the experiential component of the origins and development of Buddhist theories and practices and by attending solely to the outer expressions of those events, one may profoundly misconstrue the actual nature of the field of one's research, resulting in a biased and distorted study of Buddhism. Thus, by adhering to the principle of epistemic objectivism, the very scope of Buddhist studies becomes seriously limited.

The Buddhological de-emphasis on Buddhist experience conforms to the objectivist orientation of scientific naturalism, but it is a far cry from the provocative perspective of William James' *The Varieties of Religious Experience*, which is more often read than emulated by contemporary scholars of religion. James' treatment of Buddhist meditative experience, although well-intentioned, was inadequate due to the limited materials available to him. But with the progress in Buddhist studies since his time, scholars are no longer constrained by those limitations.

The scope of Buddhology includes the origins of Buddhist doctrines and the biographies of prominent figures in the history of Buddhism. To understand these issues, the role of Buddhist experience, including extraordinary experiences (e.g., alleged conceptually unmediated experience, paranormal abilities, and various types of extrasensory perception) needs to be addressed. Buddhist tradition states that there are two types of Buddhadharma – the Dharma of the scriptures (*āgamadharma*) and the Dharma of realization (*adhigamadharma*). If Buddhology is to study the whole of the Buddhadharma, how are Buddhologists to investigate the Dharma of realization? They can certainly study the texts that discuss this topic, but those texts are further instances of the Dharma of the scriptures, not the Dharma of realization.

It is a truism in modern natural science that if one wants to *understand* physics, for example, one must *practice* physics. Simply reading physics textbooks. studying the history of physics, and studying the lives of physicists will never suffice. If one wishes to understand theoretical physics, one must know from experience what it means to engage in the practice of theoretical physics, even if only on a rudimentary level. Likewise, if one wishes to understand experimental physics, there is no substitute for spending time in the laboratory, training under the guidance of skilled research physicists. The same is true of the study of the Buddhist Dharma of realization: without personally engaging in Buddhist theorizing and practice, this domain of Buddhism will largely remain beyond one's reach.[6]

While Buddhological literature rarely deals with subjective Buddhist experience, it even more rarely questions whether or not the insights that are allegedly derived from Buddhist practice are valid.[7]

This tendency is presumably due to the current popularity of cultural relativism and deconstructionism. Adhering to such an approach, many Buddhologists side with Gadamer in giving up the claim to find in Buddhism any truth valid and intelligible for themselves. As Gadamer declares, "this acknowledgment of the otherness of the other, which makes him the object of objective knowledge, involves the fundamental suspension of his claim to truth" (270).[8] The obvious limitation of this deconstructive, relativistic treatment of texts, however, is that as soon as this hermeneutical criterion is applied to one's own writings, one's own texts are forced to abandon their claim to utter anything that is true. On the other hand, if advocates of this viewpoint claim a privileged perspective, superior to and unlike all others, they must stand at the end of a long line of earlier proponents of all manner of religious, philosophical, and scientific theories who make the same claim.

THE BUDDHIST THEORIST

While the domain of study for a Buddhologist is the Buddhist tradition, the domain of study for a Buddhist theorist includes all manner of phenomena as they are viewed in terms of Buddhist theories. While a Buddhologist may study Buddhist theories, a Buddhist theorist uses Buddhist concepts as a means to make the world as a whole intelligible. The English term *theory* stems from the Greek *theōria*, having the meaning of *beholding*, or *viewing*, much like the corresponding Sanskrit term *darśana*. Thus, Buddhist theorists may examine not only ancient Buddhist doctrines, but modern fields of knowledge, using Buddhist terminology, theories, and logic. For example, they may analyze the assumptions underlying modern scientific views of objectivity, including scientific naturalism and scientific realism, as well as other academic disciplines and social issues from a Buddhist perspective. The domain of study for the Buddhist theorist, therefore, is greater than the domain of study for the Buddhologist as such, for the former is concerned with the whole of reality, including Buddhism, while the latter focuses academically on Buddhism alone.

Between these two approaches there are also significant differences of perspective on the study of Buddhism itself: Buddhologists are intent on learning *about* Buddhism, whereas Buddhist theorists are intent on learning *from* Buddhism. The latter are therefore more prone to use Buddhist theories to examine many of their own preconceptions and assumptions, whereas Buddhologists tend to be more interested in critiquing the preconceptions and assumptions of the Buddhist tradition. Buddhist theorists may also ask such questions that might not occur to Buddhologists. For example, what bearing might the Madhyamaka view have on contemporary problems in the ontological foundations of modern physics? How might Buddhist theories of consciousness add to and themselves be enriched by dialogue with cognitive scientific theories of mind? How do Buddhist views concerning the conceptually structured nature of experience compare with the insights of contemporary psychology?

One might suggest that one important difference between these two approaches is that Buddhologists try to adopt an objective, unbiased, and detached perspective for their study of Buddhism, while that ideal of objectivity is unattainable for Buddhist theorists since they are personally committed to a Buddhist viewpoint. This judgment is supported by the fact that scholarship by Buddhist theorists often does appear to bear a strong subjective bias. Nevertheless, the ideals of intellectual detachment, lack of prejudice, and not grasping onto views are certainly central themes of much of Buddhist philosophy; so Buddhist theorists who succumb to personal prejudice are simultaneously failing to live up to the ideals of their own tradition as well as that of modern Buddhology. On the other hand, Buddhologists who critique Buddhist assumptions without ever critically examining their own preconceptions equally fall short of the mark of true objectivity. The fact that one scholar views Buddhism from a Buddhist perspective and another views it from a modern Western perspective does not, in itself, imply that either one is more objective or rational than the other.

Using once again the previous mode of Buddhist analysis, I maintain that there is a four-point relation between Buddhologists and Buddhist theorists, which entails the existence of instances of individuals who act as (1) both a Buddhologist and a Buddhist theorist, (2) a Buddhologist but not a Buddhist theorist, (3) a Buddhist theorist but not a Buddhologist, and (4) neither a Buddhologist nor a Buddhist theorist. Rather than citing individuals by name as instances of these categories, I shall describe types of individuals.

1. A Buddhologist who is not a Buddhist may, nevertheless, at least temporarily adopt a Buddhist perspective for analyzing some aspect of the Buddhist tradition, in which case such a person would take on the role of a Buddhologist as well as a Buddhist theorist. Likewise, a Buddhist theorist may engage in the objective, scientific study of the various manifestations of the Buddhist tradition without necessarily discarding a Buddhist perspective. For the mere use of Buddhist concepts in itself is no less objective than using other

concepts familiar to modern, Western, secular scholarship. In that case, such a person would also be acting both as a Buddhist theorist and a Buddhologist.

2. A Buddhologist whose own views are incompatible with those of Buddhism and who has no interest in viewing Buddhism from anything but a non-Buddhist perspective would be an instance of someone who is a Buddhologist but not a Buddhist theorist.

3. A Buddhist theorist who is personally committed to the views of some Buddhist tradition, to the extent that he or she cannot conceive of viewing that tradition from a detached, unbiased perspective, is a Buddhist theorist but not a Buddhologist.

4. A scholar of Buddhism who is personally committed to a non-Buddhist perspective, to the extent that he or she cannot conceive of viewing that perspective from a detached, unbiased perspective, is neither a Buddhologist nor a Buddhist theorist.

If there is in fact a four-point relation between a Buddhologist and a Buddhist theorist, then both styles of scholarship should be equally welcome to the halls of modern academia. Among the four instances cited above, only the third and fourth have no legitimate place in an institution dedicated to a liberal arts education.

THE BUDDHIST PRACTITIONER

While the Buddhist theorist *views* reality in terms of Buddhist concepts, terminology, and ways of reasoning, the Buddhist practitioner *implements* Buddhist practices, such as the three trainings in ethics, meditative stabilization, and wisdom or the cultivation of the six perfections characterizing the Bodhisattva way of life. Like the relation between a theoretical physicist and an experimentalist, a Buddhist theorist is concerned with the theoretical aspects of Buddhism, whereas the practitioner is concerned with its practical applications. The ideal in many Buddhist traditions is to be both an accomplished scholar and practitioner of Buddhism. The Tibetan Buddhist tradition, for example, comments that one who meditates without having studied is like a blind man, while one who studies but does not practice is like a cripple. Nevertheless, most people within the tradition seem to emphasize one of these ideals more than the other.

While a Buddhist theorist may know only *about* the experiences that occur as a result of meditation and the like, on the basis of other people's accounts, the accomplished Buddhist practitioner comes to know the experiences themselves. Likewise, a theoretical physicist may have a fine conceptual grasp of the techniques used in a certain type of research and its results, but only those who have conducted experimental research themselves know what it is actually like to carry a research project through to the end. For the theorist, such research is something that is learned about in journals, whereas for the experimentalist, it is learned in the laboratory or the field. The Buddhist practitioner may also raise a number of questions posed by neither a Buddhologist or a Buddhist theorist. For example, are compassion and empathy qualities that can be cultivated by means of meditation? If so, can Buddhist ideas and methods be used effectively to that end in our society? If so, do the traditional techniques need to be altered to make them more effective in the modern world? A Buddhist practitioner may also address many other contemporary issues pertaining to conflict resolution, the dying process, and mental health, including dealing effectively with anger, depression, anxiety, stress, and attentional disorders.

Among the wide range of Buddhist practices, including meditation, only a small fraction of their resultant experiences are said to be generally ineffable. Many other experiences such as insight into impermanence, the realization of meditative quiescence (*śamatha*), and the experience of compassion, are not deemed inconceivable or inexpressible. Yet, it may be impossible to convey even such experiences effectively to someone who has never had them.

Following the type of analysis used previously, the relation between a Buddhist theorist and a Buddhist practitioner is a complex one. Since Buddhist tradition regards the very act of Buddhist theorizing as a form of Buddhist practice, a Buddhist theorist would therefore necessarily be a Buddhist practitioner. However, a distinction still needs to be made between *practicing* (Tib. *nyams su len pa*) and *putting into practice* (Tib. *lag len bstar ba*). For example, a Buddhist theorist who never practices meditation may study treatises on meditation, and that in itself is a type of Buddhist practice. But it is profoundly different from putting those meditation instructions into practice and witnessing for oneself the effects of the training. In terms of meditation, therefore, such a person would rightly be classified principally as a theorist and not as a practitioner. On the other hand, someone who practices simple forms of Buddhist meditation, such as the cultivation of mindfulness of breathing and mindfulness of walking, but who has little knowledge of the theoretical significance of such practices within the context of Buddhism may become an adept Buddhist practitioner, but would not be regarded as an accomplished Buddhist theorist.

Is it possible for Buddhist theorists and practitioners ever to step [illegible]eir Buddhist views and practices and examine them from [illegible] scholarly perspective? In proposing his methodology for [illegible]ditation scientifically, Frits Staal draws a strict distinction [illegible] followers of a guru, adherents of a particular sect, or peop[illegible] earch of *nirvāṇa*, *mokṣa*, or salvation and (2) genuine students of mysticism; and he maintains that the latter must sooner or later resume a critical outlook so that they can obtain understanding and make it available to others.[9] The student of meditation, he proposes, can learn the necessary techniques of meditation only by initially accepting them uncritically. This assertion runs counter to the Buddhist threefold education in hearing, thinking, and meditation, which I have discussed in the essay "The Dialectic Between Religious Belief and Contemplative Knowledge in Tibetan Buddhism," also included in this volume. Thus, Staal's assertion that the critical student must "be prepared to question and check what the teacher says, and introduce new variables and experimental variation" (146) is important for responsible Buddhist practitioners as well. He suggests that even the scientific study of meditation requires that one first suspend doubt in order to engage in meditative practice, then later on resort to analysis and critical evaluation. Without such subsequent reflection, the student of meditation will be like a sleep-walker who gains no knowledge or understanding (134). But according to the Buddhist sequence of hearing, thinking, and meditation, analysis and critical evaluation must both precede and follow the practice of meditation. Thus, Staal's claims notwithstanding (63, 148), there appears to be no justifiable reason why Buddhist practitioners in general must be less capable than Buddhologists of evolving meaningful theories about Buddhist meditation or of evaluating whether practitioners have actually attained the goals they think they have.

THE BUDDHIST

While the Buddhist tradition presents various criteria for determining who is and is not a Buddhist, it is often said that someone who takes refuge in the Buddha, Dharma, and Saṅgha is a Buddhist. The relation between Buddhist theorists and practitioners, on the one hand, and the Buddhist community as a whole may be likened to the relation between scientists and that segment of the general population that accepts the assertions of scientists largely on the basis of the authority of the scientific tradition, as opposed to their own ability to demonstrate either compelling empirical evidence or rational arguments validating those assertions. A Buddhist may or may not be a Buddhologist, a Buddhist theorist, or even a Buddhist practitioner, apart from the fact that taking refuge in the Buddha, Dharma, and Saṅgha is itself a Buddhist practice.

Must one be a Buddhist in order to adopt a Buddhist theory or engage in Buddhist practice? Clearly there are many people nowadays who accept certain aspects of the Buddhist world view or practice Buddhist meditations without considering themselves to be Buddhist and without taking Buddhist refuge. To adopt Buddhist theories or engage in Buddhist practices, must one know that those theories or practices are found in Buddhism? In other words, might the views and practices of adherents of other religions or contemplative traditions coincide with certain Buddhist views and practices? The Buddhist theorist and practitioner D. T. Suzuki, for example, claimed that Meister Eckhart's way of thinking was generally close to that of Zen Buddhism and specifically that his notion of the Godhead as "pure nothingness" was in perfect accord with the Buddhist doctrine of *śūnyatā* (Suzuki: 3, 16). The Christian theorist and practitioner Thomas Merton seemed to concur when he declared, "whatever Zen may be, however you define it, it is somehow there in Eckhart" (13).

Steven Katz, on the other hand, who, I assume, is neither a Buddhist nor a Christian theorist or practitioner, denies such claims, emphasizing that Eckhart was medieval Catholic Dominican monk and not a Mahāyāna Buddhist (57, and n. 91). Katz is certainly correct in maintaining that there were no medieval Catholic Dominican monks who were also Mahāyāna Buddhists. But this fact does not preclude the possibility that Eckhart may have gained certain contemplative experiences and insights that closely resemble those sought through the practice of Zen.

My own predilection in this regard is to rely more heavily on the authority of individuals who have deeply immersed themselves in Christian and Buddhist theory and practice than on those who know of both only on the basis of what they have read. As an analogy, to evaluate two independent, dissimilar scientific research methodologies and the theoretical conclusions drawn from such research, I believe that the theoretical and experimental scientists actually engaged in such research would generally be a more reliable source of information about the relation between their work than a philosopher, historian, or sociologist of science who knows about it only from their reports. Moreover, if two such methodologies produce similar empirical data, many scientists conclude that those methodologies were detecting a physical reality that is independent of both modes of research. A similar line of reasoning, of course, is often expressed by those who assert the presence of a "perennial philosophy" running through the great mystical traditions of the world.

In his essay included in this volume, John Makransky points out that the contemporary Buddhist tradition has taken relatively little interest in the writings of Buddhologists. Likewise, relatively few practicing scientists take much interest in the writings of philosophers of science, and some dismiss such scholarship as being irrelevant to scientific research.[10] Philosophers, they claim, only spin webs of speculation about the nature of scientific research and knowledge, without having any inside knowledge as to what it is like to actually *practice* science. Similarly, practicing Buddhists sometimes complain that Buddhologists commonly overlook the experiential aspects of Buddhism, including the practical applications of Buddhist ideas and methods, thereby ignoring the elements that are of greatest interest to them and brought them to Buddhist practice in the first place.

I believe that the dismissive attitudes of Buddhologists and Buddhist practitioners for each other is a disservice to both communities, much as the lack of appreciation of philosophy on the part of many scientists causes them to be philosophically ignorant and naive. Buddhists theorists and practitioners have much to learn from the scholarly methods of modern Buddhology. For example, the modern historical study of Buddhism might help Buddhists by demonstrating the adaptability of their own tradition as it has transformed from one culture and historical era to another. Such knowledge could help Buddhists maintain the vitality of their tradition in today's world, rather than adhering dogmatically to the forms Buddhism developed in other cultures and historical eras. Buddhologists, likewise, would have little to study were it not for the records left behind from earlier generations of Buddhist theorists and practitioners, and their scholarship may continue to benefit from the work of the present generation as well.

THE INTERDISCIPLINARY NATURE OF BUDDHISM

Since modern Buddhology strives to emulate the intellectual rigor and objectivity of the natural sciences, it is pertinent that part of the great strength of the natural sciences is that researchers from different fields frequently collaborate both in terms of their empirical methodologies and their theoretical analyses in their respective fields. We are now at a point in history at which there is rapidly increasing interest on the part of many researchers in the physical sciences, medicine, and cognitive sciences in the theories and practices of Buddhism. Much of their interest concerns the causes, nature, and effects of the phenomena of meditative experience – precisely the topics often overlooked by Buddhologists, and most strongly emphasized by Buddhist theorists and practitioners. I personally have encountered considerable interest in Buddhist techniques for training the attention, exploring the nature of the dream state, techniques for controlling one's own mind, for cultivating compassion and empathy, for relieving stress, for investigating the nature of consciousness, and for curing various physical diseases by means of Tibetan Buddhist medicine. Such collaboration provides an opportunity for Buddhologists, Buddhist theorists, and Buddhist practitioners to work together with research scientists to develop new methodologies and advance our knowledge in ways previously unimagined by any of them on their own.

In a similar vein, William James proposed a science of religion that is chiefly concerned with a scrutiny of "the immediate content of religious consciousness" (12). This approach was to be empirical, rather than rationalistic, focusing on religious experience rather than religious doctrines and institutions. Such a science, he suggested, might offer a bridge of understanding among peoples with disparate world views and bring a greater degree of coherence and intelligibility to different ways of exploring and understanding human existence (456). Perhaps the time has come when this noble challenge, proposed almost a century ago, may be taken to heart.

NOTES

1 For the Atiyoga, or rDzogs chen, account of the nature of Samantabhadra see Longchen Rabjam and also the chapter on "The Primordial Purity of the Universe" in Jamgön Kongtrul Lodrö Tayé.

2 If there were a three-point relation between Buddhism and religion, there would have to be (1) an instance of something that is both, (4) an instance of something that is neither, and instances of the above category (2) or (3) but not both. Another logical option is that instances of Buddhism and religion might be mutually exclusive, and a final option is that the sets of instances of the two might be mutually inclusive.

3 For a detailed account of medical writings and practice in early Theravāda Buddhism see Zysk.

4 As an example, note the comment by Louis de Broglie cited in Wallace 1996: 130.

5 I discuss the principles of scientific naturalism and its relation to religion and the study of the mind in Wallace forthcoming.

6 I have discussed methodologies for studying Buddhist meditation in greater detail in the chapter "Methodological Perspectives," in

Wallace 1997.

7 To take but a single example of this oversight, see Buswell and Gimello, in which Buddhist paths to liberation and enlightenment are discussed in detail, while the question of the validity of Buddhist insights rarely is addressed.

8 This statement is cited approvingly in Huntington: 13.

9 Staal: 130.

10 As an example of this dismissive attitude toward the philosophy of science, see Feynman.

REFERENCES

Almond, Philip C. (1988). *The British Discovery of Buddhism.* Cambridge: Cambridge University Press.

Buswell, Robert E. Jr. & Gimello, Robert M., eds. (1992). *Paths to Liberation: The Mārga and its Transformations in Buddhist Thought.* Honolulu: University of Hawaii Press.

Clark, Barry, trans. (1995). *The Quintessence Tantras of Tibetan Medicine.* Ithaca: Snow Lion Publications.

Capra, Fritjof (1975). *The Tao of Physics.* Boulder: Shambhala.

Davies, Paul (1992). *The Mind of God.* New York: Simon and Schuster.

Durkheim, Emile (1915/1965). *The Elementary Forms of the Religious Life.* Joseph W. Swain, trans. New York: Macmillan.

Feynman, Richard (1983). *The Character of Physical Law.* Cambridge, MA: M.I.T. Press.

Gadamer, H. (1988). *Truth and Method.* Garrett Barden & John Cumming, trans. New York. Reprint.

Güzeldere, Güven. (1995). "Consciousness: What It Is, How to Study It, What to Learn from Its History." *Journal of Consciousness Studies: controversies in science & the humanities* (II: 1) 30–51.

Harvey, Van (1981). *The Historian and the Believer.* Philadelphia: Westminster Press.

Huntington, Jr., C. W. (1989), with Geshé Namgyal Wangchen. *The Emptiness of Emptiness: An Introduction to Early Indian Mādhyamika.* Honolulu: University of Hawaii Press.

James, William (1902/1982). *The Varieties of Religious Experience: A Study in Human Nature.* New York: Penguin Books.

Jamgön Kongtrul Lodrö Tayé (1995). *Myriad Worlds: Buddhist Cosmology in Abhidharma, Kālacakra and Dzog-chen.* International Translation Committee of Kunkhyab Chöling, trans. Ithaca: Snow Lion Publications.

Katz, Steven T., ed. (1983). *Mysticism and Religious Traditions.* Oxford: Oxford University Press.

Longchen Rabjam (1996). *The Practice of Dzogchen.* Tulku Thondup, trans. Ithaca: Snow Lion Publications.

Merton, Thomas (1968). *Zen and the Birds of Appetite.* New York: New Directions.

Nagel, Thomas (1986). *The View from Nowhere.* New York: Oxford University Press.

Staal, Frits (1975). *Exploring Mysticism: A Methodological Essay.* Berkeley: University of California Press.

Suzuki, D. T. (1957). *Mysticism: Christian and Buddhist.* New York: Harper.

Wallace, B. Alan (1996). *Choosing Reality: A Buddhist View of Physics and the Mind.* Ithaca, NY: Snow Lion Publications.

Wallace, B. Alan (1997). *The Bridge of Quiescence: Experiencing Tibetan Buddhist Meditation.* Chicago: Open Court Press.

Wallace, B. Alan (forthcoming). *The Taboo of Subjectivity: A Contemplative View of Scientific Naturalism and the Mind.*

Zysk, Kenneth G. (1991). *Asceticism and Healing in Ancient India: Medicine in the Buddhist Monastery.* Oxford: Oxford University Press.

Four

The Methodological Relevance of Contemporary Biblical Scholarship to the Study of Buddhism[1]

Vesna A. Wallace

THE HISTORICAL-CRITICAL METHOD AND ITS LIMITATIONS

Over the past few decades we have observed in the West a fairly rapid increase in practical and doctrinal interests in Buddhism as well as in the academic study of Buddhism. Free-standing Buddhist schools and seminaries, which are intimately connected with newly formed Buddhist communities in the West, and Western academic institutions have charted different ways of studying Buddhism. There is very little agreement among academics and Buddhist communities with regard to what it is they are studying, how they ought to study it, and what the relevance is of their study.

Buddhist scholars within Western academia have developed diverse methods, models, and strategies for studying Buddhism and for reading Buddhist texts; and at times, we have engaged in discussions concerning which of the methods, models, and strategies should be implemented. We have also demonstrated that the historical-critical approaches – which analyze different Buddhist traditions and Buddhist texts in terms of religious and philosophical influences, textual sources, the historical development of ideas and practices, etc. – are indispensable. The historical-critical methods have helped us to avoid serious, anachronistic misapprehensions concerning ancient Buddhist texts, and they have often enabled us to reconstruct authentic Buddhist texts that require interpretation. At the same time, many scholars have failed to recognize that the historical-critical approach is neither final nor ultimately adequate. That is to say, we must still recognize that this type of methodological undertaking does not necessarily ensure a correct understanding of Buddhist texts. Although it helps us avoid ahistoric misunderstanding, it does not provide us with a satisfactory comprehension of the practical implications of Buddhist texts. As some contemporary biblical scholars[2] have rightly pointed out, the historical-critical method claims too much for itself insofar as it asserts its central role in unlocking an "objective," or "real," meaning of the text, which it places in the author's intention. In doing so, the historical-critical method scrutinizes the text as a window to some other world and focuses on the reconstruction of literary sources and events that shaped the text. In that way, it often disempowers the community of primary readers while attributing to the scholar a uniquely privileged status as its interpreter. It does not acknowledge that Buddhist texts, which are produced for and appropriated by communities of Buddhist believers, resist being reduced to a construal of a single reader, or interpreter. For these reasons, the historical-critical method is ineffective in accomplishing the interpretative task carried out by means of conversation in the context of the historical community of a particular Buddhist tradition.

By concentrating on the past, the historical-critical method often focuses on the *implied* Buddhist community behind the text and on the *other world* of the text. For example, in the study of Indo-Tibetan Buddhist *tantra*s, the emphasis of the historical-critical method has been primarily on the reconstruction of the "original" audience of Buddhist *tantra*s, on the social and religious circumstances in which those *tantra*s were taught, on their "originally" intended meaning, and on the particular manner in which their "original" audience understood them. Although the recovery of this type of information is valuable, it is frequently incomplete, and the information is invariably arranged by the interpreter in a subjective manner. Thus, the recovered information can be easily misconstrued or adjusted to the interpreter's own agenda. The presence of radically opposing views among some contemporary Buddhist scholars with regard to whether Buddhist *tantra*s are essentially gynocentric or androcentric texts is one of many instances attesting to this fact. When attempting to reconstruct the "original" Buddhist tantric audience and its socio-cultural circumstances in India, one zealous feminist scholar (Shaw) interprets the scanty and problematic historical data, as well as passages from Indo-Tibetan Buddhist *tantra*s that eulogize the feminine and validate women, as indicative of women's power and leadership in creating the Buddhist tantric movement. She does not even consider the possibility that such passages might be expressions not of women's power, but of their powerlessness. Some other scholars (e.g., Sponberg; Snellgrove) interpret the same historical data and textual passages as a reflection of the male practitioner's viewpoint, and see Buddhist tantric texts as composed primarily to benefit male tantric practitioners. However, these scholars do not acknowledge that, despite their prevalent androcentric orientation, Buddhist tantric texts may not simply reflect the socio-cultural norms of the Indian patriarchal society of the times, but also may seek to undermine some of those norms.

In a recent essay, Peter N. Gregory discusses a similar problem, that of reconstructing "original," or "early," Buddhism and the "original" teachings of the Buddha – especially when the reconstruction is approached from an exclusively textual-historical point of view, as is the case in some Japanese scholarship.[3] He skillfully articulates this problematic issue as follows:

> Although the Pāli canon may, as a whole, be closer to the Buddha's "word" than any other extant textual corpus, it is still mediated by the collective memory of the community that compiled, codified, redacted, and transmitted it orally for hundreds of years before ever committing it to writing, and even when finally put into writing, it did not remain static but continued to be modified by the tradition over the ensuing centuries. As we have it today it is thus far removed from the Buddha, and we have no way of gauging how close or how distant any given statement is to the words of the Buddha. (294–295)

A historical-critical method never can guarantee a complete and accurate picture of the "original" world behind the text, but only a partial and imagined one.

INTERPRETING WITH CONTEMPORARY BUDDHIST COMMUNITIES

Some Buddhist scholars have failed to fully detect these limitations of the historical-critical method, for several reasons. One reason is the aforementioned lack of a clearly articulated understanding as to what the critical methods are good for. The lack of such understanding stems partly from the absence of agreement about the manner in which one studies or reads a set of historically placed teachings, or texts, that are acknowledged by a large number of readers as the authentic teachings of the Buddha. Another reason is the perpetual neglect of Buddhist communities as a group of valid interpreters of Buddhist tradition and as the primary readers of Buddhist texts. In our analyses of ancient Buddhist texts, we have more frequently and in greater detail dealt with an implied Buddhist audience than a real one. For example, in analyzing the Buddhist Theravāda and Mahāyāna *sūtra*s, or Buddhist classics such as Śāntideva's *Bodhicaryāvatāra* and others, Western

Buddhist scholars almost invariably have focused on the monastic audiences of antiquity and their interpretations; they have not dealt with the contemporary audience, asking who the individuals are who actually read it. Nor have they discussed the ways in which contemporary, lay Buddhist groups in the West and in Asia are approaching these texts, the reasons for which they read or listen to them, the manner in which the hopes they bring to the text shape their understanding of the texts as they read them, etc..

So far, specific questions – who are the actual readers of the particular text, how and why do they read it, and what expectations do they bring to that text as they read it? – have been addressed almost exclusively but incompletely by scholars whose readings of Buddhist texts are determined by identity markers such as gender and social class. However, even these scholars have not sufficiently engaged in theoretical discussions about the role of the reader, especially the reader outside the realm of the academy.

TRANSCENDING THE HERMENEUTICS OF SUSPICION

The neglect of Buddhist communities as interpreters of Buddhist texts and tradition has been due chiefly to the prevalent "hermeneutics of suspicion,"[4] which frequently distrusts the subject-matter and intention of a given text and approaches it as an exercise of authority or as an expression of power. The hermeneutics of suspicion and critique has proven to be a necessary hermeneutical resource for detecting and remedying some recurring distortions in the Buddhist tradition. As David Tracy remarks, the hermeneutics of suspicion and its accompanying critical theories may be needed at the outset of the interpretative process, when the interpreter detects certain misconceptions within the religious tradition, or when she faces the cognitive ambiguities within a given text and the moral ambiguities within the tradition (1989: 52). A careful look at the history of Buddhist ideas and practices reveals that the Buddhist tradition itself repeatedly has resorted to the religious hermeneutics of suspicion when previously unconscious distortions became evident and the need for self-reformation arose. According to the Pāli scriptures,[5] even Buddha Śākyamuni himself acknowledged the propriety of suspicion with regard to dubious matters, and emphasized the experiential testing of all religious teachings, including his own. However, while applying the hermeneutics of suspicion within its own religious arena, Buddhist tradition has continued to apply other types of hermeneutics, by recovering forgotten but important elements that eventually became the basis of newly developed theories.

A similar course ought to be taken by contemporary Buddhist scholars as well. We must make sure that the hermeneutics of suspicion and critique does not remain the sole dimension of our interpretative process. If suspicion and critique simply continue as suspicion and critique, they eventually cease to be fruitful and become more destructive than constructive for our understanding of Buddhist texts and Buddhist tradition. In addition, if we are to exercise the hermeneutics of suspicion with regard to a given text, we ought to exercise it in equal degree with regard to our own preconceptions, motives, and ends as well. We ought to examine whether or not we are bending the text for our own use and twisting its meanings for our own aims. Peter Gregory writes in a similar vein in his appraisal of the critical Buddhism that is given voice in contemporary Japanese scholarship, when he asserts that critical Buddhism "demands that we be self-critical, both as scholars and as Buddhists" (297). He adds:

> Among other things, being critical means becoming aware of the assumptions on which our discussion of critical Buddhism is based. Critical Buddhism must therefore come to terms with history – especially its own history, its own historical context, and its own historical position within the history of Buddhism. Such awareness is part and parcel of what it means to be critical.

Likewise, in Western Buddhist scholarship, the hermeneutics of suspicion and critique rarely has been accompanied by self-reflection or by retrieving suppressed or forgotten elements of the Buddhist tradition that can be transformative for the tradition. Efforts to retrieve suppressed elements of the Buddhist tradition and to mediate their transformative values have been fairly small, and for the most part undertaken by Buddhist scholars who have dealt with feminist, ecological, and socio-political issues. Feminist scholars (e.g., Gross; Shaw; Klein) have focused chiefly on retrieving elements from Buddhist historical events and textual sources that empower women and that were neglected in androcentric interpretations. Other scholars (e.g., Thurman; Gómez; Swearer), inspired by charismatic Buddhist leaders and the communities of Buddhist liberation movements in Asia, have turned their attention to textual sources to retrieve elements that call for an active participation in social and political reforms. Following the example of, and collaborating with, Buddhist communities committed to social change, these scholars have engaged in a re-evaluation of Buddhist tradition and contemporary Buddhist experience in light of those elements. For example, Robert A. F. Thurman interprets certain verses of Nāgārjuna's *Ratnāvalī* ("Jewel Garland of Royal Counsels") – which expound the duties of a Buddhist king, based on Buddhist principles of identitylessness, compassion, detachment, and generosity – "as a framework on which to outline the guidelines for Buddhist social action in our modern times" (130), as well as for education, politics, distribution of wealth, etc.. Also, it is worth noting that most of the scholars who have made use of the "hermeneutics of retrieval" in their interpretations are themselves Buddhist practitioners. Scholars who are not Buddhists have ignored this hermeneutical element, perhaps in sympathy with Paul Griffiths's comment, "I am no Buddhist, and can have nothing to say of a constructive kind about the proper construal of Buddhism . . . ." (160). Or perhaps they have ignored it for fear of being labeled Buddhist apologists. Whatever the reasons for this omission, they have hindered us in reading Buddhist texts responsibly and in interpreting Buddhist tradition reliably. The hermeneutics of retrieval does not have to be limited to the aforementioned themes or to the interpretative undertakings of Buddhists alone.

Within the field of Buddhist studies, the hermeneutics of suspicion and critique also has been insufficiently and rarely followed by a conversation in which an interpreter actively engages in a genuine conversation with a text, treating it as a subject, having its own rights and integrity that ought to be respected, and not as an object to be controlled and dissected. Scholarly works that resort solely to this type of hermeneutics attest to the fact that the hermeneutics of suspicion and critique alone cannot facilitate genuine understanding or authoritative interpretation of the Buddhist tradition, nor can it provide constructive solutions for that tradition.

INTERPRETING THROUGH CONVERSATION

Postmodern biblical scholarship, which conceives understanding as a dialogue with the "other," has demonstrated that a genuine understanding of a particular religious tradition takes place only when the historical-critical method is followed by a conversation in which the "other" of the dialogue may include both the interpreter and the text. The otherness of an interpreter occurs in the conversational model of interpretation insofar as the interpreter becomes self-reflective, that is, aware of her (or his) own historical situatedness and the preconceptions and anticipations that she brings into the dialogue. The conversational model of interpretation, as put forth by postmodern biblical theologians, entails attending to what the text says about the subject-matter, to the manner in which it says it, and to the active role of the interpreter (Tracy 1989; Klemm). This hermeneutical model allows the content of a text to challenge the interpreter's preconceptions by determining whether her prejudgements are appropriate or not for a given situation. In the conversational model of interpretation, a self-reflective interpreter is aware that the horizon of her cultural preconceptions, interests, and expectations affects what she looks for and finds in the text. Thus, a contemporary interpreter is expected to be fully aware of the historicity of the text and her own historical context. Only when the interpreter becomes aware of herself as a historically and culturally situated, non-autonomous reader can she understand the complex world of her own preconceptions with regard to the subject-matter of a given text. In this way, a self-conscious interpreter is able to enter a dialogue with the text without the misguided hope of reconstructing the meaning lying *exclusively behind the text* in the mind of the author and so on or *exclusively in the text* itself. Instead, the interpreter engages in conversation with the text, seeking the meaning *in front of the text*, that is, in the subject-matter, which is now common to both the text and the interpreter (Tracy 1989; Thompson).

A prime example of the contorted and one-sided interpretation that results from the reconstruction of the meaning lying exclusively in the text is Matsumoto Shirō's interpretation of the *tathāgatagarbha* theory (see Shiro). By concentrating entirely on assertions within the *tathāgatagarbha* texts that could be interpreted as substantialistic, and by interpreting the concept of *tathāgatagarbha* as an ontological reality – a form of *dhātuvāda* that contradicts the theory of *pratītya-samutpāda*, and therefore as non-Buddhist – Matsumoto Shirō himself falls into the extreme of substantialism, which he seeks to criticize. If he had engaged in a genuine conversation with the given texts, probing his own assumptions and posing further questions to the texts to see what they might have to say about *tathāgatagarbha* in the context of *pratītya-samutpāda*, emptiness (*śūnyatā*), *nirvāṇa*, and so forth, he might have learned that *tathāgatagarbha* is neither an ontological entity, nor contradictory to *pratītya-samutpāda* – as Sallie B. King has ably argued (see King). He also might have realized that *tathāgatagarbha* does not arise as an object of the conventional mind any more than does emptiness. If one is therefore to discard *tathāgatagarbha*, one should for the same reason discard emptiness, *nirvāṇa*, etc.. In her challenge to Matsumoto Shirō's reading of the *tathāgatagarbha* notion, King engages to a certain degree in a dialogue with the texts, and thereby offers a more rounded interpretation of the *tathāgatagarbha*. However, perhaps due to the structural constrains of her essay, she seeks the meaning primarily in the text and behind the text – in the intention of the author – and does not develop her conversation with the text fully. She concludes her interpretation of the *tathāgatagarbha* concept by explaining it as a mere metaphor for the universal possibility of enlightenment, introduced for soteriological purposes, i.e., to encourage people to practice in order to reach buddhahood. She does not ask further questions pertaining to, e.g., what the texts might have to say with regard to wherefrom or wherefore the universal possibility of enlightenment arises. From one perspective, all notions of emptiness, *tathāgatagarbha*, *nirvāṇa*, etc., are nothing more than didactic devices aimed at leading contemplatives to the direct experience of the ultimate, or unconditioned. But to reduce *tathāgatagarbha* to a *mere* metaphor for the possibility of enlightenment, or a *mere* pedagogical device, may be to fall to the extreme of nihilism, which some authors of the *tathāgatagarbha* texts wished to counteract in the first place, by introducing the *tathāgatagarbha* theory. If the interpreter were to continue her dialogue with the text, perhaps she would find that *tathāgatagarbha* is not only a possibility of enlightenment, but also a condition for that possibility, i.e., the essential quality of the mind that has been referred to since the time of the *Nikāyas* as "pure" or "luminous" (Pāli *pabhassara*, Sanskrit *prabhāsvara*).[6]

In addition, by seeking the meaning *in front of the text*, the interpreter does not merely reiterate the original meaning of the text but brings in creativity in her mediation and rendering of its meaning into her own horizon. By doing so, the interpreter discerns her act of interpretation as unavoidably characterized by both her historicity her creativity, or imagination, and thereby by her finitude. The interpreter's recognition of the historicity and limitation of her own understanding leads to the insight that her understanding may differ from that of the author. However, in my opinion, this postmodern assertion does not necessarily preclude the possibility of the interpreter fathoming the meaning originally intended by the author of a text. But if and when this occurs, the interpreter's own understanding is not isolated from that of the author. This, of course, has been precisely the intent of innumerable commentators writing from within the Buddhist tradition: to gain the vision of the original author or speaker.

Moreover, respecting the Buddhist communities as the primary readers of Buddhist texts and recognizing their expectation to experience the transformative power of the texts, the interpreter should further develop the aforementioned hermeneutical model and the sense of her responsibility in the conversation with the text. If the interpreter approaches the act of interpretation not simply as a dialogue between her as a single reader and the text, but as a conversation among the real readers about the text and with the text, then the manner of that conversation, the nature of her questions, and her receptivity to the text will be shaped by multiple horizons (Küng; Tracy 1989). In this manner, the interpreter's own horizon will be expanded, her understanding of the Buddhist tradition will be enriched, and the transformative power of the text will be duly appreciated.

In order for the interpretative conversation to take place, the interpreter must be open to the attention claimed by the text and to the possibility of a genuine dialogue with the text. On the other hand, the interpreter must also recognize that the text is not an autonomous entity that does not allow the interpreter to see her questions and responses as an authentic part of that conversation. Moreover, interpretative conversation becomes possible only when the interpreter transcends the search for a unique "real" meaning behind the text in the mind of the author in the socio-historical events that shaped the text, or in the responses of the original audience.

In postmodern biblical theology, the interpretative conversation rests on the understanding that the subject matter of the text is expressed through a given literary form and in a certain kind of language. Thus, the interpreter recognizes that the process of interpretation also includes explanations of the manner in which the literary genre and linguistic and semantic structures within the text produce the world of meaning that is shared by both the text and the interpreter. These methods are also useful in preventing the interpreter from extracting diverse, spurious meanings from the text. The given form of the text and its particular kind of language put constraints on its meaning, so that it cannot be read in an infinite number of ways, despite the fact that in different eras and in different cultural settings it has been interpreted in various ways. In this way, the semiotic, structuralist, and literary critical methods of explanation rescue the interpreter from the absolute relativism of meaning.

INTERPRETING THE BUDDHIST TRADITION AND CONTEMPORARY BUDDHIST EXPERIENCE IN LIGHT OF EACH OTHER

Using various explanatory methods, the interpreter is enabled to probe, challenge, and correct her initial understanding. Buddhism, as a self-consciously pluralistic religious tradition, lends itself to an interpretative process that avails itself of a plurality of explanatory methods. However, even though diverse explanatory methods facilitate the explanation and understanding of the specific features of a given text, they are not fully adequate, nor do they necessarily induce thorough understanding of the text as a whole. A possible reason for that is that the explanatory methods do not treat the text as a subject that speaks to the primary readers – namely, Buddhist monastics and the Buddhist laity – and that induces their transformative experience whether or not they are introduced to all the information related to the text. Like our colleagues in Biblical studies, at this point, we still do not have a specific method that would enable us to treat the text as it addresses its primary readers. In consequence, we have taken Buddhist texts out of the hands of Buddhist communities; and in this way, we have disempowered these communities with respect to our interpretative context. Perhaps, our immediate task should be to search for a model of interpretation that could compensate for this shortcoming in our exploratory methods.

When we interpret texts regarded by Buddhist communities as the authentic teachings of the Buddha, we should not deliberately exclude the primary readers' questions and assumptions of truth. Instead, we ought to consider the fact that primary readers, when reading these texts as the teachings of the Buddha, implicitly include the Buddha as an additional and authoritative participant in the conversation. Some scholars may object to the inclusion of these considerations into their interpretation on the grounds that these considerations may hinder their options for interpreting the text or that they may make their interpretation too open-ended. Such a qualm may be valid to some extent. At the same time, this position prevents one from engaging in meaningful discussions concerning the ways in which the primary readers' questions and assumptions of truth may fashion the act of interpretation. It also keeps one from seeking new hermeneutical paradigms that would be appropriate for these considerations and that could bring forth a more comprehensive system of interpretation than the one presently in use. Unless we address adequately the role of primary readers and the function of their faith in reading Buddhist texts, we shall remain ignorant of the manners in which these texts shape Buddhist identity in the contemporary world. Only when we understand the ways in which a contemporary Buddhist identity is formed can we develop the mutually critical correlations between contemporary Buddhist experience and the Buddhist tradition as a whole. It seems that the most fruitful efforts to create correlations between contemporary Buddhist experience and the Buddhist tradition as a whole have been made by Buddhist scholars who have approached this issue from the perspective of social and cultural anthropology (e.g., Samuel), feminist studies (e.g., Gross), and cognitive sciences (e.g., Wallace).

As some contemporary theologians and theorists (e.g., Blank; Ricoeur) have correctly pointed out, contemporary human experience and religious tradition are two factors that are always fundamental to any religious hermeneutical enterprise, since both inevitably include hermeneutical elements. This suggests that each of the two factors is understood only by being interpreted in the light of the other. In other words, in interpreting contemporary Buddhist experience, the Buddhist tradition is already present, and the other way around. Although contemporary Buddhist experience and the Buddhist tradition are distinguishable from each other, they are clearly inseparable and mutually irreducible. Buddhists' interpretation of their contemporary experience is necessarily shaped by the history of the ideas and practices of the Buddhist tradition; whereas their interpretation of Buddhist principles is inevitably influenced by the application of those principles to their contemporary experience. For this reason, our analysis of the Buddhist tradition and contemporary Buddhist experience needs to reflect the existential inseparability of those two, even though we may approach them as two different phenomena from the methodological point of view.

Moreover, the hermeneutical aspect of contemporary Buddhist experience indicates that an interpretation is for the most part intrinsically present in that experience and in Buddhists' understanding of it. If we include the contemporary experience of Buddhist confessionals in our study of Buddhism, then the analysis of their own interpretations of their experience – which reveal its practical and spiritual dimensions – will enable us to discern the crucial correlations between an interpretation of contemporary Buddhist experience and an interpretation of the Buddhist tradition. Thus, it will help us to identify the specific instances and the degree to which the Buddhist tradition and contemporary Buddhist experience may assert their mutual identity. It will also aids us in discerning the specific cases in which contemporary Buddhist experience contradicts the earlier Buddhist formulations of truth and the cases in which the interpretation of the Buddhist tradition contradicts the predominant views resulting from contemporary experience.

If we try to establish the nature of the particular correlations between contemporary Buddhist experience and the Buddhist tradition with respect to specific issues, we may more clearly recognize the ways in which Buddhist investigations into meaning and truth, together with their methods, contribute to the continuity and interruptions within the Buddhist tradition. Also, a study of the interactions between

Buddhist faith and rationality requires that Buddhist scholars supplement historical Buddhist scholarship with other practically-oriented disciplines. Psychological and sociological examinations of Buddhist knowledge, which respectively deal with the nature and social context of that knowledge, the empirical testing of Buddhist methods leading to experiential and inferential types of knowledge, and the investigation of the effects of those types of knowledge, can be very helpful in determining the validity of Buddhist knowledge and understanding its practical implications.

For example, in her book, *Buddhism After Patriarchy*, the Buddhist feminist scholar Rita M. Gross shows in historical and theological detail that a position promoting women's equality and dignity is not merely a contemporary position advocated by Western Buddhist feminists, but is present throughout Buddhist history. Therefore, she feels that, unlike feminists in other religious traditions, Buddhist feminists "do not have to deconstruct any core teachings" (120). On the other hand, she also demonstrates that in the Buddhist tradition, this position has been normative, but seldom carried out in practice. Thus, as a contemporary Buddhist and as a woman, she views the Buddhist tradition as having a usable past, but not one that is entirely sufficient for the future. For her, "at one and the same time, it is important to know and utilize the past, while not being bound to it" (120). Thus, using traditional sources as a basis to argue for more equitable gender relations, Gross maintains the continuity of the tradition; and, at the same time, reconstructing a traditional Buddhism into a post-patriarchal Buddhism characterized by androgynous views and institutions, she clearly advocates disconnection from the androcentric views and practices of traditional Buddhism.

In a similar vein, in his book, *The Bridge of Quiescence*, B. Alan Wallace analyzes the nature of mindfulness (*smṛti*) and introspection (*saṁprajanya*) in light of modern scientific and philosophical treatments of these topics. For example, he takes the traditional Buddhist concepts of attentional stability and vividness, which are crucial to the development of meditative quiescence (*śamatha*) , and interprets them in the light of modern cognitive psychology. Wallace analyzes literary sources from the Buddhist tradition and cites accounts of contemporary Buddhist experiences that indicate that very high degrees of attentional stability and vividness can be maintained for hours on end. Consciously taking on the role of a propounder of Buddhist tradition, he criticizes modern Western skepticism about the possibility of sustained, voluntary attention and genuine introspection, and their role in examining the nature of the mind. He indicates that while most contemporary cognitive scientists downplay the role of introspection in examining mental processes, and some even deny the possibility of introspection altogether, genuine introspection does indeed occur among past and present Buddhist contemplatives, and plays a very important role in their understanding of the mind. Thus, he demonstrates the continuity between Buddhist tradition and contemporary Buddhist experience with regard to the cultivation of voluntary sustained attention. However, in these and other ways, he points out the incompatibility between, on the one hand, Buddhist tradition and contemporary Buddhist experience, and, on the other, modern scientific research and philosophical analysis, and suggests ways in which contemporary science and the Buddhist tradition may broaden each other's horizons by engaging in theoretical and practical collaboration.

CONCLUSION

By applying the types of analyses articulated above, we may find better ways of accomplishing the interpretative task of Buddhist studies and thereby enhance our understanding of this complex religious tradition. Some Buddhist scholars have shown a tendency to restrict the scope of Buddhist hermeneutics into a method of making "obsolete" Buddhist texts intelligible and acceptable to our contemporary thinking. In this way, they have frequently given to our contemporary thinking a status of an ultimate, hermeneutical perspective. If we hermeneutically privilege our contemporary thinking, we risk allowing a specific hermeneutical model to act as a filter excluding the most significant contents of a text and obscuring its richness of meanings and implications. When a hermeneutical model, rather than the subject-matter itself, becomes a chief guide in the act of interpretation, then either a given text becomes muzzled or its message becomes distorted. Some contemporary biblical scholars (e.g., Blank) already have learned that every interpretative model is selective and therefore restricted and relative. If we wish to avoid mistreating the text, we must approach hermeneutics as a complex phenomenon that includes the entire process of understanding and that consists of a series of individual elements, including the interpreter's consideration of her own attitudes and the concerns that guide her hermeneutical enterprise. As our contemporary colleagues in biblical studies often have emphasized, our own hermeneutics must subject itself to objective criticism without concealing its motivating concerns.

Also, our contemporary hermeneutics should not exclude earlier Buddhist hermeneutics, but treat it as a complementary and competing partner in a dialogue. If we ignore earlier Buddhist hermeneutics, we historically decontextualize our contemporary hermeneutics and leave it vulnerable to our own misconceptions. In a search for a more comprehensive model of Buddhological interpretation, we need to develop a religious hermeneutics that will encompass the plurality of interpretations and their histories.

Likewise, following the example of the earliest Buddhist hermeneutics, it might be fruitful for contemporary Buddhology to engage in a serious dialogue with natural sciences as even partners. As Buddhist scriptures suggest, Buddha Śākyamuni himself constructed his first hermeneutical model, namely, of the Four Noble Truths, on the example of medical science. Scientific ideas and methods of analysis may prove to be useful for developing a more comprehensive Buddhological model of interpretation. For example, a dialogue with cognitive sciences is bound to shed fresh light on the theoretical and empirical assertions concerning the nature of the mind according to the Buddhist tradition. Such dialogue may not only reveal some of the strengths and weaknesses of the Buddhist study of the mind, but also disclose the sometimes unwarranted assumptions and limited methodologies of the modern cognitive sciences.

In a similar way, Buddhist scholars should engage in conversation with confessional Buddhologists pursuing the study of Buddhism outside the university and with scholars of other religious traditions to compare their respective methods of studying religion and jointly to seek solutions to their problems. In times of the flourishing of religious and hermeneutical pluralism, the role and effectiveness of Buddhist scholarship easily can be imperiled by academic isolation and elitism, narrow specialization, and excessive individualism. To guard against these dangers, engaging in respectful dialogue with communities of believers and the scholars of the world's religions promises to yield deeper understanding of our respective roles in the areas of our study and the strengthening of Buddhist scholarship in general.

NOTES

1 Thanks to the editors, John Makransky and Roger Jackson, for their comments and helpful suggestions, and to David H. Wallace and Marianne Meye Thompson for their inspiration.

2 See Wolterstorff; Thompson; and Segovia.

3 The scholars referred to by Gregory are Hakayama Noriaki and Matsumoto Shirō, whose reconstruction of "true Buddhism," resting on

a purely textual and doctrinal approach, is sought in the *Mahāvagga*'s account of Śākyamuni's enlightenment as a discovery of *pratītya-samutpāda*.

4 According to David Tracy, the hermeneutics of suspicion is a hermeneutical model that rests on critical theories such as psychoanalysis, ideology-critique, etc., which are employed "to spot and emancipate the repressed, unconscious distortions that operate in the classic religious texts and in their history of effects through the classic religious tradition" (1989: 52).

5 In the *Kālama Sutta* of the *Aṅguttara Nikāya* (I: 189), the Buddha admonishes the Kālamas, the people of the city of Kesaputta, that they should not accept any teaching merely on the grounds of revelation, tradition, the religious authority of texts, or on the basis of mere reasoning or superficial assessment of the facts, or because it conforms with one's preconceptions, or because of the prestige of a teacher. In the *Visaṃsaka Sutta* of the *Majjhima Nikāya* (IV: 47), the Buddha encourages monks to examine the Buddha himself in order to see whether or not he is led by visibly impure mental states.

6 See *Aṅguttara Nikāya* I: 10: "Monks, this mind (*citta*) is brightly shining (*pabhassara*), but it is defiled by defilements which arrive" (quoted from Harvey: 56).

REFERENCES

Blank, Joseph (1989). "'According To The Scriptures': The New Testament Origins and Structure Of Theological Hermeneutics. In Hans Küng and David Tracy, eds., *Paradigm Change in Theology: A Symposium for the Future*. Trans. Margaret Köhl. Edinburgh: T. & T. Clark Ltd.

Gómez, Luis O. (1992). "Nonviolence and the Self in Early Buddhism." In Kenneth Kraft, ed., *Inner Peace, World Peace: Essays on Buddhism and Nonviolence*. Albany: State University of New York Press.

Gregory, Peter N. (1997). "Is Critical Buddhism Really Critical?" In Jamie Hubbard and Paul Swanson, eds., *Pruning the Bodhi Tree: The Storm Over Critical Buddhism*. Honolulu: University of Hawaii Press.

Griffiths, Paul J. (1997). "The Limits of Criticism." In Jamie Hubbard and Paul Swanson, eds., *Pruning the Bodhi Tree: The Storm Over Critical Buddhism*. Honolulu: University of Hawaii Press.

Gross, Rita M. (1993). *Buddhism After Patriarchy: A Feminist History, Analysis, and Reconstruction of Buddhism*. Albany: State University of New York Press.

Harvey, Peter (1990). *An Introduction to Buddhism: Teachings, History, and Practice*. Cambridge: Cambridge University Press.

King, Sallie B. (1997). "The Doctrine of Buddha-Nature is Impeccably Buddhist." In Jamie Hubbard and Paul Swanson, eds., *Pruning the Bodhi Tree: The Storm Over Critical Buddhism*. Honolulu: University of Hawaii Press.

Klein, Anne C. (1985). "Primordial Purity and Everyday Life: Exalted Female Symbols and the Women of Tibet." In Clarissa Atkinson et al., eds., *Immaculate and Powerful: The Female in Sacred Image and Social Reality.* Boston: Beacon Press.

Klein, Anne C. (1995). "Nondualism and the Great Bliss Queen: A Study in Tibetan Buddhist Ontology and Symbolism." *Journal of Feminist Studies in Religion* (I: 1) 73-98.

Klemm, David E. (1986). *Hermeneutical Inquiry, vol. 1: The Interpretation of Texts.* AAR Studies in Religion, no. 43. Atlanta: Scholars Press.

Küng, Hans (1989). "A New Basic Model for Theology: Divergences and Convergences." In Hans Küng and David Tracy, eds., *Paradigm Change in Theology: A Symposium for the Future.* Trans. Margaret Köhl. Edinburgh: T. & T. Clark Ltd.

Küng, Hans and Tracy, David, eds. 1989. *Paradigm Change in Theology: A Symposium for the Future.* Trans. Margaret Köhl. Edinburgh: T. & T. Clark Ltd.

Kysar, Robert (1996). "Coming Hermeneutical Earthquake in Johannine Interpretation." In Fernando Segovia, ed., *What is John? Readers and Readings of the Fourth Gospel.* SBL Symposium Series, no. 3. Atlanta: Scholars Press.

Moore, Stephen (1989). *Literary Criticism and the Gospels: The Traditional Challenge.* New Haven: Yale University Press.

Muller, A. Richard (1996). "The Significance of Precritical Exegesis: Retrospect and Prospect." In Fernando Segovia and Mary Ann Tolbert, eds., *Biblical Interpretation in the Patristic Era.* Minneapolis: Fortress Press.

Polkinghorne, John (1997). *One World: The Interaction of Science and Theology.* Princeton: Princeton University Press.

Ricouer, Paul (1989). "Response to Joseph Blank." In Hans Küng and David Tracy, eds., *Paradigm Change in Theology: A Symposium for the Future.* Trans. Margaret Köhl. Edinburgh: T. & T. Clark Ltd.

Samuel, Geoffrey (1993). *Civilized Shamans: Buddhism in Tibetan Societies.* Washington and London: Smithsonian Institution Press.

Shaw, Miranda (1994). *Passionate Enlightenment: Women in Tantric Buddhism.* Princeton: Princeton University Press.

Segovia, Fernando (1995). "'And They Began to Speak in Other Tongues': Competing Modes of Discourse in Contemporary Biblical Criticism." In Fernando Segovia and Mary Ann Tolbert, eds., *Reading from This Place, vol. 1: Social Location and biblical Interpretation in the United States.* Minneapolis: Fortress Press.

Shirō, Matsumoto (1997). "The Doctrine of *Tathāgata-garbha* is Not Buddhist." In Jamie Hubbard and Paul Swanson, eds., *Pruning the Bodhi Tree: The Storm Over Critical Buddhism.* Honolulu: University of Hawai'i Press.

Snellgrove, David (1987). *Indo-Tibetan Buddhism: Indian Buddhists and Their Tibetan Successors.* London: Serindia.

Their Tibetan Successors. London: Serindia.

Sponberg, Alan (1992). "Attitudes Toward Women and the Feminine in Early Buddhism." In José Ignacio Cabezón, ed., *Buddhism, Sexuality, and Gender*. Albany: State University of New York Press.

Swearer, Donald K. (1992). "Exemplars of Nonviolence in Theravada Buddhism." In Kenneth Kraft, ed., *Inner Peace, World Peace: Essays on Buddhism and Nonviolence*. Albany: State University of New York Press.

Thompson, Marianne Meye (1996). "After Virtual Reality: Reading the Gospel of John at the Turn of the Century." Unpublished paper, presented at the annual meeting of the AAR/SBL.

Thurman, Robert A. F. (1988). "Nagarjuna's Guidelines for Buddhist Social Action." In Fred Eppsteiner, ed., *The Path of Compassion: Writings on Socially Engaged Buddhism*. Berkeley: Parllax Press.

Tracy, David (1987). *Plurality and Ambiguity: Hermeneutics, Religion, Hope*. San Francisco: Harper and Row.

Tracy, David (1989). "Hermeneutical Reflections in the New Paradigm." In Hans Küng and David Tracy, eds., *Paradigm Change in Theology: A Symposium for the Future*. Trans. Margaret Köhl. Edinburgh: T. & T. Clark Ltd.

Tracy, David (1990). *Dialogue with the Other: The Inter-religious Dialogue*. Louvain: Peiter Press.

Vanhoozer, Kevin, J. (1995). "The Reader in New Testament Interpretation." In *Hearing the New Testament: Strategies for Interpretation*. Grand Rapids: Eerdmans.

Wallace, B. Alan (1997). *The Bridge of Quiescence: Experiencing Tibetan Buddhist Meditation*. La Salle, IL and Chicago: Open Court.

Five

Hermeneutics and Dharmology: Finding an American Buddhist Voice

Roger Corless

THE TERM

The neologism *dharmology* is suggested as the Buddhist equivalent of *theology*, a Christian term indicating that Christianity is being studied normatively, by a person who accepts Christianity as true, rather than from an academic or descriptive standpoint, in which the beliefs of the scholar, whether Christian, anti-Christian, or something else, are bracketed, in favor of a so-called objective approach.

The first problem with any neologism is how to spell it. *Theology* is clearly derived from the Greek *theos*, god, and *logos*, order, system, or principle. Since the ending is *-logos* it appears that our new word should be spelled *dharmalogy*. However, we have had the word *buddhology* around for some time, referring to the academic approach to Buddhism in western and western style universities, and here we note that the prefix *buddha-* has become *buddho-*, and that somehow, to native speakers of English, this seems more natural.[1]

This article is, in effect, about the differences between Buddhology and Dharmology, and how they might be resolved.

DHARMOLOGY

Buddhism has a reputation, at least in the West, for tolerance. But this does not mean that it is relativist or indifferentist. It is a self-confident missionary religion that, on the whole, is, simply, more polite than the other great missionary religions of Christianity and Islam. Rather than condemning non-adherents and trying to convert them so as to save them from hell, it pities them, and, employing skillful means (*upāya-kauśalya*) looks for opportunities to teach them at least the mitigated truths of Buddhism. Faced with persons who, for example, express a belief in a creator God, it adopts the stance of an adult towards a child who believes in Santa Claus. To deny Santa outright would not only be cruel, a failing of compassion, it would also destroy what little spirituality the child has. Therefore, the topic is either ignored or ways are found to re-frame Santa as "the spirit of Christmas charity."

Thus, to put it baldly, traditional Buddhism cannot accept a non-Buddhist understanding of Buddhism as anything other than a mistake. Its hermeneutic, or understanding, of reality as it truly is, makes the following assumptions:

- the Buddhas are omniscient (either actually or potentially), because they have developed (or manifested) the full freedom of body, speech and mind;
- the Buddha-dharma is true for all time-structures and world-systems;
- the trichiliocosm (*trisahasrāralokadhātava*) is the universal stage within which rebirth and liberation take place;
- reality arises interdependently (*pratītya-samutpāda*) so that propositions such as theism, atheism, realism and idealism are nonsensical.

We will briefly examine each of these presuppositions.

The Buddhas are Omniscient

All traditions of Buddhism teach that, when a living or conscious being (*sattva*) becomes a Buddha, the entity has access to all knowledge. Whether this access is constant, or is dependent upon applying the mind to a certain topic, is a controversy that divides Mahāyāna and Theravāda, leading to different interpretations of, for example, the decision of Śākyamuni Buddha to begin teaching. When Brahmā tells the Buddha that there are beings with little dust on their eyes, who could therefore be expected to understand the Dharma, Theravāda interprets this to mean that the Buddha did not initially know this but, on directing his *dhamma-cakkhu* (the "eye" or supernormal insight that sees reality directly and truly) towards the issue, was able to see for himself that this was the case. Mahāyāna, on the other hand, claims that the Buddha knew the truth all the time and, out of compassion, was merely pretending not to know so as to allow Brahmā to gain an enormous amount of merit by being the one who triggered the renewal of the Dharma in this world-cycle. The theoretical difference, at least as Mokṣākaragupta explains it, is between whether the Buddhas are potentially omniscient (*sarvajña*) or actually omniscient (*sarvasarvajña*) (Kajiyama: 134–137). The practical difference, for our purposes, is slight. Whatever can be known, says Buddhism, the Buddhas know it.

The omniscience of the Buddhas has consequences for the ordinary practitioner of Buddhism. The anthropology of Buddhism is one of perfectibility (Katz). A human, qua human, mis-takes reality due to ignorance or, perhaps better, unawareness (*avidyā*), but this unawareness is not inherent. The true nature of mind is pure, wise, and compassionate. Mahāyāna tends to regard pure mind as something already existing (*amalajñāna*) and waiting only be to be discovered or uncovered, while Theravāda prefers to say that ordinary mind is defiled but can be completely liberated, or separated from pollution (*cittavimutti*). Thus, although we may discover that we are not omniscient, this is merely because we have not yet fully manifested (Mahāyāna) or gained (Theravāda) our full potential.

The Buddhadharma is the Eternal Truth

If the Buddhas are omniscient, it follows that what they teach, the Buddha-dharma, is true in the same universal way as, for instance, it is claimed that the laws of physics are true. One may believe or not believe the tenets of some religion or other, but one cannot gainsay gravity. In the same way, if one denies the validity of the Four Noble Truths, etc., one is not merely exercising one's constitutional right, as an American, to believe in another religion, one is simply stupid. A consequence of this position is that Buddhism cannot be considered, from the Buddhas' point of view, to be a religion: it is the Truth, the way things are.

The Trichiliocosm Is The Universal Stage Within Which Rebirth And Liberation Take Place

As there is no form of traditional Buddhism in which the Buddha is regarded as nothing more than a human who founded an interesting school of philosophy, so there is no form of traditional Buddhism that does not assume, as a matter of course, that the world of humans in which Śākyamuni Buddha manifested is nothing more than a tiny part of a very large or (according to the *Lotus Sūtra*) infinite universe brimming with many different living and conscious beings (*sattva*), many of whom are invisible or otherwise inaccessible to each other, but all of whom are, eventually, reborn as each other, and that in these different realms, time proceeds at different rates. On what we call earth, Buddhism regards humans as beings of a hoary antiquity far beyond what we are told by modern paleontologists. Any attempts to reduce this *trisahasrāralokadhātava*, or trichiliocosm as Edward Conze called it, to the cozy anthropocentric world of Aristotle, or to the grim, largely dead and empty universe of Newton, are incompatible with any previously known form of Buddhism. A consequence of this position is that life and consciousness are not accidental epiphenomena, they are intrinsic to reality as it truly is. And since what is meant by consciousness is, ultimately, Buddha-consciousness (according to the Mahāyāna) or liberated, unconditioned consciousness (according to the Theravāda), this means that reality, seen truly, is great compassion (*mahākaruṇā*) and great wisdom (*mahāprajñā*).

Reality Arises Interdependently

Buddhism slides between the philosophical puzzles of theism, atheism, realism, and idealism, as well as free will and determinism, with the observation of interdependent arising (*pratītya-samutpāda*).[2] A consequence of this position is the famous, not to say notorious, claim of Nāgārjuna to have no philosophical or metaphysical position (*dṛṣṭi*). This is, of course, something of a leg-pull, since he has to claim *śūnyatā* (emptiness or, better, transparency, the lack of inherent existence, or, in western terms, *quidditas*, in anything that exists or does not exist) as the nature of reality, and so he has to hold *some* view, but what he seems to mean is that claiming *śūnyatā* leaves the claimant with no subjective ground to stand on (*apratiṣṭhita*) and no objective reality to point to (*niḥsvabhāva*). Thus, if the maneuver has worked, one is philosophically unassailable.

BUDDHOLOGY

The academic study of Buddhism, known as Buddhology, as it has been developed in western universities and in Western-style universities in Japan and elsewhere, is opposed to, or incompatible with, the presuppositions of Dharmology at almost every point, to the extent that we can ask whether Buddhism can be legitimately studied at Western universities (Corless 1990).

On the surface, Buddhology, as an enterprise of the selfless search for truth as it came to be understood in the European Renaissance and Enlightenment periods, is very tolerant, accepting the Buddhist world-view with the same open arms with which it accepts every other world-view. But that is the first problem: it is relativist and indifferentist, whereas Dharmology is self-assured and absolutist.

The second problem is more subtle. The claims of openness, tolerance, and objectivity are actually dogmas masquerading as universally acceptable axia. They are, indeed, no more than *claims*, and they are claims which Dharmology not only denies but traces to the confused operation of unawareness, particularly the "identify, draw and label" aspect of confused mind which it calls *vikalpa*. Its main principle of operation is the so-called rational classification of so-called objective data. Its main intellectual assumption is that the pinnacle of the human mind is manifested in tenured professors at the major universities. Put baldly, it is the vehicle for the triumphalism of the researcher with a Ph.D. From this perspective, Wilfred Cantwell Smith can unabashedly assert "Whether we should . . . call [the Buddha's faith] faith in God, depends entirely on what we think of the universe, *not on what he thought of it*" (Smith: 32, italics original).

Thus, the professor displaces the Buddha as the central object of worship and the true locus of refuge, and we are left with the universe which Alfred North Whitehead pilloried as "matter hurrying endlessly."

It is not difficult to see how this world-view arose. The Black Death was a catastrophe incompatible with a God who was all-loving, all-knowing, all-powerful, and accessible to the human mind.[3] The thinking person therefore had two options: to retain a belief in God, but to allow God's intelligibility to retreat into the incomprehensibility of Catholic Nominalism or Protestant Fideism, thus separating religion from the general sphere of human investigation, which appropriated the name science (formally the broader concept of *scientia*) to itself; or to reject God and seek an explanation of the universe based entirely upon material forces, either dismissing any discussion of values, mind, and spirit, or (as Descartes did quite explicitly) shuffling them off into the realm of theology.

This maneuver of the Western Mind, which was nothing more than the petulant afterglow of the panic that arose when it realized that its world-view had been shattered, left us unable to deal with anything other than clocks, and things that resembled, or were thought to resemble, or were thought to suppose to resemble if they behaved themselves, clocks.

The poverty of this world-view is now apparent, yet after suffering intellectually lethal attacks from Freud, Marx, and Derrida, it stubbornly survives in the mythological world of the television commercial in which actors in white coats try to convince us of the superiority of a product because, they say with conviction, "It's *scientific*!" Why? Because, I assume, it allows the professors, that is, those who invented the materialistic world-view, to fill the place held in the Middle Ages by the Church, controlling ideology and, therefore, the way we are supposed to view reality and truth.

As Buddhists, we can understand this as a grasping (*tṛṣṇā*) which attempts to preserve the collective constructed self of professors in the Academy, but we need not take it seriously as a view of reality.

THE TENSIONS

However, any ruling ideology demands that it be taken seriously: that is why it is a ruling ideology. So, we experience, in western academics, the tension between Buddhology, which is respectable, and Dharmology, which is respectable only as a private option: if we suggest that it be put publicly on the level of Buddhology, our colleagues in the Academy are at best embarrassed, and at worst they ensure that we do not get a tenured post at a major university – the modern equivalent of excommunication.

When we teach Buddhology we must do so with an "unholier than thou" attitude, asserting, or pretending if necessary, that we do not practice the Dharma, ignoring the ethical (*śīla*) and meditational (*samādhi*) aspects, and reducing the wisdom aspect (*prajñā*) to philosophy. We concentrate on texts, and on the textual features of texts (philology, authorship, provenance, date) rather than on their content. At the beginning of the modern period of academic Biblical study it was said "We treat the Bible like any other book" with the result that Biblical specialists now routinely claim that it is none of their business to speak about whether or not there is a God and whether or not there is a God who does anything. And Buddhologists have caught the infection. The Buddhist world-view is a myth which we study objectively and rationally, and we exalt the historical-critical approach above the doctrinal, or Dharmological.

A prominent scholar of Tibetan Buddhism was repeatedly denied promotion because, it was said, he *merely* (my italics) translated the commentaries of the lamas (i.e., pursued basic research), he did not criticize them. A scientist, on the other hand, would not expect to be criticized for "merely" doing basic research, because the scientist would be presumed to be acting within the parameters of the ruling ideology.

This tension between public denial (masquerading as neutrality) and private affirmation manifests in Japanese universities, where the western academic system has been, according to the Japanese tradition, both imported and adapted, as separate departments (or faculties), one dealing with Buddhology (*Bukkyōgakubu*) and one with Dharmology (e.g., in a Shinshū aligned university, *Shinshūgakubu*): the relationship between these departments is, apparently, often a matter of great delicacy.

A DHARMOLOGICAL BUDDHOLOGY

Making Buddhism Sound Like Christianity

The title of the published version of Alfred Bloom's dissertation, *Shinran's Gospel of Pure Grace* (1965), immediately makes the Western reader think of Christianity, and indeed the book has many explicit references to Martin Luther.[4] Certain Christian terms are used, not only by Bloom, but by practically every Buddhologist, as if they were unproblematic. No-one, for example, seems to have difficulty referring to "Zen monks," even after finding out that they are all married, and Buddhist *vihāras*, *gompas*, and *teras* are all called monasteries – or, sometimes, temples. When the Buddha became the Buddha he is said to have obtained "enlightenment" – not a Christian term indeed, but a borrowing from the alien world of German Rationalism. And in Shin Buddhism, we have that little word *shin* which, until recently, we blithely translated as "faith" and then, thinking we were on to something, compared it with Christian "faith."

The history of the transmission of the Dharma to China tells us that there is a certain usefulness to this practice. By taking an unfamiliar, not to say barbaric, Buddhist technical term and matching it with a vaguely similar Confucian or Taoist technical term, in a process called *k'o-i* (stretching the meaning), the early translators were able to soften up the Chinese for the time when Kumārajīva came along and suggested, for instance, that instead of using the homey Taoist character *wu* (non-being) for *śūnyatā* they should use the strange, but ultimately more accurate, character *k'ung* (vacuity), and that some foreign words (such as *buddha*) were better left as they were and, however unlovely the resulting compounds, merely transliterated.[5]

It took the Chinese about four hundred years to go from An Shih-kao to Kumārajīva, but history moves faster now, and after – how long shall we say? one hundred years after the European colonial discovery of Buddhism? – we are now in a position to give up *k'o-i*, recognizing, as the Chinese eventually did, that it encourages false comparisons (as, for example, in our case, between Zen *sō* and Benedictine monks) and propose or invent perhaps stranger, but more precise, terms of our own.

A feature of modern English not shared by classical Chinese is its willingness to accept foreign words as its own, with little change save a bowdlerizing of the pronunciation. Buddha has been an English word for so long it hardly sounds foreign any more, as has nirvana, Zen, and so forth. Each edition of Webster's English Dictionary contains a larger crop of "Buddhist" words now accepted as English. So, people no longer do Insight Meditation, they practice Vipassanā (which they re-pronounce as Vipassāna, the stress being in a place unusual for English) and it does not seem odd to refer to a *rōshi* (pronounced *rosshy*) or a *bla ma* (pronounced *lāma*), although such persons are often still given quasi-Catholic titles such as Venerable, Eminence, and Holiness. Maybe the day will dawn when we will no longer use the terms *monk* and *nun* in Buddhism.

I suggest that, whenever possible, a technical Buddhist term with no obvious English equivalent should be imported in some form of transliteration that will make it reasonably easy to [re-]pronounce, and in this regard I applaud the decision of the Shin Buddhism Translation Series Committee to import *shinjin* as *shinjin* and not to try to make it mean "faith."[6]

In cases where, despite our best efforts, the transliterated word refuses to stick in English, we need to think very carefully about the *context* of the term and choose an English term referring to a similar *context* (for example, is a particular *gompa* more like a temple, a monastery, or a university?). If even that fails, we will need to invent a word: such as, let us say, Dharmology.[7]

An American Buddhist Voice

And now, at last, our feature presentation. Skillful translation of terms is not enough to indigenize the Dharma, we need to find out how it might best fit with American culture.

A Plurality of Methods

The first thing to note about American culture is that there isn't one. Not that there is no culture, but that there is not only *one* culture. The U.S.A. was founded on pluralistic assumptions, epitomized in the separation of church[es] and state. But pluralism is, Americans discovered, uncomfortable, and it has consistently been in danger of being abbreviated. The Chinese Exclusion Act may be a distant memory at 1882, but the "reds under the bed" scare-mongering of Sen. Joseph McCarthy is barely forty years past. Today, in reaction to the modest liberalism of the Clinton administration, the religious right is gearing up to convert us all, if it can, into fundamentalist Christian heterosexual Republicans.

In the face of this, it behooves Americans to change the symbol of Americanism from the melting pot, inside which all differences blend into the flavor of the majority, to the rainbow, which is a unity not in spite of, but precisely because of, its diversity. The rainbow, which has been suggested as a symbol of racial diversity by Jesse Jackson, and is used as a symbol of diversity of lifestyle by gays and lesbians, is a common symbol of liberation in Tibetan Buddhism. It can be used by Dharmologists to proclaim a plurality of methodologies, for it is not necessary to defeat the world-view of academic Buddhology, only to dethrone it by showing its limitations.

In a sense, academic method has dethroned itself. As has already been hinted, Freud has shown that a philosopher's philosophy is psychologically conditioned, Marx has shown that it is culturally conditioned, and Derrida has shown that it is, well, conditioned: and Einstein and Bohr have shown, in very different ways, that there isn't any matter in the ordinary and common sense of the word. The shock waves from these conclusions have not yet reached all academic disciplines, but the process is well advanced, and Dharmologists can be in the forefront of helping their colleagues absorb the news in a positive and sophisticated way.

For, indeed, it is not news to Buddhism. The conditioned nature of reality and its emptiness of inherent existence have been cornerstones of the Dharma since the time of its rediscovery in this world-cycle. The ideas come as a shock to westerners only because they have for so long believed in essences (*svabhāva*) – what the Deconstructionists call Logocentrism – and they make the mistake of thinking that the deconstruction of Logocentrism results in Nihilism. A little lesson from the Dharmologist on the differences between *Nityavāda*, *Ucchedavāda*, and *Śūnyavāda* should help our learned colleagues to return to sanity.[8]

Myth as Fact

In Bernardo Bertolucci's film *Little Buddha* Lama Norbu asks the father of a potential tulku (note: I purposely say tulku, not "reincarnation") of Lama Dorje if he has read thc story of the Buddha. "Yes," replies the father, "I have read the myths." "A myth," says Lama Norbu "is one way of telling the truth."

Myths have come a long way since they were regarded, by rampant Rationalism, as mere lies. Max Müller's suggestion that myths were diseased language and that we should "translate" them to restore their true, rational meaning, was quaint but at least it gave them some form of credence. Then came Jung, and the possibility that myths could be real, but they were only inside us as psychological realities, not outside us as objective (and therefore rational) facts. Now, perhaps, we are ready to see myths as equally real as so-called facts, since both are conditioned realities. The conditions are different, but only reality-as-it-is is unconditioned. Facts are a sort of myth as myths are a sort of fact.

We have been softened up for this by science fiction. Who can say that Kirk, Picard, and successive versions of *The Enterprise* do not exist at all? Do we not, through *Star Trek*, learn a great deal about life and its possibilities that we could learn in no other way? Perhaps this is why (as it is rumored) the Dalai Lama instructs some of his *bhikṣus* to watch *Star Trek*.[9]

Within this perspective of a plurality of logospheres, or realms of meaning, we can, for example, accept both the truth that Dharmākara Bodhisattva practiced under Lokeśvararāja Tathāgata and that, paleontologically speaking, they would have been dinosaurs.

Recognition of Superconsciousness

The most astonishing hubris of academic method is its assumption that anybody with a reasonably high I.Q. not only has the right to philosophize (a privilege we might grant even to the certified insane) but the right, having philosophized, to be taken seriously. Thus Descartes, without any prior training in analytic meditation,[10] launched upon a cosmological introspection simply because he had been stranded somewhere and had nothing else to do. He did surprisingly well – he seems to have identified the *vijñāna-skandha*[11] – but he made the elementary mistake of identifying the flow of self-consciousness processes (*vijñāna*) with an inherently existing self which is conscious of itself (*ātman*) – the kind of entity which some Hindu systems call the "I-sayer" or "I-maker" (*ahaṃkāra*).

The Dharmologist must insist that for the mind to investigate reality without mis-taking it, it must be properly trained, and that this training does not consist in stuffing the mind with information but in sharpening, clearing and transforming it through the triple practice of *śīla*, *samādhi* and *prajñā*.

What would the annual meeting of the American Academy of Religion be like if it resembled a meeting of Geshes or Roshis more than a tumbling of footnotes yearning to become text? Perhaps ordinary people would listen to us, and the phrase "it's academic" would be a compliment rather than an insult.

Actually Doing It

This article has not attempted to give an example of what an American Dharmology might look like, but it has prepared the way for such by making explicit the implicit presuppositions of Buddhology and Dharmology. When this has been done, we can take both disciplines seriously. One person can certainly function as both a Buddhologist and a Dharmologist, changing their approach according to the audience. A dual Dharmologist-Buddhologist, in conversation with themselves, will probably find that they can use both methods more confidently and clearly. Not being committed naively and irrevocably to the Buddhological *Weltanschauung*, they can suggest scholarly innovations that would otherwise never occur to them. Being aware of the methods and conclusions of Buddhology, they can re-examine, in the light of the fruits of their triple practice, the tenets of what Paul Griffiths calls *Buddhalogy*, and, in constructing a Dharmology, distinguish the baby from the bath water.

So, my learned colleagues, let's do it. Who wants to be first?

NOTES

1 I first came across the term in Alfred Bloom (20), where it appears in the form "dharmalogically." Al tells me he got the term from Taitetsu Unno, who spelled it *dharmology*, but Al changed it to the apparently more correct *dharmalogy*. The term *buddhalogy*, as distinguished from *buddhology*, is used by Paul Griffiths (1994) to refer to emic accounts of the Buddhas, apparently as a Buddhist equivalent of the Christian term *Christology*.

2 The term literally means "occurring next to, or in association with, one another." Starting with any event, or the existence of any animate or inanimate object, we observe (or at least, we do so observe when we observe with meditative insight) that it arises within a matrix of other events and animate and inanimate objects, which, we further observe, arises within a broader matrix of yet other events and animate and inanimate objects. No end is found to this process. It is an infinite regress, but it is a regress of mutual conditioning or interdependence, not a regress back in linear time, so it escapes the charge of logical absurdity customarily leveled by theists at cosmologies that fail to identify a First Cause. Thus, it is neither a theist nor an atheist position. And because mind and matter are also observed to arise interdependently, it is neither a realist nor an idealist position.

3 For the lasting philosophical effects of the Black Death, see Tuchman. Although the Plague was equally physically devastating in China, it

had no philosophical effects since it was ascribed, not to Divine Providence, but, probably quite accurately, to the Mongols, who notoriously did not wash, and, moreover, were not Chinese, and thus an obvious source of imbalance for all under Heaven.

4 Al informed me that the Protestant Christian flavor was an *upāya*. As a teenager, and a committed Christian, he was giving an evangelical address to a Japanese audience and, although he used an interpreter, he knew enough Japanese at that time to realize that the interpreter had said, in regard to a Christian's faith in Jesus, "this is like faith in Amida." Al was taken aback, since he had been taught that faith in Jesus was unique, and he began to question his commitment to Christianity and to move towards Buddhism. Years later, he decided to direct his book at theologians, and to give it the title he did, "as a monument to that moment" and in the hope that information about faith in Amida might change the thinking of theologians about Christian faith the way it had changed his. However, since the book was published in a series of predominantly social science monographs, his words did not reach their intended audience. (Personal communication, September 24, 1994, Berkeley, California.)

5 Hsüan-tsang listed five terms which he transliterated rather than translated: "the esoteric; those with several meanings; those without equivalent in China; old-established terms; and those which would be less impressive when translated." Soothill and Hodous: 123 (sub *wu-chung pu-fan*).

6 *Faith* is a word with a rich history in Western religion and philosophy, but none of its many uses has very much to do with *shinjin* as used by Shinran and his successors. *Shin*, the first character of the compound, means something like trustworthiness, especially in a Confucian context, and somebody somewhere decided that it was equivalent, in a Buddhist context, to Protestant Christian faith (as understood, particularly, by Martin Luther). *Shinjin* was then over-literally translated as "faithful mind" or "the mind of faith," rendering the compound either trivial or meaningless. *Shinjin* is, for Shinran, the absolutely certain realization that one's own, human, defiled, and limited mind is non-dual with the pure and limitless mind of Amida Buddha. It is an action of Amida, not of the human. There does not seem to be any direct parallel to this in Christianity: therefore, the term should be left untranslated.

7 For more thoughts on translation and transliteration, see Corless 1989.

8 For five not-so-easy pieces relating to this lesson see Loy. The Sanskrit terms mean, respectively, Eternalism (the view that things have inherent existence or quiddity and that nothing ever really goes out of existence), Nihilism (the view either that nothing really exists or that, finally, everything vanishes without trace into a cosmic void), and "Transparency-ism" (the middle path, or the viewless view that nothing has inherent existence and that therefore reality is

fundamentally open, joyous, and free).

9 I cannot substantiate this rumor, but fondness for science fiction amongst Tibetan teachers is not unusual. I personally knew a high lama who would not willingly miss an episode of *The Incredible Hulk.* Perhaps it reminded him of some of the *sādhanas* (visualization liturgies) in which peaceful and wrathful forms of a deity transform into each other.

10 Although he went to school with the Jesuits, there is no evidence that he was trained in the *Spiritual Exercises* of their founder, St. Ignatius Loyola.

11 Buddhism identifies the apparently indivisible body-mind complex as a sort of committee with five sub-committees or aggregates (*skandha*): *rūpa* (form), *vedanā* (sensory input), *sajñā* (concept formation), *saṃskāra* (habitual reactions) and *vijñāna* (self-reflective activity, often misleadingly called consciousness). This last aggregate is the cluster of mental processes which reflects on the flow of body and mind and therefore provides a basis for the illusion of the existence of a self-conscious self.

REFERENCES

Bloom, Alfred (1986). *Shoshinge: The Heart of Shin Buddhism.* Honolulu: Buddhist Study Center Press.

Corless, Roger (1989). "How Do You Say *Anuttarasamyaksaṃbodhi* in English?" *Buddhist-Christian Studies* (9) 237–239.

Corless, Roger (1990). "How is the Study of Buddhism Possible?" *Method & Theory in the Study of Religion* 2.1: 27–41.

Griffiths, Paul (1994). *On Being Buddha: The Classical Doctrine of Buddhahood.* Albany: State University of New York Press.

Kajiyama Yuichi (1966). *An Introduction to Buddhist Philosophy: An Annotated Translation of the Tarkabhāṣā of Mokṣākaragupta.* Kyoto: Memoirs of the Faculty of Letters, Kyoto University (10) 134–137.

Katz, Nathan (1982). *Buddhist Images of Human Perfection.* Delhi: Motilal Banarsidass.

Loy, David, ed. (1996). *Healing Deconstruction: Postmodern Thought in Buddhism and Christianity.* Atlanta: Scholars Press.

Smith, Wilfred Cantwell (1979). *Faith and Belief.* Princeton: Princeton University Press.

Soothill, William Edward and Lewis Hodous (1937). *A Dictionary of Chinese Buddhist Terms.* London: Kegan Paul, Trench, Trübner.

Tuchman, Barbara W. (1978). *A Distant Mirror: The Calamitous 14th. Century.* New York: Knopf.

PART II

EXERCISES IN BUDDHIST THEOLOGY

Six

Historical Consciousness as an Offering to the Trans-Historical Buddha[1]

John J. Makransky

Although Religious Studies, including Buddhist studies, has begun to shed light on the historical nature of Buddhist traditions, only Buddhist traditions can reflect critically upon the implications of such findings for their own systematic understandings, practice and relevance to our time.

For the most part, however, Buddhists East and West have hardly begun to assess the implications of historical consciousness for their own self-understanding. For example, many of the most learned Asian Mahāyāna teachers continue to speak as if the historical Buddha personally taught the Mahāyāna Buddhist scriptures, in spite of much evidence to the contrary. And long time Western students of such teachers, who have begun to teach Zen or Tibetan practice in the West, often do the same. They do this, I believe, not so much to deny the historical evidence, but because they do not yet know what to make of it, what implications it may have for the self-understanding of their own tradition. Meanwhile, diverse forms of Buddhist practice plant roots more deeply into our culture, eliciting widespread and serious interest which appears to be growing exponentially.

We seem to find ourselves today in a confusing position analogous to China of the first centuries CE or Tibet from the eighth century: an early period of encounter between several Buddhist traditions at once with a new culture, a period in which intense exchange occurs in some sectors of the new culture even as barriers go up in other sectors. In contemporary Western academic culture, Religious Studies (or History of Religions) seeks to protect its hard-won status as "detached observer" that was necessary for it to emerge as a discipline distinct from Theology in the academy, and contemporary Buddhist studies inherits that ethos, enabling it to uncover historical and cultural data from an "objective" distance that renders it impotent to evaluate the implications of its findings for a tradition which still remains largely unaffected by them.

Buddhist Studies scholars have been taught how to critically analyze traditional Buddhist understandings of text, lineage, tradition, etc., but only to "bracket" (and therefore leave unexplored) what underlying truth or value in Buddhism may be left untouched by the critique, or may even be better revealed through such critique. Yet it is precisely Buddhism's possible truth and transformative value that has elicited so much of the contemporary world's interest in it. Since these are not the primary interests of the secular academy in which the discipline of Buddhist Studies has come to be situated, the latter has, more than it yet recognizes, rendered itself irrelevant to our historical moment.

Yet, as this volume demonstrates, there is a newly emergent movement in the academic study of Buddhism, including both Asian and Western Buddhist scholars, which seeks to address this need, a movement referred to here as "Buddhist Theology." Like Christian theologians who critically analyze elements of Christian tradition to clarify its truth and power for a new time, Buddhist scholars of Buddhism can now increasingly appropriate the academy's critical tools for the use of Buddhist tradition: to shine new light upon its historically conditioned patterns of thought and practice, to learn better how those inherited patterns have worked to communicate, or sometimes obscure, the truth and transformative power of Dharma, and thus, in what new ways the Dharma may need to be understood and expressed in our time.

The large and growing number of people in contemporary cultures with serious interest in Buddhism do not look to it primarily as a basis for fascinating discussions (a primary criterion of topic selection for Religious Studies forums), but for its truth and transformative potential. They include not only those who may identify themselves as contemporary Buddhists, but prominently also Christians, Jews and others who find that Buddhist teaching or practice sheds further light for them upon the truths of their own traditions, or upon possibilities for integration of those truths into life. For this reason, I believe, critical methods applied to Buddhism will make a greater contribution to Western culture and knowledge through their appropriation *by* Buddhist tradition – which uses them to clarify its truth and power for our time – than if they remain, as up to now, largely restricted in their application to the limited and arbitrary purposes of secular academic culture.

In this essay, I seek to provide one distinctly Buddhist approach to historical and constructive "theology." My own formation has occurred in Tibetan Buddhism, which is a form of Mahāyāna Buddhism within the Tibetan cultural sphere. Here, I will try to talk about Mahāyāna Buddhism in ways broadly relevant to all its cultural spheres, while standing both within Mahāyāna tradition and within historical consciousness. What follows is a critique that applies to all scholastic traditions of Mahāyāna that have legitimized their systematic perspectives by projecting them back upon Śākyamuni Buddha (or other figures constructed upon his paradigm), thereby absolutizing their systematic thought and repeatedly obscuring the historico-cultural specificity and diversity of expressions intrinsic to continuing Mahāyāna revelation. Such legitimizing and absolutizing procedures, shared by most scholastic Mahāyāna traditions, are driven by cultural assumptions that are not shared by contemporary scholars. Yet, in subtle ways, they continue to effect contemporary attempts to understand and articulate Buddhism in our time.

The purpose of this critique, then, is to argue for a new appreciation of the tremendous wealth of methods for and perspectives upon awakening bequeathed to us from diverse, culturally specific communities of practice experience, as Buddhism and our culture enter a process of mutual transformation that will require us to draw upon a diversity of approaches founded upon the long experience of prior traditions. Another purpose is to demonstrate the inevitability of new authentic embodiments and expressions of Dharma in our culture, emergent now and in the future, as a phenomena in long continuity with the ancient process of ongoing (never closable) Mahāyāna revelation that has always been specific to time and place.

Mahāyāna as a distinct, self-aware movement within Indian Buddhism begins near the beginning of the Common Era (four to five centuries after the historical Buddha), with the appearance of new texts promulgated by their own adherents within the Saṅgha, the Buddhist religious community. Each text begins with the traditional phrase: "thus have I heard" marking it as "*sūtra*," a scripture of teachings given or certified by the historical Buddha, Śākyamuni. In what follows, I focus upon Mahāyāna *sūtra*s to discuss the origins of their power for Mahāyānists, the needs met by prior ahistorical understandings of them, and the problems such understandings now pose for us. Although my focus here is just Mahāyāna *sūtra*s, each Mahāyāna tradition's ahistorical pattern of understanding with regard to its *sūtra*s and other inspired texts has effected its systematic thought at every historical stage, in ways yet to be analyzed in detail by any tradition.

As contemporary scholars have noted, neither in the Mahāyāna nor in prior Buddhist traditions was the Buddha's official teaching limited only to what Śākyamuni, the historical Buddha, spoke. Prior non-Mahāyāna traditions accepted some teachings as scripture (*sūtra*) if they were inspired by Śākyamuni Buddha and certified by him (Davidson: 310). Mahāyāna *sūtra*s, although they appear centuries after the historical Buddha, use a literary device to fulfill that criterion:

they mythologize history to place the scripture back into the time of Śākyamuni Buddha, so he can inspire and certify it.

Yet the actual source of teaching authority has clearly shifted. For often in these *sūtras* it is not Śākyamuni Buddha himself who is the first or primary teacher of the Dharma, but one of his disciples, in dialogue with others. And it is that bodhisattva disciple's own appropriation of the Buddha's teaching in practice experience which actually empowers him or her to stand in for the historical Buddha Śākyamuni as the teacher of the new scripture.

These two aspects of scriptural legitimation, the historical myth and the actual source of the teaching in practice experience, are intertwined in Mahāyāna texts, through the concept of buddha's power or authority (*buddhānubhāva*, *adhiṣṭhāṇa*). Does the power and authority to teach in the Buddha's place come from the Buddha as enlightened *other*, or through the disciple's own internalization of the Buddha's enlightenment?

As example, we turn to the beginning of the *Aṣṭasāhasrikā-prajñā-pāramitā Sūtra* (eight thousand verse perfection of wisdom scripture, henceforth abbreviated "*Aṣṭa.*") a key text in the development of early Mahāyāna literature. This text centers upon the perfection of wisdom, *prajñāpāramitā*, which it identifies as the guiding principle of the bodhisattva path and the source and content of highest enlightenment.

The opening words, "thus have I heard," mark the text as scripture set in the historical Buddha Śākyamuni's time. The Buddha speaks first, but not to give the teaching. Rather, he requests Subhuti, one of his disciples, to teach the perfection of wisdom, on his behalf:

> "Make it clear now, Subhuti, to the great bodhisattvas starting from perfect wisdom, how the great bodhisattvas enter into perfect wisdom."

Śāriputra, another disciple of Śākyamuni, now wonders whether Subhuti will teach perfect wisdom by his own power or through the power of the Buddha. Subhuti, knowing his mind, says to Śāriputra:

> "Whatever, Śāriputra, the Buddha's disciples teach, make known, explain, proclaim, reveal, all of it is to be known as the Tathāgata's [the Buddha's] work, for they train themselves in the Dharma taught by the Tathāgata, they realize its true nature (*dharmatā*) directly for themselves (*sākṣātkṛ*) and take possession of it. Having realized its true nature directly, and taken possession of it, nothing that they teach, make known, explain, proclaim, or reveal is inconsistent with the true nature

> of the Dharma. It is just the outpouring of the Tathāgatha's demonstration of Dharma. Whatever those sons of the family demonstrate as the true nature of Dharma, they do not bring into contradiction with that nature."[2]

Thereafter, it is Subhuti, rather than the Buddha, who teaches most of the early portion of the *sūtra* on perfect wisdom.

From the perspective of prior (pre-Mahāyāna) tradition, the certification to speak with the Buddha's authority can come only from the historical Buddha as the enlightened *other*. To meet that expectation, Śākyamuni Buddha is put in the scene as other than Subhuti, to certify him as the bodhisattva disciple who may speak in his place. But this literary device also enables something new to be said: that the Buddha's authority and power comes *not* just from the historical Buddha, but from the wisdom of enlightenment itself, now located within other persons in the religious community, the Saṅgha, who have realized the perfection of wisdom that the Buddha had realized.

In contrast to the historical Buddha Śākyamuni, we might call the perfection of wisdom itself, the wisdom of enlightenment embodied in the practice experience of accomplished members of the Saṅgha, the "trans-historical Buddha."

Another quote from the *Aṣṭa.* sheds further light on this:

> "Any bodhisattva who, after he has deceased in other world systems where he has honored and questioned the buddhas, ..., is reborn here, would, when he hears this deep perfection of wisdom being taught, identify this perfection of wisdom with the Teacher, and be convinced that he is face to face with the Teacher, that he has seen the Teacher [the Buddha]" (Conze: 138).

The perfection of wisdom is the trans-historical Teacher that speaks through any teacher who has authentically embodied it. To recognize the real import of the *sūtra* is to meet the trans-historical "Buddha," the perfection of wisdom that inspired its composition and now communicates itself to the disciple prepared to encounter it. The perfection of wisdom is a direct, non-dual, liberating awareness of the real, undivided, insubstantial nature of all phenomena (*dharmatā*). It therefore comes to be designated in this and other Mahāyāna texts as "*dharmakāya*": embodiment (*kāya*) of the real nature of things (*dharmatā*) in direct, non-conceptual knowledge. It is a knowledge that takes spontaneous expression in compassionate self-communication to those who have not yet awakened to it. Because, according to these texts, bodhisattvas have awakened to such knowledge in many places and times, we can understand *dharmakāya* as a trans-historical principle that persons of many cultures have uniquely embodied as agents of awakening (*rūpakāya*).

Dharmakāya, understood in this sense, has spoken through persons of flesh and blood throughout history. For this reason, although non-conceptual in nature and therefore literally inconceivable to us, its voices have always been those of historically and culturally conditioned persons, for whom liberating awareness was evoked and expressed through culturally specific concepts, images, practices, and languages.[3]

Like the *Aṣṭa.*, numerous Mahāyāna *sūtra*s characterize the knowledge and teaching of Dharma as the outflow of direct experience that has been elicited by many kinds of practice: elaborate rituals for serving and honoring the buddhas and bodhisattvas, purification practices, devoted recollection and invocation of the qualities of buddhahood (*buddhānusmṛti*), visualization practices, visions and dreams of buddhas and bodhisattvas, many levels of meditative attainment (*samādhi*s), the formal taking up of bodhisattva vows, long practice of the perfections (*pāramitā*s) and other components of the path, recurrent references to unconditional compassion (*mahākaruṇā*), skillful means (*upāya*) and the perfection of wisdom. The precise relations between all such practices, and their relation to the liberating awareness of awakening that issues from them, are diverse and often ambiguous, expressed differently between *sūtra*s and within different parts of *sūtra*s, as we would expect from the diversity of practice communities in which the texts emerged.

In sum, composers of Mahāyāna *sūtra*s employed the literary device of the historical Buddha Śākyamuni to permit the trans-historical Buddha, liberating wisdom emergent in the practice experience of diverse religious communities (Saṅgha), to teach in new times and places.[4] As the *Vimalakīrti Sūtra* declares: "It is dualistic to say Buddha, Dharma, and Saṅgha. The Dharma is itself the nature of Buddha. The Saṅgha is itself the nature of Dharma . . . ." (Thurman: 75).

The Mahāyāna doctrine of skillful means, *upāya-kauśālya*, both emerged from and further informed this understanding. In the *Aṣṭa.*, skillful means are the diverse and often subtle activities through which bodhisattvas progress on their path and elicit the wisdom of enlightenment (*prajñāpāramitā*) in others.[5] In many other scriptures, such as the *Avataṃsaka* and *Vimalakīrti sūtra*s, the concept is expanded and much further developed: skillful means includes the infinite scope of activities and methods through which buddhas and bodhisattvas communicate Dharma in the precise ways appropriate to the capacities of all living beings. Skillful means, in such texts, is an infinitely vast, incomprehensible mystery, for the methods that buddhas and bodhisattvas employ to reach beings are as diverse as beings themselves, and are operative through all space and time.

Some *Avataṃsaka* quotes as example:

> "Buddha turns the wheel of true teaching, which is infinite and has no bounds; the truth taught is beyond compare: the shallow can not fathom it." (Cleary: 164)

> "Their compassion and pity extends to all – they know the mind of every sentient being, and expound to them in accord with their predilections, infinite, boundless enlightening teachings." (437)

> "Just as no beings in the universe can count the drops of rain pouring from great clouds, and would go crazy if they tried, . . . in the same way the Buddha . . . showers a great rain of teachings that no sentient beings, seekers of personal salvation, or self-enlightened ones can know, and they would surely go mad if they tried to assess them in thought; only the great enlightening beings, lords of all worlds, by the power of awareness and intellect cultivated in the past, comprehend every single expression and phrase, and how they enter beings' minds. . . ." (975)

> "Just as the great clouds rain water of one flavor, yet there are innumerable differences according to where it rains, in the same way Buddha appearing in the world rains water of teaching of one flavor of great compassion, yet his sermons are infinitely variegated according to the needs of the situation." (976)

> "Just as the ocean water flows under the continents and islands, so that all who drill for water find it, yet the ocean does not form any notion of itself giving out water, in the same way the water of Buddha's ocean of knowledge flows into the minds of all sentient beings, so that if they examine things and practice ways of entering truth, they will find knowledge, pure and clear, with lucid understanding – yet the knowledge of Buddha is equal, nondual, without discrimination; but according to the

differences in sentient beings' mental patterns, the knowledge they obtain is not the same." (999)

"In this world there are four quadrillion such names to express the Four Holy Truths, in accord with the mentalities of beings, to cause them all to be harmonized and pacified. . . . [And] just as in this world... there are four quadrillion names to express the Four Holy Truths, so in all the worlds to the east – hundreds of thousands of billions, countlessly, innumerably, boundlessly, incomparably, incalculably, unspeakably, inconceivably, immeasurably, inexplicably many worlds, in each there are an equal number of names to express the Four Holy Truths, to cause all the sentient beings there to be harmonized and pacified in accordance with their mentalities. And just as this is so of the worlds to the east, so it is with all the infinite worlds in the ten directions." (276, 281)

Skillful means in such texts, as the infinite self-communication of undivided and unlimited enlightened awareness, is as vast a mystery as the Judeo-Christian God. If we take it seriously both from within historical consciousness and within Mahāyāna Buddhist tradition, it is the vast mystery through which authentic Mahāyāna experience has been made possible across diverse cultures through so many centuries. And it is precisely because accomplished members of diverse Buddhist communities through history have been the primary source of skillful means that skillful means have been so skillful: enabling the trans-historical Buddha, wisdom embodied in accomplished Saṅgha of new places and times, to speak again and again, always with fresh, intimate voices – to speak directly from and to the hearts of Central Asians, Indians, Chinese, Koreans, Tibetans, Japanese, Vietnamese – to speak to each in precise ways that uniquely invoke a wisdom and love beyond self-clinging in each culture and time.

The vast meaning of skillful means articulated in *sūtra* passages like those above, understood within historical consciousness, becomes a doctrinal resource for contemporary Mahāyāna traditions (each of which has tended to view itself as the "pure" repository of the Dharma) to reflect with new seriousness upon the possibilities of truth to be found in other Buddhist cultures throughout history.[6]

Skillful means, explicitly or implicitly, provided the rationale for the very appearance of new *sūtras*, and by extension, for the very rise of the Mahāyāna as a distinct movement, for it enabled the trans-historical Buddha to speak newly again and again. So the anonymous author of the *Aṣṭa.* passage earlier quoted does not have the *historical*

Buddha Śākyamuni himself begin the teaching on perfect wisdom, but has him request *Subhuti* to teach. The anonymous author, in his literary imagination, invokes the historical Buddha Śākyamuni to request *himself*, with Subhuti as his textual persona, to reveal the trans-historical Buddha's new teaching, to communicate the Dharma in newly effective ways necessitated by intervening centuries of development in thought and practice set within culture. And so new *sūtra*s continued to appear over centuries.

The anonymous authors of Mahāyāna *sūtra*s, then, by employing the literary device that put the historical Buddha in the text, liberated the wisdom of enlightenment in them to speak in new ways. But in ancient Indian culture where the new *sūtra*s appeared, to experience the power of the texts to elicit the very awareness they expressed was to take *literally* the device that legitimized them: to believe that such texts had *actually* come from the historical Buddha Śākyamuni.

Now, as the new *sūtra*s themselves make clear, Buddhist Saṅgha members who conservatively adhered to prior tradition did not accept the new *sūtra*s as scripture (many passages in the new *sūtra*s prophesy their own rejection, describe the persecution of those who will promulgate them, explain why only some persons will be capable of recognizing their truth and others not, etc.). The Mahāyāna movement was composed of those who *did* find the new *sūtra*s convincing and efficacious, and therefore, from within their ahistorical world view, scriptures to be defended as Śākyamuni Buddha's own teaching. But then, so their ahistorical understanding entailed, if only some members of the present Buddhist community can recognize the truth of these texts, while others are unable to do so, that must be because the historical Buddha Śākyamuni had provided these texts for similarly perceptive disciples of his own time, even as others were unable to recognize their truth.

The literary device of Śākyamuni Buddha in the new *sūtra*s had projected the past into the present for legitimation. This now entailed that the very different ways the *sūtra*s were received in the present had to be projected back into the past. The historical Buddha in his lifetime, so the logic went, must have given different kinds of teachings to followers of different capacities: Mahāyāna teachings to those with the greater capacity to understand them; less profound, "Hīnayāna" teachings to those with lesser capacity. And as more Mahāyāna sutras emerged within different communities of practice, whose messages therefore differed from each other, this too had to be explained by reference to the differing capacities of Śākyamuni Buddha's followers, in a mythical past now absolutized as the differing capacities of all Buddha's followers in all times.

This, in turn, conditioned a much narrower understanding of skillful means then we find in the quotes above.[7] Different thinkers identified a different teaching or set of *sūtras* as the truest, the one that represents the historical Buddha's own final perspective; while other teachings were characterized as the Buddha's *lesser* means which he taught only to lead persons of lesser capacity to the highest teaching upheld by the new tradition. This much narrower, rigidly hierarchical understanding of skillful means makes diverse messages of scripture consistent by superimposing a single interpretive scheme upon them, and gives that scheme the aura of absolute finality by imputing it to Śākyamuni Buddha. Scriptural basis for this narrower sense of skillful means also occurs in the *Avataṃsaka* as in many other Mahāyāna *sūtras*, but appears in developed form in the *Saṃdhinirmocana Sūtra*, which places a hierarchical scheme of "three turnings of the Dharma wheel" into the mouth of the historical Buddha Śākyamuni.

Thus, even as the doctrine of skillful means (understood as infinite mystery) permits the transcendent (perfect wisdom) to take new expression, the new tradition that it gives rise to constructs a narrower sense of skillful means, not mysterious at all, to establish its authority vis a vis prior tradition. As new expressions of transcendent knowledge continue to unfold, and further reflection, each new tradition's systematic understanding establishes a new hierarchy of prior teachings leading to its own, which are de-historicized and absolutized in the same way: by projecting them back upon Śākyamuni Buddha as his own view. Each new tradition legitimizes itself by seeking to defeat the infinitely wide sense of skillful means that had enabled it to emerge, by using a narrower meaning of "skillful means" to absolutize its own historically conditioned understanding in the name of the Buddha.

Thus, the need for transcendent knowledge to take new expression in new places and times, which the doctrine of skillful means permitted, is actively obstructed sooner or later by every new tradition it gives rise to. By thereby controlling the doctrine of skillful means, each sub-tradition seeks to control transcendence, once and for all – to stop the process of ongoing revelation that gave rise to itself *at itself* – to stop the self-communication of eternal truth at its own understanding of it.

Notice, where the doctrine of skillful means is narrowed and absolutized, how the diverse historical origins of the new *sūtras* become further obscured, hiding the historical nature of their power. Mahāyānists had experienced their own *sūtras* as uniquely powerful *not* because they came from Śākyamuni Buddha centuries before, but precisely because they came to them through religious communities and cultures much closer to their own place and time that could express enlightenment in much more intimate and fresh ways. And Saṅgha members who rejected those *sūtra*s did so not just because of differences in their own intrinsic capacity, but because they were conservative adherents of prior norms.

Nevertheless the Mahāyāna's ahistorical understanding of its sources, together with the narrow sense of "skillful means" that rationalized it, has been presupposed by its scholastic traditions of India, Tibet, and East Asia. Scholastic disagreements over soteriology, for example, have been conducted, in part, by subsuming Mahāyāna *sūtra* messages of immediate transcendence and spontaneity under messages of gradualism and human effort, or vice versa. Similarly, scholars who have disagreed over the meaning of buddha-nature (*tathāgathagarbha*) blithely subsume messages of intrinsic purity under messages of potential purity, or vice versa, simplistically marginalizing many parts of *sūtra*s and *śāstra*s that contributed to the concept, as if the tension between messages is not the expression of diverse practice communities and contexts, but of an eternal hierarchy of Buddha's skillful means, which the exegete, pretending to inhabit Śākyamuni Buddha's perspective, identifies as his own. Along similar lines, overly simplistic conclusions have been reached as to which methods of practice described in Mahāyāna *sūtra*s are the only ones that lead directly to ultimate awareness, which conceptual understandings of (non-conceptual) reality are final, which ways of conceptualizing (inconceivable) enlightenment are final, etc.[8]

Scholars' systematic choices in each place and time occurred largely in ignorance of their own historical conditioning and of the historical nature of the inspired texts upon which they drew. A diversity of expressions from a diversity of prior practice communities were homogenized into the single ordered expression of one person, Śākyamuni Buddha, through narrow schemes of skillful means absolutized as the only ladder to enlightenment. *Sūtra*s such as the *Saṃdhinirmocana*, which put such schemes into Śākyamuni Buddha's mouth, enabled scholars of each later tradition, in the name of the Buddha, to think of their own, conditioned decisions as transparent windows upon the Buddha's unconditioned perspective, making it routine for their systematic writing to contain the implicit claim to know the absolute scheme to enlightenment for all living beings through all time (enshrined in *p'an-chiao*, *grub mtha'* and related schemes in Buddhist cultures of East Asia and Tibet).

Such habits for interpreting sacred text, driven by Asian assumptions concerning authority and legitimation, carry over from early Mahāyāna into scholastic interpretations of later inspired texts such as the tantras, the origins of Zen teachings and the origins of Tibetan treasure texts, distorting the systematic Mahāyāna understandings of all its traditions.[9]

Because these ahistorical understandings give the sectarian views of each sub-tradition the aura of unique and absolute authority, they support each in its competition with others for social and institutional support, from which has come great social pressure in Tibet and East Asia to argue for one such understanding over the others. And this pressure continues to operate as these traditions now enter our culture, promoting a narrowness with regard to possibilities of liberating truth both within the diverse traditions of Buddhism and within other traditions.

Contemporary Buddhist academics and teachers of Dharma (East and West) are still prone to this error. By failing to fully recognize the historically conditioned nature of our own perspectives and needs, and those of the past, we still fall into the habit of pretending to the ahistorical view of Śākyamuni Buddha in order to promulgate a relatively narrow systematic perspective that oversimplifies the Mahāyāna's complex history of doctrinal development and thereby stunts the future possibilities of our tradition. And this may be masked not only by old sectarianism assumptions, but also by the more contemporary rhetorics of critical method.

D. Seyfort Ruegg criticized two such developments in a recent article. The first development is the recent taking up of Tibetan sectarian positions by contemporary scholars, such as *rang stong* (empty of self) versus *gzhan stong* (empty of anything extrinsic), to argue for one doctrine over the other with the sectarian assumption that they are "opposed theories located on the same level of discourse," an assumption partly based upon the ahistorical hermeneutics of prior Tibetan systematicians (who followed the *Saṃdhinirmocana Sūtra*'s "three turnings of Dharma" hierarchical scheme noted above). Ruegg suggests that much historical and philosophical work needs to be done to explore the extent that elements of these doctrines may have been complementary in Indian and Tibetan thought and practice, or may have functioned as incommensurables ("located on different levels, or within distinct universes of religious and philosophical discourse"). Ruegg continues: "What is needed in Buddhist studies is not enlistment in campaigns and polemics with other schools of Buddhist thought, but careful descriptions and analyses of the various traditions establishing their sources and religio-philosophical problematics and identifying how each dealt with the philosophical and hermeneutical questions that arose in their respective schools" (168).

From a theological perspective, I would add, such "careful

descriptions and analyses" are important not just to uphold scholarly standards for the secular academy, but to meet the present and future needs of Mahāyāna tradition. For example, based upon such research, future Mahāyāna systematicians, freed from the ahistorical hermeneutics of prior tradition, may not need to construct a rigid dichotomy from those elements of Indo-Tibetan thought that some have dichotomously constructed as *rang stong* versus *gzhan stong*. Rather, instead of seeking to construct one architectonic, hierarchical scheme (based on an ahistorical re-construction of Śākyamuni Buddha's teaching career), future systematicians will study roles of context-specific practice experience and uses of language by diverse communities in the development of varied doctrinal discourses. And this information can then be applied to re-evaluate how elements of ancient doctrine and practice might be incorporated into newly effective systems of understanding and praxis for persons of the present and future. It is time, in other words, within our historical consciousness, to lay the foundation for new constructive, systematic work, rather than to argue for one prior systematic scheme in toto over another, each such prior scheme having been designed to address the problems and needs of other places and times, based upon hermeneutic assumptions some of which we do not share.

The second recent development that Ruegg critiques does constitute new systematic analysis, but analysis that falls far short of the mark by failing to avoid prior sectarian traditions' worst habits of ahistorical criticism, and by largely ignoring praxis as a force in doctrinal development. I refer to the "Critical Buddhism" movement in Japan, which portrays the buddha-nature doctrine (*tathāgathagarbha*) as non-Buddhist (169). "Critical Buddhists" simplify the internally complex discourses of buddha-nature that emerged from diverse Buddhist practice communities and cultures into a reified philosophical construct, project that reified understanding back upon the whole prior history of Buddhism, and argue against it in the name of an equally narrow philosophical re-construction of Śākyamuni's "real teaching" (*pratītyasamutpāda*, dependent arising) that is supposed to contradict it.

As Ruegg notes, however, ". . . in totally rejecting [buddha-nature] . . . as non-Buddhist ["Critical Buddhists" of Japan] seem to have overshot the mark by giving scant attention to the explications of the *tathāgathagarbha* theory by Buddhist thinkers who, outside Japan, have at the same time accepted *pratītyasamutpāda* as basic." Ruegg points to a Tibetan figure, Gung thang dKon mchog bstan pa'i sgron me, as example of such a thinker. But it should also be noted that the buddha-nature doctrine is complex in its Indian development, evolving out of many practices and doctrines that may have developed in synergy, prominently including Prajñāpāramitā thought and praxis for which pre-Mahāyāna and evolving Mahāyāna concepts of *pratītyasamutpāda* are foundational. Ironically, in its very attempt to challenge Buddhist tradition, the new "Critical Buddhism" of Japan falls into the tradition's own worst habit of constructing from within the relatively narrow viewpoint and concern of its own place and time an ahistorical, absolutist version of Buddhism naively legitimized as Śākyamuni's original view (Swanson: 120, 121, 127–128).

The same basic pattern of narrow ahistorical absolutism in the name of Śākyamuni Buddha finds a different kind of contemporary expression in a recent essay by Stephen Batchelor, who asserts a Buddhism purified of the accretion of all beliefs and religious practices which, he argues, would have been abhorrent to the version of Śākyamuni Buddha that he has constructed as the historical Buddha (Batchelor, "Buddhism without Beliefs"). Batchelor, like prior traditional scholars who, unaware of their own historical conditioning, were unable to recognize the transformative power of Buddhist beliefs and practices of places and times other than their own and rationalized their exclusivism by projecting it upon a "Śākyamuni Buddha" they had constructed in their own image, asserts a new hegemony over Dharma by re-constructing it narrowly within the presuppositions of his own place and time (in his case, a post Western enlightenment agnosticism) projected back upon Śākyamuni.

A historically responsible detailed construction of "the real" Śākyamuni Buddha will likely never be possible, given the limitations on historical materials of ancient India. But the recurrent desire to make such a construction in the specific form needed to authorize one's current perspective is the ahistorical habit we have inherited from prior Buddhist tradition. It is a bad habit: a repeated falsification through which we hide from ourselves the complex historical conditions of doctrinal transformation within Buddhist communities of practice and the historically conditioned nature of our own systematic work within current communities of practice.

Like systematic Buddhist thinkers of the past, we too must identify the basic principles of thought and practice that can serve as criteria to judge the authenticity of any systematic Buddhist understanding of any place and time, including our own. And the underlying principles identified must be consistent with what we know of Śākyamuni Buddha's teaching mainly through textual sources that date centuries after him. *Equally important*, however, are the developments in practice and thought that contributed to authentic doctrinal development and transformation in all periods from

Śākyamuni to the present. Without falling into the ahistorical error sketched above, we do have enough from such sources to agree upon a few core principles readily discernible both within Śākyamuni Buddha's teaching and, through their repeated reinterpretation, within the Buddhist traditions of cultures of Asia.

The previous *Avataṃsaka* quote that alludes to the "four quadrillion names" of the Four Noble Truths identifies those core principles. In the Buddha's teaching of the Four Noble Truths we have the essential criterion through which we can analyze and argue over the adequacy and authenticity of any Buddhist system of thought and practice past or present. This criterion does not deny the re-interpretability of those Truths in accord with the real problems and needs of thought and practice in each new place and time. Indeed, the Mahāyāna doctrine of skillful means as articulated in texts such as the *Avataṃsaka* would argue for the necessity of such repeated reinterpretation: so as to make the nature of suffering, its connection to self-clinging, and the possibility of its transcendence through specific forms of practice intimately accessible to the variety of dispositions and world views of real persons situated in different cultures and times.

In other words, we must learn to eschew the traditional habit of seeking to absolutize our own sectarian (or agnostic) view through detailed re-construction of Śākyamuni Buddha in our own image. Instead, we should adopt a more minimal understanding, that the Buddha taught the Four Noble Truths, that he sought the liberation of persons from self-clinging and consequent suffering, that he sought their awakening to a penetrating wisdom and unconditional love free from such clinging. On that basis alone, I would argue, Śākyamuni would likely have approved of the many methods through which precisely what he sought for others *has* been accomplished in so many places and times quite different from his own: a vast array of practices of devotion, offering, repentance, recitation, ritual purification, sacred memory, holy visions, contemplative practices, sacramental feasts, etc. many of which (contra Batchelor) have been both deeply religious and transformatively effective; many of which (*contra* "Critical Buddhism") have functioned as ritual-contemplative means to express and evoke deep experiential intuitions of buddha-nature (not just to speculate about it).[10]

Which of this vast treasury of beliefs and practices may help elicit similar liberating awareness now and in the future remains to be seen. People, as ever, possess a wide variety of dispositions situated in diverse cultures. It would be lethal for us to assume that we further the tradition by seeking to marginalize or erase many of its past practices and all the beliefs that have motivated them, whether the quest to do so is rationalized in terms of the sectarianisms of past traditions ("only the practices of my tradition lead to complete awakening") or the new parochial sectarianisms of agnostic modernism or "Critical Buddhism" ("only agnostic inquiry avoids clinging and leads to awakening, not religious understandings and practices," or "never practices informed by the buddha-nature doctrine").

Contrary to the sectarian assumptions of our various sub-traditions past and present, the history of Buddhist praxis and doctrine would indicate that there has *never* been only one narrowly delimited way to awaken, and that *any* means to awaken is also a potential object of clinging. That the doctrine of buddha-nature has become, to some degree, a superficially understood rationale for social inertia in contemporary Japan does not mean that it has been such always or everywhere else. That agnosticism is experienced by some (like Batchelor) as a liberating method does not preclude its becoming a stultifying absolutism for others, discouraging them from drawing upon the more highly developed capacities they may have for self-transcendence through faith or devotion.

As Mahāyāna traditions enter our culture, they already begin to transform it in ways whose long term outcomes we can hardly imagine. Reciprocally, each Mahāyāna tradition will now need to undergo the deeper transformations in its own self awareness that its entry into contemporary culture's historical consciousness ought to elicit. Based upon the preceding discussion, and speaking from within Mahāyāna tradition, here are a few of the principles I suggest should guide this process:

*1. We should recover the wider understanding of skillful means (*upāya-kauśalya*) revealed in Mahāyāna scriptures*

Mahāyāna understanding of skillful means must shift away from the narrow, ahistorical interpretation that absolutized each of our traditional systems of thought and practice, cutting us off from the historical sources of our inspired texts and putting us into sectarian competition with each other based in large part on mutual ignorance.

Instead, if we re-examine the doctrine of skillful means from within historical consciousness, as we must, our attention is shifted to the much vaster sense of the concept found in other parts of the Mahāyāna textual corpus: skillful means as the infinite means through which enlightened ones lead beings to awaken, suited to the vast diversity of their capacities and mentalities. This is the wide sense of "skillful means" that both permits and encourages us to look with wonder upon the great diversity of ways, situated within each place, time, and culture, Mahāyāna practice has elicited an ultimate awareness in persons that transcends egocentrism and expresses itself in unconditional concern for all.

2. We should pay new attention to the historical conditions of ongoing revelation and doctrinal development, contextualized in the practice of communities, to provide Mahāyāna tradition much more knowledge to evaluate its present and future possibilities.

To understand skillful means in this vaster way, rather than in the narrow, hierarchical way of past interpretive schemes, points us toward, rather than away from, the actual historical conditions for inspired texts like the Mahāyāna *sūtras* and the implications of such conditions for the present and future of our tradition. Instead of repeatedly gazing upon ahistorical images of Śākyamuni we ourselves have constructed to legitimize our current perspectives, we can put new emphasis on exploring the diverse ways enlightened wisdom has uniquely emerged in accomplished members of practice communities of different times and cultures, sensitizing us to the possibility of new expressions already emerging and to come. If Mahāyāna revelation specific to our place and time is already emergent, nothing could be more traditional.

In addition, by shifting our attention *away* from previous ahistorical ascriptions of doctrines to Śākyamuni Buddha *toward* the ways diverse communities have appropriated the Dharma in practice experience accompanied by doctrinal change, current Buddhist communities receive more light to discern the nature of authentic doctrinal transformation. This can shed light for us upon analogous processes already operative in the present of which we are as yet only dimly aware.[11] We authentically follow upon prior tradition neither by precise imitation of prior systematic understandings, nor by rejecting them wholesale (a la Batchelor), but by learning how to enter into the same synergy of practice experience and long reflection upon received doctrines through which such understandings came to be newly constructed in other places and times.

3. We should recognize the limitations of all systematic schemata, past and present. We should also recognize the likelihood of an irreducible pluralism of valid Mahāyāna perspectives, while continuing to uphold the Four Noble Truths as criteria for judging their authenticity, adequacy, and transformative effectiveness.

By adopting the wider understanding of skillful means over the narrower, I do not argue for a new uncritical and equal acceptance of all past practices of Buddhist cultures. Buddhism's own moral imperative to investigate what is convincing and effective from the perspective of one's own time and place must never be abandoned.

Rather, I argue that whatever systematic conclusions we reach now, as in the past, are conditioned and incomplete. In our world alone, says the *Avataṃsaka Sūtra*, the Four Noble Truths have four quadrillion names! The Four Noble Truths hold, but precisely how it is that each individual in each place and time comes to profound recognition of their meaning is not something we should ever pretend to fully know again. Rather, historical awareness shines light for us on the plurality of ways the Four Truths have been repeatedly reinterpreted to meet hermeneutic needs specific to each culture and period, so they may be authentically and freshly reappropriated. Effective appropriation of the Four Noble Truths in practice experience has never been monolithic, and is never figured out once and for all for all cultures and times in the abstract, no matter how clever one's reconstruction of Śākyamuni Buddha or Buddhist history to mask the limitations of one's abstraction. Nor is fresh and authentic appropriation of them ever guaranteed by simply repeating the now archaic idioms of past Buddhist cultures.

Roger Haight, a contemporary Roman Catholic theologian, has recently made observations regarding the pluralism of christologies observable in the New Testament and throughout the history of Christian reflection that are highly relevant to the present discussion. He says:

> New Testament christologies differ because they are historical: the texts making up the New Testament were written by different authors, representing different communities, writing for different audiences, facing different problems. These different communities had different cultures, with different traditions, interests, and styles of speaking and understanding. Also, the subject matter, Jesus, displays any number of different facets of religious mediation. Historically, then, each New Testament text is historically situated and contextualized; it is the product of the inculturated interpretation and appropriation of Jesus of Nazareth. . . . [C]hristology should be a pluralistic discipline today because Jesus Christ must be interpreted and culturally appropriated by particular communities today even as he was in the formation of the New Testament. . . . To summarize the point in a sharp phrase, the New Testament does not merely tolerate a situation of pluralism in christology, it prescribes it.
>
> . . . In a pluralistic situation one cannot consider one christology as exclusively authentic and valid so that all others must conform to it. This does not mean that all christologies are equally legitimate. Nor does it imply that certain standards

> and norms cannot be established to govern all christologies; they can. But it does imply that authority must appeal to more than simply the citation of an objectively defined christology (44–45).

The pluralism of interpretations of Buddhist principles in Mahāyāna texts are the products of communities of practice even more diverse than those that produced the New Testament. We must agree with Haight, though here with reference to the pluralism of Mahāyāna understandings starting from its *sūtras*, that we cannot responsibly view one such understanding as "exclusively authentic and valid so that all others must conform to it." This does not mean that all systematic understandings are equally legitimate. The standard and norm remains the Four Noble Truths, to which systematic thought and practice has been held accountable in Mahāyāna as in pre-Mahāyāna traditions.[12] But like Haight's Jesus, the Four Noble Truths have displayed "any number of different facets of religious mediation." And, as the *Avataṃsaka* so eloquently intimates, those Truths take expression in a limitless variety of ways found effective for experiential appropriation by a diversity of communities of practice and reflection. This leaves us with an irreducible pluralism of systematic perspectives that have supported awakening in and through the differing capacities, needs and cultural conditionings of diverse communities. We have no basis for arguing that all others conform to one systematic viewpoint where they can authentically defend their own viewpoint by reference to the Four Noble Truths and experience it as more transformatively effective.[13] We should therefore get out of the habit of inserting our own current systematic perspective into Śākyamuni Buddha's mouth in the mistaken attempt to force such conformity.

Such has been the repeated misuse of our reverence for Śākyamuni Buddha. Accomplished members of practice communities in all Buddhist cultures past and present are the actual source of our wisdom through history, yet each of our traditions has repeatedly submerged or erased many of their voices, voices of the trans-historical Buddha, for ahistorical re-constructions of Śākyamuni that support our own exclusive understanding of the moment. If indeed Śākyamuni sought for others to awaken and teach the Dharma, the better way to demonstrate reverence for him would be to pay new attention to the plurality of voices of awakening he inspired: the "lion's roar" of the trans-historical Buddha that has echoed for so many centuries from Śākyamuni's time to our own.

An increased capacity to hear and revere Buddhist perspectives that had previously seemed alien from our own may also help us enter more seriously than in the past into dialogue with other religious and cultural traditions of our time. Perhaps some of the "four quadrillion names" of the Four Noble Truths can only be heard if we learn the mindfulness that permits echoes of the trans-historical Buddha's voice to be heard in the words of non-Buddhists.

In sum, this stage of Buddhist entry into our culture is a time to receive as much as we can from all sources of doctrine and practice, without cutting off prematurely something the tradition may need for its future by uncritically adopting the absolutizing and totalizing habits of *any* of the sectarian schemes of interpretation now promulgated in each of the traditions we inherit. This entails a critical re-examination of all prior systems of thought regarding the extent of their dependence on inadequate interpretive methods, accompanied by new systematic work that breaks from the ahistorical absolutism of many of those systems. If done in conformity with principles like those suggested here, this will constitute critical and constructive theological work. For the purpose of criticizing some prior methods of tradition is precisely to recover or re-emphasize other key principles of its thought and praxis in the light of historical consciousness. While doing this, however, we should be on our guard to avoid the modern (and very seductive) temptation to create new absolutisms that naively dismiss too much of a past we know too little of in the name of a narrow contemporary direction for Buddhism whose long term value may be quite limited.

This puts us in a ticklish position vis a vis the Buddhist traditions in which we continue to train. From one perspective, we seek to be profoundly, utterly formed by them. From another perspective, for us, as for all who have come before us, to take possession of the tradition is to find its authentic expression within our own place and time, in and through our historical and cultural being, including historical consciousness. As contemporary Mahāyāna thinkers, this is not just the responsibility to find our own authentic Buddhism. If we proceed wisely, it will be our culture's precious offering, through us, to the ancient Mahāyāna tradition we love. May it become such an offering, to be received and returned as a blessing upon our culture and our world.

NOTES

1 This essay is an extended rumination following upon recent completion of a book (Makransky, *Buddhahood Embodied*, 1997). In the following notes, reference is made to sections of that book to further contextualize or exemplify topics under discussion here.

2 English translation mine, from Vaidya: 2–3. For Conze's translation, see Conze: 83–4. Compare also *Prajñāpāramitā-Ratnaguṇasaṃcayagāthā* 1.2–4 (Conze: 9), and *Aṣṭa.* passages 1.25 (Conze: 91–92), 2.44 (100), 3.74–75 (109), 4.99 (118), 11.251 (170), 16.321 (199). Compare also *Mahāratnakūṭa Sūtra*, Chang: 110–111.

3 For a fuller explanation of the evolving concept of *dharmakāya* in *prajñāpāramitā sūtra*s and Mahāyāna *śāstra*s, see Makransky, chapters 3–5.

The assertion of a "trans-historical" principle of awakening (*dharmakāya*) may be controversial for scholars who adhere to more radical versions of postmodern thought, which assert absolute uniqueness and diversity among cultures and historical periods, highly skeptical of meta-narratives that assert any over-arching unity. But such a perspective is too one-sided, and possibly self-contradictory. Can a contemporary critic rule out the possibility that persons of different places and times have had a direct awareness of the impermanent and insubstantial nature of phenomena, an awareness that liberates from self-clinging and takes expression in unconditional love? From what frame of reference would such certainty come? A Western post-Enlightenment assumption of universal human limitation, imputed as meta-narrative upon all cultures and history?

There are not only dissimilarities, but also similarities among the diversity of human experiences in history and cultures. Sexual love, hatred, envy, grief are unique in each culture and time, but not entirely unique. Similarly, the dynamics of self-clinging, the expressions it takes, the sufferings it elicits, the possibility of freedom from it, and the means to that freedom (the Four Noble Truths) may be, in certain ways, uniquely experienced by persons of different places and times, without being absolutely unique.

The expression "trans-historical Buddha" used in this essay is inspired by Mahāyāna messages like that of the *Vimalakīrti Sūtra* (quoted below). Members of Saṅgha in each place and time who awaken to the Dharma recurrently re-introduce the ultimate meaning of "Buddha" to their own place and time.

I use the expression "trans-historical Buddha," then, not to refer to an unchanging, substantial essence literally carried across cultures or time, but to an awareness of insubstantiality and unconditional love accessible to every place and time that is always unique in some respects, since elicited and expressed in culturally specific ways through unique individuals.

4 For a more detailed analysis of the apparent role of inspired speech as an expression of liberating awareness in original expositors of Mahāyāna *sūtras*, see MacQueen, 1981, 1982.

5 See, for example Conze: 250–251.

6 It is also a doctrinal resource for new Buddhist reflection upon the availability of its liberating truth within other religious traditions. See for example *Laṅkāvatāra Sūtra* 192–193 on the Tathāgatha's manifestation as the various divinities of Hinduism; *Lotus Sūtra* chapter 24 on Avalokiteśvara's manifestation as such; *Śikṣāsamuccaya* 325, 332 on great bodhisattvas maturing beings by following non-Buddhist ways, including manifestation as leaders of non-Buddhist traditions, and by teaching the Dharma through all cultures and in all languages (Bendall and Rouse: 290, 295).

7 The historical order of development of wider and narrower expressions of skillful means is unclear. Often both occur in different portions of the same texts. In these paragraphs, I merely point out the different expressions and some of the understandings behind them.

8 So, for example, Tibetan traditions tell of a council during the reign of the eighth-century Tibetan king Khri srong lde brtsan to determine which form of Buddhist understanding and practice was to be officially sanctioned in Tibet: the gradualist perspective expounded by the Indian scholar Kamalaśīla or the simultaneist perspective of immediate access to awakening expounded by the Chinese Ch'an teacher Hva-śang Mahāyāna. The historicity of the council may be uncertain, but Tibetan writings and materials found at Tun Huang have repeatedly expressed the concern among Buddhists to argue for one perspective over the other, based again on the assumption that Śākyamuni Buddha personally taught all the Mahāyāna sūtras in which a confusing diversity of messages concerning gradualism and immediacy appear. Kamalaśīla and his subsequent defenders have thought they were arguing for the one final view of Śākyamuni: gradualism, with all *sūtra* messages of immediacy requiring interpretation, while Hva-śang Mahāyāna and his defenders based their argument on the opposite view, that Śākyamuni's final understanding was immediacy (Gómez 1983a, 1983b; Ruegg).

But if, as argued here, diverse *sūtra* messages of gradualism and immediacy represent the expressions of diverse practice communities with very different needs, they express not the point of view of one ca. fifth century BCE North Indian figure, but diverse experiential findings of what has been found convincing and transformatively effective in many different places and times. Then the meaning of the "debate" between Kamalaśīla and Hva-śang Mahāyāna must be entirely different for us than for past interpreters. It is no longer a matter of who has properly understood Śākyamuni's message in toto and who got it wrong and must be banished to preserve the Dharma's purity. Rather, the question becomes which elements of thought and practice, convincing and transformatively effective for diverse prior communities, may inform and empower practice and thought now and in the future. We are no longer concerned to determine Śākyamuni Buddha's one final intention of an exclusive, absolutized paradigm, but rather to uncover alternative models for systematic practice and thought already found effective by others, elements of which, taking new expression, may speak powerfully to the specific conditions of our place and time, thus contributing to the ongoing reconstruction of systematic understanding. So, for example, some contemporary Buddhist teachers have noted that many Westerners suffer both from intense guilt and lack of self-confidence on the one hand, and a naive expectation for instant spiritual gratification on the other. If so, our culture may need to draw heavily upon both gradualist and simultaneist elements of prior Buddhist systems. For only if we sensed the immediate accessibility of the real power of awakening could we find the delight of discovering it afresh in each moment of a life-long discipline (Śāntideva: "Enthusiastic perseverance is delight in the virtuous").

9 Those elements of Mahāyāna traditions that more openly express the ongoing nature of continuing Mahāyāna revelation, exemplified in "Pure Vision" revelations of Tibet (which play an important role in all Tibetan sects), escape the critique of this essay, for they more transparently reveal the actual dynamics of continuing revelation that have always been operative. See Mayer: chapter 1.

10 One colleague who read this paragraph asked if I had not fallen prey here to the very "Śākyamunification" against which I had argued in the rest of the essay. Any follower of the Buddha must have some concept of what the Buddha was in support of his or her understanding and practice. I do not argue against having any such concept, but rather for a minimal concept in keeping with the little we know: primarily that he sought and provided means for others' awakening appropriate to his own place and time. What I argue against is a detailed concept of Śākyamuni that is filled in primarily with the details of one's own (or the founder of one's sect's) world-view projected back upon him, obscuring from our view many other embodiments and expressions of awakening potentially relevant to our place and time.

11 This is part of the reason contemporary critical tools applied to study of Buddhism will make more of a contribution to contemporary culture through their appropriation by Buddhist tradition than through their exclusive use by and for the secular academy. In this regard, see for example Makransky: Preface, chapters 1, 13. The discussion there represents an attempt to shed some light on future Mahāyāna doctrinal possibilities by using critical tools to illuminate the historical and structural nature of some past doctrinal developments around buddhahood.

12 For example, the bodhisattva resolve of *bodhicitta* (the resolve to fully awaken for all beings) constitutes a Mahāyāna response to the

First Noble Truth of suffering with particular focus on its universality and ultimate undividedness. Mahāyāna teachings of emptiness/perfection of wisdom are deconstructive responses to the Second Noble Truth, the self-clinging that causes suffering, and diverse means of eliciting and expressing such wisdom comprise the paths (Fourth Truth) to full awakening and freedom (Third Truth) for several traditions of North and East Asia. Mahāyānists have understood the Four Truths as foundational, while repeatedly reinterpreting them in conformity with the specific features of inculturated, i.e. living, practice experience.

13 The Four Noble Truths in their mutual relations have had a diversity of interpretations that are not merely speculative but intimately related to the practice experience of diverse communities. On the Mahāyāna quest for authentic reinterpretation of the Four Noble Truths as a driving force behind doctrinal transformation in light of practice experience, see Makransky, chapter 13.

REFERENCES

Batchelor, Stephen (1997). "Buddhism without Beliefs." *Tricycle* (6: 3) 18–23.

Bendall, Cecil and W. H. D. Rouse, trans. (1971). *Śikṣā-Samuccaya: A Compendium of Buddhist Doctrine Compiled by Śāntideva.* Varanasi: Motilal Banarsidass (reprint).

Chang, Garma C. C. (1983). *A Treasury of Mahāyāna Sūtras: Selections from the Mahāratnakūta Sūtra.* University Park, PA: Pennsylvania State University Press.

Cleary, Thomas, trans. (1993). *The Flower Ornament Scripture.* Boston: Shambhala.

Conze, Edward, trans. (1973). *The Perfection of Wisdom in Eight Thousand Lines.* Bolinas, CA: Four Seasons Foundation.

Davidson, Ronald (1990). "An Introduction to the Standards of Scriptural Authenticity in Indian Buddhism." In Robert Buswell, ed., *Chinese Buddhist Apocrypha.* Honolulu: University of Hawaii Press.

Gómez, Luis O. (1983a). "Indian Materials on the Doctrine of Sudden Enlightenment." In Whalen Lai and Lewis R. Lancaster, eds., *Early Ch'an in China and Tibet.* Berkeley: University of California Press.

Gómez, Luis O. (1983b) "The Direct and Gradual approaches of Zen Master Mahāyāna: Fragments of the Teachings of Mo-ho-yen." In Robert Gimello and Peter Gregory, eds., *Studies in Ch'an and Hua-yen.* Honolulu: University of Hawaii Press.

Haight, Roger (1997). "On Pluralism in Christology." *Budhi: A Journal of Ideas and Culture* (1) 31–46.

MacQueen, Graeme (1982). "Inspired Speech in Early Mahāyāna Buddhism II." *Religion.* (12) 49–65.

Makransky, John (1997). *Buddhahood Embodied: Sources of Controversy in India and Tibet.* Albany, NY: State University of New York Press.

Mayer, Robert (1996). *A Scripture of the Ancient Tantra Collection: The Phur-pa bcu-gnyis.* Oxford: Kiscadale Publications.

Ruegg, D. Seyfort (1995). "Some Reflections on the Place of Philosophy in the Study of Buddhism." *Journal of the International Association of Buddhist Studies* (18) 145–181.

Ruegg, D. Seyfort (1989). *Buddha-nature, Mind and the Problem of Gradualism in a Comparative Perspective: On the Transmission and Reception of Buddhism in India and Tibet.* London: SOAS, University of London.

Swanson, Paul L. (1993). "'Zen is not Buddhism': Recent Japanese Critiques of Buddha-Nature." *Numen* (40) 115–149.

Thurman, Robert A. F., trans. (1976). *The Holy Teaching of Vimalakīrti: A Mahāyāna Scripture.* University Park, PA: Pennsylvania State University Press.

Vaidya, P. L., ed. (1960). *Aṣṭasāhasrikā-prajñā-pāramitā-sūtra.* Buddhist Sanskrit Texts no. 4. Darbhanga, India: Mithila Institute.

Seven

Truth in Buddhist Theology[1]

José Ignacio Cabezón

CONTEXT

In an earlier essay in this volume I set forth my views concerning the nature of Buddhist theology as an academic enterprise. There I mentioned that I take this kind of theology to be a form of normative discourse that situates itself explicitly and self-consciously within the Buddhist tradition, and that, abiding by accepted scholarly norms, critically plumbs the tradition with a view to making relevant in a public and open fashion the meaning and truth of Buddhist doctrine and practice. Such a view of theology implies that it is, as it were, bifocal: attending, on the one hand, principally to the tradition as its chief source of intellectual and spiritual nourishment, and, on the other, to the exigencies of human existence that it seeks to address. These exigencies are of course many and varied. They range from very practical concerns, like what constitutes proper sexual conduct, to highly theoretical ones, such as the nature of knowledge. Whether practical or theoretical, the issues that preoccupy the academic Buddhist theologian are generally of two types. Some will emerge from, and hence be immediately recognizable to, the tradition (for example, the question of what constitutes valid knowledge). These we can call emic questions.[2] Others will emerge from outside of the tradition, and, even if not immediately recognizable to it, will become familiar to the tradition through a process of dialogue and translation, though this process is often complex and, in any case, not immediate. These latter types of questions we can call etic. Theoretical etic questions can arise from a number of sources: from other religious/theological traditions and from the secular, intellectual realm. This essay seeks to bring the resources of the Buddhist tradition to bear on one very important theoretical etic question that emerges from the discipline of Western philosophy: what is truth? Or, more specifically, what is it that we are saying when we say, of a particular doctrine, for example, that it is true?

The Indo-Tibetan Buddhist tradition throughout its history has been concerned with questions of truth. There the word *satya* (Tibetan *bden pa*; lit. "truth") has been used in a variety of hermeneutical, ethical, and theological contexts, and some of the speculation that emerges around the use of the word satya in these various contexts will be relevant to the present discussion. But this essay is clearly motivated principally by an etic agenda as regards the question of truth. The Western philosophical tradition has speculated at length concerning this issue. In particular, there have arisen a number of theories of truth that attempt to explain what is required of a proposition when we say of it that it is true. Three such theories – the correspondence, coherence and pragmatic theories – stand out prominently among the various options as being the most important, and it is the purpose of this essay to continue the conversation whose aim is to situate the Indo-Tibetan tradition vis a vis these three theories.

Why should Buddhist theologians be concerned with the question of truth? In particular, why should they be concerned with situating their tradition with respect to the question of truth as it is understood in Western philosophy? It is possible, I suppose, to engage in the task of Buddhist theology without explicitly declaring what theory of truth undergirds one's discourse: after all, the Buddha did so, as did the great Mahāyāna theologians of old. However, contemporary academic theologians have a responsibility to respond to the intellectual climate of our times. In an age where the notion of truth is itself so contested, with the options clearly demarcated and with different advocates of these options entrenched and ready for battle, not to situate oneself amidst those options is hardly an alternative for the academic theologian, Buddhist or otherwise.[3] Any contemporary Buddhist theology that attempts to be systematic must therefore face the issue, and this is what I propose to do here.

I take as a point of departure for the discussion that follows Roger Jackson's detailed and lucid treatment of the issue in his *Is Enlightenment Possible?* Jackson begins his analysis by presenting the major contemporary Western options regarding what makes a proposition true: (1) its correspondence to a real state of affairs in the world, (2) its pragmatic utility or (3) its coherence within an accepted framework. Jackson then plumbs the Buddhist tradition for evidence concerning Buddhist attitudes to truth, and while realizing that evidence for all three views can be gleaned from the Buddhist sources, he opts for the correspondence theory as being the Buddhist – and more generally the religious – theory of truth par excellence. To Jackson's credit it must be mentioned at the outset that he does take pains to point out the complexity of the issues involved, for example, the way in which all three theories are, both in the Buddhist and the

Western sources, insidiously interrelated. Moreover, in opting for the correspondence theory, on which more below, Jackson attempts to modify the latter so as to take into account objections that might be raised from the other two camps. It might be claimed then that my painting a picture of Jackson as a correspondentist sloughs over the subtlety of his analysis, and this may well be true. But regardless of Jackson's own stance, it is certainly the case that there are those who would uphold the view that the correspondence theory is the best approximation to an Indo-Tibetan theory of truth. In this sense perhaps it is more honest to point out that Jackson's analysis provides me here with an object of critique, whether or not the view being criticized is Jackson's own.

It might also be worth noting at the outset that there is also another major difference between Jackson's analysis and my own in this essay. Although there are normative elements in Jackson's analysis – times at which he seems to show his own clear preference for one view of truth as opposed to another – his work is principally descriptive and philosophical rather than theological, his goal being to elucidate what view was espoused by the classical Indian Buddhist tradition. This type of descriptive-philosophical analysis is certainly relevant to my own undertaking here, but does not exhaust it, given that my goal is theological.

The trinitarian view of truth that forms the basis for Jackson's inquiry – and my own here – is the result of an analysis of truth that emerges out of a Western philosophical context, and it must be understood that the fit with the Buddhist sources will not be exact. In particular, whichever of the options one considers to best represent the Buddhist view, it still remains incumbent upon one to reformulate the view, as it were, from the Buddhist sources up, an enterprise that will yield an authentically Buddhist theory of truth. This constructive exercise is especially important for the Buddhist theologian, whose task is not the mere description of such a theory, but (a) its normative espousal and (b) its use as the basis on which to demonstrate both the cogency of Buddhist doctrines and their relevance to contemporary life. This, then, represents something of the context and the reasons for what follow.

RELATIVISM

Whether or not there are religious/theological traditions that assume a relativist theory of truth – where the tenets of the religion, for example, are seen as true only intrareligiously, that is, applicable only to adherents – is, I suppose, an empirical question that falls within the purview of inquiry of the historian, or comparative philosopher, of religion. With the exception of certain strands of liberal (and perhaps post-liberal) Christianity, I know of no religious tradition that upholds a relativist theory of truth in regard to its doctrines.[4] Certainly, the Indo-Tibetan Buddhist tradition does not subscribe to such a view, maintaining instead the universal validity of its fundamental doctrines across linguistic, temporal and cultural boundaries. The truth of fundamental Buddhist doctrines – like the four noble truths, emptiness, the possibility of human perfection, the soteriological efficacy of meditation, and so forth – are seen to be independent of historical or cultural context. If these doctrines are true, they should be true for everyone everywhere: as true for us today, as they were for the Indian and Tibetan masters who formulated and expounded on them centuries ago. This is not to deny that there are some doctrines that are context-specific (that is, true at most only in specific historical or cultural contexts); nor is it to deny that even fundamental doctrines will have to be explained and defended in context-specific ways. Nonetheless, the validity of Buddhism as a religious tradition requires that there be some set of fundamental doctrines whose truth is not relative to time or place. At the same time I must emphasize that I do not intend this claim to be unchallengeable. What these fundamental doctrines are, and whether or not (and in what sense) they are true, will have to be shown, and not simply assumed. Indeed, it is precisely the theologian's task to do so. But any theology that is content to abandon the universal validity of its fundamental doctrines in favor of some brand of relativism will have failed as a theology through its complicity in the destruction of tradition.[5]

In the last two decades we have seen many philosophical criticisms leveled against relativism (see, e.g., Davidson; Mandelbaum; Harris; Rosemont), but I take the chief theological critique to be a pragmatic one: (1) religious traditions function for people; (2) relativism brings about the demise of traditions; (3) therefore, relativism is false. But again let me emphasize that I am setting forth the argument here only schematically, without defending the individual premises. Such a defense, I realize, is necessary, and, in the case of the first premise at least, is coterminous with the very task of theology.

What of the claim that the Buddhist sources subscribe to a kind of relativism, say in their espousal of the doctrine of dependent arising (Sanskrit *pratītya-samutpāda*; Tibetan *rten 'brel*, sometimes translated "relativity," better translated "dependent arising")? This objection can simply be dismissed as a misunderstanding of this particular doctrine, the result of faulty translation. However, another objection is not so easily dismissed. It might be claimed that the doctrine of *upāya*, or "skillful means," represents (or at least implies) a kind of relativism, one in which the truth of doctrine is indexed not to cultures or historical periods but to individuals! The argument might be framed as follows. The tradition recognizes that different individuals have different psychological and intellectual predispositions. That is precisely why the Buddha taught a variety of – sometimes radically inconsistent – doctrines. A doctrine that is true for an individual A will not necessarily be true for an individual B whose mental predispositions are different from those of A. Hence, truth is relative to individuals' mental predispositions and capacities, and not universal.

Let me dispel the notion that the doctrine of *upāya* represents a Buddhist brand of relativism. First, it must be remembered that the doctrine of skillful means is essentially a doctrine related to soteriology and not (at least directly) to questions of truth. It does not claim that different doctrines are unconditionally true for different individuals, but that different doctrines are differently efficacious for different individuals with different mental predispositions.[6] Even though all doctrine is considered efficacious, there are degrees of efficacy. Hence truth, to the extent that it can be equated with soteriological efficacy (something that I will argue for below), is also a matter of degree. That a doctrine – like the doctrine of three final vehicles, a classical example of a provisional doctrine – may function as a temporary device for some individuals (and is therefore true in the limited sense that it leads to the spiritual progress of those individuals) does not mean that that doctrine will be ultimately efficacious even for those individuals. In fact, many doctrines that are provisionally useful at one stage of the path will have to be repudiated in its later stages (just as the doctrine of three final vehicles is repudiated by the affirmation of the doctrine of only one final vehicle – Sanskrit *ekayāna*). But though this is the case for many doctrines, it is not the case for all. In particular, it is not the case for doctrines that are unconditionally true. The doctrine of emptiness in its most subtle formulation is one such doctrine. It is incontrovertible – that is, it is not superseded by any doctrine that contradicts it; and its understanding is a necessary and universal prerequisite for enlightenment. Unconditionally true doctrines are not true for – that is, they are not true relative to – a certain limited group of individuals. It is not the case that a doctrine x can be unconditionally true (*lege* ultimately efficacious) for individual A and that its contrary x' is unconditionally true for individual B. Unconditionally true doctrine represents a set of (presumably consistent) propositions that all individuals must eventually understand, believe and internalize if they are to attain enlightenment. Even if, along the way, there are doctrines that contradict ultimately true doctrines and that, serving some temporary spiritual purpose, might therefore be considered provisionally efficacious and therefore partially true, these are not unconditionally true for any individual. Hence, provisional truth may be relative to individuals, but unconditional truth is not.

The doctrine of *upāya* neither presumes nor does it imply a relativist theory of truth. Indeed, relativism of any kind is incompatible with the universalistic character of Buddhism.

AGAINST CORRESPONDENCE

Jackson argues that Buddhism, like all religions worthy of the name,[7] espouses a correspondence theory of truth: "when we analyze the sorts of truth-claims made in Buddhism, correspondence (though not named as such, of course) turns out to be the most fundamental criterion . . . the Buddha asserted the four noble truths and their cosmological and philosophical presuppositions in a literal or 'hard' sense" (43). Now Jackson here, and elsewhere in his work, I think conflates literalness and correspondence. A pragmatist, for example, might argue that Buddhist metaphysics and cosmology should be taken literally – for example, that Buddhists should live as though there existed past and future lives – while bracketing the question of whether or not rebirth corresponds to some external state of affairs in the world. Treating Buddhist doctrines as useful devices whose sole purpose is the mental purification of individuals, in the process refraining from judgments as to whether or not they correspond to objective states of affairs, in no way entails a non-literal view of doctrine, for, as Jackson himself acknowledges, Buddhists have nowhere actually claimed such correspondence. Put another way, correspondence, pragmatism and coherence are options regarding the truth of doctrines, while literalness and non-literalness are options regarding their meaning.

Apart from this issue, it seems to me that there are independent reasons for arguing against the fact that Buddhists – at least certain Indo-Tibetan Buddhists – hold principally to a correspondence theory of truth. Here are some arguments framed as a response to the case made by Jackson.

1. Jackson argues (32–33), rightly, that a correspondence theory requires the existence of a "'real world' that is independent of human mental activity and human symbolic language" (32–33), that "statements to be 'true,' must 'correspond' to some reality beyond the

conceptual scheme in which they are found" (34). Now whether or not the existence of a world independent of human thought and action is possible for some Buddhists – and the fact that the world is the result of the collective karma of beings should be enough to bring *even this much* into doubt – it seems clear that this is highly problematic for others, especially for Mādhyamikas. It is precisely Mādhyamikas who claim that the world is the imputation of conceptual thought and language; and that the only reality it has is the conventional one given to it by linguistic-conceptual construction. So if a correspondence theory of truth requires an independently existing world, then such a theory is ruled out at the very least for Mādhyamikas, and, given the implications of the theory of karma, perhaps more generally for all Buddhists. Of course, it might be claimed – and Jackson, to his credit, is not unaware of such a move – that a modified Buddhist correspondence theory could be constructed wherein claims that are candidates for truth correspond not to an independently existing world, but an interdependent, conventionally existing one. But though the latter is certainly more acceptable to, say, Mādhyamikas than the former, it might still be maintained that the issue is not resolved. For example, to what does the object seen as water by humans, as pus and blood by *pretas*, and as fire by hell beings, to take a classic example, correspond? The kind of object that a correspondence theory requires must simply be too objective (that is, not sufficiently subjective) to allow for the malleability required by the theory of karma.

2. Although the issue of truth in Dharmakīrti is complex, as Georges Dreyfus (1995) has recently demonstrated, the fact that the problem for Dharmakīrti and his commentators is framed principally in epistemological rather than ontological terms is further support of my claim that a correspondence theory of truth is problematic for Indo-Tibetan Buddhist philosophers. For Dharmakīrti, it is not correspondence to an actual external state of affairs that makes something true. Rather, truth, to the extent that it is a problem for him at all, can be characterized (at least by us, given our concerns) as the content of valid knowledge. What makes something true then is the fact that it is validly cognizable, and this, as we shall see, does not entail correspondence but rather the ability of such knowledge to fulfill a human purpose (*puruṣārthasiddhi*) (see Nagatomi: 55ff.) A great deal could be said in this regard. Suffice it to point out that (at least according to some Indian and Tibetan interpreters) there is no external world independent of conceptual construction with which to come into contact in the case of inference (valid knowledge of the conceptual kind). To quote Dreyfus, "if one understands such a [correspondence] theory to posit truth as a metaphysical correspondence between

concepts and a reality determinable in abstraction from any conceptual scheme, then Dharmakīrti is not committed to such a theory" (687). The issue, however, is complex, and the correspondentist could claim that there is another strain in Dharmakīrti's thought that speaks of valid knowledge as being induced by the power of actual entities (*vastubalapravṛtti*). In my reading of Dharmakīrti, however, it is the pragmatic criterion which I see as predominating.

3. Jackson (47–48) cites in support of a correspondence theory of truth in Buddhism the fact that the Buddha is repeatedly described in Buddhist sources as someone who perceived the truth, and that that truth or order exists "whether or not Tathāgatas arise or do not arise." But that buddhas perceive the truth, and that this truth is true regardless of whether or not there are buddhas, does not necessarily support the correspondence view. There is, as is well known, a long-standing tradition in Buddhism that states that the truth or reality taught by the Buddha – his doctrines – are linguistic constructs invented by the Buddha as a way of counteracting the afflictions that plague sentient beings. Hence, doctrine is true because it serves, practically, to bring about the mental purification of living beings. Consider, for example, the Abhidharma claim that the 84,000 portions of doctrine were taught in order to counteract the 84,000 afflictions; or the claim that the "wheel of the doctrine" corresponds not to some independent state of affairs in the world, but to the realizations that exist in the mental continua of saints; or, again, the more radical claim, put forward by the early Tsong kha pa, for example, that Buddhist truths "exist *only* within the disciples' frame of reference (*gzhan snang*)," that is, only as they manifest in the minds of those who hear them.[8] Hence, the truth may exist whether or not Tathāgatas arise, but it does not exist separate from the human predicament which it was meant to address. There is a real sense in which the truths taught by the Buddha are considered mere inventions created for the sake of solving the specific problem of suffering, and not objective, free-floating, metaphysical facts independent of the human predicament.

As with the correspondence theory, there are also problems in maintaining that the Indo-Tibetan tradition subscribes to a coherence theory of truth. According to the coherence theory, a proposition (or doctrine) is true if it coheres with a designated set of beliefs.[9] Given the incommensurate nature of the belief systems of the Buddhist tradition, even one as circumscribed as the Indo-Tibetan tradition, coherence is simply not sufficient to guarantee the truth of a doctrine. Buddhist doctrine – even in this one sub-tradition – is extremely diverse, and at times even contradictory. This being so, mere internal consistency with some portion of the corpus of Buddhist doctrine will not guarantee a doctrine's truth, since it is quite possible that a doctrine that is supported in one portion of the canon will be repudiated in another.[10] Therefore, independent criteria, over and above coherence, are considered necessary in determining which doctrines are unconditionally true.

THE PRAGMATIC THEORY OF TRUTH

The classical pragmatic theory of truth has been variously formulated in the Western philosophical tradition.[11] In its most general form it states simply that a proposition <*p*> is true if and only if it is useful to believe that *p*. Analytic philosophers have further refined the idea of usefulness by introducing the notion of degrees and of comparative usefulness. Hence, in another formulation, a proposition <*p*> is true if and only if it is useful at least to degree *l* to believe that *p*; and in yet another case the theory has been stated such that a proposition <*p*> is true if and only if it is more useful to believe that *p* than to believe that not-*p*. Given what I said earlier in the context of the doctrine of *upāya*, it should be clear that introducing comparative degrees of usefulness to the theory will be seen as a welcomed refinement by the Buddhist theologian. I leave it as an exercise for the reader to determine the whys and hows of this.

Of course, Buddhist theology cannot simply accept a Western formulation of the pragmatic theory uncritically and *in toto*. It must come to its own formulation by way of a dialogue with the Western sources. Let me state briefly what I believe some of the conclusions of such a dialogue might be. First, Buddhist theology is not concerned with developing a *general* pragmatic theory of truth, one that explicates the truth value of all propositions pragmatically. It is concerned instead with a very small subset of all propositions, namely doctrinal ones. Whether and how the truth of other, non-religious, claims is to be explained simply falls outside of the purview of Buddhist theological speculation. This is not a trivial observation, for many of the problems faced by the pragmatic theory of truth as formulated by Western philosophers occur precisely because it attempts to be all-encompassing. Limiting the scope of the theory to doctrinal claims, therefore, allows the theologian to circumvent many of the objections that might be raised in regard to a more general theory of truth. Second, Buddhist theology will want to formulate the theory so that the truth of a doctrine is dependent *either* on the usefulness of *believing* it, *or* on the usefulness of *acting* in accordance with it, or on the usefulness of *internalizing* it in the process of meditation. There may be a variety of doctrines whose usefulness emerges not from simply believing them, but from the fact that they serve as the basis for certain actions (or as the basis for avoiding certain actions), or as the result of their being yogically intuited in the process of meditation. This particular slant on the theory is, of course, due to the fact that the Buddhist tradition will insist on considering activities other than belief (action, mystical intuition) as being pertinent to the question of truth. Finally, the particular Buddhist version of the theory will define *usefulness* in quite specific ways that go beyond the cognitive and behaviorist definitions often found in the Western sources.[12]

Jackson, following Walter Kaufmann, himself acknowledges the appeal of the pragmatic theory as an alternative, citing the parables of the raft and the arrow, the doctrine of skillful means (*upāya-kauśalya*) and the hermeneutical doctrine of provisional vs. definitive meaning as all indicative of pragmatic tendencies within the tradition. But while acknowledging that these may be indicative of a practical, pragmatic, and even pragmatist, strain within Buddhism, he insists, following Jayatilleke (47, 53), that it does not represent the espousal of a pragmatic theory of truth, for the latter requires that a belief be considered "true if it is useful and false." But such a formulation of the pragmatic criterion is at the very least confused, and at worst sophistic. Pragmatists do not claim that beliefs are "true if they are useful and false" – a contradiction – but that the truth of doctrines lies precisely in their pragmatic utility. The word "false" in the expression "useful and false" is of course appealing to (and hence assuming) a correspondence (or some other) theory of truth, making its use in the formulation of the pragmatic criterion disingenuous.[13]

Now apart from the various examples cited by Jackson that are suggestive of the overall pragmatic leanings of the Indo-Tibetan tradition, there is perhaps another worth mentioning. Buddhists engage in a variety of meditative exercises for the purpose of mental transformation, and in many of these exercises the object of the meditator often corresponds to no real object in the external world. To deepen their realization of the impurity of the world, for example, Buddhists cultivate a state of meditative stabilization in which the world is experienced as being filled with bones. Similarly, there are *samādhis* that have as their objects other unreal objects: consider, for example, the visualization of oneself as a deity, which is the fundamental practice of the generation stage of the *anuttarayoga tantra*. Though this is a debated issue, there is considerable consensus, at least in the Madhyamaka textual tradition, that such meditative states are neither wrong nor mistaken.[14] This implies that the state of affairs experienced in such states is in some sense true. What makes these states unmistaken, and their respective objects true? It is of course their pragmatic usefulness in the process of self-transformation. Once again, pragmatism triumphs over correspondence.

Although Jackson and Dreyfus disagree, as we have seen, on the question of whether or not Buddhism (and more specifically Dharmakīrti) is committed to a correspondence theory, in all fairness to Jackson, it must be pointed out that Dreyfus sides with him in claiming that, though Dharmakīrti's philosophy may be pragmatic in tone, it does not offer a pragmatic theory of truth. Dreyfus, following certain Indian and Tibetan commentators, argues that Dharmakīrti offers a pragmatic description of non-deceptiveness, but is not a pragmatist in the sense of the American pragmatist tradition that begins with Peirce, James, Dewey and (arguably) continues in Rorty. But Dreyfus's point is really a hermeneutical one: that there is no one-to-one correspondence between Buddhist and American theories of pragmatism, and this is certainly true. As I have already mentioned, to suggest that Buddhists are pragmatists – that they offer a pragmatic theory of truth – is not the end of a comparative analysis, but the beginning of a conversation in which the specifically Buddhist version of pragmatism can begin to be formulated from the Buddhist sources up. Put another way, noticing the pragmatic tendencies of Buddhist thinkers leads to a decontextualized notion of pragmatism which can then be brought into conversation with the reality of Buddhist texts to formulate an authentically Buddhist version of this tradition. That it will not be Jamesian is of course true, but even granting that, this still leaves open the question of the *extent* to which it is or is not Jamesian.[15] More important, not being Jamesian or Rortyan is no more a reason for eschewing the appellation "pragmatist" than not being Christian is a reason for eschewing the term "theological." The meaning of words are neither restricted to their histories nor reducible to their etymologies.

BUDDHIST PRAGMATISM

Pragmatists have often been accused of being relativists. The charge is not altogether unfounded, for pragmatists have often indexed their criteria for what constitutes pragmatic efficacy to specific groups of individuals (cultures, religions, conversation partners, etc.). Some pragmatists would claim that a particular notion (a religious doctrine, say) may be efficacious (and therefore true) in one setting, and yet lack such efficacy (and therefore lack truth) in another.[16] To avoid the charge of relativism, the pragmatist must propose crit efficacy that are valid across temporal, geograp boundaries. Christian theologians with strong pragma Gordon Kaufman (1993) have attempted to do this, a Kaufman's case his hyper-historicism leaves him open to the cha a certain, albeit weaker, form of relativism.[17] However othe traditions argue for their pragmatic norms, and how they craft these norms so as to avoid the charge of relativism, it seems to me that Buddhist theological pragmatists will have to do so by fashioning criteria of pragmatic efficacy which they hold to be universal. This means that the efficacy of at least certain doctrines will have to be held to be independent of time, place, language, culture and conversations.

What will a universal, pragmatic theory of truth look like for Buddhist theology? Presumably the creation of such a theory will involve the crafting of criteria of pragmatic utility that are Buddhist in character. Here mere physiological efficacy – the fact that doctrines or techniques of mental cultivation function to relieve stress, for example – will not do; neither will mere intellectual efficacy – the fact that particular ways of thinking enhance a conversation or a research program in some significant way. What is called for in a Buddhist theory are criteria of efficacy that are consonant with the ultimate Buddhist goal of human perfection. Whatever else we may wish to include among the qualities that make candidates for truth pragmatically efficacious (and therefore true), it is clear that reference will have to be made to a doctrine's ability to effectuate the positive transformation of individuals.[18] But to stop here would be to beg the question, for what precisely constitutes positive transformation? In this regard, the Buddhist tradition has a great deal to say. To put it in a particularly *Mahāyāna* Buddhist way, we might formulate the notion of positive mental transformation in terms of the *upāya/prajñā* (method/wisdom) dyad, for example. Doctrines that lead to the enhancement of the qualities of compassion/altruism and wisdom would then be truths for Mahayana Buddhism. As mentioned above, this still leaves open the possibility of degrees of efficacy, and therefore of truth, but despite the fact that certain doctrines will be at most provisionally true, the universalistic character of Buddhism requires a core of unconditionally true doctrines the intellectual understanding and direct meditative intuition of which are prerequisites to the enlightenment of all beings.

Once criteria for what constitutes pragmatic efficacy have been formulated, the Buddhist theologian's task is of course far from finished. The criteria themselves must be defended. And, of course, there remains the work of demonstrating how Buddhist doctrines fulfill these pragmatic criteria and how other doctrines fail to do so (the work of apologetics). At least the first of these latter two tasks – demonstrating the pragmatic efficacy of Buddhist doctrine – has in large part been done by the classical Buddhist tradition itself. For example, the Tibetan *lam rim* tradition has set forth – largely in pragmatic terms – the need for engaging in a series of sequential meditations each of which practically serves as a necessary prerequisite for the next, culminating in the meditations on the Mahayana doctrines of altruism and wisdom. In these texts, then, what guarantees the efficacy or truth of doctrines lower in the contemplative scheme, the pragmatist would assert, is not their correspondence to a specific state of affairs in the world but the fact that they are practically required as stepping stones to higher ones.

All of this, I realize, represents only the bare bones of a Buddhist theological theory of pragmatic truth, but it is, nonetheless, a starting point. Or that, at least, is my hope.

CONCLUSION

Up to this point I have argued that from among the three major Western theories of truth – correspondence, coherence and pragmatism – it is the last of these, the pragmatic theory, that represents the most promising option for the Buddhist theologian. By "promising option" I mean, of course, that the pragmatic theory, because it resonates well with the Buddhist sources, offers the Buddhist theologian the most fruitful starting point for the formulation of an authentically Buddhist theological theory of truth, a very preliminary version of which I have attempted to outline above. My decision to adopt a pragmatist perspective has therefore been partially based on the fact that of the three options it is the pragmatist option that represents the best fit with the Buddhist textual sources, a fact that must be seriously taken into account by any theologian who considers himself or herself responsible to the tradition. But aside from being responsible to the tradition, the Buddhist theologian is also responsible to the truth. This leads to the following important question: what makes the pragmatic theory (or indeed any theory) of truth true? Put another way, what criteria (what theory of truth) does one use to adjudicate between different theories of truth?

[illegible] theories of what makes a first-order proposition (a [illegible]ne, for example) true are viable, that is, if they are [illegible]es of truth, then one would expect that they should be capable of offering us guidance as regards the second order question of what it is that makes a theory of truth itself true. If a theory is plausible in regard to first order questions, it should also be plausible in regard to the meta-question of adjudicating between the theories themselves, a property which I call transitivity across the meta-theoretical boundary. Thus, a true theory of truth should be transitive. It should provide us with insight not only in regard to why first order propositions are true, but also in regard to why the theory itself is true vis a vis the other theories. Of the three alternatives, I claim that it is only pragmatism that exhibits the property of transitivity. To what could a theory of truth correspond in order for it to be true under a correspondence model? With what could a theory of truth cohere for it to be true under a coherence model? I do not see answers to these questions as forthcoming. Only pragmatism, it seems to me, provides us with good reasons for adjudicating between theories of truth: for determining one theory (pragmatism itself) to be true. This is tantamount to saying that there are good pragmatic reasons for opting for pragmatism, or, alternatively, that the pragmatic theory of truth is, from among the options, the most practically efficacious.

But efficacious for whom? Who makes use of theories of truth? Theologians, of course, make use of such theories. Let me now conclude with a few remarks concerning the pragmatic efficacy of pragmatism as a theory of truth for Buddhist theologians (or at least for *this* Buddhist theologian).

There are of course many Buddhist theologians who will be content to espouse and defend the traditional metaphysical beliefs of Buddhism – karma, rebirth, the theory of enlightenment – from a correspondence perspective, maintaining that these are doctrines that actually mirror real states of affairs in the world. While feeling a certain respect and even nostalgia for this perspective, I find myself unable to subscribe to it as a mode of theological expression. Instead, I find myself in the position of being metaphysically alienated, unconvinced of the metaphysical (*lege* correspondence version of the) truth of a good deal of Buddhist doctrine, while still profoundly convinced of the validity of the Buddhist tradition as a whole. For alienated Buddhist theologians like myself – skeptics who find problematic the espousal of the metaphysical truth of Buddhist doctrines like karma and rebirth – pragmatism offers a method of finding truth in the tradition, even in those portions of the tradition which would otherwise be unacceptable. Herein lies the pragmatic value, and hence the validity (the truth) of pragmatism for the Buddhist theologian.[19]

This still leaves unanswered many fundamental questions. How exactly are doctrines like karma, rebirth, and the possibility of enlightenment pragmatically useful? How are they conducive to positive human transformation in ways that rival doctrines are not? Is the mere belief in their pragmatic efficacy psychologically sufficient to bring about the desired goal of human transformation? To what extent can we will ourselves to believe, act upon and internalize doctrines whose metaphysical reality we doubt? It is answers to questions like these that will serve as the framework for Buddhist theological pragmatism, but that is the subject of another essay.

NOTES

1 This essay was first delivered as a paper in the Theology and Religious Reflection Section of the 1996 annual meeting of the American Academy in New Orleans. The author would like to express his thanks to the editors of this volume and to my colleague, William Dean, for their valuable suggestions. Special thanks to Roger Jackson for his willingness to challenge many of my observations, which in several instances has led to substantial revisions.

2 On the emic-etic distinction as developed in anthropology see Harris; Garbarino: 82–84, 98; Marcus and Fischer: 180–181.

3 As with the question of truth, there are a number of other issues that have emerged in Western theology and the philosophy of religion that it will be important for Buddhist theologians to address by either situating themselves along the spectrum of options or else by critically rejecting the possible options. Whatever tack is taken, it seems clear to me that these are issues that in any case cannot be avoided. Among these are the questions of foundationalism /deconstruction, empiricism/rationalism, historicism/ahistoricism, realism/idealism and public/private. For an excellent overview of some of the possible options regarding these important questions see Frankenberry.

4 So-called "ethnic" religious traditions like Native American religions, Judaism and Hinduism, while maintaining that "membership" or central participation in cultic life may be restricted to a limited group of people as defined by a variety of factors like race, ethnicity or land, nonetheless hold certain truths to be universal, and therefore true for all. The fact that not all people are or can be Hindus does not mean that Hindus believe that the truths of Hinduism apply only to Hindus.

5 A tradition that is universalistic, like Buddhism and Christianity, requires that at least a subset of its doctrines be true universally. Relativism, by challenging the universal validity of doctrine, casts aspersions on the universalistic character of tradition, thereby leading to their demise.

6 Given that I will be arguing below for a kind of pragmatist theory of truth in Buddhist theology, in which the truth of a doctrine is determined by its soteriological efficacy, it behooves me to say a few words about the nature of that efficacy at this point. That logically inconsistent doctrines can be soteriologically efficacious would seem to imply that logically inconsistent doctrines can be true. However, the tradition distinguishes between doctrines that are necessary to enlightenment (e.g., compassion, the Prāsaṅgika Madhyamaka interpretation of emptiness, and so forth) and those that, though helpful for some, are not necessary (the doctrine of three final vehicles, the Yogācāra interpretation of emptiness, etc.), and indeed must eventually be left behind in favor of the former. Necessary or unconditionally true doctrines serve as the real antidotes to the suffering of self and others. All other doctrines, while temporarily effective for some practitioners in that they advance them along the spiritual path, do not serve as real – that is, permanent – antidotes. For example, as regards the various interpretation of emptiness, all views except for that of the Prāsaṅgika Madhyamaka are considered provisional (*neyārtha*; *drang don*). All of these views are meant to lead to the acceptance and internalization of the Prāsaṅgika view, which is considered definitive (*nītārtha*; *nges don*). The former do not represent the Buddha's ultimate purport or intention (*dgongs pa thar thug pa*), the latter does. Hence, the former may be true in a limited sense that is due to their provisional efficacy, but they are not true in the unqualified way that the definitive view – the ultimately efficacious one – is true, that is, unconditionally. See Cabezón: 53–70.

7 I would argue, therefore, for the rather traditional view that a religion is not fully a religion unless it claims universality and refers to a metaphysical realm and/or entities, and that the compromises wrought in religion by a pragmatic or coherence theory of truth rob it of some of its most vital characteristics" (40). As will be seen from the discussion that follows, I will be arguing here for a universalistic version of pragmatism.

8 For a discussion of these various claims see Cabezón: 29–52.

9 This set of beliefs is often identified as the beliefs which an individual or group of individuals is epistemically justified in having, but it is unnecessary to go into this aspect of the theory here.

10 Consider, for example, what Tsong kha pa says about the attempt to decide which doctrines are provisional and which definitive (that is, which provisionally true and which unconditionally true) based on criteria of coherence qua consistency with scripture: "Regarding the way of distinguishing between these two options, it cannot be done simply by (relying) on scripture . . . since there are many inconsistent ways of explaining the provisional and the definitive in the canon. Given that in general one cannot posit something as being the case simply because a scriptural passage says so, that is, given that this relationship (between a scripture's claim and the truth) does not hold,

the particular case of distinguishing between provisional and definitive can also not be adjudicated by the words (of a particular sūtra) . . . In the end, this distinction must be made by relying (not on scripture) but on stainless reasoning" (340).

11 For a useful and concise overview of the various formulations, with a more extensive critique of the theory, see Schmitt.

12 "A belief is behaviorally useful when it empowers us to satisfy our desires. Such empowerment may encompass any number of abilities – to manipulate or acquire objects, to predict the future, to convince others to do things, or to communicate information to others. A belief is cognitively useful when it equips us to organize, predict and explain our experience . . . [W]e may assume here, as James apparently does, that usefulness is some combination of behavioral and cognitive usefulness" (Schmitt: 79).

13 Jackson himself seems to acknowledge this (47, notes 13, 14), but this does not seem to stop him from following Jayatilleke on this point (as in the discussion on p. 53).

14 For a brief and excellent overview of the issues, see Lati Rinbochay and Napper: 113–115.

15 Powers explores this very issue, though he is concerned more with demonstrating the parallels between Dharmakīrti and the radical empiricism of James than with the question of pragmatism. Powers's work is illuminating and provocative, though I believe that he goes too far in attempting to demonstrate similarities between Buddhism and the American radical empiricist tradition. Powers's essay is worthy of a more full response, which unfortunately is not possible here. Nancy Frankenberry (1–4), who also sees significant parallels between Buddhism and American radical empiricism (see her chapter 5), begins her work by analyzing some of the implications and presuppositions of an empiricist view of the world: (1) that experience "is the touchstone of all theories and all claims to knowledge," (2) that the limits of knowledge are defined by the limits of what is experienced, so that as a method of inquiry empiricism becomes a way of organizing and interpreting the data of investigation, a method that is instrumental, operational and experimental, and (3) that empiricism appeals to experience in the establishment and justification of claims, with an appeal to the given over and above the rationally constructed. Without getting into detail here, let me simply point out that a perusal of my 1994 work should make it clear that each of these three "tenets" would be problematic for Indo-Tibetan Buddhism. For the latter similar problems also exist with regard to accepting less generic versions of empiricism, say of the Deweyan and Jamesian kinds. For discussions of portions of these latter two perspectives that in my view are especially important to the dialogue with Buddhism, see Frankenberry: 44–45, 83–89.

16 It might be claimed that Richard Rorty's version of pragmatism is relativist in this vein, though to argue for this here would take us too

far from our central concern.

17 Kaufman sets forth the normative criteria for his brand of pragmatic historicism in chapter 10 of *In Face of Mystery* (1993: 125–140). It is perhaps ironic that Kaufman eschews relativism precisely by invoking a kind of historical relativity: we no longer live in an age where relativism is useful, though it may perhaps have been at one point (1993: 118–123). This generally soft stance on relativism (it is false for us today, but not generally), together with his hyper-historicism, leads to his work's becoming infused with a relativism that his initial disavowal of this position fails to dispel. Consider, for example, his claim that "what is 'optimal' for one sociocultural situation or natural setting will be quite different from what is 'optimal' in other significantly different contexts" (1993: 128). For other similar passages in Kaufman see 1993: 129, 136, 162, 165.

18 It is clear that the Buddhist vision of what constitutes the ideal state of sentient being-ness (that is, enlightenment), with all of its ancillary qualities, will have to be defended as part of this project. That this cannot simply be taken for granted – for example, that a state of being non-mistaken in regard to the real nature of things, or that desirelessness, cannot simply be assumed to be constitutive elements of human perfection – can be seen from Gordon Kaufman's provocative critique of these very notions, a response to which I hope to publish shortly. See Kaufman 1996.

19 My position here is in marked contrast to the position of, for example, Stephen Batchelor, who maintains that the appropriate response of the metaphysically alienated Buddhist is one of agnosticism: "*I do not know*"; see Batchelor: 38. Although this is certainly not the place to engage Batchelor's views, suffice it to say that I believe Buddhist theological pragmatism to represent a more adequate response to skepticism than mere agnosticism, if for no other reason than that it takes the data of tradition more seriously.

REFERENCES

Batchelor, Stephen (1997). *Buddhism Without Beliefs: A Contemporary Guide to Awakening.* New York: Riverhead Books.

Cabezón, José Ignacio (1994). *Buddhism and Language: A Study of Indo-Tibetan Scholasticism.* Albany: State University of New York Press.

Davidson, Donald (1973–4). "On the Very Idea of a Conceptual Scheme." *Proceedings of the American Philosophical Association* (47) 5–20.

Dreyfus, Georges (1995). "Is Dharmakīrti a Pragmatist?" *Asiatische Studien/Études Asiatiques* (49: 4) 671–691.

Frankenberry, Nancy (1987). *Religion and Radical Empiricism.* Albany: State University of New York Press.

Garbarino, Merwyn S. (1977). *Sociocultural Theory in Anthropology: A*

Short History. Prospect Heights IL: Waveland Press.

Harris, James F. (1992). *Against Relativism: A Philosophical Defense of Method*. La Salle, IL: Open Court.

Harris, Marvin (1968). *The Rise of Anthropological Theory: A History of Theories of Culture*. New York: HarperCollins Publishers.

Jackson, Roger R. (1993). *Is Enlightenment Possible?: Dharmakīrti and rGyal tshab rje on Knowledge, Rebirth, No-self and Liberation*. Ithaca: Snow Lion Publications.

Kalupahana, David J. (1986) "The Epistemology of William James and Early Buddhism." In Joseph Runzo and Craig C. Ihar, eds., *Religious Experience and Religious Belief: Essays in the Epistemology of Religion*. Lanham, MD: University Press of America.

Kaufman, Gordon D. (1996). "Some Buddhist Metaphysical Presuppositions." In *God, Mystery, Diversity: Christian Theology in a Pluralistic World*. Minneapolis: Fortress Press.

Kaufman, Gordon D. (1993). *In Face of Mystery: A Constructive Theology*. Cambridge, MA: Harvard University Press.

Lati Rinbochay and Elizabeth Napper (1980). *Mind in Tibetan Buddhism*. Valois, NY: Gabriel/Snow Lion.

Mandelbaum, Maurice (1979). "Subjective, Objective and Conceptual Relativisms." *The Monist* (62: 4) 403–423.

Marcus, George E. and Michael M. J. Fischer (1986). *Anthropology as Cultural Critique: An Experiment in the Human Sciences*. Chicago: The University of Chicago Press.

Nagatomi, Masatoshi (1967–8). "Arthakriya." *The Adyar Bulletin* (31–32) 52–72.

Powers, John (1994). "Empiricism and Pragmatism in the Thought of Dharmakīrti and William James." *American Journal of Theology and Philosophy* (15: 1) 59–85.

Rosemont, Jr., Henry (1989). "Against Relativism." In Gerald James Larson and Eliot Deutsch, eds., *Interpreting Across Boundaries: New Essays in Comparative Philosophy*. Delhi: Motilal Banarsidass (reprint of the 1988 Princeton edition).

Schmitt, Frederick J. (1995). *Truth: A Primer*. Boulder: Westview Press.

Tsong kha pa bLo bzang grags pa (1987). *rJe Tsong kha pa chen po'i gsung 'bum bzhugs so*. mTsho sngon mi rigs dpe skrun khang.

Eight

The Lack Of Self: A Western Buddhist Psychology

David R. Loy

(I)

Buddhism, it is often claimed, has thrived in foreign cultures (and perhaps been co-opted in its birthplace) because of its adaptability, a flexibility consistent with its emphasis on impermanence and essencelessness. Then what is Buddhism adapting to today, as it infiltrates Europe and America?

Some may point to the Buddhist-Christian dialogue, now an established site of interreligious conversation; others to Hollywood (for Tibetan Buddhism, at least). Yet it seems to me that Buddhism's main port of entry into Western culture has become Western psychology, especially psychotherapy, the tradition of "talking cure" that more or less began with Freudian psychoanalysis and has since ramified into an unclassifiable plethora of therapies. This interaction is all the more interesting because psychoanalysis and most of its offspring remain marked by an antagonism to religion that is the legacy of the Enlightenment, which defined itself in opposition to myth and superstition. Doctor Freud, who never gave up his hope of grounding psychoanalysis in physiology, understood his legacy to be a rudimentary branch of medical science, and reserved some of his harshest words for the "collective neurosis" of religious belief.

While the importance of this creative dialogue has become undeniable, it remains unclear where it is heading. Do (or can) some Buddhist meditative practices function in ways similar to some forms of therapy? If so, how do they differ? Or does the former begin where the latter ends: i.e., is the psychotherapeutic treatment of "neurosis" a good preliminary for Buddhist practice aimed at the "higher goal" of enlightenment?

I am not aware that any consensus is forming regarding the answers, yet such questions keep recurring within many Buddhist meditation circles and for many Western Buddhist teachers, some of whom are also professional therapists. In any case, the concern of this essay is more theoretical. I believe that the interaction between

Western psychology is an opportunity for comparison in the best sense, in which we do not merely wrench two things out of context to notice their similarities, but can benefit from the different light that each casts upon the other. While Western psychology brings to this encounter a more sophisticated understanding of the ways we make ourselves unhappy, Buddhist teachings imply a deeper insight into the source of the problem.

One could criticize such comparisons by arguing that, in contrast to Buddhist-Christian dialogue, the Western psychologizing of Buddhism may secularize it so much that it loses its soteriological thrust, to end up, say, promoting techniques aimed at nothing "higher" than reducing day-to-day anxiety. One way to reply to this is to question the secular/sacred dualism which the objection takes for granted: such a dichotomy is less problematical for Buddhism (especially in its Mahāyāna version, for which saṃsāra is not other than *nirvāṇa*) than for Christianity (rendering to Caesar what belongs to Caesar). To put it another way, the objection is turned back upon itself by all the traditional and ongoing debates about what that soteriology amounts to: a transcendental exit from *saṃsāra* or a this-worldly transformation of the way we perceive it? By no accident, then, has this become a main issue in the encounter between Buddhism and psychotherapeutics, and it may well be that Buddhism has more to offer soteriologically to a medically-modeled psychology that has powerful insights into the nature and etiology of mental dis-ease but little vision of what mental *health* involves. Perhaps Western psychotherapy today is still too indebted to Freud's questionable libido theory, which by no coincidence (given the influence of Schopenhauer in the late nineteenth-century) bears more than a passing resemblance to Schopenhauer's pessimistic understanding of the Will. Perhaps, also, our Western vision of human possibility is too deeply colored by the now-pervasive nihilism that Nietzsche predicted for the twentieth-century due to the death of God and His values.

If there is a case for the criticism that such a psychologized Buddhism is unfaithful to the lofty goals of its own tradition, this objection might also apply to what happened in China, where the Mahāyāna encounter with Taoism (and Confucianism) led to forms of salvation that Śākyamuni may have had trouble recognizing; and certainly in Japan, where Zen taught the samurai how to die and how to kill, and where contemporary Buddhist temples are preoccupied with the lucrative profits from funeral services. If these East Asian versions of Buddhism are still recognizable as Buddhist, why should we deny that claim for what is happening in the West? Doesn't the criticism assume an "essence" to Buddhism, which emphasizes "essencelessness"?

On the other side, though, does *śūnyatā* really imply that it is *never* possible to throw out the baby with the bath water? An approach that stresses continuity through change may not be enough to ensure that the final product is Buddhist, if we accept Śākyamuni's statement that his enlightenment revealed something exceedingly difficult to realize – and therefore presumably easy to misunderstand. We can imagine cases where a student does not clearly understand the teacher yet nonetheless goes on to teach what he thinks is his teacher's teaching; in fact, there may have been many such cases, raising more questions about retrospective lineages such as that precious to the Chan/Zen tradition, which traces the purity of the salvific experience back through the "sixth patriarch" and Nāgārjuna to the pure source of Śākyamuni himself.

Perhaps Nāgārjuna's approach is relevant here. His deconstruction of causal relations refutes not only the self-existence of things but the other extreme of "momentariness", the view that there is no relationship at all between separate moments or manifestation-instants. If, due to the Western-influenced influence of such interpreters as D. T. Suzuki, our previous understandings of Buddhism have erred on the side of essentialism and universalism, today we seem to suffer from the opposite tendency, an emphasis on difference and particularity that frustrates the continuity necessary to understand relationship. Today it is increasingly difficult to talk about "Buddhism" in general terms, the way I am doing, and that development is not all bad. But the movement from one extreme to the other highlights the essential question of what knowledge, whether general or particular, is for. What do we seek from it? What motivates our will-to-truth? If sameness has meaning only in relation to difference, and difference only in relation to sameness – in more Buddhist terms, if continuity requires change and vice-versa – what does that imply for the present encounter of Buddhism with a psychologized West where "hang-ups" have replaced sin, and therapy the role of prayer? What is the similarity in that difference?

Consider, for example, Dōgen (1200-1253), whose *Shōbōgenzō* many consider the finest work of Japanese religious philosophy. Some recent scholarship has been emphasizing that our understanding of the *Shōbōgenzō* must be situated in its particular historical context. For example, in *Chan Insights and Oversights*, Bernard Faure focuses on its sectarian concerns, especially Dōgen's rivalry with the *Dharumashu* school. This is an important corrective to earlier readings that perceive only a dehistoricized philosophy. Yet approaches to Dōgen that stress his difference from us – easy to do, since he is almost as strange to contemporary Japanese – tend to lose sight of the fact that this difference is important to us only insofar as it mediates the *continuity* between Dōgen's fundamental concerns and ours: the problems of death and time, self and other, delusion and realization, and so forth. Why should we (as human beings, not just as scholars) be interested in him or in any other Buddhist figure unless their writings provoke something in us that is confronted by those same essential human concerns? In the final analysis, Dōgen's differences from us are important to us for the same reason his similarities are important: because they help to illuminate something about our human situation, which is different from his yet nonetheless fundamentally similar to it.

The basic life problem of our human condition, our mutual *genjō kōan*, can be framed in terms of this tension between sameness and difference, between continuity and change. On the one side, "I" experience my sense-of-self as stable and persistent, apparently immortal; on the other side is growing awareness of my impermanence, the fact that "I" am growing older and will die. This *aporeia* is essentially the same one that confronted Dōgen and Śākyamuni himself, when, as the myth has it, he ventured out of the protected palace compound to encounter an old man, an ill man, and finally a corpse. This suggests it is *the* problem that motivates the religious quest; that may be to simple, yet insofar as this problem also motivates the psychotherapeutic quest to understand ourselves and the meanings of our lives and our deaths, there is affinity between the two. Most traditional religions resolve the *aporeia* by claiming that the soul is immortal. Buddhism does the opposite, not by simply accepting our mortality in the usual sense, but by offering a path that emphasizes realizing something hitherto-unnoticed about the nature of that impermanence; and insofar as Western psychotherapeutics cope with our death fears not by denying death but by making us more aware of those fears and what they mean for our life, there is further affinity between the two. In psychological terms, both emphasize that what passes for normality (*saṃsāra*) is a low-grade of psychopathology, unnoticed only because so common; that the supposedly autonomous ego-self is conditioned in ways we are normally not aware of (karma, *saṃskāras*); and that greater awareness of our mental processes can free us (*samādhi, prajñā*).

Yet such similarities have meaning for us only in relation to their difference; for why else should we be interested in *both*? If psychotherapy today has greater insight into the dynamics of mental *duḥkha* (repression, transference, etc.), Buddhism points more directly at the root of the problem: not dread of death, finally – a fear which still keeps the feared thing at a distance by projecting it into the future

– but the more immediate and terrifying (because quite valid) suspicion each of us has that *"I" am not real right now. Anātman* thus implies a subtle yet significant distinction between fear of death and fear of the void – that is, terror of our own groundlessness, which we become aware of as a sense of *lack* and which motivates our compulsive but futile attempts to ground ourselves in one way or another, according to the opportunities for self-grounding that our particular situations provide.

The rest of this paper will explore these similarities and differences in two ways. First, we shall adumbrate them by considering what *anātman* implies for such psychoanalytic concepts as repression, the Oedipal complex, and guilt, followed by what Buddhist meditative practices imply about the resolution of these problems, about how to ground our groundlessness. Afterwards we shall look at what such an approach means for some recent postmodern and post-colonial critiques of Buddhism and Buddhist Studies, especially those presented in *The Curators of the Buddha.* Here the dynamics of *anātman* and groundlessness come home to roost: for if our *śūnyatā* – what the next section will call our *lack* – is not only a personal problem but a collective one (especially for a culture such as ours, which has become alienated from its spiritual roots), what does that imply about the Western attraction to, and perspective on, Buddhism? The problem for most postmodern and subaltern approaches, I shall argue, is that their hermeneutics have not been sensitive enough to the situation of the Western "interpreter" at the end of the second millennium. Whatever insights they yield into the history of Buddhism are compromised by their use of Western methodologies which reinscribe the problems they reveal, and which overlook the special hermeneutical possibilities that the Buddhist tradition offers.

(II)

Śākyamuni Buddha did not use psychoanalytic terms, but in trying to understand the Buddhist claim about *anātman*, the denial of self, we can benefit from the concept of repression and what Freud called the return of the repressed in symbolic form. If something (a mental wish, according to Freud) makes me uncomfortable and I do not want to cope with it consciously, I can choose to ignore or "forget" it. This allows me to concentrate on something else, yet what has been repressed tends to return to consciousness anyway. What is not consciously admitted into awareness irrupts in obsessive ways – symptoms – that affect consciousness with precisely those qualities it strives to exclude.

Existential psychologists such as Ernest Becker and Irvin Yalom argue that our primary repression is not sexual desires, as Freud believed, but the awareness that we are going to die. Does *anātman* imply a different perspective on this process?

Buddhism analyzes the sense-of-self into sets of impersonal mental and physical phenomena, whose interaction creates the illusion of self-consciousness – i.e., that consciousness is the attribute of a self. The death-repression emphasized by existential psychology transforms the Oedipal complex into what Norman O. Brown calls an Oedipal *project*: the attempt to become father of oneself, i.e., one's own origin. The child wants to conquer death by becoming the creator and sustainer of his/her own life. Buddhism shows us how to shift the emphasis: the Oedipal project is more the attempt of the developing sense-of-self to attain autonomy, to become like Descartes' supposedly self-sufficient consciousness. It is the quest to deny one's groundlessness by becoming one's own ground: the ground (socially conditioned and maintained yet nonetheless illusory) we "know" as being an independent self.

Then the Oedipal project derives from our intuition that self-consciousness is not something "self-existing" (*svabhāva*) but a mental construct. Consciousness is more like the surface of the sea: dependent on unknown depths that it cannot grasp because it is a manifestation of them. The problem arises when this conditioned consciousness wants to ground itself – i.e., to make itself *real*. If the sense-of-self "inside" is a construct, it can attempt to real-ize itself only by stabilizing itself in some fashion in the "objective" world. The ego-self is this never-ending project to objectify oneself, something consciousness can no more do than a hand can grasp itself.

The consequence of this perpetual failure is that the sense-of-self has, as its inescapable shadow, a sense-of-*lack*, which it always tries to escape. The ineluctable trace of nothingness in our being, of death in our life, is a feeling of *lack*. The return of the repressed in the distorted form of a symptom shows us how to link this basic project with the symbolic ways we try to make ourselves real in the world. We experience this deep sense of *lack* as the feeling that "there is something wrong with me,? but that feeling manifests, and we respond to it, in many different ways. In its "purer" forms *lack* appears as an ontological guilt or anxiety that gnaws on one's very core. For that reason ontological guilt wants to become guilt *for* something, because then we know how to atone for it; and anxiety is eager to objectify into fear *of* something, because we have ways to defend ourselves against particular feared things.

The problem with objectifications, however, is that no object can ever satisfy if it is not really an object that we want. When we do not understand what is actually motivating us – because what we think we want is only a symptom of something else (according to Buddhism, our desire to become real, which is essentially a spiritual yearning) – we end up compulsive. Then the neurotic's anguish and despair are not the result of his symptoms but their source; those symptoms are necessary to shield him from the tragedies that the rest of us are better at repressing: death, meaninglessness, groundlessness. "The irony of man's condition is that the deepest need is to be free of the anxiety of death and annihilation; but it is life itself which awakens it, and so we must shrink from being fully alive" (Becker: 66). If the autonomy of self-consciousness is a delusion which can never quite shake off its shadow-feeling that "something is wrong with me," it will need to rationalize that sense of inadequacy somehow.

This shifts our focus from the terror of future annihilation to the anguish of a groundless-ness experienced now. On this account, even fear of death and desire for immortality symbolize something else; they become symptomatic of our vague intuition that the ego-self is not a hard-core of consciousness but a mental construction, the axis of a web spun to hide the void. Those whose constructions are badly damaged, the mad, are uncomfortable to be with because they remind us of that fact.

In more Buddhist terms, the ego-self is delusive because, like everything else, it is a temporary manifestation arising out of the twelve factors of *pratītya-samutpāda* (which encompass everything), yet *it feels separate from that interconditionality.* The basic difficulty is that insofar as I feel separate (i.e., an autonomous, self-existing consciousness) I also feel uncomfortable, because an illusory sense of separateness is inevitably insecure of itself. It is this inescapable trace of nothingness in my "empty" (because not really self-existing) sense-of-self that is experienced as a sense-of-*lack*; in reaction, the sense-of-self becomes preoccupied with trying to make itself self-existing, in one or another symbolic fashion.

According to Otto Rank, contemporary man is neurotic because he suffers from a consciousness of sin (read *lack*) just as much as pre-modern man did, but without believing in the religious conception of sin, which leaves us without a means of expiation. In the rituals of archaic man a sense of indebtedness was balanced by the belief that the debt could be repaid; today we are oppressed by the realization that the burden of guilt is unpayable (Rank: 194). In *Civilization and its Discontents*, Freud understands a heightening sense of guilt as the price we pay for advances in human culture, but the price is so high that guilt has now become "the most important problem in the development of civilization." He traced guilt back to the biologically-transmitted memory of a prehistoric primal deed, sons banding together to kill their autocratic father. With each generation this process is internalized anew in the Oedipal complex; the same instinctive wishes recur and cannot be concealed from the superego, producing guilt.

If, however, the Oedipal *project* is the sense-of-self's attempt to become self-grounding and to end its dependence on others by becoming autonomous (i.e., self-conscious), then the guilt that arises need not be traced back to ambivalent wishes, for it has a more primordial origin in the sense of *lack* deriving from the repressed intuition of self-consciousness that it does not self-exist. Such basic "guilt" is not neurotic but ontological. It is not a consequence of something I have done, but of the fact that I "am"– sort of. Ontological guilt arises from the contradiction between this socially-conditioned sense that *I am* and the suspicion that *I am not.* Their clash is the sense-of-*lack*, which generates the *I should be* . . . The tragedy is that I "awaken" into being only to be confronted by my lack of being. Schizophrenics sometimes feel guilty just for existing because this contradiction is less repressed for them.

The prehistories of *Genesis* and Freud's primal deed mythologize the fact that this mode of awareness is not some natural way of experiencing the world but historically-conditioned. According to Erich Neumann, the full emergence of the ego abolishes the original paradisal situation; this "is experienced as guilt, and moreover as original guilt, a fall" (114). The evolution of *homo sapiens* into self-consciousness has alienated the human species from the rest of the world, which became objectified for us as we became subjects looking out at it. This original sin is passed down to every generation as the linguistically-conditioned and socially-maintained delusion that each of us is a consciousness existing separately from the world. Yet if this is a conditioning there is the possibility of a reconditioning or a deconditioning, such as Buddhism emphasizes.

Why do we need to feel guilty, and accept suffering, sickness and death as condign punishment? What role does that guilt play in determining the meaning of our lives? I am reminded of a definition offered somewhere by Nietzsche: "Original sin: a new sense has been invented for pain."[1] Even the feeling of wrongdoing gives us some sense of control over our own destinies, because an explanation has been provided for our sense of *lack*. "The ultimate problem is not guilt but the incapacity to live. The illusion of guilt is necessary for an animal that cannot enjoy life, in order to organize a life of nonenjoyment" (Brown: 270). Since nothing is more painful to endure than pure *lack*, we need to project it onto something, because only thus can we get a handle on it. If that object is found outside we react with anger, if directed inside it becomes guilt (introjected anger, according to psychoanalysis). In "Some Character Types met with in Psychoanalytic Work" (1916), Freud describes "criminals from a sense of guilt" whose guilt feelings are so powerful that committing a misdeed actually brings relief – which makes sense, if what they crave is something specific to be able to atone for. Guilt implies responsibility, which is preferable to helplessness, however uncomfortable that guilt may be.

In contrast to the Semitic religions, Buddhism does not reify the sense of *lack* into an original sin, although our problems with attachment and ignorance are similarly historically-conditioned. Śākyamuni Buddha declared that he was not interested in the metaphysical issue of origins and emphasized that he had one thing only to teach: *duḥkha* and the end of *duḥkha*, our suffering now and the path to end that suffering. This suggests that Buddhism is best understood as a way to resolve our sense of *lack*. Since there was no primeval offense and no expulsion from the Garden, our situation turns out to be paradoxical: our worst problem is the deeply-repressed fear that our groundlessness/no-thing-ness is a problem. When I stop trying to fill up that hole at my core by vindicating or real-izing myself in some symbolic way, something happens to it – and to me.

This is easy to misunderstand, for the letting-go that is necessary is not directly accessible to consciousness. The ego cannot absolve its own *lack* because the ego is the other side of that *lack*. When ontological guilt is experienced more "purely" – as the unobjectified feeling that "something is wrong with *me*" – there seems to be no way to cope with it, so normally we become conscious of it as the neurotic guilt of "not being good enough" in this or that particular way. On the Buddhist path, the guilt expended in these situations is converted back into ontological guilt, and that guilt endured without evasion; the method for doing this is simply awareness, which meditation cultivates. Letting-go of the mental devices that sustain my self-esteem, "I" become vulnerable. Such guilt, experienced in or rather as the core of one's being, cannot be resolved by the ego-self; there is nothing one can do with it except be conscious of it and bear it and let it burn itself out, like a fire that exhausts its fuel, which in this case is the sense-of-self. If we cultivate the ability to dwell as it, then ontological guilt, finding nothing else to be guilty for, consumes the sense-of-self and thereby itself too.

From a Buddhist perspective, then, our most problematic duality is not life against death but self versus non-self, or being versus non-being. As in psychotherapy, the Buddhist response to such bipolar dualisms involves recognizing the side that has been denied. If death is what the sense-of-self fears, the solution is for the sense-of-self to die. If it is no-thing-ness (i.e., the repressed intuition that, rather than being autonomous and self-existent, the "I" is a construct) I am afraid of, the best way to resolve that fear is to become nothing. Dōgen sums up this process in a well-known passage from *Genjōkōan*:

> To study the buddha way is to study the self. To study the self is to forget the self. To forget the self is to be actualized by myriad things. When actualized by myriad things, your body and mind as well as the bodies and minds of others drop away. No trace of realization remains, and this no-trace continues endlessly. (Dōgen: 70)

"Forgetting" ourselves is how we lose our sense of separation and realize that we are not other than the world. Meditation is learning how to become nothing by learning to forget the sense-of-self, which happens when I become absorbed into my meditation-exercise. If the sense-of-self is a result of self-reflection – of consciousness attempting to reflect back upon itself in order to grasp itself – such meditation practice makes sense as an exercise in *de-reflection.* Consciousness unlearns trying to grasp itself, real-ize itself, objectify itself. Enlightenment occurs when the usually-automatized reflexivity of consciousness ceases, which is experienced as a letting-go and falling into the void and being wiped out of existence. "Men are afraid to forget their minds, fearing to fall through the Void with nothing to stay their fall. They do not know that the Void is not really void, but the realm of the real Dharma" (Huang-po: 41). Then, when I no longer strive to make myself real through things, I find myself "actualized" by them, says Dōgen? This process implies that what we fear as nothingness is not really nothingness, for that is the perspective of a sense-of-self anxious about losing its grip on itself. According to Buddhism, letting-go of myself and merging with that no-thing-ness leads to something else: when consciousness stops trying to catch its own tail, I become no-thing, and discover that I am everything – or, more precisely, that I can be anything.

Is this nothingness or being? Groundlessness or groundedness? If each link of *pratītya-samutpāda* is conditioned by all the others, then to become completely groundless is also to become completely grounded, not in some particular but in the whole network of interdependent relations that constitutes the world. The supreme irony of my struggle to ground myself is that it cannot succeed because I am already grounded in that totality, because the infinite set of differential "traces" that constitutes each of us is nothing less than the whole universe itself. "The self-existence of a Buddha is the self-existence of this very cosmos. The Buddha is without a self-existent nature; the cosmos too is without a self-existent nature" (*Mūlamadhyamakakārikā* 22: 6). What Nāgārjuna says here about the Buddha is equally true for each of us and, indeed, everything; the difference is that a Buddha knows it. I am groundless and ungroundable insofar as delusively feeling myself to be separate from the world; yet I have always been fully grounded insofar as the whole world manifests in (or *as*) me. With that conflation, the no-thing at my core is transformed from sense-of-*lack* into a serenity that is imperturbable because there is nothing to be perturbed: "When neither existence nor non-existence again is presented to the mind, then, through the lack of any other possibility, that which is without support becomes tranquil" (Śāntideva).[2]

How does this solve the problem of desire, our alternation between frustration and boredom? A consciousness that seeks to ground itself by fixating on something dooms itself to perpetual dissatisfaction, for the impermanence of all things means no such perch can be found. But since it is our *lack* that compels us to seek such a perch, the end of *lack* allows a change of perspective. The solution is a different way of experiencing the problem: in Hegelian terms, the "free-ranging variable" which always has some finite determination yet is not bound to any particular one. The "bad infinite" of *lack* transforms into the "good infinite" of a variable that needs nothing. In Buddhist terms, this transforms the alienation of a reflexive sense-of-self always trying to fixate itself into the freedom of an "empty" mind that can become anything because it does not need to become something.[3]

(III)

If understanding the *duḥkha* of *anātman* as the sense-of-self's sense-of-*lack* gives us insight into our individual human condition, can it also shed light on the dynamics of societies and nations? If, as Nietzsche suggests, madness is something rare in individuals – but is the rule in groups, parties, peoples, and ages, has a group dynamic of *lack* been working itself out in history?

For all their wretched poverty and violence, medieval societies had a security that we today can scarcely imagine, for they were grounded less in a catholic church than in an organic world-view that explained everything – including our sense of *lack* and how to resolve it – and assigned its place in the great chain of being. Today we lack such a collective *lack* project and no longer understand why we feel *lack*. The unsurprising result is that, despite our wealth and comfort, our lives suffer from a *lack* of meaning that disguises itself as consumerism and a host of other addictions. Having lost our spiritual grounding in the Judeo-Christian God and the moral code He enforced, and more recently our faith in technological progress as an alternative mode of self-grounding, we experience our groundlessness as an unbearable lightness of being. The tragic dialectic between security and freedom reasserts itself: having attained some measure of *self*-determination and confronted the *lack* at its core, we now crave the grounding that would connect our own aspirations with something greater than ourselves.

I emphasize the obvious because it has obvious implications for the attraction of Buddhism to Westerners and less obvious implications for some recent critiques of Buddhist cultural history (Faure) and Buddhist studies (Lopez et al.). This final section will develop those implications as a response to *Curators of the Buddha*, in particular, not as an attempt to "refute" it (for its perspectives on the academic history of Buddhist Studies are invaluable) but with the intention of deepening its self-reflection on the source of colonialist motivations.

Curators of the Buddha is clearly inspired by Edward Said's *Orientalism*, for it attempts a similar critique by emphasizing "the importance of understanding the history of Buddhist Studies in the west under the larger categories of colonial and post-colonial cultural studies, to see the emergence of the academic study of Buddhism in Europe and America within the context of the ideologies of empire" (2–3). The problem that recurs in its essays, however, is that the motivations they expose in the history of Buddhist Studies do not quite fit into such a post-colonialist model, for the Western fascination with Buddhism is more complex; in fact, it is not too strong to say that most of the essays end up subverting such a straightforward subaltern approach. The most important contribution of the book is less its application of Foucault's and Said's insights to our understanding of Buddhism, than the contrast it unwittingly reveals between how the West has understood Islam and how the West has understood Buddhism – or, more precisely, the different ways it has misunderstood them both. If the syndrome Said described is Orientalism, the Western reception of Buddhism is better characterized as counter- or reverse-Orientalism.

Western Orientalism was also somewhat ambivalent, so the difference is a matter of degree; but the difference is considerable. If reverse-Orientalism remains a type of Orientalism, it is a different type that requires deeper sensitivity to the complicated and contradictory motivations of its Western interpreters. Especially with regard to Buddhism, the issue of Orientalism/reverse-Orientalism needs to be raised within the context of the West's problematic relationship with its own religious roots: the Renaissance and Reformation challenges to them, the Enlightenment attempt to dispense with them, and the return of that repressed desire for spiritual grounding in various ways, including its projection onto exotic foreign cultures. If religion is how we cope with our *lack*, a civilization that turns its back on religion will need to discover or create other ways to cope with that *lack*. God could die in the eighteenth and nineteenth centuries because there was an alternative myth: the dream of technological and social progress. For those suspicious of such attempts at self-grounding, or still feeling the need for religious supplement, Buddhism offered much that was attractive. If Buddhism has constituted what Robert Young calls "a form of dislocation for the West" (Lopez: 20), it is because the West was already dislocated; Buddhism provided the exotic alterity for that projection, the possibility of a spiritual salvation from the East. As the essays in the Lopez volume make clear, whatever intellectual *hubris* was involved in colonizing and civilizing the Theravāda cultures of South Asia was largely offset by a compulsive need to extract an alternative spiritual grounding from them.

Consider, for example, the West's colonization of Asian *history*, in which "the past of this Orient is regarded with nostalgia, the present with contempt", by inventing an "authentic Buddhism" – a Victorian religion of reason – which is attributed to a "classical age" that is then contrasted with its degeneration into, e.g., modern Tibetan Buddhism. Since Europe created such a Buddhism, it could also control it, making it the standard by which to judge all contemporary instantiations of that Buddhism as lacking (Lopez: 252, 7). To quote Robert Young again, "Those who evoke the 'nativist' position through a nostalgia for a lost or repressed culture idealize the possibility of that lost origin being recoverable from its former plenitude without allowing the fact that the figure of the lost origin, the 'other' that the colonizer has repressed, has itself been constructed in terms of the colonizer's own self-image" (Lopez: 282). Yet we need to ask why we constructed that figure and what we hope to gain from it. Emphasizing the *lack* that motivated this invention provides a more nuanced perspective. To see the present as a corruption of the past may be used to justify the "civilizing process" of colonialism but it is also one response to a religious projection that senses that Buddhism as presently "instantiated" cannot save us, that it no longer seems to provide what is needed to solve our spiritual problem. The search for "pure origins" was determined as much by unconscious spiritual need as by desire for control.

The fragmentation of Christendom eventually led to disillusionment with religious institutions as sources of grounding, and that eventually led, more recently, to the theological search to recover "pure", i.e., original Christianity. It is one way of responding to the realization that modern European "instantiations" of Christianity too no longer offer a convincing way to overcome *lack*: if such institutions do not correspond to our image of the founder and his community, the tradition must have deteriorated. The problem is that every such attempt to rediscover the "pure essence" only succeeds in producing new and original versions incommensurable with the preceding ones. Such nostalgia for a pristine classical period has a long tradition in Europe – only in the last few centuries has it been superseded by belief in progress – but such an attitude was not limited to the Christian West: East Asian belief in *mappō*, the gradual decline of the Dharma, comes to mind, and "Theravada Buddhists themselves subscribed, at least at times, to a similar 'metaphysics of origin'" (Charles Hallisey, in Lopez: 43). Rather than ascribe this tendency simply to colonialism, we need to ask what makes a "metaphysics of (pure) origins" attractive in the first place. If the present reality cannot ground us, maybe the lost origin could, if only we can return to its former plenitude (which, we have been led to believe, suffered from no *lack*).

The Buddhist myth of pure origin and plenitude is found most purely in its central metaphor of transmission, the belief that there is a Dharma that has been passed down over the centuries, from teacher to student, from culture to culture, and from one language to another language, without its "essence" being lost or distorted. In his concluding essay, "Foreigner at the Lama's Feet," Lopez describes his struggle to negotiate between two very different models of such transmitted authority, the oral teachings of his lama and the classical written texts privileged by Buddhology. He gives a moving account of his realization that his work on a Tibetan text involved participating "in the Buddhist myth of the essential presence of the [self-identical] dharma to be translated and transmitted," while at the same time claiming a special hermeneutical perspective from which to observe the text, "not on the surface of the timeless and hence ahistorical present I imagined my teacher to inhabit, but with an X-ray vision that allowed me to see into the depths of its history, even to its origin, most hidden yet most fundamental, giving myself over to one authority while claiming another, all the while remaining blind to the practices of domination of which I was both agent and object.. In that way he sought to gain the traditional authority of the lama's words while simultaneously controlling the production of the text. But, quoting de Certeau, "this discourse, in writing the Fable that authorizes it, alters it" (Lopez: 282, 285).

From my own Buddhist perspective, which emphasizes the possibility of our non-duality with situations, Lopez's perceptive account of his hermeneutical situation is also striking because it lacks any "fusion of horizons" between himself and the lama or the text they work on together – either before or after his realization. The result is that Lopez's commentary on what happened between him and his lama reinscribes the dilemma he analyzes. The lama's commentary on the text implied the unspoken claim that he knew the intention of the original speaker, the Buddha; Lopez knows better, that all such attempted "participation in origins" fails because commentaries always change the meanings they purport to uncover. His account is still "colonial" in the sense that *now* he – but still not the benighted lama – understands what was really happening in their encounter. Contrast this with the type of dialogue Todorov speaks of, "in which no one has the last word" and where "neither voice is reduced to the status of a simple object" (Dallmayr: 32). Lopez's later perspective does not approach this ideal any better than his original understanding did; the movement from one to the other merely reproduces his superior understanding of the situation. But how is it possible for scholars today, with their toolbox of sophisticated hermeneutical techniques, not to do that? A problem especially pertinent for someone offering a psychotherapeutic interpretation of Buddhism that, one might retort, purports to explain *duḥkha* better than Śākyamuni did.

The basic problem, for all of us, is the impossibility of escaping the hermeneutic circle. Whether or not we ever escape Orientalism, the solution is not to be found in an attempted "objective" understanding of Buddhism that transcends our particular historical situatedness or our general human condition. There is no such Archimedean point from which to study Buddhism. Such objectivity cannot be attained and would be meaningless to us if it could be. The answer is not an escape from our prejudices but greater awareness of them – in this case, of the craving for spiritual grounding that has motivated so much of the Western interest in Buddhism. Even as the search for a "true" Buddhism prior to our interpretation is a false chimera, so is the search for "true" knowledge untainted by our *pre-judice* – by the pre-judgment motivating our quest for that particular knowledge. What is necessary is to clarify the interpretive strategies we bring with us and look through, which we may hope will enable us to minimize negative filters such as Orientalism. A critique of colonialist approaches will never uncover a true, i.e. objective Buddhism waiting for us behind them. We cannot avoid bringing our own presuppositions to our encounter with Buddhism, and in particular we cannot escape the problem of the West's spiritual confusion – its groundlessness – at the end of the second millennium. In that sense the teachings of Buddhism *must* be ahistoricized and universalized, so that we may learn from them whatever can speak to our human situation today, individually and collectively. We are compelled by our need to appropriate what Buddhism (and "the East") can offer us, and the real issue is whether that appropriation will be done consciously and respectfully in dialogue with the other, or unconsciously in projection and transference.

What does this imply about the way to conduct this search for understanding across cultures? It is one thing to notice how Lopez (like most of us) reinscribes the hermeneutical dilemma he describes, another to figure out how to escape it. Although it addresses Hinduism rather than Buddhism, I think Fred Dallmayr's *Beyond Orientalism* points in the right direction. Himself a Heidegger scholar, Dallmayr quotes the Indian philosopher J. L. Mehta, on the Heidegger-like claim that what is needed is "a renunciation of the voluntaristic metaphysics of the will to interpret the other, a willingness to let the other be, only inviting him to engage in the exciting and creative task of reappropriation that lies ahead, for him and in respect to his own tradition" (xxiii). Derrida also refers to a necessary turn from purposive-teleological striving to a kind of reciprocal happening or disclosure (57), presumably of the sort in which no voice is reduced to an object and no one has the last word. Dallmayr himself speaks of "a willingness to enter the border zones or interstices between self and other, thus placing oneself before the open 'court' of dialogue and mutual questioning." Such exegesis needs "to steer a middle course between understanding and nonunderstanding, by offering a careful account which yet leaves blank spaces intact. . . . [T]he point is not to render transparent what is (and must remain) concealed, but rather to comprehend and respect the complex interlacing of transparency and nontransparency in poetic [and presumably religious] texts" (47, 44).

Lopez could respond, quite rightly, that he was not in a position to engage in this kind of dialogue with his respected Geshe; his role was to receive the oral and textual transmissions and preserve them in a different language and culture. What I think Dallmayr's very apposite reflections imply, then, is a challenging distinction between the type of dialogue he recommends and religious conversion. His argument raises questions about what it means for us Westerners to become Buddhists if that forecloses the sort of dialogical encounter which is able to leave blank spaces intact in the open court of mutual questioning. We cannot dwell comfortably in such spaces and questioning if there is strong need to grasp a salvific truth – that is, if my sense-of-*lack* needs the security that comes from embracing a foreign religion and affirming its exotic spiritual claims. Needless to say, however, there is more to Buddhism than that.

This brings us to a final irony of academic Buddhism. Despite the fact that Buddhist Studies scholars are often practitioners as well, the implications of this practice for their scholarship have been largely ignored. For example, although Faure's *Chan Insights and Oversights* is a painstakingly detailed attempt to apply postmodern approaches to Chan thought, his study provides another oversight of its own by overlooking the most important and obvious contribution that Chan/Zen makes to the hermeneutical process: meditation itself (*zazen*, etc.). A *Buddhist* hermeneutics includes a trilateral interplay among practice (*samādhi*), insight (*prajñā*), and text (*sūtra*, etc.). Perhaps the usual emphasis on enlightenment being a non-conceptual experience distracts us from identifying samadhi and prajna as parts of the hermeneutic process. The ambiguity of the term *dharma* – both "teaching" and "reality" – reminds us that in Buddhism the quest for textual understanding cannot be separated from the larger quest to understand the world and how we dwell "in" it. Those of us who practice should know better than to make that mistake.

NOTES

1 Also: "'Sin' . . . constituted the greatest event in the entire history of the sick soul, the most dangerous sleight-of-hand of the religious interpretation" (Nietzsche: 277).

2 *Bodhicaryāvatāra* 9: 35. Cf. *Mūlamadhyamakakārikā* 7: 16: "Any thing which exists by virtue of relational origination is quiescence itself."

3 The comparison adumbrated in this section is developed more fully in Loy 1996.

REFERENCES

Becker, Ernest (1973). *The Denial of Death*. New York: Free Press.

Brown, Norman O. (1961). *Life Against Death*. New York: Vintage.

Dallmayr, Fred (1997). *Beyond Orientalism*. Albany: State University of New York Press.

Dōgen (1985). *Moon in a Dewdrop: Writings of Zen Master Dōgen*. Ed. K.

Tanahashi. San Francisco: North Point Press.
Faure, Bernard (1993). *Zen Insights and Oversights.* Princeton: Princeton University Press.
Huang Po (1958). *The Zen Teaching of Huang Po.* Ed. John Blofeld. London: Buddhist Society.
Lopez, Donald, ed. (1995). *Curators of the Buddha.* Chicago: University of Chicago Press.
Loy, David (1996). *Lack and Transcendence.* Atlantic Highlands, NJ: Humanities Press.
Neumann, Erich (1973). *The Origins and History of Consciousness.* Princeton: Princeton University Press.
Nietzsche, Friedrich (1956). *The Birth of Tragedy and The Genealogy of Morals.* Tr. F. Golffing. New York: Doubleday Anchor.
Rank, Otto (1958). *Beyond Psychology.* New York: Dover.

Nine

Critical Synergy: The Context of Inquiry and the Project of Buddhist Thought

Mark T. Unno

"In the realm of possibility, anything is possible."
Soren Kierkegaard (a.k.a. Anti-Climacus)

INTRODUCTION

In the preface to this volume Roger Jackson and John Makransky enunciate the need for Buddhist theology as a two-way venture: first, critical reflection on normative Buddhist self-understanding in light of non-Buddhist discourse, and second, critical reflection on the contemporary world from within a perspective grounded in Buddhist tradition. While I find myself somewhat uncomfortable with the term "Buddhist theology" because of the various connotations of theology and would rather speak of Buddhist thought,[1] the former nonetheless seems appropriate in helping to frame certain questions and issues that are timely, both in ways that Buddhist thinkers might become self-critically constructive in the academy and that might stimulate critical reflection within the non-Buddhist academy. Specifically, the idea of a Buddhist theology suggests significant parallels with Christian theology which (despite the presence of other theologies) has been largely responsible for shaping the contours of normative religious discourse in interaction with other disciplines within the academy, particularly in the North American context.[2] Buddhist thinkers such as Anne Klein and Kenneth Kraft have just begun to offer responses to the same critical challenges posed by feminist and environmental thinkers that Christian theologians have been considering for some time (Klein; Kraft). They, as well as contributors to the present volume, may be regarded as pioneers in the field of Buddhist theology as defined by the editors.

Examining the context of inquiry will help to illuminate the possibilities and limits of this emerging discourse. If we outline selected moments in the historical context of Christian theology, then key ideas and problems can be brought into relief, and a trajectory can be traced that involves theology and religious studies, one that moves from apologetic defense of the faith to a recognition of radical religious diversity. On the Buddhist side, I focus my discussion on selected ideas from two thirteenth-century Japanese thinkers, the Kegon and Shingon monk Myōe Kōben (1173-1232) and the well-known Zen figure Dōgen Kigen (1200-1253); specifically, I examine three key issues: the relation between the discursive intellect and nondual awakening, the issue of single versus plural practices, and the problem of karmic evil. Bringing together the problematics of Christian theology and the Buddhist understandings of such figures as Myōe and Dōgen, the present essay offers not so much a Buddhist theology of its own (something that would be too ambitious for the scope of this essay as well as the author at this stage in his reflections) but considerations and perspectives for the possibilities of Buddhist thought illuminated by the relevant concerns of academic discourse.

More concretely, I suggest that the Buddhist thinker, faced with the challenges of a radically diverse world of religious understanding, may fruitfully reflect on the place of discursive logic in Buddhism to formulate conceptions of practice within an awareness of karmic limitations. Such an interplay between Buddhist thought and the wider world of intellectual inquiry holds the promise of a critical synergy, in which the encounter between normative Buddhist understanding and the larger universe of ideas and experiences is seen as a moment of creative potentiality.

CHRISTIAN THEOLOGY AND RELIGIOUS STUDIES

As much as theologians and scholars of religious studies set themselves apart from one another, the work of the latter is very much an outgrowth of the former, and a historical trajectory can be traced to illustrate this fact. Sumner Twiss provides a helpful outline of this trajectory in his essay, "Shaping the Curriculum: The Emergence of Religious Studies," in which he identifies four major phases, adapting categories introduced by other scholars, most notably Frank Reynolds: Early Modern Theological (roughly 1800-1900), Transitional Ethnocentric (roughly 1900-1950), Late Modern Critical-Scientific (roughly 1950-1975), and Postmodern Hermeneutical (roughly 1975-1997) (Twiss: 29–38). Without going into any detail, one can see just by examining these rubrics that there has been a movement away from the apologetic, theological agenda of early work in the study of religion towards the critical awareness of postmodern diversity. Twiss's identification of these four phases reflects his own postmodern hermeneutical disposition:

> . . . this context involves the vivid and self-conscious awareness of pluralization within American society–as represented, for example, by the increasing size and "voice" of minority groups–and a vivid and self-conscious awareness of an interdependent global world order–as reflected, for example, in global concerns about the natural environment, the legacy of the nuclear arms race, the extent of starvation and suffering throughout the world (Twiss: 35).

Furthermore, this awareness has been accompanied by the displacement of "the Enlightenment myth of monolithic objective reason" by a "rather more humble sense of the reaches of context-dependent rationality and the historical and social location of all human endeavors." This does not mean that theology in the classical, apologetic sense has disappeared altogether, not by any means. However, it does signal the widespread recognition that constructive religious thought must be responsive to the complex challenges of a multicultural world. On the one hand, this awareness of postmodern diversity and context-dependent rationality is precisely what is making possible the emergence of Buddhist thought as a viable contributor to the normative discourse on religion in the West. On the other, this same awareness also tends to relativize Buddhist thought as just one form of rationality among others with its own historical and social limitations.[3] The fundamental challenge faced by the would-be Buddhist theologian is: How can one be responsive to the great diversity of human life, religious or otherwise, without losing the normative force of his or her own Buddhism? Is there a way of becoming truly responsive in a manner that expands the horizons of Buddhist theology rather than rendering it ineffectual and self-enclosed? In important ways, answers have already begun to appear in the affirmative. Not only are there scholars such as Klein and Kraft who identify themselves with particular strains of Buddhist thought, but there are institutional Buddhist figures who have begun to engage in sophisticated interaction with the larger intellectual world, such as the Dalai Lama and the Vietnamese Buddhist monk Thich Nhat Hanh. Yet, it is far from clear to what extent the work of these figures will lead to the articulation of a comprehensive Buddhist theology as envisioned by Jackson and Makransky. We turn to an examination of selected moments in the historical development of Christian theology in order to understand more fully the possibilities and potential roadblocks that lie ahead for Buddhist thinkers.[4]

THE GREAT HOPE OF WESTERN REASON

Despite what Twiss describes as a situation of "context-dependent rationality and the [relative] historical and social location of all human endeavors," David Tracy states that theologians "can continue to give ourselves over to the great hope of Western reason" (Tracy: 113).

> But that hope is now a more modest one as a result of the discovery of the plurality of both language and knowledge and the ambiguities of all histories, *including the history of reason itself*. . . (emphasis in italics mine). (Tracy: 113)

> That hope is this: that all those involved in interpreting our situation and all those aware of our need for solidarity may continue to risk interpreting all the classics of all the traditions.[5] And in that effort to interpret lies both resistance [against ignorance and the evils of the world] and hope [for true understanding and a harmonious world] (Tracy: 114).

Because he is a Christian theologian, Tracy's hope for reason is, of course, undergirded by faith, a faith in his Christianity as, paradigmatically, articulated by the gospels. Thus, his great hope lies in reason and faith, but faced with the radical diversity of postmodernity, it is to reason that he turns as the means of negotiating the complexity of his world, as the bridge between faith and the world at large, and this in spite of the fact that he sees the history of this reason as itself but one among many histories fraught with ambiguity. It is a hope shared by other Christian and Christian-oriented thinkers, such as Alasdair MacIntyre, Charles Taylor, and Jeffrey Stout, all of whom despite their recognition of essentially the same plight of reason in postmodernity seek to affirm this reason as the means of establishing and articulating the basis of a viable Christian self-understanding in a diverse universe of understandings.

This exercise of reason now taking placing in the setting of the secular, liberal, democratic university with its ideal of public, equal access to objective bodies of knowledge, however, is rooted in the classical European education of medieval Christian academies where the hierarchical mentor-disciple relationship and personal charisma lay at the heart of the transmission of knowledge. In such a setting where we might find an Anselm articulating his proof for the existence of God, reason was not so much an independent faculty that might challenge faith but more an embellishment to the latter, a means to glorify what was taken to be axiomatic. Theology as the queen of the sciences was rooted in a seemingly secure faith, and thus grounded, the function of theology was not to answer the challenges of the various sciences but grant them validity through a reason which served as its handmaiden.

Likewise in the case of Buddhism, monasteries have served largely as centers of education where various disciplines from psychology to medicine developed under the umbrella of a Buddhist world view. Just as the Buddha is said to have told his disciples that enlightenment is logically coherent but that reason could not by itself grasp enlightenment, for much of Asian Buddhism religious knowledge, the truth about Reality, was thought to be elucidated in *bodhi,* the highest and ultimate source of knowledge transmitted and confirmed through the master-disciple relationship. From the austere setting of the early Indian monastic communities to the large and complex monasteries of pre-modern Japan, these key elements in the nature and function of religious knowledge remained in place. Even today, if one goes to Dharamsala or Kyoto, one will find the basic structure of the master-disciple lineage and the personal transmission of religious knowledge remarkably unchanged from centuries past, at least as the form of orthopraxy. The discursive intellect may be used to interpret how *bodhi* is to be attained, but the soteriological reality of *bodhi* is never called into question.

In the West, however, a different history evolved alongside this classical mentor-disciple model which one still finds in seminaries and divinity schools.[6] As Walter Capps explicates in his narrative history of religious studies, the Cartesian turn in Western religious thinking opened the door to reason as a systematic faculty of doubt, a doubt that at least in principle could call into question the very existence of God (Capps: 2–5).

The emergence of reason as an autonomous factor has turned out to be a double-edged sword that has sustained theology and the study of religion ever since. Descartes systematically introduced doubt in order to confirm belief, but critical questioning and faith have become more and more equal partners in the articulation of religious self-understanding. Thinkers coming from different perspectives, such as Charles Taylor, whose *Ethics of Authenticity* is informed by a kind of Thomistic method, Carolyn Merchant, who examines the *Death of Nature* as a feminist thinker, and Nishitani Keiji who in *Religion and Nothingness* treats Western philosophical and theological problems in light of Buddhist (especially Zen) concepts have, even while acknowledging Descartes' insights, tended to emphasize the limitations and negative effects of Cartesian disengaged, disembodied reason. These limitations notwithstanding, it is questionable, as Capps suggests, whether the kind of open, critical inquiry that takes place in today's multicultural academy would have been possible without the autonomous reason inaugurated by Descartes, a kind of reason that generally has not existed in the history of Buddhist Asia before the nineteenth century.

If Descartes and his contemporaries opened the door to critical inquiry as we know it today, Kant formalized the structure of reason and sought to complete the separation of reason from direct knowledge of its objects, including God. Taylor goes so far as to suggest that, ever since Kant, it has been impossible to know a thing directly (Taylor: 377). The universalizability of theoretical paradigms, at least in principle; critically distanced yet morally and humanistically relevant examination of texts; the rational evaluation of diverse positions–all of which lie at the heart of modernism and the idea of the modern, secular university–would not have been possible without the articulation of an autonomous reason such as we find in Kant. This formalization of reason by Kant the philosopher, moreover, was effected in the service of establishing the rational grounds of belief for Kant the theologian; the autonomy of reason became coterminous with the autonomy of faith. And it may have been with a kind of controlled Kantian passion that many scholars of Buddhist studies have raised questions about various matters, including textual authenticity, historical factuality, the role of state in religious institutions, and the status of religious lineages that have usually not been asked about by Buddhists to the degree and breadth found in the Western academy. These scholars have often done so because they were moved to clarify the normative significance of Buddhist discourse, but as the editors of this volume note, these scholarly endeavors have not for the most part led to the kind of constructive, "theological" creativity that has been perceived to be taking place within the Christian context.[7]

POSTMODERN OBJECTIVITY

From a postmodern perspective, however, Kant's practical (ethico-religious) reason has not turned out to be any more universal or truly critical than the Newtonian physics which provided the model for the formalization of his theoretical reason. Instead, the very notion of a unified, systematic objectivity and the possibility of a universally coherent faith have been called into question. Yet, this has not led to the demise of objectivity. In the case of quantum mechanics and Heisenberg's Uncertainty Principle, the idea of the total, static objectivity of the outside observer was displaced by an understanding of a contingent objectivity inseparable from the act of observation, and this was effected by taking the objective scientific method beyond its previous limits. Just as the notion of detached objectivity has been called into question objectively in quantum physics, objectivity in the humanities and social sciences has also been deconstructed and problematized through discursive analyses. Catherine Bell's study of *Ritual Theory, Ritual Practice* and Pierre Bourdieu's critique of sociological objectivity in *The Logic of Practice*, to name just two instances, both appeal to objectivity and discursive self-reflexivity as criteria for establishing the truth.

Bourdieu's own account of the way in which he began to seek out sociological objectivity is telling on this account. Disturbed by what he saw as ethnocentrism in the scholarship on Algerian society as he himself began his researches on Algiers, he came to the realization that (he as) the sociologist could not ignore his own subjectivity if he were to attain to a satisfactory degree of sociological objectivity: "In the social sciences, the progress of knowledge presupposes progress in our knowledge of the conditions of knowledge. That is why it requires one to return persistently to the same objects; . . . each doubling-back is another opportunity to objectify more completely one's objective and subjective relation to the object" (Bourdieu: 1).

Scholars such as Bourdieu and Bell do not deny the inevitable influence of their own subjective biases. Indeed, they analyze their own and others' subjectivities as part of a larger objectivity in an analytical, objectified mode of reflection. Insofar as they find the subjective significance of their work elucidated through an appeal to objective, discursive methods, they are the postmodern heirs to Kant's critical method. Without this objectivity which relativizes all subjectivity, the radical recognition of diversity which has emerged in the postmodern context probably would not have been possible.

POSTMODERNITY: THE RELIGIOUS RESPONSE

Much of postmodern discourse in the humanities has taken Western thought, specifically so-called male-dominated Protestant Christianity, to task for the hegemonic suppression of other voices which would include Buddhism. Thus, in the postmodern, multicultural West, the Christian theologian often finds himself besieged for his patriarchal, colonialist hegemony, in ideology as well as in practice. Buddhist thinkers have begun to exploit this postmodern refrain as an opportunity to introduce Buddhist thought as a normative alternative.

One such thinker who, although working largely within a modernist narrative, identified himself as a postmodernist alternative to Western philosophical and theological paradigms, was the Zen thinker Hisamatsu Shin'ichi. Yet, as a number of scholars have begun to suggest, Hisamatsu and other Japanese Buddhist philosophers and theologians may have been naive or blind to the ways in which they themselves co-opted a kind of Enlightenment belief in linear progress from the West with the consequence that their thought bears hegemonic undertones and ramifications (Ketalaar; Maraldo and Heisig). Hisamatsu's postmodern consciousness differs in this sense from that of Twiss and Tracy mentioned earlier. For Hisamatsu, Zen Buddhism potentially succeeded Western theology and philosophy with their modernist shortcomings; the decline of the latter signaled the ascent of the former.

More recently, the likes of C. W. Huntington, Jr., in *The Emptiness of Emptiness* and David Loy in *Nonduality* have directed significant attention to potential resonances between Buddhist thought and post-structuralists such as Derrida. They are clearly more aware than Hisamatsu of the difficulties involved in a direct hierarchical articulation of a normative Buddhist position in relation to Western thinkers such as Wittgenstein, Heidegger and Derrida. Although it remains to be seen whether they will provide cogent Buddhist responses to post-structural critiques involving issues of, for example, Buddhist notions of history and gender, their treatment of Western thought is more thorough and informed than that of earlier generations.[8] On the one hand, they are less concerned with critiques of Western thought than some earlier Buddhist thinkers and more focused on identifying fruitful resonances. On the other, the normative evaluations they offer are often more critically informed and balanced than that of their predecessors. Without going into a detailed discussion of the specific strengths and potential weaknesses of their work, however, more general questions pose themselves: What are the ramifications of their projects in Buddhist thought, both theoretically and practically? Are they ultimately aiming for a synthesis of Buddhist and Western thought, and if so, what kinds of practices will lead to the realization of this synthesis? Is their work to be understood in a more comparative light,[9] and if so, what are the normative implications of their comparisons?

The answers to these questions have an especially important bearing on ethical life, both at the levels of individual and social practices. If Buddhist thought does not at least potentially prescribe a set of personal and social practices, then what are the practical fruits of their normative reflections? If they do circumscribe a set of appropriate practices, then does this mean that eventually all people would ideally follow such practices?

It is in the realm of practice, of individual and social ethical life, that the concrete ramifications of any potential Buddhist theology come to light, an arena that is just beginning to be investigated by scholars–with the work of individual Buddhists such as the Dalai Lama and Thich Nhat Hanh as well as collaborative enterprises such as the electronic *Journal of Buddhist Ethics.*[10] The need to examine the practice of Buddhism has increasingly become clear, both in relation to Asian institutions and Western Buddhist communities as their form and function continue to undergo various challenges and changes. The focus of the present discussion, however, is restricted to one main problematic, the complex intersection between Buddhist thought and practice in a religiously diverse world.

As encounters between different religions turn out to be increasingly real and not merely notional, as Bernard Williams would say (160-161), the normative claims of Buddhists and other religionists must face their real tests in the realm of practice. As this has already been a question of central importance for a number of Christian and Christian-oriented thinkers, it may be helpful to consider some of their more prominent responses, on this occasion three cases of religious virtue theorists:[11] Alasdair MacIntyre, Charles Taylor, and Jeffrey Stout.

Alasdair MacIntyre

In *After Virtue,* Alasdair MacIntyre describes a world of diverse practices where the true knowledge of ethics has been lost. He uses the metaphor of a society bereft of scientific knowledge in which individuals and small groups attempt to piece together the lost body of theories and data. His fundamental presupposition is that there is a single, universally applicable ethics, albeit with a certain degree of openness, one based in Aristotelian and Thomistic virtue theory, which can and once did provide the sufficient basis for individual and communal life. The present diversity of practices is a result of confusion and loss, and the proper course of action lies in preserving pockets of sanity and waiting for the present "dark ages" to pass so that the truth can once again re-emerge:

What matters in this stage is the construction of local forms of

> community within which civility and the intellectual and moral life can be sustained through the new dark ages that are already upon us. And if the tradition of the virtues was able to survive the horrors of the last dark ages, we are not entirely without grounds for hope. (MacIntyre: 261)

On the one hand, MacIntyre tells us that viable practices do not exist outside of established traditions, that the lives of individual communities and persons are inevitably shaped by tradition. Furthermore, he argues that the traditions of each community are largely unintelligible from an etic perspective; this logic is designed to provide a measure of protection against reductionistic understanding of the Other. On the other hand, he looks to a single, specific tradition as being the only real hope for humanity. Recognizing the current situation of radical diversity, he resorts to a strategy of conservative seclusion in order to preserve the universality and integrity of his own inner normative self-understanding. In this strategy of seclusion or conservation, however, MacIntyre's Aristotelian/Thomists find themselves isolated and claiming universality for their positions without being able to engage other traditions and practices in a truly meaningful way; here, the recognition of diverse practices leads not to a creative, constructive theology but to a more conservative, apologetic understanding.[12]

Charles Taylor

Similarly faced with the diversity of religious perspectives and philosophical views, Charles Taylor recognizes many of the same issues as MacIntyre as being key to the resolution of postmodern religious and ethical life, including the problem of moral intelligibility and the role of religious virtues at the intersection of individual and social life. Unlike MacIntyre, Taylor makes his own normative Thomistic position less explicit and leaves more room for dialogue and interaction with other positions, at least in principle. In order to do this, Taylor takes a multi-faceted approach of which three aspects are of particular interest here:

(1) In *Sources of the Self,* he provides a narrative history of the modern and postmodern Western conception of the self. In doing so, he brings to light what he sees as the various dimensions of selfhood within the historical and cultural context of the West.[13] This account suggests the necessary parameters for full selfhood without explicitly prescribing them, such as critical reasoning, the life of the emotions,

the relationship to nature, and so on.

(2) In *The Ethics of Authenticity,* he delineates what he sees as the predominant contemporary notion of ethical selfhood and its various potentials and shortcomings. Here again, he suggests but does not prescribe the postmodern contours of the Western self. Unlike MacIntyre, he does not see a return to a golden age and even recognizes the creative potentiality of the uniquely individual postmodern self, but he does raise serious questions about the ethical condition of a self that recognizes no higher truth or reality beyond itself.

(3) In a series of essays in *Human Agency And Language,* Taylor defines the formal logic behind his conception of selfhood, based on the ultimate existence of hypergood (in opposition to all evil) as the source of religious and moral life and the principle of articulacy as the measure of any viable religious or philosophical world view. That is to say, all comprehensive systems of thought carry assumptions about the moral life that can be made discursively explicit; once these assumptions are brought to light, they can and should be measured against that which is ultimately or hyper-good.

This discursive method of establishing the highest good lies at the heart of Taylor's conceptions of religious selfhood, and the various historical narratives and cultural analyses he offers in such works as *Sources of the Self* and *The Ethics of Authenticity* are designed to bring to light the practical virtues of the self that conforms to this good. Herein also lies the basis of comparing one view of the self and its attendant world with that of another and thereby establishing the strengths and weaknesses of any particular conception.

Jeffrey Stout

In *Ethics after Babel* Jeffrey Stout, like MacIntyre and Taylor, seeks to establish the practice of virtues as the basis of the religious and moral life. Unlike them, he sees the possibility of a shared social ethic that does not exclude a diversity of personal virtues. Individual persons and communities can bring disparate sets of virtues and understandings to the larger whole and yet successfully contribute to the *telos* of a common overall good.

> We can make good use of Aristotelian and civic republican talk about the virtues and politics as a social practice directed towards the common good without supposing that this sort of moral language requires us to jettison talk of rights and

> tolerance. We can use this talk by thinking of liberal political institutions as oriented towards a provisional *telos*–a widely shared but self-limiting consensus on the highest good . . . . But this telos justifies a kind of tolerance foreign to the classical teleological tradition. And it rightly directs our moral attention to something our ancestors often neglected, namely, the injustice of excluding people from social practices because of their race, gender, religion, or place of birth. (Stout: 292)

There is an Augustinian turn in Stout's thinking that shows itself in his simultaneous awareness of the continual potential for corruption in human beings and of the human potential for self-cultivation. In this sense, there is more possibility in his logic to doubt the consistency of his own rationality than in the case of either MacIntyre or Taylor. In fact, Stout sees the practical life of *homo religiosus* as one of experimentation and adaptation, an organic process in which continual adjustments contribute to the realization of a potentially harmonious whole:

> Our task, like Thomas Aquinas's, Thomas Jefferson's, or Martin Luther King's, is to take the many parts of a complicated social and conceptual inheritance and stitch them together into a pattern that meets the needs of the moment. It has never been otherwise. The creative intellectual task of every generation, in other words, involves moral *bricolage* (Stout: 292)

MacIntyre's response to the problem of religious and moral diversity in *After Virtue* might be characterized as one of conservative retreat, that of Taylor as one of progressive reform based on the hierarchical articulation of moral and religious goods, and that of Stout as a constructive bricolage. All three responses offer important suggestions for the Buddhist theologian who must weigh the practical ramifications of any constructive project of thought in a tradition where theologizing and philosophizing have so often been inseparable from questions of practice.

MacIntyre's strategy of conservative retreat would be applicable to normative systems of Buddhist thought that prescribe a tightly bound set of pre-established practices that are seen to be threatened by a confused, diverse world of practices. One example of this might involve a someone who sees an established set of precepts, such as the list of 250 precepts for monks and 348 precepts for nuns as the ideal mold for realizing the four noble truths, the eight-fold noble path, and so on. Like MacIntyre, such a thinker faces the challenge of placing his or her faith in the idea that, sometime in the future, the golden age of the Dharma will return to prevail over the world and the theoretical difficulty of justifying the ways in which such a position is and is not intelligible to others.

Taylor's stance of progressive reform based on the hierarchical articulation of moral and religious goods offers interesting parallels with East Asian Buddhism's *p'an-chiao,* or hermeneutical systems of hierarchical classification. Like Taylor's *Sources of the Self,* each school's system of classification acknowledges insights offered by other schools within a narrative history of Buddhist thought. As in *The Ethics of Authenticity,* there is usually an analysis of the contemporary situation. A Buddhist counterpart to Taylor's philosophical method of hierarchical articulacy, such as T'ien-t'ai Chih-i's manner of establishing *chung,* the middle, provides the logical thread running through the various accounts and the means for determining the highest truth. Any Buddhist theology that draws on these East Asian hierarchies would involve a marriage of East Asian and Western narratives and a combined analysis of contemporary religious concerns. Out of this meeting of histories might emerge a new synthesis, one that integrates various Asian, Western, feminist, and queer histories, among others.

Stout's constructive bricolage entails a recognition that any thought-construction is provisional and created to meet the needs of the moment. In this sense there is a similarity with the Buddhist notion of *upāya* or skillful means. Both Stout's bricolage and Buddhist *upāya* appeal to a higher truth whose expressions vary according to the moral, socio-political, and cultural needs of the present. Furthermore, like East Asian *p'an-chiao*, this does not negate a teleological narrative; it does, however, require an acknowledgment of the limits of each theological enterprise even within its own situation. Theology in this view needs to be flexible enough to delimit its own relative position among other theological perspectives, and yet to offer a comprehensive view of the self and world in relation to ultimate reality, to be both particular and universal, not just in theory but as living thought. That is to say, theology must itself be a kind of practice that is continually open to the diverse intellectual landscape, inviting previously unrecognized voices to not only participate in framing the ideas and practices that will shape self and society but to inform and transform the contours of theology's own self-articulation.

Doubt as a formal principle of inquiry, critical reason as an autonomous faculty of systematic thinking, and the self-reflexive location of subjectivity as integral to a larger, discursive objectivity are three important moments in the development of theology and religious studies in a diverse postmodern world. Strategies and methods of conservative retreat, progressive reform, and constructive bricolage represent three prominent responses on the part of normative Christian thinkers that reflect a recognition of these elements of postmodern understanding. The significance of Buddhist theology within the Western academy will depend partly on the kinds of responses offered in light of the same conditions of postmodern intellectual practices.

BUDDHIST THOUGHT–DŌGEN AND MYŌE

The choice of Dōgen and Myōe for exploring possibilities for a Buddhist theology no doubt reflect the particularities of my own intellectual history, but among various Buddhist figures I have encountered thus far, I believe there are certain aspects of their thinking that are especially suggestive for the kinds of issues being considered here.

Dōgen And The Relation Between Discursivity And Nondual Awakening

This examination of Dōgen is restricted primarily to the *Genjōkōan* fascicle of the *Shōbōgenzō*,[14] widely considered to be one of the most prominent passages in his major opus. Of interest here is the relation between the functioning of the discursive intellect and nondual awakening, specifically in terms of three aspects: Dōgen's implicit understanding of the dialectical relation between the discursive intellect and nondual awakening, his affirmation of discursive difference within the framework of this relationship, and the manner in which this relation is appropriated in praxis. The significance of these three aspects becomes apparent when considered in light of the problem of radical religious diversity outlined above.

In general, Dōgen does not use the classical terminology of the two-fold truth, of *zokutai* and *shintai,* mundane truth and highest truth, *shiki* and *kū*, form and emptiness; nevertheless, he articulates two major aspects of emptiness theory throughout much of his work, namely, the lack of any fixed essence or intrinsic identity (Sanskrit *asvabhāva*) and going beyond illusory distinctions of self/other, life/death, and so on, thereby awakening to the interdependent arisal of provisional forms, of relative existence (Sanskrit *pratītya-*

samutpāda). For example, not only is a flower devoid of any fixed essence, but the practitioner realizes the truly empty reality of the flower when he or she also awakens to the non-duality of self and flower.

There are two primary classes of dharmas or things that are regarded as empty: 1) the conventional world of mental and physical objects, such as the desire for food and flora and fauna, and 2) the Buddhist teachings. Dōgen adds a twist to this common understanding by stating that it is virtually impossible not to be attached to the illusory distinctions of form even when one has attained enlightenment.

All of this is succinctly expressed in the first four lines of the *Genjōkōan*, following the form of the classical Indian tetralemma or *catuṣkoṭi*.[15]

> [1] When all dharmas are the Buddha Dharma, there is illusion and enlightenment, practice, birth, death, buddhas and sentient beings. [2] When myriad dharmas are without self, there is no illusion or enlightenment, no buddhas or sentient beings, no generation or extinction. [3] The Buddha Way is originally beyond fullness and lack, and for this reason there is generation and extinction, illusion and enlightenment, sentient beings and buddhas. [4] In spite of this, flowers fall always amid our grudging, and weeds flourish in our chagrin (Waddell and Abe: 133).

Line [1] negates the fixed existence of the usual world of mental and physical objects as illusion and affirms the Buddha Dharma as the realm of enlightenment. Line [2] negates the fixed existence of both the Buddha Dharma and the usual world of mental and physical distinctions: both are empty. Line [3] affirms the relative existence of the conventional world of form and of the Buddha Dharma precisely because both are illuminated as empty, as "beyond fullness and lack."

In the common formulation of the fourth line of the tetralemma, neither the relative existence of form and Buddha Dharma nor their emptiness is affirmed, since "form," "Buddha Dharma," and "emptiness" are themselves nothing more than empty, conceptual designations; that is, to understand that conventional reality is empty *as a discursive proposition* is not true understanding. In the *Genjōkōan*, however, line [4] does not at first seem to signify such a transcendence of discursivity or conceptuality; rather, Dōgen appears to regress to the world of attachment to distinctions: "In spite of this, flowers fall always amid our grudging, and weeds flourish in our chagrin."

Taken at face value, this implies that even one who grasps the third level of the tetralemma is bound to fall back into delusory, discursive consciousness. If, in contrast, this last line is read as a transcendence of discursive consciousness in emptiness or *samādhi*, then it is precisely by recognizing or becoming mindful of one's attachments in the present moment that they are dissolved in nondual awakening.

Stated more positively, there is a complementary relationship between attachment and awakening; without the former, the latter does not take place. Becoming one with attachment to the flower in the present is inseparable from the illumination of emptiness that brings that attachment into focus, simultaneously resolving and dissolving the experience of the flower in the field of emptiness.

This second reading accords with the next four lines:

> [5] To practice and confirm all things by conveying one's self to them, is illusion; [6] for all things to advance forward and practice and confirm the self, is enlightenment. [7][Those] who greatly enlighten illusion, are buddhas. [8][Those] who are greatly deluded about enlightenment, are sentient beings.

That is, [5] if one attempts to practice by bringing one's preconceptions to the world, then this is illusion; [6] if one allows the world of phenomenal distinctions to enter one's empty awareness, then there is awakening. [7] Thus, those who illuminate illusory distinctions in nondual awakening are buddhas. [8] Those who merely think discursively about enlightenment are deluded sentient beings.

Such a view of the practice of the two-fold truth is potentially fruitful for engaging the world of radical religious diversity. For the Mahāyāna Buddhist who subscribes to emptiness, one way to manifest empty awareness is to embrace the world of diversity, to identify with it, yet not become entangled in its confusion; in fact, one who is able to identify with various forms of religious thought and life from the perspective of emptiness may be able to broaden not only the horizon of his or her intellectual and experiential world but also to increase and deepen the repertoire of his or her *upāya*. At that level, what initially appeared to be competing discourses, Buddhist and Christian, religious and non-religious, turn out to be streams within a field of critical synergy where knowledge of the other in emptiness enlarges one's world and refines one's understanding.

A similar approach is expressed in the *Vimalakīrti Sūtra* when Mañjuśrī asks the layman Vimalakīrti where emptiness should be sought, and the latter replies, "Mañjuśrī, emptiness should be sought in the sixty-two heretical teachings" (Thurman: 44). If one attempts to confirm the doctrine of emptiness discursively by imposing it on non-Buddhist "heretical teachings," this, in Dōgen's view, is delusion. If, however, one is open to the Other in nondual awareness, then, what previously appeared to be heretical and to stand in irreconcilable opposition to one's self-understanding turns out to confirm one's awakening to emptiness.

Thus, Dōgen states,

> The sixty-two viewpoints are based on the self; so when egoistic views arise, just do zazen quietly, observing them. What is the basis of your body, of its inner and outer possessions? . . . Mind, discriminating consciousness, knowledge, and dualistic thought bind life. What, ultimately, are exhaling and inhaling? They are not the self. There is no self to be attached to. The deluded, however, are attached to self, while the enlightened are unattached. (Yokoi: 49)

Of course, here, Dōgen is treating the sixty-two non-Buddhist views as heretical, but this statement should apply equally to Buddhist views, according to the reading of the *Genjōkōan* given above. As long as one is attached to any conceptual construct, of self or no-self, Buddhist or non-Buddhist, this is delusion: "mind, discriminating consciousness, knowledge, and dualistic thought, bind life."

Dōgen articulates the relation between nondual awakening and discursive consciousness as follows: "When the Dharma is still not fully realized in [one's] body and mind, [one] thinks it is already sufficient. When the Dharma is fully present in body and mind, [one] thinks there is some insufficiency" (Waddell and Abe: 137). That is, if one is attached to discursive logic, and one's realization of the Dharma is therefore incomplete, then one is driven to assert and to try to convince oneself and others of one's understanding, as if discursive knowledge were all there is. If, however, there is the full realization of the Dharma, of the two-fold truth, in body and mind, then one thinks there is some insufficiency, an insufficiency in discursive consciousness which is illuminated by the full realization of the Dharma.

Insofar as it involves discursive, conceptual work, any theological enterprise Buddhist or otherwise is, from this view, "incomplete," and the recognition of this incompleteness entails a certain kind of humility. More importantly, Dōgen suggests that there is a means of dissolving this sense of incompleteness and resolving the discursive discrepancies between divergent perspectives: "The sixty-two viewpoints are based on the self; so when egoistic views arise, *just do zazen* quietly, observing them."

As with some of the Christian thinkers examined above, Dōgen proposes a practice to deal with problems of conceptual difference. His practice of just doing zazen, or sitting-only, *shikan taza,* moreover, becomes central to his entire world view, his so-called theology, as it were. As such, *shikan taza* bears ontological, epistemological, and ethical consequences.[16]

Sitting-only is the practice whereby one enters the world of the *samādhi* freely manifested, *jijiyū zammai,* the highest expression of which is the king of *samādhi*s *samādhi*s, *zammai ō-zammai.*

Ontologically and epistemologically, this leads to the realization that all things manifest the Dharma interdependently, including birds and sky, fish and water, sentient beings and buddhas: "We can realize that water means life [for the fish] and the sky means life [for the bird]. It must [also] be that water means life [for the sky], and the fish means life [for the water]" (Waddell and Abe: 137).

Ethically, the practice of seated meditation, sitting-only, becomes the focal point for the practice of doing all things single-mindedly in *samādhi*; this is concretely expressed in the various regulations prescribing everything from the duties of a Zen cook to the administrative structure of the Zen monastery, compiled by later generations into the *Eihei shingi.*[17] This integral relationship between different dimensions of Dōgen's thinking can be seen in the concept of *shushō ittō,* practice as enlightenment, where ontology is inseparable from epistemology and ethics.

As simplified as this view of Dōgen is, centered on the *Genjōkōan* and overlooking the complex, evolving character of his thinking, it reveals several features of his thought that carry implications for Buddhist theology. First, Dōgen's approach can be seen in light of all three responses to religious and moral diversity outlined in the earlier examination of Christian thinkers: conservative retreat, progressive reform, and constructive bricolage. Second, it brings to light the particular problems of Buddhist thought that looks to the two-fold truth as a means of responding to the problem of radical religious diversity.

Dōgen is himself aware of the problem of diversity within Buddhist tradition, but depending on one's reading, this awareness leads him to respond in a more exclusive or inclusive manner.

For example, his advocacy of sitting-only is a call for a return to the "original" Buddhism of Śākyamuni against the rising tide of diverse, heretical practices as much as it is a formulation of practice as awakening, and he seeks to implement this strategy of conservative retreat by creating a remote community of pure practice, the mountain monastery of Eiheiji.

His accounts of the teachings transmitted by his own teacher Ju-ching and his formulation of various monastic practices represent adaptations of previous understandings and practices, and in this sense take the form of progressive reform. In fact, he rejects the literal acceptance of the early Indian monastic codes contained in the *Vinaya* in favor of the *shingi,* which represent a reconfiguration and elaboration of Chinese Ch'an *chinggui,* which were not designed to be comprehensive in the way that Dōgen came to conceive them (Unno: 76-78).

Yet, Dōgen's new formulations of practice and awakening may also be regarded as constructive bricolage; he not only repositions the *shingi* as central to his world view but creates many new practices to suit his particular situation. Moreover, in his later thought, he incorporates ideas from the Lotus Sutra and relaxes his emphasis on seated meditation as the heart of orthopraxy. This more eclectic approach is inherited and expanded by his successors who go onto incorporate various other elements, including Shingon esotericism.[18]

Depending upon what aspects of Dōgen's thought and writings one regards as central to his religious world view, he may be regarded as a conservator, reformer, or innovator, and this has implications for the ways in which he becomes a resource for any project of Buddhist theology. The more his contribution as a conservator is emphasized, the more the Zen Buddhist thinker who draws on him as a normative point of reference conflicts with divergent perspectives. The more his work as an innovator as responding to the diverse conditions of his cultural and religious milieu are emphasized, the more he becomes a model for constructive synthesis with its creative potentialities and attendant ambiguities.

The heart of the problem remains, in any case, the relationship between the two-fold truth as a conceptual model for bringing together Buddhist awakening to emptiness and the affirmation of religious diversity. As long as the discussion is limited to the relatively general terms of the *Genjōkōan,* it is fairly easy to see the recognition of the insufficiency of discursive understanding as a positive point of entry into nondual awakening. This recognition entails a sort of humility that one has not only in relation to the religious truth of emptiness but also in the face of the emptiness of one's religion. However, due to the fact that this (trans-)theological framework requires specific forms of practice for its realization, there is a tension between the more theoretical dimensions of this model of Buddhist awakening and the particularity of the forms of practice articulated throughout Dōgen's texts. For someone like Dōgen who both wishes to assert the pan-Buddhist character of his own grasp of tradition and to criticize views and practices he regards as heretical to the two-fold truth (Faure; Dumoulin: 69-71), the challenge of recognizing the insufficiency of his own discursive self-expression takes on immediate urgency in his day-to-day life, since the theoretical perspective that encourages humility vis-à-vis all conceptual constructs cannot be realized outside of particular forms and therefore formulations of practice.

Narrowly defined, sitting-only constitutes the core of a tightly knit set of practices that excludes engagement with other practices, but this creates a tension with Dōgen's non-dualist philosophy as articulated in the *Genjōkōan.* More openly rendered, sitting-only could become the focal point for an expanding set of practices. The insufficiency of discursive consciousness is recognized and dissolved as the Buddhist theologian comes to know the Other through appropriating his or her practices within a non-discursive, non-ideological framework. Even when actual practice is limited or at least different, as in the case of a male thinker approaching and appropriating feminist thought, the willingness to admit the karmic limitations of discursive understanding and to attempt to analogically and imaginatively enter an unknown sphere of life and practice maximizes the possibility for creative encounter.[19] In this sense, non-dual implies that any given idea or practice be applied to the Buddhist thinker him or herself to unmask preconceptions and assumptions and be conveyed to the Other in a non-hegemonic, inclusive manner.

As difficult as this seems, we know that many have found the journey across boundaries of culture and tradition to be fruitful if challenging. Such Christian thinkers as Thomas Merton or Aelred Graham not only engaged Buddhist thought but were transformed by Buddhist practices. The two-fold truth as we find in the likes of Dōgen and, as we shall see, Myōe, seem to invite a similar engagement with Christian and other non-Buddhist practices on the part of Buddhist thinkers when translated into the critically self-reflexive framework of postmodern understanding.

Myōe Kōben And The Problem Of Diverse Practices

The depth and complexity of this problem is perhaps brought into even greater relief in the case of Dōgen's contemporary Myōe Kōben. Although Dōgen may have grappled with the diversity of practices, much of his struggle takes place on the notional plane as he remains ensconced in his mountain monastery through the mature period of his career. Myōe, in contrast, travels between various centers of practice throughout his life; like the postmodern theologian encountering his or her colleagues at various academic and non-academic venues, Myōe's encounters with diverse practitioners are consistently quite real. The heir to multiple traditions by birth as well as by study, he responds to the diverse landscape of religious ideas and practices with his own diverse repertoire of skillful means.

Myōe explicitly identifies the two-fold truth as the cornerstone of his self-understanding, of "the two kinds of emptiness, human beings and phenomena, of which I, [Myōe,] so often speak" (Unno: 163). One of the most striking passages on the provisional nature of conceptual truth can be found in a work advocating the practice of the Kōmyō Shingon, the Mantra of Light, entitled *Kōmyō Shingon dosha kanjinki.* In this passage, he compares the Buddhist teachings to intoxicating mushrooms. A monk, while intoxicated, sees a vision, a hallucination, in which another monk brings the mushrooms to him accompanied by the latter's mother.

> Last year one of the monks living here became intoxicated after eating some mushrooms. After he awoke, he related the following story. He said that the lowly monk who picked the vegetable and gave it to him had come with his mother and would not leave his side. He apparently had to return to his far away home but remained standing nearby. [The monk who had fallen ill] said that he had great difficulty remembering the episode. (Unno: 116)

Myōe likens the monk bringing the mushroom and his mother to buddhas. When the intoxicated monk awakens, he is cured of his hallucination (of thinking that the Buddhist monk and his buddha-mother were real); thus, Buddhism itself turns out to have been nothing more than a dream. Paradoxically, the intoxicated monk could not have awakened from such a hallucination unless the monk and mother had brought him the mushrooms, that is, unless they *were* real.

> If the mother had not given birth, then there would have been no monk to pick the mushrooms. If there were no monk, then he would not have picked the mushrooms and come. If the mushrooms had not existed, then [no one] would have eaten them. Then the original mind would neither have become intoxicated, seen the monk, nor seen the mother. This is the true and real original mind. [Yet,] truly one ought to know. This intoxication was like a dream or phantasm. (Unno: 117)

The empty reality of the monk, the mother, and the mushrooms is correctly realized when the monk who eats the mushrooms awakens from his vision/hallucination and realizes their empty nature. This awakening, however, leads not to a celebration of attainment but to an awareness of karmic evil:

> The person who is protected by all of the Tathāgatas of the ten directions is like the one who had the monk and his mother at his side. When conditions overturning this come together, then one becomes a sinner. All of this is due to the power of interdependent origination difficult to fathom. (Unno: 117)

At the moment of awakening from this vision, the monk emerges into a discursive consciousness that distinguishes between the previous hallucinatory state and the present awakened one. Yet, this discrimination between before and after is itself illusory, and the moment that the monk recognizes his karmic attachment to this distinction, he realizes that he has "become a sinner." This is akin to Dōgen's recognition of insufficiency wherein discursive consciousness is illuminated by nondual emptiness, although Myōe's formulation is more dramatic in the way that he emphasizes the illusory nature of Buddhism as a conceptual construct. Discursive consciousness is always illusory, in a dream-like state. Buddhism is the dream within a dream that awakens one out of the dream. However, discursive consciousness finds itself in yet another dream after awakening; only now, consciousness is continually illuminated by a larger awareness in which it is creatively dissolved and resolved.

As a practical consequence of these views, Myōe adopts a framework of diverse practices. He tests and recommends a wide range of practices to his disciples, from the *nembutsu* of invoking the name of Amida Buddha to the mantra practice of the Kōmyō Shingon and the counting of breaths found in the seated meditation of Zen. He even encourages his followers to seek out teachers of various schools if they do not find his own instruction to be sufficient: "If there is something that one cannot understand by studying one's own school, then one may obtain the view [of the matter as taught in] the Zen school and thus benefit by consulting a Zen priest, or by relying on [other] Buddhist teachings, or [some other] person. Do not be confined to one-sided views" (Kawai: 47).

In this sense, Myōe is magnanimous in his attitude towards diverse practices and schools of thought; this is in accord with the spirit of skillful means through which he seeks to find appropriate practices for himself and others in accord with varying circumstances.

There is, however, one thing he cannot tolerate, exclusivism, something he sees in the work of his contemporary Hōnen, the prominent Pure Land Buddhist master who advocates the single-minded practice of Pure Land *nembutsu* and the abandonment of all other practices as heretical.[20] In an unusually scathing critique of Hōnen entitled *Zaijarin* ("Tract Destroying Heresy"), Myōe severely takes Hōnen to task for denying others the full range of practices that might help them. From the perspective of his inclusive, contextual approach, one which resonates with Stout's model of constructive bricolage, he cannot tolerate Hōnen's exclusivity and dogmatism. In fact, he formulates his practice of the Mantra of Light as a non-exclusive alternative to Hōnen's *nembutsu* as a means of attaining birth in Amida's Pure Land.

Yet, even in criticizing Hōnen he comes to recognize the negative effects of denying an exclusive position: an inclusivity that excludes exclusivity is still discursively one-sided. Conversely, there may be times and places that a certain exclusivity is necessary or even desirable; inclusivity can be just as ideological and problematic as exclusivity. Although Hōnen is ideologically exclusive, he is purposely excluding the practices of what he regards as corrupt ecclesia in order to embrace the suffering masses with a socially inclusive practice. Myōe has no choice but to criticize Hōnen, yet he is aware of the insufficiency of his critique: "By nature I am pained by that which is harmful. I feel this way about writing the *Zaijarin*" (Unno: 175).

The path of the Buddhist adept, the ideal articulated by Mahāyāna Buddhist thinkers such as Dōgen and Myōe, is one of living in the karmic world but not being of it, freely entering *saṃsāra* yet just as freely moving beyond to *nirvāṇa*; paradoxically, however, one who engages the diverse world of human endeavors necessarily becomes entangled in its insufficiency. Myōe, the monk who has been extolled as "the purest monk in the land," and who once cut off his ear as a sign of protest against the corrupt ecclesia of his time, saw that in the depths of his own being, the karmic suffering of his contemporaries was inseparable from his own: "The path of the Dharma-master is [ideally supposed to be] outside of the six realms of transmigration. [However,] I, [Myōe,] have fallen into the path of the Dharma-master and am now afflicted with suffering. What can be done with the evil ways of the Dharma-master?" (174).[21]

Like Dōgen's reference to weeds and flowers, this statement can be taken either at face value as an admission of failure, or as the affirmation of difference–within Myōe's own practice of Buddhism. In the latter case, this discrepancy between his philosophical ideal and his karmic reality is transformed into a positive recognition of insufficiency illuminated within the larger unfolding of the Dharma beyond words. Instead of the desperate question of a confused theologian, the question, "What can be done with the evil ways of the Dharma-master?" becomes, like Vimalakīrti's illness, an expression of identification with the suffering of all beings, the bodhisattva spirit speaking through Myōe and willingly entering the difficulties of this saṃsāric world. This is because the recognition of his own karmic limitation comes out of his attempts to meet the needs of the people of his time, and one senses in his voice the critical synergy of his bodhisattva-like creativity and his flawed humanity, a synthesis that renders him more fully human in a positive sense. This does not mean that we should overlook the problematic dimensions of his world view as we attempt to appropriate elements of his or any other Buddhist thought for our time. If Buddhism does not exist apart from actual Buddhists, then it is the lived practices of the Buddhist theologian that give life to his thought. From their efforts and failures we learn about our own; errant detours increase our knowledge of the contours of *saṃsāra* and deepen our compassion even as we remain answerable to karmic consequences.

This examination of Myōe, like that of Dōgen, barely begins to uncover the implications of their thought for Buddhist theology. There are many issues of individual and institutional practice as well as epistemology, ontology, and cosmology that remain to be examined. Yet, even this brief foray into issues of theoretical and practical concern offer glimpses into the creative possibilities as well as difficulties faced by the Buddhist thinker in a radically diverse world.

CONCLUSION

The power to doubt thoroughly, to examine critically, and to recognize the truly radical character of intellectual, cultural, and religious diversity in a multicultural world are integral to the project of Buddhist thought in a postmodern world. By considering these discursive principles and faculties within the framework of the two-fold truth as articulated and practiced by thinkers such as Dogen and Myoe, we may start to understand the creative potential for constructive religious thought as well as the challenges and limitations of Buddhist theology as an contemporary intellectual and practical endeavor.

Of course, we must not underestimate the historical, cultural, and intellectual distances that lie between the context of thirteenth-century Japan and religious discourse in postmodernity. Feminist thinkers such as Martha Nussbaum have developed cogent critiques of current practices while acknowledging both the limitations of and indebtedness to Aristotle. American discourse on social justice is similarly indebted to and is critical of the ideas of the "founding fathers." Critical historical understanding is important for engaging in the project of constructive religious thought so that we may learn from the past and avoid mistakes in the future.

An awareness of the relationship between discursive consciousness and nondual awakening, a recognition of karmic limitations and the insufficiency of discursive logic, and a framework in which the practices of both self and other can inform and transform one another opens up the possibility for a truly fruitful mutual encounter between Buddhist thought and the intellectual world at large, an encounter which is already beginning to take place through the work of authors in this volume and elsewhere.

Integral to this understanding is that, depending on the person, time, and place, any given situation may not be conducive to such a mutal transformation. I believe that the emergence of Buddhist theology cannot be forced or held back but must take place on its own time. It may seem as though I am advocating a Buddhist correlate to Stoutís method of constructive bricolage, and I do believe that a similar approach may be fruitful for Buddhist theology as envisioned by the editors of this volume. For some individuals, however, a more MacIntyrean strategy of conservative retreat may be in order. For others, a Taylorean approach of progressive reform may provided a needed balance between adherence to tradition and responsivenss to the changing present. Or perhaps, some other approach or a combination of approaches will open further possibilities. Each of us must do our best to understand and meet the challenges of our multicultural world in a manner that befits our own abilities and experiences as well as that of others, weighing the consequences of our thoughts and actions whose problematic nature itself becomes the fertile ground of creativity.

This paper will more than fulfilled its function if it has served to stimulate reflection on that task.

NOTES

1 While Buddhism has contained a rich pantheon of deities throughout its history, especially in Mahāyāna and Vajrayāna developments, the non-self or empty nature of these deities, the primacy of dharma over buddha as purportedly enunciated by Śākyamuni, and other factors must be taken into account in considering the appropriateness of

theology as a term describing normative, constructive Buddhist thought.

2 My understanding of this volume is that the targeted audience is primarily although not limited to scholars and religious thinkers in the West. For this reason, the concerns addressed here deal primarily with issues and contexts within Western intellectual history. For a historical treatment of some of the ways that religious thinkers, specifically Japanese Pure Land, Buddhists have engaged various intellectual and social concerns in the twentieth century such as race, class, and nationalism within Asian Buddhism, see Unno 1998.

3 Naturally, "Buddhist thought" is no more monolithic than "religious thought." The range and diversity of the former has, in fact, been highlighted by the meeting of various strains of Buddhism in the West, very often for the first time.

4 The narrative outlined below is only one of many possible narratives; yet, it reflects accounts that have been articulated by many diverse thinkers, East and West, feminist, post-structuralist, and the like, such that it bears significant intellectual currency, whatever its objective status. See, for example, Capps, Bourdieu, Foucault, Merchant, Taylor 1989.

5 Tracy here limits his discussion of the sources of religious knowledge to texts with a special emphasis on classics. The question of non-textual, or at least non-literate, sources of religious knowledge remains unaddressed.

6 Of course, this is a over-simplified dichotomy. The mentoring model of the personal transmission of knowledge is still important generally in the academy. However, a different model has emerged both formally and in practice that alters previous understandings as described below.

7 The normative limitations of some of these efforts may be due precisely to the fact that they carry Kantian presuppositions. While it is beyond the scope of this essay to explore this question fully, related issues are examined later in this essay.

8 David Loy addresses issues of gender in Loy 1996.

9 David Loy (1988) explicitly casts his work as a study in comparative philosophy involving various strains of Asian and Western thought. Issues of normative understanding are nevertheless involved in *Nonduality* By articulating what he sees as the essential identity of Advaita Vedānta, the Taoism of Lao Tzu and Chuang Tzu, and Zen Buddhism, he is laying claim to a constructed and constructive unity of the three which supersedes any historical differences asserted by thinkers identifying themselves as representatives of these traditions.

10 http://jbe.la.psu.edu

11 A strong case for deontological ethics as the basis for the practical unity of diverse religious perspectives is presented by Sumner B. Twiss in his work on universal human rights. One possible appeal of

virtue ethics in contrast to deontological ethics in a religiously diverse world is its at least partial basis in individual practice rather than a commonly shared set of binding principles of action, but there are obvious limitations of virtue ethics in relation to problems of human rights. A synthesis of deontological and virtue ethics may hold some promise for religious practice in a world of diversity. It can be argued that various strands of Buddhism already bear the seeds of such a synthesis with *pratītya-samutpāda,* dependent co-origination, as its deontological principle and the six *pāramitā* as its fundamental virtues. Although potentially relevant to the present discussion, a consideration of this line of thinking is beyond the scope of this paper.

12 MacIntyre makes his normative position on religious morality even more explicit in *Three Types of Moral Inquiry;* his position has continued to evolve since the publication of this work and *After Virtue*, but the latter work which attained widespread critical acclaim, represents a distinctive position that is particularly worth examining here.

13 Conspicuous by their absence in his account are the voices of women generally and feminist thinkers in particular, African American, native American and other ethnic and religious minorities, and other groups excluded from elite intellectual discourse.

14 As a number of scholars have begun to note, Dōgen's views of Buddhism evolved over time with potentially important changes in his philosophical understanding. Here I focus on passages from the *Genjōkōan*, fully aware that the ideas expressed there are by no means representative of the whole range of his conceptions. See, for example, David Putney (1996).

15 Although there is nothing out of the ordinary in the interpretation that follows, I have not seen the beginning of this passage interpreted in precisely this manner. Waddell and Abe give a similar but more complex reading without reference to the *catuṣkoṭi.* It should also be added that each line of this passage represents an existential as well as logical position. Full understanding of the significance of each line implies practical realization. See, for example, Yasutani's interpretation of the *Genjōkōan* (14–18).

16 Anne Klein, dealing with issues of feminist and gender theory, similarly offers the practice of the Great Bliss Queen as providing both an ontological and epistemological framework for considering the challenges of postmodern understanding, and her central notion of "correlative emptiness" reflects the advocacy of both a theoretical and a practical orientation.

17 For an account of the primacy of sitting practice and its relation to the *shingi*, see Bodiford (169); Bielefeldt.

18 See Bodiford, as well as Dumoulin (51–153).

19 James Fredericks (1997) suggests that interreligious friendship as a theological virtue is one way that a Christian thinker might address

religious ìdiversity creatively and responsibly. His work offers potentially fruitful suggestions for Buddhist theology and has influenced reflections contained in this paper.

20 For a detailed discussion of this issue, see Unno (93–94, 106–107) and Tanabe (84–115).

21 The status of karma is an important issue in considering the metaphysical implications of Buddhism in interaction with non-Buddhist thought, an issue that lies beyond the scope of the present paper. On the one hand, karma must be just as empty as any other Buddhist notion given the analysis of the two-fold truth presented above. On the other, karma remains problematic for Western forms of thought that do not recognize moral causality beyond the life of the discursively defined body; yet, it may be precisely in offering a vocabulary of continuous moral causality that Buddhist notions of karma have something to offer to Western religious and ethical understanding.

Problems tend to arise in the application of karma theory around issues of responsibility and accountability. When applied objectively and discursively as a discourse of moral calculus, either to others or to oneself, karma becomes a category of moral accountability. When applied intersubjectively and nondualistically to the relationship between self and other, karma becomes a discourse of responsibility. The ethical uses and abuses of karma may correspond to some extent to terms of accountability and responsibility. I believe abuses occur more often when karma is applied as a discourse of accountability, especially when it is used to blame others for their own circumstances. I think more creative uses are found in the intersubjective realm of responsibility. For a discussion of various aspects of morality in terms of accountability and responsibility in the context of Western ethical theory, see Tong, especially Chapter 6 on Nel Noddings's relational ethics.

REFERENCES

Bielefeldt, Carl (1985). "Recarving the Dragon: History and Dogma in the Study of Dōgen." In William LaFleur, ed., *Dōgen Studies*, 21-53. Kuroda Institute Studies in East Asian Buddhism 2. Honolulu: University of Hawaii Press.

Bodiford, Will. M. (1993). *Sōtō Zen in Medieval Japan*. Honolulu: University of Hawaii Press.

Bourdieu, Pierre (1990). *The Logic of Practice*. Trans. Richard Nice. Stanford: Stanford University Press.

Capps, Walter H. (1995). *Religious Studies–The Making of a Discipline*. Minneapolis: Fortress Press.

Dumoulin, Heinrich (1990). *Zen Buddhism: A History–Japan*. New York: Macmillan Publishing.

Foucault, Michel (1976). *The Archaeology of Knowledge.* Trans. A. M. Sheridan Smith. New York, Pantheon Books

Fredericks, James (1997). "Interreligious Friendship–A New Theological Virtue." Unpublished paper delivered at The National Meeting of the Catholic Theological Society. Minneapolis.

Heisig, James and John Maraldo, eds. (1995). *Rude Awakenings: Zen, the Kyoto School, & the Question of Nationalism.* Honolulu : University of Hawaii Press.

Huntington, Jr., C. W. (1990). *The Emptiness of Emptiness.* Honolulu: University of Hawaii Press.

Kawai, Hayao (1992). *The Buddhist Priest Myōe: A Life of Dreams.* Trans. Mark Unno. Venice, CA: Lapis Press.

Klein, Anne Carolyn (1995). *Meeting The Great Bliss Queen: Buddhists, Feminists, and the Art of the Self.* Boston : Beacon Press.

Kraft, Kenneth (1992). *Inner Peace, World Peace.* Albany: State University of New York Press.

Loy, David (1988). *Nonduality.* New Haven: Yale University Press.

Loy, David (1996). "Sky-Dancing at the Boundaries of Western Thought: Feminist Theory and the Limits of Deconstruction," in David Loy, ed., *Healing and Deconstruction.* Atlanta: Scholars Press.

MacIntyre, Alasdair (1984). *After Virtue.* 2nd ed. Notre Dame, IN: University of Notre Dame Press.

MacIntyre, Alasdair (1990). *Three Rival Versions Of Moral Enquiry: Encyclopedia, Genealogy, And Tradition.* Notre Dame, IN: University of Notre Dame Press.

Merchant, Carolyn (1989). *The Death of Nature: Women, Ecology, And The Scientific Revolution.* New York: Harper & Row.

Nattier, Jan (1992). *Once Upon a Future Time.* Berkeley: Asian Humanities Press.

Nishitani Keiji (1982). *Religion and Nothingness.* Berkeley: University of California Press.

Okubo Doshu, ed. (1971). *Dōgen zenji zenshu* I. Tokyo: Chikuma Shobo.

Putney, David (1996). "Some Problems In Interpretation: The Early and Late Writings Of Dōgen." *Philosophy East and West* (46: 4) 497-531.

Stout, Jeffrey (1988). *Ethics after Babel: The Languages of Morals and Their Discontents.* Boston: Beacon Press.

Tanabe, George (1992). *Myōe the Dreamkeeper.* Cambridge, Mass. : Council on East Asian Studies, Harvard University : Distributed by the Harvard University Press.

Taylor, Charles (1989). *Sources of the Self: The Making Of The Modern Identity.* Cambridge: Harvard University Press.

Taylor, Charles (1992). *The Ethics of Authenticity.* Cambridge: Harvard University Press.

Taylor, Charles (1985). *Human Agency And Language* Cambridge: Cambridge University Press.

Tong, Rosemarie (1993). *Feminine and Feminist Ethics.* Belmont, CA: Wadsworth Publishing.

Tracy, David (1987). *Plurality and Ambiguity: Hermeneutics, Religion, Hope.* San Francisco: Harper and Row.

Twiss, Sumner. B (1995). "Shaping the Curriculum: The Emergence of Religious Studies." In Mark Hadley and Mark Unno, eds., *Counterpoints: Issues in Teaching Religious Studies.* Providence: Department of Religious Studies, Brown University.

Unno, Mark Ty (1994). *As Appropriate: Myōe Kōben And The Problem Of The Vinaya In Early Kamakura Buddhism.* Unpublished Dissertation. Stanford University.

Unno, Mark Ty (1998). "Shin Buddhist Social Thought in Modern Japan." In Kenneth K. Tanaka and Eisho Nasu, eds., *Engaged Pure Land Buddhism: Challenges Facing Jodo Shinshu in the Contemporary World*, 67-87. Berkeley: WisdomOcean Publications.

Waddell, Norman and Masao Abe, tr. (1972)."Shobogenzo Genjokoan," by Dōgen Kigen. *The Eastern Buddhist* (New Series) (5: 2) 129-140.

Williams, Bernard (1985). *Ethics and the Limits of Philosophy.* Cambridge: Cambridge University Press.

Yasutani, Hakuun (1996). *Flowers Fall–A Commentary on Zen Master Dōgen's Genjōkōan.* Tr. Paul Jaffe. Boston: Shambhala.

Yokoi, Yuho, with Daizen Victoria, trans. (1990). "Gakudō Yōjin-shū," by Dōgen Kigen. In Yokoi and Victoria, *Zen Master Dōgen: An Introduction with Selected Writings.* New York: Weatherhill.

Ten

The Dialectic Between Religious Belief and Contemplative Knowledge in Tibetan Buddhism

B. Alan Wallace

I would like to present this essay as an example of a Buddhist theoretical critique of the relation between religious belief and contemplative knowledge in Tibetan Buddhism, and I shall contrast this with Steven Katz's and Paul Griffiths's academic analyses of mysticism and Buddhist insight practice. A tension has long existed in the Tibetan Buddhist tradition between religious belief based upon scriptural authority and contemplative knowledge drawn from first-hand, personal inquiry. While many of the great scholars and contemplatives of Tibet have emphasized the importance of a balance between these two themes, when a contemplative tradition degenerates, this tension is lost: scholars devote themselves exclusively to textual study, disclaiming the present possibility of experiential knowledge; while contemplatives disdain textual knowledge as dry intellectualism, thereby reducing their tradition to a system of theoretically barren techniques.

The very possibility of genuine contemplative inquiry and insight has been called into question by modern scholars of mysticism and Buddhism. Steven Katz, for example, claims that religious images, beliefs, symbols, and rituals define, *in advance*, the types of experiences a contemplative wants to have and does eventually have (1978: 33). In a similar vein, Paul Griffiths states that the Buddhist cultivation of contemplative insight (Pāli *vipassanā-bhāvanā*) consists of "repeated meditations upon standard items of Buddhist doctrine . . . until these are completely internalized by practitioners and their cognitive and perceptual habit-patterns operate only in terms of them" (13). Thus, according to the above interpretations, mystical experience in general and the Buddhist cultivation of insight in particular entail no genuine, open-minded inquiry, but rather a self-imposed form of indoctrination (Griffiths: 15). I shall argue, however, that this description characterizes Buddhist meditation only in its more degenerate forms and is therefore a misleading depiction of the tradition as a whole.

Within Tibetan Buddhism, the sect that most readily lends itself to the critique of Katz and Griffiths is probably the dGe lugs order, which over the past few centuries has become highly scholastic in theory and practice. Its appeal to scriptural authority and rational argument can be traced to the writings of Tsong kha pa (1357-1419), the founder of this order. For example, in his classic work entitled *The Great Exposition of the Path to Awakening*[1] his erudite discussions of the cultivation of meditative quiescence (*śamatha*) and insight (*vipaśyanā*) are based almost entirely upon the Buddhist canon, including *sūtras* attributed to the Buddha and Sanskrit commentaries composed by the patriarchs of Indian Mahāyāna Buddhism. The accounts of these two fundamental approaches to Buddhist meditation are standardized and essentially normative, with virtually no descriptions of contemplatives' own first-hand accounts of their individual experience. Moreover, these presentations include almost no references to the written accounts of Tibetan contemplatives, even though, by Tsong kha pa's time, the techniques for developing meditative quiescence and insight had been practiced in Tibet for more than five hundred years.

Advocates of the dGe lugs order defend this reliance upon textual authority and rational analysis in terms of the traditional, threefold sequence of Buddhist praxis, namely hearing, thinking, and meditation. Understanding derived from hearing (including textual study) consists of the intellectual comprehension of Buddhist doctrine; understanding derived from thinking (including the practice of rational analysis and debate) reveals whether that doctrine is internally consistent and whether it conforms to valid experience (*pratyakṣa*); and understanding derived from meditation is gained by attending to the *realities indicated by Buddhist teachings, and not to the assertions of the doctrine itself.*

The goal of the second phase of that training – namely, thinking – is not merely *belief* (*manaḥ-parīkṣā*) in the validity of Buddhist doctrine, but *inferential knowledge* (*anumāna*) of the realities presented in that doctrine. The goal of the third phase of that training – namely, meditation – is perceptual knowledge (*pratyakṣa*) of those same realities. The first two of those types of understanding can be acquired during one's training in a monastic university under the guidance of erudite scholars. But to acquire the knowledge derived from meditation, one is advised to seek out a master who can teach from his own contemplative experience and that of the oral lineage of his own teachers. Such guidance therefore vitalizes the scholastic presentations of meditation with oral accounts of the personal experiences of generations of accomplished contemplatives. Moreover, the meditation master should also have the wisdom, drawn from experience, to help each student choose the most suitable techniques for his own cultivation of quiescence and insight. Without such personal guidance from an experienced teacher, it is argued, even the most lucid texts on meditation by themselves will provide inadequate guidance to the aspiring contemplative.

That system of training is said to be effective when a scholarly presentation of meditation is used by an experienced contemplative as a basis of practical guidance for his students. But when the teacher has no experience, then the text alone gives the impression that there is no significant variation in the ways individuals pursue the practices for cultivating quiescence and insight. That tradition further degenerates when teachers admonish their students that the era of contemplative realization is past, and that the most students can hope for in the present day is scholastic comprehension of the classical treatises and their commentaries.

The above description of the sequence of hearing, thinking, and meditation may be taken as evidence in support of Katz's and Griffiths's assertion that Buddhist contemplative practice consists of nothing more than the adoption of cognitive and perceptual habit-patterns that accord with the principles of Buddhist doctrine. The phase of thinking about the doctrine, in their view, may be nothing more than an intellectual exercise aimed at personally validating that doctrine. This may especially appear to be the case when the scholastic training in dGe lugs monasteries lasts as long as twenty-five years during which there is little time for experiential inquiry by way of one's own meditative experience. Indeed, a similar critique of this approach was made by Karma chags med (1613-1678), an eminent scholar and contemplative of both the rNying ma and bKa' brgyud orders of Tibetan Buddhism. In his view, such a primary emphasis on extensive intellectual learning and debate may actually impede first-hand, empirical inquiry into the nature of the mind and the realization of a primal state of awareness in which conceptual constructs are transcended. This, he asserts, is the central issue in the Buddhist cultivation of insight. In accordance with the Mahāmudrā and Atiyoga traditions of Buddhist meditation, he proposes that one proceed swiftly to the experiential examination of the mind, such that one's view of the nature of awareness can be derived from one's own personal experience (Karma chags med: 376–377; trans. Karma Chagmé: 100–101).

While the dGe lugs order relies primarily on the Buddhist *sūtra*s and *tantra*s and their authoritative Indian and Tibetan commentaries, the rNying ma order also relies heavily on *gter ma*s, secret teachings which are believed to have been composed and hidden by the eight-century, Indian Buddhist adept Padmasambhava, who was instrumental in bringing Buddhism to Tibet. Some of these were written manuscripts (*sa gter*) purportedly hidden in caves and discovered centuries later, in the manner of "spiritual time-capsules," when the time was ripe for them to be revealed. One classic *gter ma* is the meditation manual entitled *The Profound Dharma of The Natural Emergence of the Peaceful and Wrathful from Enlightened Awareness.* Like the writings of Karma chags med, this treatise emphasizes first-hand empirical investigation over rational analysis, as indicated by the following passage:

> According to the custom of some teaching traditions, you are first introduced to the view, and upon that basis you seek the meditative state. This makes it difficult to identify awareness. In this tradition, you first accomplish the meditative state, then on that basis you are introduced to the view. This profound point makes it impossible for you not to ascertain the nature of awareness. Therefore, first settle your mind in its natural state, then bring forth genuine quiescence in your mind-stream, and observe the nature of awareness. (Padmasambhava: 320-321)[2]

The theme expressed in the above passage – of being introduced to a theory of consciousness *after* one has experientially accomplished the meditative state – is also expressed by Paṇ chen blo bzang chos kyi rgyal mtshan (1570-1662), a prominent authority in the dGe lugs order, and the spiritual mentor of the Fifth Dalai Lama. In his meditation manual entitled *The Highway of the Victorious Ones: A Root Text on Mahāmudrā* he writes:

> Thus, among the two traditions of seeking meditative experience
> On the basis of the view, and seeking the view
> On the basis of meditative experience,
> This accords with the latter tradition.[3]

The dGe lugs order as a whole accepts in principle the possibility of authentic *gter mas*, but it is uneasily aware of the likelihood of counterfeits either knowingly or unknowingly being passed off as genuine teachings of Padmasambhava. This is all the more a concern in the case of "mind treasures" (*dgongs gter*) – teachings allegedly hidden by Padmasambhava in the mind-streams of contemplatives, who in subsequent lifetimes discover them in the course of their own meditative development. One relatively recent example of such a mind treasure is a treatise entitled *The Vajra Essence: A Tantra Naturally Arisen From the Nature of Existence From the Matrix of Primordial Awareness of Pure Appearances*,[4] revealed to and written down by the nineteenth-century, Tibetan Atiyoga master bDud 'joms gling pa. This work, consisting of more than 260 folios, records a discussion of many points of theory and practice between Samantabhadra, the primordial Buddha, and a circle of his bodhisattva disciples. The cultivation of quiescence and insight is a prominent theme of this *tantra*, but unlike the *normative* accounts presented by Tsong kha pa, the discussion here presents a description of the wide *variety* of experiences that individual practitioners may have in the course of this meditative training (bDud 'joms gling pa: 31–47).

Padmasambhava, Tsong kha pa, and Karma chags med all agree that the attainment of quiescence is indispensable for the achievement of contemplative insight. Tsong kha pa cites a common analogy to explain the relation between quiescence and insight: in order to examine a hanging tapestry at night, if you light an oil-lamp that is both radiant and unflickering, you can vividly observe the depicted images. But if the lamp is either dim, or – even if it is bright – flickers due to wind, you would not clearly see those forms (Tsong kha pa, Pha: 134B–135A; trans. Wallace: 118). Likewise, the aim of the training in quiescence is to counteract the alternating laxity and compulsive agitation of the mind and to bring forth a high degree of attentional stability and vividness. Only when the awareness is trained in this fashion is it said to be a suitable instrument for the contemplative investigation of the nature of the mind and other phenomena.

This view of quiescence stands in sharp contrast to the interpretation of Paul Griffiths, who writes that such training is designed to focus the awareness upon a single point so that ultimately all mental activity is brought to a halt and no experience of any kind is able to occur (13–15). If that were indeed the aim of the cultivation of quiescence, there would be good grounds for his conclusion that the goal of this training is incompatible with that of the cultivation of insight. But in reality, it would be hard to find any Tibetan Buddhist contemplative who would endorse his interpretation of quiescence, let alone seek to realize it. The cultivation of quiescence is no more incompatible with the cultivation of insight than the development of telescopes is incompatible with the observation of the planets and stars.

The goal of Buddhist meditation in the view of all the Tibetan Buddhist adepts cited in this paper is to gain non-dual, conceptually unmediated insight into the nature of ultimate reality that transcends all conceptual frameworks. This reality, they maintain, is not the product of their doctrines, nor is its realization the culmination of only one type of contemplative training. On the contrary, Paṇ chen blo bzang chos kyi rgyal mtshan maintains that although many different techniques and types of terminology are used in diverse contemplative disciplines within Tibetan Buddhism, if they are examined by erudite, experienced contemplatives, they are found to converge upon the same reality (2). Karma chags med goes a step further in approvingly citing O rgyan Rin po che, a renowned contemplative of the bKa' brgyud order, who claims that Buddhist selflessness (*nairātmya*), the middle way (*madhyamaka*), the essence of the Tathāgata (*tathāgatagarbha*), the total-ground (*ālaya*), the absolute nature of reality (*dharmadhātu*), and even the Self (*ātman*) posited by certain non-Buddhist, Indian contemplative schools all refer to the same reality! (Karma chags med: 386–387; trans. Karma Chagmé: 107).

Certainly not all Tibetan Buddhists make such inclusivist appraisals of contemplative experience. On the contrary, some dGe lugs pa scholars claim that only the authors of the textbooks of their own monastic colleges have come up with the one correct interpretation of the Madhyamaka view; other dGe lugs pa scholars have strayed from the one true path, and other doctrines concerning Mahāmudrā and Atiyoga, for instance, are regarded as being profoundly flawed and ineffective for the attainment of *nirvāṇa*. Likewise, some rNying ma pa scholars deny that contemplatives following dGe lugs interpretations of the Madhyamaka view penetrate to anything beyond a "partial" or "trivial" emptiness (Tibetan *stong nyid nyi tshe ba*), which is nothing more than an artifact of their doctrine. Nevertheless, as indicated by the above references to Paṇ chen blo bzang chos kyi rgyal mtshan and O rgyan Rin po che, Katz is simply wrong in claiming that the non-exclusivist perspective is something primarily derived from "non-mystics of recent vintage for their own purposes" (1978: 46). According to Paṇ chen blo bzang chos kyi rgyal mtshan, such a perspective has long been held by contemplatives who are both experienced in their own tradition and learned in the traditions of others. Such individuals have always been rare.

This inclusivist position stands in stark contrast to that of Katz, who claims that all contemplative states of consciousness are thoroughly structured by the conceptual, religious frameworks in which such experiences are sought. Indeed, one of his initial premises is that conceptually unmediated experiences are impossible in principle, for human experience invariably involves memory, apprehension, expectation, and language (1978: 26, 33, 59). That human experience normally operates under those conditions can hardly be contested, and it is a fact long known by many scholars in the Buddhist tradition. But the central point of Buddhist contemplative training is to achieve a type of insight that is profoundly unlike ordinary human experience. To argue that conceptually unmediated experience is impossible on the grounds that it is inaccessible to non-contemplatives is like claiming that knowledge of the infinite density of the zero-point energy of the electromagnetic vacuum is impossible on the grounds that it is inaccessible to non-physicists.

When addressing the possibility of ineffable knowledge, the question must be asked: ineffable for whom? If Jack has never tasted anything sweet, Jill would be at a loss to find no words to convey to him the taste of Belgian milk chocolate, let alone the difference between that and Swiss chocolate. Likewise, wine connoisseurs have a terminology that is quite intelligible among themselves, but that conveys little to teetotalers. Evidently there are many kinds of knowledge and experience that cannot be conveyed in words to outsiders, and are, therefore, in ineffable in some contexts. Once this point is acknowledged, we may consider whether two accomplished Mahāmudrā adepts might converse about the nature of emptiness and primordial awareness in ways that would convey meaning in that context, but not for those lacking such experience.

I suspect that Katz's refusal to entertain the possibility of knowledge or experience unmediated by language or concepts stems from his adherence to the Kantian metaphysical assumption that if there is some noumenal reality that utterly transcends human percepts and concepts, it cannot be known directly; at best, one can only think about it. But this is precisely the assumption that Buddhist contemplatives refute, some of them on the basis of their own experience. Since they cannot directly demonstrate the nature of their knowledge to others, they take great pains to show others how to acquire such knowledge for themselves. But Katz insists that experienced contemplatives are in no better a position to evaluate their experience than are non-contemplatives (1983: 5). Thus, he discards the only feasible way for us to get at the nature of contemplative experience for ourselves so that we can speak of it from first-hand knowledge. Of course, if his initial Kantian premise is correct, his methodological position would also be sound. But such reasoning is obviously circular.

It must also be mentioned that within the context of Buddhist contemplation, most experiences and insights are *not* said to be ineffable or inconceivable. While ontological knowledge of ultimate reality (Tibetan *ji lta ba mkhyen pa'i ye shes*) is said to be ineffable, in contrast, contemplative, phenomenological knowledge of conventional reality (Tibetan *ji snyed pa mkhyen pa'i ye shes*) can be articulated; and the latter may be verifiable by other means of inquiry. Now when Katz claims that contemplatives' beliefs and practices define, *in advance*, the types of experiences they want to have and do eventually have, it would seem that he is denying the possibility of *any* real discoveries being made by means of contemplative inquiry. At this point, Katz's claim that his account does not "begin with a priori assumptions about the nature of ultimate reality . . ." (1978: 66) seems highly suspect.

Katz's attitude is remarkably similar to that of the scholastic clerics of Galileo's time who refused to look through his telescope to view the craters on the moon. Since Aristotle's metaphysics denied the possibility of such blemishes on the moon's surface, they were convinced *in advance* that even if they were to see the alleged craters, any such appearances would have to be due to distortions of the lenses of the telescope. Thus, experimental scientists, in their view, were in no better a position to evaluate the nature of scientific discoveries than were scholastic theologians.

From a similar vantage point, many Buddhist scholastics assume that conceptually unmediated knowledge is possible and has been achieved in the past; but they, too, find justification for refusing to put their assumption to the test of experience. Thus, despite the differences in their initial assumptions, the orientations of Katz and Buddhist scholastics are strikingly similar.

For all their differences, proponents of the rationally-oriented dGe lugs order and the empirically-oriented rNying ma and bKa' brgyud orders unite in advocating conceptually unmediated realization of ultimate reality as the goal of contemplative practice. While this experience is said to be of supreme value in and of itself, the authenticity of such experience is validated by its enduring fruits – namely the spontaneous emergence of unprecedented, unconditional love, intuitive wisdom, and freedom from fear and suffering. While dGe lugs pa contemplatives commonly prepare for such realization by means of extensive, intellectual analysis, and rNying ma contemplatives commonly adopt a more empirical approach, the end result, many of them claim, is identical. The progression, as in many other contemplative traditions, is from religious faith and belief to contemplative insight and knowledge.

This raises the fundamental question whether unbiased inquiry ever occurs within contemplative practice, when practitioners are following in the footsteps of earlier teachers who have shown the way to achieving their state of knowledge and enlightenment. This religious approach appears to be fundamentally different from the dominant modern paradigm of effective inquiry and genuine discovery, namely the scientific enterprise. If the ideal of science is to challenge repeatedly even the most widely accepted beliefs and practices of past researchers and to discover truths never before known to humanity, is this not diametrically opposed to the religious ideal of first believing wholeheartedly in the doctrines of one's tradition and then seeking to realize those truths for oneself?

There are certainly important differences between these two models, but there may be more similarity between them than first meets the eye. Buddhism advocates the cultivation of three types of faith: (1) the faith of admiration (Tibetan *dang ba'i dad pa*) for the personal qualities, insights, and deeds of the great practitioners of the past; (2) the faith of belief (*yid ches pa'i dad pa*) in the validity of their insights; and (3) the faith of aspiration (*mngon par 'dod pa'i dad pa*) to realize those same qualities and insights for oneself. While the term *faith* is not commonly associated with the scientific tradition, it is certainly true that many people are drawn to a career in science out of an admiration for the great scientists of the past and their discoveries. Moreover, it is the faith of aspiration that moves them beyond admiration alone to the active pursuit of scientific training and research. As for belief, during the first fifteen or twenty years of one's training in a discipline such as physics, a student is expected to believe in the integrity of the physicists of the past – that they did not fudge their data or perform sloppy analyses – and one must believe that the technology one uses in the laboratory will actually perform as the engineers who created it have claimed. Only in this way can a scientist "stand on the shoulders of their forebears" and make unprecedented discoveries of their own; and, of course, only a small minority of scientists seriously challenge the prevailing scientific views of their time. Nevertheless, the ideal of unwavering belief in religion and the ideal of fundamental skepticism in science do appear to radically segregate these two enterprises; and I suspect that it is this difference that leads Katz and Griffiths to adopt a thoroughly constructivist interpretation of contemplative knowledge.

From a Mahāyāna perspective, however, this issue cannot so easily be laid to rest, for – as Tsong kha pa discusses at considerable length (Tsong Khapa 1984) – given the great diversity of mutually incompatible philosophical doctrines within the Buddhist tradition, belief in the validity of the teachings of the Buddha is no simple matter. While some of these doctrines were intended to be taken literally (Sanskrit *nītārtha*), as clearly representing the nature of reality, other were intended solely as pedagogic devices (*neyārtha*) that may be *instrumentally* effective in leading certain trainees to greater understanding, but which do not accurately *represent* reality. To make this issue all the more problematic, there is no universally accepted Buddhist scripture that distinguishes, once and for all, which among the Buddha's teachings correspond to reality and which are merely pedagogical in nature. Thus, Buddhist practitioners must finally resort to their own reasoning powers and experience to determine which Buddhist theories and practices actually represent reality and lead to valid knowledge. To do so, some degree of skepticism towards one's own tradition seems to be indispensable. In the final analysis, the challenge before Buddhist contemplatives is not so very different from that facing scientific researchers. This fact is obscured, however, when contemplative inquiry is overwhelmed by the scholastic emphasis on preserving a tradition.

The role of belief is also a complex one when it comes to engaging in contemplative practice. While the techniques for cultivating quiescence can be described in precise detail, the types of experiences individuals will have during their own training are unpredictable; and the actual nature of the achievement of quiescence cannot be accurately imagined by those who have not experienced it. Moreover, the conceptually unstructured state of awareness that is purportedly experienced due to the cultivation of insight cannot possibly be grasped with the conceptual mind, so all one's learned ideas about it finally have to be left behind. Even though practitioners first believe in the validity and value of the insights of their contemplative tradition, if they fail to engage in genuine inquiry of their own, those salvific insights will never be achieved; and those practitioners will never become true contemplatives in their own right. Thus, genuine rational and empirical inquiry are indispensable, even though they take place within an accepted belief system.

If Griffiths were thoroughly justified in his conclusions about the nature of insight practice, then Katz would be right about the utterly constructed nature of mystical experience in Buddhism. And historically speaking, their conclusions do often hold true with respect to contemplative traditions that are either dead or dying. However, drawing on the wit of Mark Twain, reports of the demise of the Buddhist contemplative tradition have been somewhat exaggerated.

When the vitality of a contemplative tradition is no longer sustained by accomplished adepts, it may degenerate into dry scholasticism, in which religious beliefs gradually come to appear radically different from empirical knowledge. Moreover, if even textual knowledge of contemplation is lost, then the tradition may be reduced to a scattered array of techniques and miscellaneous claims of altered states of consciousness that are also far removed from verifiable empirical knowledge. According to the fourteenth Dalai Lama, religious writings may be likened to paper currency, while religious experience and especially contemplative experience are like gold reserves.[5] To the extent that such experience is no longer current or considered to be of value, religious texts appear to the outsider to have no validity; and an entire dimension of human experience – from a contemplative point of view, the most important dimension – is sacrificed as a result.

NOTES

1 Tsong kha pa. *Byang chub lam rim che ba.* Collected Works, Vol. Pa.
2 This passage occurs in the section on "Revealing the Nature of Awareness" in Padmasambhava 1997.
3 *Phyag chen rtsa ba rgyal ba'i gzhung lam* ACIP S5939F.ACT, p. 2. In his autocommentary to this text, he explains that according to the tradition he is advocating here, one should first cultivate meditative quiescence and then proceed to the cultivation of insight.
4 Tibetan title: *Dag snang ye shes drva pa las gnas lugs rang byung gi rgyud rdo rje'i snying po.* Sanskrit title: *Vajrahṛdayaśuddhadhutijñānahāreśrīlaṃjātiyātisma.* Collected Works of H.H. Dudjom Rinpoche. Vol. 1. I am presently translating this entire text into English.
5 H. H. the Dalai Lama drew this analogy during a private conversation I had with him in 1980, at his home in Dharamsala, India.

REFERENCES

bDud 'joms gling pa (n.d.). *The Diamond Heart Tantra: A Tantra Naturally Arisen From the Nature of Existence From the Matrix of Primordial Awareness of Pure Appearances.* (*Dag snang ye shes drva pa las gnas lugs rang byung gi rgyud rdo rje'i snying po*) (*Vajrahṛdayaśuddhadhutijñānahāreśrīlaṃ-jātiyātisma*). Collected Works of H. H. Dudjom Rinpoche. Vol. 1.

Griffiths, Paul J. (1986). *On Being Mindless: Buddhist Meditation And The Mind-Body Problem.* La Salle, IL: Open Court.

Karma Chagmé (1997). *A Spacious Path to Freedom: Practical Instructions on the Union of Mahāmudrā and Atiyoga.* Commentary Gyatrul Rinpoche, trans. and ed. B. Alan Wallace. Ithaca: Snow Lion.

Karma chags med (1984) *Meaningful to Behold: The Essential Instructions of Avalokiteśvara on The Union of Mahāmudrā and Atiyoga* (*Thugs rje chen po'i dmar khrid phyag rdzogs zung 'jug thos ba don ldan*) Bylakuppe: Nyingmapa Monastery.

Katz, Steven T. (1978). "Language, Epistemology, and Mysticism." In Steven T. Katz, ed.. *Mysticism and Philosophical Analysis.* New York: Oxford University Press.

Katz, Steven T. (1983). "The 'Conservative' Character of Mystical Experience." In Steven T. Katz, ed., *Mysticism and Religious Traditions.* Oxford: Oxford University Press.

Padmasambhava (n.d.). *The Profound Dharma of The Natural Emergence of the Peaceful and Wrathful from Enlightened Awareness: Stage of Completion Instructions on the Six Transitional Processes (Zab chos zhi khro dgongs pa rang grol gyi rdzogs rim bar do drug gi khrid yig),* a *gter ma* of Padmasambhava revealed by Karma gling pa. Volume 3 of the edition of the Kar gling zhi khro cycle from the library of Dudjom Rinpoche (I-Tib-1440, 75-903780).

Padmasambhava (1997). *Natural Liberation: Padmasambhava's Teachings on the Six Bardos.* Commentary Gyatrul Rinpoche, trans. and ed. B. Alan Wallace. Boston: Wisdom Publications.

Paṇ chen blo bzang chos kyi rgyal mtshan (n.d.). *The Highway of the Victorious Ones: A Root Text on Mahāmudrā* (*Phyag chen rtsa ba rgyal ba'i gzhung lam*). ACIP S5939F.ACT.

Tsong kha pa (n.d.). *A Great Exposition of the States of the Path of Awakening.* (*Byang chub lam rim che ba*) Collected Works, Vol. Pa.

Tsong kha pa (n.d.). *A Small Exposition of the Stages of the Path to Awakening* (*Byang chub lam gyi rim pa chung ba*). Collected Works, Vol. Pha.

Tsong Khapa (1984). *Tsong Khapa's Speech of Gold in the Essence of True Eloquence: Reason and Enlightenment in the Central Philosophy of Tibet.* Trans. Robert A. F. Thurman. Princeton: Princeton University Press.

Eleven

In Search of a Postmodern Middle

Roger R. Jackson

PRELUDE: ON BEING A POSTMODERN BUDDHIST

What does it mean to be Buddhist in the midst of postmodernity? The preposition notwithstanding, "postmodernity" is certainly not a place, and, despite the singular noun, it is not one thing, or even a thing at all. Rather, it is a complex spiritual condition, a range of attitudes, a set of perspectives shaped by the acute hermeneutical self-consciousness that has come, at the turn of the second millennium, to frame nearly every field of human inquiry. Indeed, one of the characteristics of postmodernity is precisely that those subjected to it are in certain respects placeless, without a fixed or final abode in which to secure themselves, without a "thing" to which to cling. In postmodernity, the ancient cosmological and social certainties provided by traditional world-views are left behind, but so, too, are the more recent complacencies of modernism: perpetual social and intellectual progress, the triumph of rationality, the apotheosis of science – that is why it is *post*modernity. Postmodernity is marked above all by a loss of stable identity, and by the concurrent recognition that the world, and human life, are irreducibly characterized, to use David Tracy's terminology, by plurality and ambiguity (see, e.g., Tracy; Lyotard; Lakeland). The more we learn about the varieties of human culture, the idiosyncrasies of our fields of inquiry, the structures of our languages, and the complexity of our self-awareness, the greater becomes our appreciation for the essential plurality of the world and our perspectives upon it. And, when we recognize that each perspective developed within a particular culture or field of inquiry is itself historically situated, grounded in temporally contingent assumptions and purposes, then we are forced to concede that our attitudes and efforts, our words, perhaps our very identities, however certain and compelling they may seem to us, are ultimately relative, provisional, and quite ambiguous: as T. S. Eliot puts it in "East Coker," they "slip, slide, perish, decay with imprecision, will not stay in place" (121). In a world fundamentally plural and ambiguous, there is no Archimedian point: "reality," "truth," "goodness," "self," "happiness" – all the classic absolutes – fall under suspicion, and the Son of Man, or the Daughter of the Buddha, has no place to lay her head.

Postmodernity is not a place, but there are fewer and fewer places where it is not recognized; it is not a thing, but there are fewer and fewer people who remain untouched by it, not only in the greatest cities, but in the remotest villages, as well. This is due largely to of the exponential growth, in the twentieth century, of human systems of transportation and communication. The world may or may not be on the way to becoming the "global village" envisioned by Marshall McLuhan, but it is probably safe to say that never before have so many people been so aware of so many cultures and ideas outside those into which they were born. This awareness of plurality does not, of course, always entail an acceptance of ambiguity – it is entirely possible to declare that, in spite of the plurality of cultures and perspectives around us, there still remain absolute truths, and that our own religion, or field of inquiry, or ideology provides the standard against which all others may be measured and judged. It is, however, increasingly difficult to sustain a purely intellectual defense of such a claim, for the very grounds of certainty that once were seen to provide the foundations for philosophy and the various natural and social sciences, hence for definitive knowledge, have themselves been severely eroded – to the point where it is difficult, if not impossible, to make absolute claims in any other way than dogmatically.

Religious people face a particularly vexing set of problems in their confrontation with postmodernity, just as they did with the onset of modernity. Religions, after all, traditionally have provided encompassing explanations for the nature of the cosmos and how we are to live in it. In pre-modern settings, encounters with a plurality of religious perspectives were common, but generally raised questions only of *how* one might be religious, i.e., what form one's religiousness might take. Modernity, however, with its progressivism, scientism, and epistemological and economic optimism, threatened everywhere that it took hold to replace traditional religious views and values with a secular alternative that was made all the more persuasive by its association with vast military, economic, and political power. For people confronted with modernity, therefore, the question became not *how* to be religious, but *whether* to be religious at all.[1] The last half millennium of European and North American history certainly bears witness to the subversive effects that modernity may bring to traditional religions, and there is ample evidence from the more recently modernizing cultures of Asia, Africa, and Latin America that religious people confront the same difficulties there. Responses vary, of course, ranging from the abandonment of religion altogether, to a turn to fundamentalism, to attempts to assign religion and modernity to separate, incommensurable spheres, but the implications of modernism are nearly impossible to ignore.

In certain respects, the subversion of modernist certainties that is reflected in postmodernism would appear to be good news for the religiously inclined, for the secularist alternative declared by many to have superseded traditional world-views itself has been relativized, as its historical contingency, philosophical limitations, and imperialist presumptions all have been exposed. This would seem to imply that modernist ideas are no more compelling or true than traditional religious perspectives, and that acceptance of the latter is at least as reasonable as embrace of the former (see, e.g., Wolfe; Spretnak). However, the turn to postmodernism equally implies that modernist ideologies cannot be overridden by religious perspectives, either, and religious perspectives tend by their very nature to be totalistic, intended as they are to subsume all other outlooks by providing a comprehensive, metaphysically-grounded view of the world and our place within it. If, from a postmodernist perspective, a given religious outlook can at best be regarded as one plausible alternative among many – no better or worse than secularist or other religious outlooks – then postmodernism provides little more comfort than does modernism, and we should not be surprised that the postmodern relativization of religion has been resisted nearly as strongly as the modernist attempt to replace it outright.

It often has been argued that, of the world's religious traditions, Buddhism is uniquely exempt from the challenges of modernity and postmodernity, because of the uncanny match between philosophical perspectives at the heart of its wisdom literature and outlooks developed in the West in the twentieth century. Thus, it has been suggested by many recent writers, both Western and Asian, that even in its traditional homelands and previous eras, Buddhism was prospectively modernist because of its focus on an impersonal, dynamic, causal, and broadly ecological explanation for the operations of the cosmos, such that more recent scientific explanations simply have filled out, rather than conflicted with, Buddhist accounts (see, e.g., Rahula, Ambedkar, Hayward). Still others (more typically Westerners) have suggested that traditional Buddhism prefigured postmodernity because of the centrality to it of such doctrines as dependent origination, no-self/emptiness, mind-only, and non-abiding *nirvāṇa*, all of which appear to relativize all entities and concepts, while at the same time precluding the possibility that any entity or concept could possess a fixed identity, nature, or abode – hence to foreshadow the postmodern concern with plurality, ambiguity, and the deconstruction of all absolutes (see, e.g., Magliola; Glass; Loy).

However, even if the radical ideas cited as proto-modern or proto-postmodern are now and always have been quite basic to Buddhism, and even if they may more or less reasonably be matched with modernist or postmodernist concepts – each of which is an arguable claim – such ideas never have been sufficient to define what it means to "be Buddhist." For one thing, these implicitly "deconstructive" or "ecological" Buddhist ideas must be seen as related to and in many ways motivated by more conventional metaphysical or religious concepts and concerns, such as the attainment of a state of unassailable spiritual security, *nirvāṇa*, in – or beyond – a cosmos whose every inhabitant is subject to greater or lesser suffering in multiple lives; this condition, *saṃsāra*, is rooted in turn in the ignorant, acquisitive and aggressive actions of the inhabitants themselves. Furthermore, "being Buddhist" has almost never been explicable merely in terms of ideas, whether radical or more conventional; rather, as with religious people everywhere, Buddhists have drawn identity and inspiration as much from affect as from intellect, as much from the resonance of a song as from the force of an idea, as much from stories as from syllogisms, as much from a questioning of the invisible as from an analysis of the seen. Buddhism, in short, has been as shaped by faith and feeling as by philosophy and meditation, and, like adherents of other religions, the vast majority of Buddhists have – the rhetoric of their wisdom traditions notwithstanding – sought a locus of genuine stability in an otherwise capricious universe, whether in the three jewels of refuge, the silence of samādhi, the advice of a guru, the life of the saṅgha, the words of a *sūtra*, or the vision of a buddha radiant just beyond the horizon, or just beyond this life.[2] Understood in this way, rather than on the basis of selected radical ideas, traditional Buddhism appears considerably less modern, or postmodern, and considerably more like other religions.

But, if modern thought has superseded much of traditional cosmology, and if postmodernist perspectives have relativized all possible viewpoints, both religious and secular, it hardly seems possible any longer to "be Buddhist" in the traditional manner. Past and future lives appear at best to be speculations backed by ambiguous evidence. The concept of karma, asserted to be both invisible and ubiquitous in the operations of the cosmos, seems, like the traditional Christian concept of God, to explain so much with so little evidence that it ends by explaining nothing at all. The ideal of *nirvāṇa* – especially within this life – seems to imply a kind of human perfectibility of which most of us have grown suspicious. Religious practices, from meditation, to chanting, to donation to the saṅgha, may change an individual life or even a whole society, but that they bring ultimate peace to either is far less obvious. Guru after guru has proven to be human – and in many cases, all-too-human. Texts have been contextualized, hence relativized, by other texts, and by our knowledge of their historicity. Visions are scarce, and, like nearly all other religious experiences, subject to psychological, or even physiological, explanations that belie the extraordinariness usually claimed for them within traditions. Would it not be better, then, for Buddhists, and other religious people, simply to cut their losses by a thorough demythologization, abjuring ideas that no longer seem plausible, while focusing on those few, crucial concepts that allow them to remain flexible and effective in the contemporary ideological world-bazaar? Why not simply emphasize a good, postmodern perspective like the wisdom realizing emptiness, add to it a socially responsible interpretation of the ideal of compassionate action, call that Buddhism, and be done with it?

The answer to these questions may depend in turn on the way we choose to answer one of the hoariest questions Westerners have asked about Buddhism: Is it a philosophy or a religion? If Buddhism simply is a set of broadly construed ideas and ideals – the truth of emptiness, the value of contemplation, the cultivation of a compassionate heart and nonviolent action – then to "be Buddhist" in the midst of postmodernity is not difficult at all; what is more, the very generality of these ideas and ideals means that Buddhism itself becomes a virtually unrestricted tradition, such that, as Jorge Luis Borges puts it, "[a] good Buddhist can be a Lutheran or Methodist or Presbyterian or Calvinist or Shintoist or Taoist or Catholic; he may be a proselyte of Islam or of the Jewish religion, all with complete freedom" (59). Conversely, to the degree that he or she values emptiness, contemplation, and compassion, the Lutheran, Taoist, or Jew – or, for that matter, the secular humanist – may with equal conviction claim to be a Buddhist. If that is all there is to it, if Buddhism is simply an infinitely protean postmodern philosophy, then it is little more than a cipher, bereft of distinctive content, applicable everywhere, hence nowhere. If, on the other hand, Buddhism is understood as not just an ideology but a religion, then it is not enough simply to subscribe to certain general ideas or values of Buddhist provenance, and declare oneself a Buddhist; rather, one must, to quote Borges again, "*feel* the four noble truths and the eightfold path" (59), *tell* the Buddha's story, *do* the things that Buddhists always have done; one must, in short, form one's life through the myths, symbols, metaphors, and ritual acts of Buddhist tradition. And, to the degree that from a postmodern perspective not just religions, but ideological systems and analytical processes, too, are understood to be human constructions rooted in myths, symbols, metaphors, and ritual acts, philosophy itself never can be self-sufficient, for it turns out to be inextricable from mythopoetic processes fundamental to human language, thought and society.[3] In this sense, being Buddhist in postmodernity begins to look a lot like being Buddhist in a traditional setting – but without the philosophical certainty.

This lack of certainty may seem to open a huge gulf between traditional and postmodern Buddhists, but I would maintain that this is so only if we insist that such certainty is fundamental to religiousness. To assert that it is seems to require precisely the sort of reduction of religion to philosophy, and philosophy to the attainment of definitive knowledge, that no longer seems possible, given the state of our understanding of how both "religion" and "philosophy" actually work. Indeed, it is tempting, given postmodern perspectives, to argue that we might with justification reduce philosophy to a form of religion, but that is not a line I wish to pursue here. Rather, in the light of the preceding discussion, I simply want to assert that, (a) in both its traditional and postmodern settings, a religion is *not* most usefully understood as a set of doctrines that must be either true or false, (b) to "be religious" is above all to approach life through a certain *aesthetic*, found primarily but not exclusively in specific myths, symbols, metaphors, and ritual acts, (c) Buddhism, in both its traditional and postmodern settings, must be understood as a religion, (d) to "be Buddhist" is to live primarily within the aesthetic constellation formed by such myths as the Jātakas or the story of the Buddha, such symbols as the *stūpa* or the monk, such metaphors as the wheel or the middle way, and such ritual acts as prostration or meditation; and (e) in this aesthetic view of Buddhism, such doctrines as *saṃsāra* and *nirvāṇa*, dependent origination and emptiness, are still quite important, but, rather than definitive of the tradition, they are seen as one aspect among many, and, rather than propositions to be proved or refuted, they are seen as metaphors or images that help to form the imaginative and affective landscape in which Buddhists live and move and have their being.

A fuller justification of my aesthetic definition of religion in general and Buddhism in particular will have to await another forum.[4] Here, I simply want to take that definition as a working hypothesis, and explore, from two different angles of approach, its usefulness for understanding what it means – and has meant – to "be Buddhist." My first approach will be autobiographical; an account of my own resolution of the problem of being Buddhist will perforce be anecdotal, but may nevertheless be instructive, if for no other reason than revealing the personal sources of my hypothesis. The second approach will be metaphorical; through an analysis of an exemplary Buddhist image, that of "the middle," I hope to show how a particular metaphor has "worked" for Buddhists from the tradition's inception and may continue to work for them in a postmodern setting. Neither of these approaches will prove my hypothesis, but if they stimulate others to think along similar lines, my essay will have served its purpose.

AN AUTOBIOGRAPHICAL APPROACH: WRESTLING WITH DHARMAKĪRTI

I was raised, in the fifties and early sixties, in Europe and the New York suburbs, in a good, but non-religious family. My father was a lapsed Southern Baptist, my mother a freethinker. They slept late on Sundays, and let my brother and me do so, too. In my teens, I passed through a number of intellectual phases typical of precocious adolescents of the era: Marxist, existentialist, nature mystic. I arrived at college considering myself more or less a Buddhist, but in the course of four years I read only a few books on Buddhism (D. T. Suzuki, Herbert Guenther, Frederick Streng on Nāgārjuna[5]) and meditated hardly at all. Like virtually my entire peer group, I experimented with psychedelics; like many, I had experiences that I was convinced were tantamount to enlightenment. The sense of enlightenment wore off, but the desire to explore my mind did not. After graduation, I moved to the San Francisco Bay Area, but even a year in that spiritually vibrant locale did not alter my relation to Buddhism, which remained almost purely intellectual.

My introduction to real Buddhist practice came in the spring of 1974, at Kopan Monastery, near Kathmandu, Nepal, where I attended a one-month intensive course taught by two English-speaking Tibetan lamas of the dGe lugs tradition, Thubten Yeshe and Thubten Zopa Rinpoche. The heart of the course was the lamas' lectures on the *lam rim*, or stages of the path to enlightenment, a system of meditation that involves a progressive inculcation of the basics of the Tibetan Buddhist world-view: the fundamental purity of the mind, the importance of the spiritual master, the rarity and usefulness of the human rebirth, the certainty and unpredictability of death, the ineluctable functioning of karma, the dire experiences awaiting those born into *saṃsāra*'s lower realms, the unsatisfactoriness of even the higher realms, the enchainment of the twelve links of dependent origination, and, above all the crucial importance of taking refuge in the Buddha, Dharma and Saṅgha, and developing, in turn, renunciation toward *saṃsāra*, the altruistic spirit of enlightenment, *bodhicitta*, and the realization of emptiness as the final nature of all *dharmas*.[6] These topics were, for the most part, presented quite traditionally and literally, and, considered within the larger course context of dawn precepts, heavy incense, prostration and chanting, long meditation sessions, and intensive group discussions (not to mention crowded conditions, little sleep, and bad food) they represented for most of us a radically different way of understanding, and living in, the world. The course was, quite simply, an invitation to total immersion in Buddhism, and I, overwhelmed by the teachings and deeply impressed by the lamas, took the plunge, shaving my head, going for refuge, and taking my first tantric initiations. I went into retreat for a time after the course, making meditation part of my daily routine, then traveled to Dharamsala, India, to study for the summer with Geshe Ngagwang Dhargyey at the library established there by the Dalai Lama. In the fall, I returned to Kopan for another one-month course, which only deepened my sense that I had found my path, and the teachers to guide me along it.

Out of funds, I knew that return to the U.S. was inevitable. Wanting to continue my Dharma studies in as intensive a manner as possible, I enrolled in the Buddhist Studies program at the University of Wisconsin-Madison, under the tutelage of Geshe Lhundup Sopa, a highly respected Tibetan master who also happened to be one of my Kopan lamas' most important teachers. It undoubtedly would be an exaggeration to say I arrived in Madison wrapped in dogmatic slumber, for I had a number of uncertainties about key points of Buddhist doctrine, but for the most part those uncertainties were in abeyance, suspended in the service of practicing Buddhism zealously, learning as much as I could from texts and teachers, and working to help found a meditation center in Madison. A college friend who visited me soon after I moved to Madison wondered what I found so appealing about a "medieval" world-view, but for me, that vision, though far from proved, was full of possibilities, and at least as compelling as what the modern West had to offer. Why could there not be past and future lives? Why might not karma be a real force in the cosmos, working in the ways described by Buddhists? Why couldn't humans attain states of mind in which ignorance, anger, and greed would never arise? Why couldn't Buddhist practices utterly transform one into the sort of person described in the hagiographies? With time, however, my uncertainties grew, or, rather, reasserted themselves. Where was the proof? Certainly, the reality of *saṃsāra* and *nirvāṇa*, of rebirth, karma, and buddhas, were far from self-evident, and what right, I began to ask myself, had I to practice as if they were? My dilemma was aggravated by the fact that Buddhism claimed to be a non-dogmatic tradition, open to empirical and rational inspection, yet the more I inspected, the less certain I became that basic Buddhist doctrines were anything more than another form of science fiction. Basic metaphysical issues aside, I also was less and less satisfied by the ways in which Buddhism addressed a variety of emotional and social issues that seemed to me vitally important, from the place of anger and sexual love in human life, to the Buddhist's relation to the political order. My practice waned, my certainty that I was really was a Buddhist wavered.

Over five years of serious Buddhist study, whenever I had expressed doubts to my teachers, they had referred me to the same work: the great seventh-century Indian treatise on logic and epistemology, the *Pramāṇavārttika* of Dharmakīrti, which had exercised immeasurable influence over later Indian, and all Tibetan, Buddhism. In particular, the *Pramāṇavārttika*'s second chapter, on the establishment of authority (*pramāṇasiddhi*), was said to contain a demonstration of the reality of past and future lives, the plausibility of the Buddha's attainment of enlightenment, and the truth of the Four Noble Truths that could stand up to any attempt at disproof. Since the time had come for me to find a dissertation topic, I resolved to focus on the second chapter of the *Pramāṇavārttika*, as elucidated in the greatest of all dGe lugs pa commentaries on the text, by the fifteenth-century Tibetan master, rGyal tshab rje. What followed was four years of thinking, reading, consultation with lamas, writing, more consultation, more thinking, reading, and writing, and still more consultation. By the time I produced my gargantuan, 1020-page dissertation – half philosophical analysis, half translation and annotation of rGyal tshab's commentary[7] – I had decided that Dharmakīrti's arguments did not, in fact, work. As sophisticated as they were, they required both the distortion of opposing views and the presumption of certain problematic axioms, above all, the mind's fundamental purity and independence of particular bodies. They could not, therefore, be said conclusively to demonstrate the reality of past and future lives, the Buddha's attainment of enlightenment, or the truth of the Four Noble Truths.

At this point, nine years after taking refuge, my belief in the basics of the Buddhist world-view – of those metaphysical doctrines I first had imbibed at Kopan, and sought for a decade to comprehend – had almost completely evaporated. Logically, I should have stopped being a Buddhist. But I did not. Indeed, I reached the end of my long skeptical inquiry, and found that my sense of "being Buddhist" was nearly as strong as ever. How could this be? Shouldn't my painful awakening from religious dogmatism have spelled the end of my relation to Buddhism? That it did not is due, I believe, to at least three separate factors, which may not be entirely idiosyncratic to my own personal history.

First, while over the course of time my confidence in the literal accuracy of Buddhist metaphysical claims weakened, other aspects of Buddhist doctrine and practice continued to seem irrefutable. In particular, I still found utterly compelling, and endlessly fruitful, (a) the central Mahāyāna philosophical claim, that all entities and concepts are empty of self-existence because they are dependently originated, (b) the basic Mahāyāna ethical injunction, that one ought to be a compassionate bodhisattva, working as much as possible for the benefit of others, and (c) the basic Buddhist claim that meditation – whether concentrative or analytical, complex or formless – is the best tool yet developed for disciplining one's mind, hence of altering one's way of seeing the world and living within it. All three of these perspectives, it seemed to me, were valuable quite independently of whether there are or are not multiple lives, does or does not exist a universal karmic law, is or is not a transcendent perfection like that ascribed to buddhas. In certain respects, to focus on emptiness, compassion, and meditation, while letting Buddhist metaphysics go, is to make a move very much like that chosen by many Christians in the last two centuries: demythologizing one's tradition, and selecting from it certain doctrines that, whether or not they can be upheld in a traditional manner, seem existentially meaningful and useful, regardless of one's cultural or historical situation (see, e.g., Batchelor 1983, 1997). The advantage of such a demythologized, bare-bones Buddhism is that it permits one to preserve a core set of Buddhist beliefs and practices without having to subject oneself to the cognitive dissonance involved in trying to subscribe to "medieval" beliefs while living in a world shaped by modernity; its disadvantage is that it threatens to deprive Buddhism of the majesty of its vision, the mystery of its great narratives, the resonance of its art and rituals. Indeed, bare-bones Buddhism has precious little to differentiate it from secular humanism; one may as well read Camus as the *Dhammapada*.

There was, however, a second, crucial dimension to my sense of being Buddhist in a post-metaphysical mode, which put some flesh back onto those bare doctrinal bones. Not only had my confidence in certain key perspectives survived my skeptical inquiry, but so, too, had my "feel" for the myths, symbols, and metaphors, the sights, sounds, and sensations of Buddhism. Subtly, inexorably, years of exposure to and internalization of these "aesthetic" aspects of the tradition had brought me to a point where they became the most powerful single lens through which I viewed myself and the world, a paradigm to which I had grown so accustomed that it seemed to form an a priori condition for much of my experience. So, my confidence in emptiness, compassion, and meditation was *not* deprived of its rich, surrounding context; indeed, such doctrines and practices were for me quite inseparable from the scent of juniper incense on a cold morning, the sense of rightness I felt when prostrating to an image or circumambulating a *stūpa*, the shiver sent through me by the very word *śūnyatā*, the sweet possibilities conjured by certain ritual songs, the mystery contained in the smile on Buddha statue from Borobudur. Nor, despite my skepticism, did I separate those basic doctrines from the rich vision and language of traditional Buddhist metaphysics: I still could recite the Buddha's life-story, Māra and all, though I knew it bore little relation to what historians accept; could praise enlightened beings for qualities I doubted they, or anyone, literally could possesses; could vow to liberate sentient beings in future lives I was not certain thcy would experience; could contemplate as primordially pure a mind I was not convinced was more than a byproduct of the brain. This "aestheticized" but non-metaphysical Buddhism has the advantage over the demythologized version of thoroughly engaging not just the intellect, but all of one's imaginative and sensory powers, thereby providing a fuller context and greater incentives for belief and practice (see, e.g., Guenther; Trungpa). It is possible, on the other hand, to interpret such an aestheticized Buddhism as a mere exercise in nostalgia and self-delusion, a predictable by-product of the perpetual human need to create a vision, with reinforcing experiences, that will help make sense of a chaotic world. On such a view, an aestheticized but non-metaphysical Buddhism is the result a cowardly compromise, in which one has the courage neither to accept traditional metaphysics in the face of modernist doubts, nor to rest satisfied merely with those doctrines that stand up to the rigorous empirical and logical tests to which they, like all truth-claims, must be subjected.

The inadequacy of this critique of an aesthetic Buddhism lies, I believe, in a third factor of which I had become aware by the time I finished my dissertation: the postmodernist discovery of (a) the impossibility of determining finally the "truth" of *any* particular world-view or vision, whether traditional or modern and (b) the inadequacy of defining religion on the basis primarily of core metaphysical doctrines, or determining the meaningfulness of a religion on the basis of the "correspondence to reality" of those metaphysical doctrines. If all world-views or religious visions are understood to be complex human constructs, relative to particular cultural and historical circumstances and to people's interactions with other people and the world around them, such views or visions begin less to resemble science, in the traditional sense of an objective description of the human and natural world, and more to resemble art, as a selective and creative interpretation of human experience. Science itself increasingly comes to be seen as a sort of art, as does philosophy; what, then, to say of the avowedly less objective realm of religion? Where all modes of inquiry turn out to be "art," decisions about truth become far more problematic. At the very least, alternative visions of the cosmos and human possibility, e.g., secular or religious, Christian or Buddhist, no longer seem to be in direct competition, but, rather, to represent one or another imaginative manner of organizing human knowledge, experience, and aspirations. The choice of one or the other, therefore, turns out not to be based on its greater ultimate plausibility or on any complete correspondence to objective reality – for no such plausibility or correspondence can finally be established – but on its capacity to provide a coherent paradigm for thinking about and acting within the world in an effective and meaningful manner. The choice, in short, is an aesthetic one, for that may be the only sort of choice that, in a postmodern setting, remains open. Thus, to be a Buddhist may be as reasonable as to be a Christian or a secular humanist, for each of these is simply an aesthetic, an imaginative and effective way of organizing one's life and thought. One may tell the stories one enjoys, sing the songs that move one, perform the acts that seem required, and even proclaim the doctrines that seem to reflect one's sense of the true. One may, in fact, do, think, and say all the things that traditionally religious people have done, thought, and said, and may do so with the deep conviction derived from traditional authority or personal experience – as long as one does not fall into the trap of believing that one's commitment is anything more than a strong aesthetic preference: a celebration of possibility, perhaps even probability, but never of absolute certainty.

The advantage of this approach to "being Buddhist" is that it permits a contemporary person to participate unapologetically and conscientiously in the full range of the tradition's dimensions: mythological, doctrinal, ritual, ethical, institutional, and experiential. The disadvantages, it may be objected, are that it (a) denies the very essence of religiousness, which is absolute conviction in a total explanation of the cosmos and (b) succumbs too readily to a postmodern relativism that is philosophically self-contradictory and subversive of all notions of progress in the attainment of truth.[8] These are serious concerns, which do not admit of simple replies. The essence of religiousness *is* quite difficult to separate from a sense of absolute conviction in a total explanation of things, yet I would argue that such a definition is quite limited, shaped as it is by post-Enlightenment Western philosophical concerns with the centrality of rationality in all matters, and failing as it does to account for the richer, more complex and "aesthetic" ways in which humans – traditionally and in postmodernity – actually experience and express religiousness. The eschewal of absolute truth for one's own religious or ideological stance *does* open the door to a certain degree of relativism, but I would urge that the relativism is not thoroughgoing, precisely because various religious and ideological communities, in their inevitable encounter, create a natural system of "checks and balances," whereby their assertions are counterpoised both to one another and to the powerfully consensual assertions of both science and common sense – a process that leads to the provisional acceptance of certain truth claims as, in David Tracy's phrase, "relatively adequate" (22 *et passim*). Can I, or any Buddhist, live comfortably with the sense that his or her tradition may be "only" relatively adequate in its description of, and approach to, the way things are? The question is not easily answered, but I want to suggest, through the following exploration of the Buddhist metaphor of the middle, that the tradition itself provides good grounds for thinking so.

A METAPHORICAL APPROACH: *MEZZO DEL CAMMIN* AND THE *MADHYAMA PRATIPAD*

In the West, to find oneself in the middle is generally unfortunate. While it is true that our languages contain such expressions as "golden mean" and "happy medium," far more often the middle is depicted as a locus of uncertainty, a condition in which resolution is impossible because one is not committed to one "side" or the other, or no longer where one was, but not yet where one is bound. We speak of being "caught in the middle," and find the sense of such expressions as "middle class," "middle age," "middle west" or "middle reliever" only in relation to the more definite extremes to which they are relative: rich and poor, youth and old age, east and west coast, starter and closer. It also is an index of underachievement: the English word "mediocrity" contains the image of the middle, and we speak of a less than towering literary figure as a "middling" poet or novelist, while in Italian, something or someone that is "so-so" is said to be "mezzo-mezzo" ("middle-middle"). By the canons of classical aesthetics, tragedies must start *in medias res*, in the midst of an ongoing crisis, whose seeds are in the past and whose dénouement has yet to be worked out; the middle from which the play begins is where the situation is most inchoate. In the epic realm, Dante begins his *Commedia* with one of the most famous, and expressive Western descriptions of what it means to be in the middle: "In the middle of my life's path / I found myself in a darkened wood, / For the direct way was lost" (5). He is quite consciously echoed by T. S. Eliot, who writes in "East Coker" of being "[i]n the middle, not only in the middle of the way / But all the way, in a dark wood, in a bramble, / On the edge of a grimpen, where is no secure foothold, / And menaced by monsters, fancy lights, / Risking enchantment" (125). Eliot writes in the same poem of finding himself ". . . in the middle way, having had twenty years – / Twenty years largely wasted . . . – / Trying to learn to use words, and every attempt / Is a wholly new start, and a different kind of failure" (128). For the Westerner, in short, the middle is where one's way is lost.

For the Buddhist, on the other hand, the middle is precisely where the path is found. From the very inception of the tradition, the middle has served as one of the handful of fundamental Buddhist metaphors, along with such images as the wheel (whether of rebirth or of Dharma, or, later, as a *cakra* within the tantric subtle body), the river (*saṃsāra*'s flow and the spate of defilements, or the effortless flow of primordial mind), seeds and fruits (a model for the functioning of karma), space (a meditative attainment, or an index of the ultimately empty and/or mind-based nature of things), the path (a continual sequence of acts conducive to enlightenment), *nirvāṇa* (the extinction – as of a fire – of suffering and its causes), and, not least, *buddha* (which invests the terms for the tradition, Buddhadharma, its founder, the Buddha, and its normative ideal, buddhahood, with the imagery of awakening, as from a sleep of ignorance, a deluded dream). All of these (and many other) metaphors have been subject to constant elaboration and reinterpretation over the centuries, and provide us, in their transformations, with a fascinating way of understanding the growth of Buddhist tradition, through time and across cultures.[9] None is more ancient, richer in interpretive lore, or more resonant in the postmodern age, than the metaphor of the middle.

If we accept the nearly universal Buddhist claim that the Buddha's first "formal" discourse following his enlightenment is reflected in the themes – if not necessarily the exact wording – of the *Dharmacakrapravartana Sūtra* ("*Sūtra* Turning the Wheel of Dharma"), then the proclamation that founds the entire Buddhist tradition is of a "middle way." At the very beginning of the *sūtra* the Buddha identifies two extremes (*anta*) that are not be practiced by renunciants: indulgence in sense-pleasures and devotion to self-mortification, i.e., hedonism and asceticism; he then adds that, avoiding these extremes, he has realized a middle path or middle way (*madhyama pratipad*), which is conducive to vision, knowledge, tranquillity, insight, and enlightenment, and which consists of the Noble Eightfold Path, namely, right views, intentions, speech, action, livelihood, effort, mindfulness, and concentration.[10] This initial articulation will help to frame all subsequent Buddhist discourse about the middle: the combination of negative and positive rhetoric, in which one identifies two extremes to be avoided and the characteristics of the middle between them, will be basic to the tradition ever afterward. Indeed, to the degree that the eightfold noble path covers fully what it means to "be Buddhist," we might, with only slight exaggeration, regard all subsequent Buddhist literature as a set of footnotes to the *Dharmacakrapravartana Sūtra*, as an attempt to work out where the middle is to be found with respect to views, intentions, speech, action, livelihood, effort, mindfulness, and concentration. Nevertheless, within the context of the *sūtra* itself, it is really only right action that receives any kind of detailed treatment; in that sense, the earliest detailed articulation of the metaphor of the middle deals with what we might call the ethical middle, i.e., a way of life that steers between the extremes of hedonism and asceticism.

Understanding the middle in terms of other elements of the eightfold noble path was worked out elaborately in subsequent literature, either implicitly or explicitly. Thus, for instance, right livelihood for lay people might be defined as avoidance of the extremes of, on the one hand, unrestricted participation in the occupation of one's choice and, on the other, prohibition of any occupation that involved the slightest harm to sentient beings. Right speech might be defined as avoidance of the extremes of, on the one hand, speech heedless of subject, style of delivery, or truthfulness and, on the other hand, silence. Right concentration might be defined as avoidance of the extremes of mental scattering and sinking. And meditation (*bhāvanā*), comprised of right mindfulness and right concentration, might be defined as avoidance of the extremes of, on the one hand, only placement meditation, which lacks the correct view, hence wisdom, derived from analysis, and, on the other hand, only analytical meditation, which lacks stability and depth. Indeed, it became a standard view early on that proper Buddhist meditation must *combine* the two elements that, taken on their own are inadequate; this notion of "right meditation" displays another aspect of Buddhist discourse about the middle, which would gain special importance in a Mahāyāna setting, namely, the middle as a *combination* of elements that, taken in isolation, would be considered extreme.

The aspect of the eightfold noble path that probably received the most extensive articulation in terms of the metaphor of the middle was that of right views, which might include views about such diverse, but basic, topics as rebirth, karma, causation, and existence and non-existence. Thus, the *Milindapañhā* ("Questions of [King] Milinda") articulates early Buddhist ideas of rebirth and karma through a series of similes (e.g., the connection of a fire to the fire that lit it, the transformation of milk to yogurt, the protestations of a mango thief) that are intended to demonstrate that the relation between the different rebirths or karmic causes and effects of a single "individual" is neither identity nor difference. The text does not explicitly cite the metaphor of the middle, but by positing two extremes, each of which is unacceptable, and suggesting a way of avoiding those extremes, it strongly implies that we can understand rebirth or karma only if a middle position can be reached.[11] More explicit in its identification of the basic Buddhist view as a middle way is the *Mahākatyāyana Sūtra* ("*Sūtra* [Spoken] to Mahākatyāyana"), which begins with the assertion that most people hold to a belief in either existence (*sat*) or non-existence (*asat*), in this case meaning eternalism or nihilism with respect to the duration and ontological status of things. Each of these, however, is identified as an extreme view, based on a partial, ill-motivated apprehension of reality. On the other hand, one who, "in light of the highest knowledge," sees that things arise, will not be prone to deny their existence absolutely, while one who apprehends the converse, that all things that arise inevitably cease, will not be prone to affirm their existence absolutely, either. The middle way taught by the Buddha is asserted to avoid these extremes, and is specifically identified with the teaching of the twelve links of dependent origination: ignorance, formations, consciousness, name-and-form, sense-faculties, contact, sensation, craving, grasping, becoming, rebirth, and aging and death. This teaching avoids the extreme of non-existence because it affirms that each factor arises in definite dependence upon the factor that precedes it in the "chain"; it avoids the extreme of existence because it affirms that each can cease upon the cessation of the factor on which it depends.[12]

The *Mahākatyāyana Sūtra*'s concern with avoiding ontological extremes is self-consciously taken up, extended, and radicalized by Nāgārjuna in his fundamental text on Mahāyāna wisdom, the *Madhyamakakārikā*, or "Stanzas on the Middle Way." In chapter fifteen, "Examination of Self-Existence," one of the pithiest and most important in the text, Nāgārjuna cites the *Mahākatyāyana Sūtra* as a canonical source of the Buddha's refutation of the extremes of "is" and "is not" (15: 7), and goes on to paraphrase the *sūtra* in support of his claim that the very concept of self-existence (*svabhāva*) inevitably pushes one toward eternalism or nihilism, neither of which is tenable in a cosmos governed by causes and conditions (15: 10-11) (see, e.g., Inada: 99–100; Garfield: 222–224). Unlike the *Mahākatyāyana Sūtra*, Nāgārjuna does not specify that the course between "is" and "is not" is a middle way, though any educated reader would quickly draw the inference. Rather, his one specific reference to the metaphor from which his text draws its name is found in the twenty-fourth chapter, "Examination of the Four Noble Truths." There, in response to a critic's claim that his analysis of all entities and concepts as empty precludes causation and all other conventions, as well as the efficacy of the Buddha's teachings (24: 1-6), Nāgārjuna introduces the crucial distinction between the two truths, superficial (*saṃvṛti*) and ultimate (*paramārtha*), each of which has its proper sphere of application, and each of which is in harmony with the other (24: 7-10); indeed, it is only if entities are ultimately empty that they can function conventionally, for the alternative to emptiness, self-existence, obviates all change, hence all conventional arising and ceasing (24: 14-17). In short, Nāgārjuna asserts, "We declare that whatever is dependent origination is emptiness, and that [latter], a dependent designation, is itself the middle path. Since there is no dharma that is not dependently originated, there is no dharma that is not empty" (24: 18-19) (see, e.g., Inada: 143–148; Garfield: 292–308). The "middle" decreed by Nāgārjuna here is, taken negatively, a path between the "is" implied by interpreting the cosmos in terms of self-existence and the "is not" implied by applying emptiness in too thoroughgoing a manner; stated more positively, it is the mutual implication between dependent origination and emptiness, whereby understanding that entities and concepts arise conventionally in dependence upon causes and conditions entails automatically that they are ultimately empty, while the recognition that their ultimate nature is emptiness means that they must be conventionally established dependent arisings. In this sense, Nāgārjuna's middle avoids the extremes of eternalism and nihilism taken as absolutes, but permits the assertion of "is" and "is not" as conventional designations as long as *both* of the two truths are kept in mind.

The philosophical schools inspired by Nāgārjuna took their common name, Madhyamaka, from the title of his greatest work, but they were far from unanimously agreed on where, precisely, the middle described by the term ought to be located, for the conceptualizations of the eternalist and nihilist extremes to be avoided varied with time and circumstance. Thus, Svātantrika Mādhyamikas, such as Bhāvaviveka, Jñānagarbha, Śāntarakṣita, and Kamalaśīla (6th-8th centuries CE), tended to believe that nihilism would be incurred if conventional entities were not asserted to have their own conventional self-natures (e.g., as radically momentary, or mind-only), and independent (*svatantra*) syllogisms framed to establish ultimate and conventional truths; the Svātantrika middle, therefore requires a more "positive" approach to philosophy, in which the two truths are blended, though not indistinguishably. Prāsaṅgika Mādhyamikas, on the other hand, such as Buddhapālita, Candrakīrti, and Śāntideva (6th-8th centuries CE), maintained that such assertions and modes of argument opened the door to eternalism, and that all constructive philosophy and argumentation had to be eschewed in favor of critical analysis of the consequences (*prasaṅga*) of other schools' positions; the Prāsaṅgika middle, therefore, requires a more negative approach, in which the two truths are kept distinct, though never utterly disconnected.

In the view of Seng-chao, Chi-tsang and other Chinese Mādhyamika masters of the San-lun ("Three Treatise") school (6th-7th centuries), the two truths is a crucial concept, but prone to misunderstanding: taken separately, the conventional truth conduces to eternalism, and the ultimate to nihilism, while taken in contradistinction, they breed dualistic habits of thought; this requires the positing of a *tertium quid* in which the extremes and the dualism implied by traditional ways of stating the two truths are transcended, permitting one to arrive at the San-lun "middle," in which neither *saṃsāra* nor *nirvāṇa*, existence nor non-existence, duality nor non-duality, extreme nor middle, can be maintained, and so principle (*li*) is perfectly upheld (see, e.g., Chan: 360 ff.). The Great Madhyamaka (*dbu ma chen po*) outlook associated with certain Tibetan proponents of Other-Emptiness (*gzhan stong*), such as Rang 'byung rdo rje, Dol po pa shes rab rgyal mtshan, and 'Jam mgon kong sprul (13th-18th centuries), begins with the contention that the thoroughgoing application of emptiness to both conventional *and* ultimate phenomena, so typical of both Prāsaṅgikas and Svātantrikas, leads to the nihilistic conclusion that buddhahood is empty in the same way that conventional entities are, whereas, although saṃsāric conventionalities are empty of self-existence, e.g., because they are dependently originated, buddhahood is empty only of those conventionalities, while its natural purity, luminosity, and gnosis are eternally established and independently existent; thus, the Great Madhyamaka middle involves negating the self-existence of conventional entities and concepts, but not of the ultimate buddha-mind, which, more than merely a soteriological goal, is the very basis of both *saṃsāra* and *nirvāṇa* (see, e.g., Gyamtso Rimpoche: 76; Hookham: 157–159).

Mādhyamikas were far from the only Buddhists to claim that they had located the true middle view intended by the Buddha; the ideal of the middle has helped to shape the articulation of nearly all Buddhist philosophical positions,[13] to the point where even the much-deplored "Personalists" maintained that the concept of *pudgala* they posited to account for personal continuity avoided nihilism because it was a positive entity, and eternalism because it was defined as neither permanent nor impermanent. One non-Madhyamaka text that explicitly employs the metaphor of the middle is the fourth-century *Madhyāntavibhāga* ("Distinguishing the Middle From the Extremes"), a verse treatise variously attributed to Maitreya or Asaṅga that is couched primarily in the language of Yogācāra. Regarding the Mādhyamika insistence upon emptiness as a species of nihilism, the *Madhyāntavibhāga*'s author opens with the assertion that "[t]he imaginer of the unreal (*abhūtaparikalpa*) exists: there is no duality in it, but emptiness exists in it; therefore, all [entities] are neither empty nor non-empty, because of the existence [of the imaginer of the unreal], the non-existence [of duality], and the existence [of the emptiness of the imaginer of the unreal] – and that is the middle path" (1: 1-2). This gnomic utterance would prove deeply influential on Yogācāra philosophy; it is capable of multiple interpretations, at least one of which, suggested by the *Madhyāntavibhāga* itself, is in terms of the familiar concept of the three natures, the imputed (*parikalpita*), dependent (*paratantra*), and the absolute (*parinispanna*), of which the first is utterly unreal, the last is utterly real, and the second is, depending upon one's perspective, either real or unreal; the middle, thus, consists in being able to distinguish, with relation to dependently originated phenomena, what is unreal – imputations of duality or externality – from what is real – the non-existence of any imputed duality or externality.[14] Unsurprisingly, Yogācāra and Madhyamaka themselves came eventually to be seen as extremes between which a middle must be found: later Svātantrika Mādhyamikas defined Yogācāra assertions of the mind's ultimate reality as eternalism, and alleged Prāsaṅgika denials of the mind's conventional existence as nihilism, suggesting that conventionally, all entities must be seen as "mind-only," but that ultimately, the mind was no more self-existent than its objects.

The explicit or implicit articulation of a middle between undesirable extremes also is a hallmark of much of Mahāyāna *sūtra* literature, as, for instance, in the *Vimalakīrtinirdeśa Sūtra*'s indication of a "Dharma door of non-duality" opening between any possible set of extremes (chapter 9, tr., e.g., Thurman: 73–77), the *Laṅkāvatāra*'s assertion that self-realization is "devoid of being and non-being, oneness and otherness, bothness and non-bothness, existence and non-existence, eternity and non-eternity [and] has nothing to do with the false imagination" (24: 89, tr. Suzuki: 78), and the *Prajñāpāparmitā sūtras*' repeated assertions (most famously, in the *Heart Sūtra*) that the bodhisattva is free from clinging either to form or to emptiness, since the two are not, finally, different from one another: all forms are empty, but emptiness invariably is predicated of forms (or sensations, perceptions, formations, or consciousness). The literature also characterizes the bodhisattva's practice positively, in terms of the need to conjoin the wisdom realizing emptiness with a compassionate commitment to the welfare, material and spiritual, of all sentient beings, wherever they may be. The layman Vimalakīrti's ability to involve himself in worldly affairs for the sake of others, while at the same time being detached from them on the basis of his renunciation and wisdom, is regarded as epitomizing the bodhisattva ideal, and there are countless other examples of such practices in other Mahāyāna *sūtras*. Thus, in certain respects, practice of the Mahāyāna path involves *avoiding* extremes, while in other respects, it involves *conjoining* positive, paired qualities. Each of these, in its way, helps to define the middle.

In much of the preceding, the emphasis has been placed on aspects of the middle *path*. Buddhist articulations of the goal of the tradition, however, especially in Mahāyāna, also are evocative of the metaphor of the middle, though seldom explicitly. Thus, one of the most common Mahāyāna articulations of the "location" of the buddha (or bodhisattva), is that he or she finds an abode neither in the turmoil of *saṃsāra* nor in the quiescence of the arhat's *nirvāṇa*, but, rather, in a non-abiding *nirvāṇa* (*apratiṣṭhitanirvāṇa*) in which each of those extremes is avoided. In a typical passage, the poetical summary of the Perfection of Wisdom known as the *Ratnaguṇasaṃcayagāthā* ("Verse Collection of Precious Qualities") explains that the Buddha "himself was not stationed in the realm which is free from conditions, / Nor in the things which are under conditions, but freely he wandered without a home: / Just so, without a support or a basis a Bodhisattva is standing. / A position devoid of a basis has that position been called by the Jina" (2 : 3, tr. Conze: 13; see also Williams: 181–184). In other words, the buddha (or bodhisattva) is "in the world, but not of it." This sort of paradoxical description of the Mahāyāna buddha is carried forward in other ways, as well. Thus, fully enlightened buddhahood is classically defined as consisting of two "bodies" (*kāya*), an utterly unchanging, transcendent, luminous, and omniscient gnosis (*dharmakāya*), and variable, circumstantial, spontaneously manifesting forms that assist suffering beings (*rūpakāya*) – the two would seem to preclude one another, yet they are inseparable, and invariably coordinated. Similarly, the gnosis of a buddha is said uniquely to be capable of cognizing simultaneously both ultimate and conventional truths, both emptiness and forms, both "is not" and "is" (see, e.g., Williams: chapter 8; Griffiths 1994: chapter 6; Makransky: chapter 13).

This Mahāyāna notion of the enlightened state as a simultaneous embrace of apparently contradictory qualities is dramatically elaborated in Buddhist tantric traditions, especially those of the Highest Yoga Tantras (*anuttarayoga tantra*). There, the graphic depictions of male and female deities in sexual embrace symbolize the enlightened adept's non-dual conjunction (*yuganaddha*) of coemergent (*sahaja*) factors: bliss and emptiness, creation and perfection, song and silence, method and wisdom, passion and compassion, breath and mind. The conjunction of each pair is at the same time an avoidance of falling to one extreme or the other, and therefore the implicit location of a middle. Explicitly, traditions of Highest Yoga Tantra speak of "the middle" in quasi-physiological terms, in reference to the central channel (*madhyama*, *avadhūti*) of the subtle body, which is the locus for the most advanced yogic practices, the "place" where the various mental and physiological forces that are the true basis of *saṃsāra* and *nirvāṇa* are manipulated and merged, and the path brought to completion in the conjunction, *yuganaddha*, that is buddhahood. Those who have mastered their psycho-physiology in the middle channel, or *avadhūti*, are sometimes referred to as *avadhūtipa*s; they are regarded as having transcended all conventional notions of white or black karma, virtuous or non-virtuous, and to have been freed thereby to act spontaneously however they wish, in accordance with their unsurpassable compassion and wisdom, their perfect comprehension of the forms of things, the needs of beings, and the emptiness of themselves and all they survey. This may appear to lead to "extreme" behavior, but is, in fact, a kind of middle between asceticism and heedless sensualism, with an accent on motivation, rather than behavior, that is typical of certain Mahāyāna approaches to ethics (see Guenther; Jackson 1991).

With the image of the unconventional, spontaneous *avadhūtipa*, our brief overview of the Buddhist metaphor of the middle has come nearly full circle, for in tantric literature, as in the Buddha's very first discourse, the articulation of the middle has a strongly ethical component: the metaphor is used to signal the sort of behavior that is expected of an enlightened person. How far, though, does the ethical middle seem to have shifted between the sober moderation enjoined in the *Dharmacakrapravartana Sūtra* and the enlightened sensuality espoused in the *tantras*! It is a matter of profound disagreement among Buddhist traditions whether the shift is real or apparent; what is important for our purposes is that there certainly is a shift in rhetoric, as there was a shift from one philosophical school to another over which extreme views were to be avoided, and a shift between Hīnayāna and Mahāyāna traditions over where the middle path was to be found, or how enlightenment was to be constituted. From a historical perspective, then, it becomes evident that the Buddhist "middle" is a constantly shifting locale, defined by the different ways in which theoreticians and practitioners have felt compelled to articulate the extremes that must be avoided or the qualities that must be combined. In short, the Buddhist middle turns out to unfixed: it is simply the compromise between extremes or dualities as they have been defined in one circumstance or the other. This pattern would seem to suggest that, whatever the situation, a middle is always available, but that no particular version of the middle enjoys completely definitive status. How can we judge the tantric ethical middle superior or inferior to, more or less "truly Buddhist" than the middle evoked in the Buddha's first sermon, or Nāgārjuna's definition of a philosophical middle better or worse than that of a Personalist or Yogācāra? Each responded to a particular set of conditions and was based on idiosyncratic perceptions, which can perhaps be understood, evaluated to some degree, but never utterly validated or invalidated, except in relation to our own contingent, conventional perspectives and purposes. At the end of our search for the traditional Buddhist middle, then, we may not find ourselves so far after all from the ambiguous "dark wood" of Eliot and Dante, where the way is easily lost, one's foothold is insecure, and one enters at one's peril – though enter one must.

As there are differences among traditional Buddhist definitions of the middle and the extremes it avoids, so there will certainly be differences between one or another traditional definition, and the sorts of accounts that might be framed in a modern or postmodern Western context. Thus, for instance, the detached ethical middle defined by the *Dharmacakrapravartana Sūtra* – especially when it is understood to entail monastic life – may appear to many inhabitants of laicized Western societies to constitute an ascetic extreme, while the passionate/compassionate ethical middle defined in the tantras, may be regarded, in societies lacking a tradition of "crazy wisdom," as constituting an irresponsible hedonistic extreme; a postmodern ethical middle might be located in the detached engagement in his or her vocation by a lay contemplative. Or, the metaphysical middle allegedly achieved by the *Milindapañhā*'s description of rebirth without identity, may, in a world less prone to accept traditional metaphysical claims, seem to represent the extreme of eternalism, while the contemporary materialist assertion that the mind is either identical to brain-states or an adventitious, impotent by-product of the brain, may now seem to represent the extreme of nihilism; the postmodern metaphysical middle might be located in the exploration of the powers of consciousness by a student/meditator uncommitted to belief in rebirth. Or, those trained in recent philosophy may regard traditional Buddhist – or Western – foundational claims that there is a definite way things really exist and reliable epistemic authorities for ascertaining that reality, as falling to the extreme of realism, and the negative, deconstructive rhetoric of much traditional Buddhist wisdom literature – or recent Western philosophy – as falling into paradox, hence an implicitly relativistic extreme of nihilism; the postmodern philosophical middle might be located in the deliberate attempt to balance – or oscillate between – conventional ways of knowing and describing the world and an ultimate recognition that any such convention is merely a conceptual construction, quite empty of independent validity.

These are simply suggestions; since traditional articulations of the Buddhist middle turn out to be quite various, we can be certain that postmodern versions will be equally diverse, if not more so. Indeed, we cannot predict *what* middles will emerge in the course of postmodern Buddhist reflection – only that it will be a guiding metaphor in the future as it has been in the past, and that it will be the attempt to locate a middle, rather than any specific notion of that middle, that will be at least one important way in which Buddhists will mark themselves off from proponents and practitioners of other religions or ideologies. And, if it is the process of finding a middle, rather than any specific formulation of the middle, that turns out to be at least partially definitive of Buddhism, then Buddhism cannot so easily be regarded as a religion focused on specific doctrinal *content*. Rather, it is the *forms* followed by Buddhists, from invoking the Buddha, to building stūpas, to sitting in meditation, to seeking the middle way, that define it. If, in turn, aesthetics involves reflection upon and activity in relation to forms (as well as the formless), then we may not be far from understanding how Buddhism, or any religion, may finally be an aesthetic – a way of employing myths, symbols, metaphors, and rituals to reform habitual patterns of thought and behavior, conform to reality as it truly may be, perform our lives in the most meaningful possible way, and, perhaps, transform ourselves from "bound" to "liberated" beings – all the while doubting, yet all the while, in Eliot's words, "risking enchantment."

CODA: TRADITION, POSTMODERNITY, AND THE MIDDLE

A traditionalist might at this point observe: It's all quite interesting to undertake a social, cultural, and philosophical analysis of concepts like tradition, modernity, and postmodernity, philosophy and religion; or compose one's spiritual autobiography; or survey millennia of Buddhist thought with the historian's detached eye. But, none of these is undertaken with the warrant or authority of Buddhist tradition, so the whole exercise is little more than the self-indulgent ramblings of yet another deracinated modern intellectual. What is required is that one begin one's cultural analysis from a firmly Buddhist conceptual base, and then move out to consider concepts more modern and Western; that one subordinate one's autobiographical impulses to the greater wisdom of the tradition and the exemplary men and women who have helped to shape it; and that one eschew the historian's pontification in favor of struggling with Buddhist formulations of the extremes and middle, and locating oneself appropriately. What is more, the traditionalist might add ironically, to be postmodern, one must be hermeneutically self-conscious enough to recognize that such modes of inquiry as cultural analysis, autobiography, and historical survey are themselves historically conditioned developments, hence possibly subject to correction by other, more "relatively adequate" approaches to understanding and conducting human affairs – some of which, like trust in the sustaining and communicative power of an ultimate reality or absorption in non-conceptual introspective states, might turn out to be deeply rooted in pre-modern traditions.

The traditionalist's complaint is not without merit. It is true that the historian's general overview belies the fact that there are very few Buddhists who do not begin from a quite specific base of practice and thought, in which the human problematic is defined distinctly, certain practices are promoted and others shunned, and the middle located quite precisely. It is also true that the problem of authority is a serious one for postmodern Buddhists, who often are disposed neither culturally nor personally to accept some of its traditional forms – whether scripture, or the word of a teacher, or even yogic experiences – with the same degree of confidence as their predecessors did. Indeed, innate or learned skepticism about such forms of authority may prove a major obstacle to the sorts of "faith" or "confidence" (*śraddhā*) that has been a cardinal virtue for Buddhists from the earliest times. Furthermore, it is true that the suspicion of tradition that modern and postmodern perspectives tend to engender is itself a product of particular historical and cultural forces, hence no better guarantor of absolute truth than tradition, and such suspicion may in the long term come to be seen as less warranted by "the facts" of the cosmos, and less fruitful in human lives, than now is commonly supposed.

Yet, the traditionalist's argument is problematic. While postmodern Buddhists still will tend to identify themselves with a particular tradition of Buddhism rather than Buddhism as a whole, they cannot remain blind to the perspectives offered by traditions other than their own, whether Buddhist or non-Buddhist, and must be willing to question their own assumptions accordingly. While "faith" in some authority is probably inseparable from what it means to be Buddhist, we must recall that that "faith" has varied in intensity and focus from era to era, and need *not* be tied to assurances of absolute authoritativeness, so much as to confidence in the trustworthiness of a text, teacher, or experience relative to the time in which one lives. While postmodern styles of reflection and discourse are explicitly quite different from those of most traditional Buddhists, it is far from clear that traditional Buddhists have *not* implicitly approached their heritage through what we would call social, cultural, and philosophical analysis, autobiographical reflection, or historical study of particular themes. Indeed, there is ample evidence that Buddhists have been doing these things from the very start, whether in the form of critiques of the ideas and practices of Buddhists and non-Buddhists; written or unwritten reflections on the results of their individual attempts to take seriously the Buddha's invitation to "come and see" (*ehi passako*) for themselves whether the Dharma makes sense; or efforts to understand and rank Buddhist positions through historical contextualization.

To take an example just of the latter, in chapter seven of the *Saṃdhinirmocana Sūtra*, the Buddha articulates a conception of "three turnings of the wheel of Dharma," in which each successive revelation (Hīnayāna, Mādhyamika, Yogācāra) is appropriate to the spiritual needs and abilities of its audience, and supersedes that which preceded it (see, e.g., Lamotte).[15] Because all Buddhist doctrines and practices must be linked directly or indirectly to the Buddha, all three teachings are put into his mouth, though from a historian's perspective, of course, this simply represents an attempt to justify a much later idea by giving it the imprimatur of original authority; as such it reflects a hermeneutical move common to theologians everywhere, whose practice, in Walter Kaufmann's words, is "the systematic attempt to pour the newest wine into the old skins of denomination" (221). The more idiosyncratically Mahāyāna Buddhist aspect of the move is the insistence that every teaching attributable to the Buddha is true in the sense of being situationally appropriate. This view, in turn, is vitally linked to the crucial Mahāyāna doctrine of skillful means (*upāya-*

kauśalya), whereby buddhas and bodhisattvas, motivated by compassion, speak and act in ways that are suited to the needs and abilities of their audience. Those ways of speaking and acting may appear to contradict other teachings, or even "objective truth" or "morality." The contradiction, however, only will be genuine if notions of objectivity and morality can stand up to rigorous analysis – but they cannot: they are conceptual constructions, dualistic formulations that are relative, empty, and unfixed. Thus, any teaching or action by an enlightened being is, in the light of perfect wisdom, ultimately baseless, while in the light of perfect compassion and skill, it may be relatively adequate to describe a state of affairs or advance the spiritual interests of a sentient being. If all statements and acts are relative to a particular situation, then Buddhist tradition *cannot* ever be fixed, and a modern or postmodern Buddhist's articulation of it *cannot* be invalidated by appeal to tradition – for tradition itself turns out to be without moorings – not only from the perspective of a modern historian, but on its own, traditional grounds.

But if tradition is unmoored, what is left of "Buddhism"? Might it not simply drift on the open sea of postmodernity, losing all distinctiveness, along the lines suggested earlier by Borges' remarks? The concern should be as real for postmodernist as for traditionalist Buddhists. It admits of no easy solution, but, one last time, the metaphor of the middle may provide at least some guidance. We might regard a total fixation on tradition and traditional doctrines, even in the face of the insights of modernity and postmodernity, as one extreme; and the utter deconstruction of tradition, such that no Buddhist identity remains, as the other extreme. The middle between them, I would suggest, lies in maintaining one's appreciation for the unfixed, relative nature of Buddhist truth and tradition, while continuing (a) to frame one's sense of this ultimate appreciation in terms that are primarily Buddhist – e.g., no-self, dependent origination, emptiness, non-duality, *dharmakāya*, mind-only, buddha-nature – and (b) to construct one's conventional life primarily through the myths, symbols, metaphors, and ritual acts employed by Buddhists in the past and present – e.g., telling the Buddha's story; analyzing karma and *dharmas*, or conventional and ultimate truths; prostrating to one's teacher; reflecting on the Four Noble Truths; longing for the farther shore of *nirvāṇa*; performing *pūjā*; engaging in philosophical debate; acting compassionately; conjoining meditative concentration and insight.

In short, postmodern Buddhists must, in David Tracy's phrase (18–19), remain in conversation with their classics. And, the notion of "classic" is not limited to texts: a visualization of a buddha, going on pilgrimage to Bodh Gaya, a donation to the saṅgha, the attempt to locate the middle, a recitation of the *Heart Sūtra*, or a session of sitting meditation: each of these is a "classic" that, to find the postmodern middle, a Buddhist may engage. The Buddhist knows that these classics are ultimately fictions, components of a complex aesthetic. But if fictions are all we have, then we cannot avoid thinking and living through one or another or some combination of them – we cannot avoid constructing an aesthetic. We know that, ultimately, all such constructs are groundless, but know, too, that, conventionally, they may be relatively adequate approximations of the ways things are. What is more, some have proven to be deeply valuable, making them, in Wallace Stevens' phrase, "supreme fictions," which, empty and unfounded though they may be, nevertheless give shape to the deepest human yearnings for a sense of what reality, truth, goodness, self, or happiness might be like. The Buddhadharma is such a supreme fiction, and the contemporary Buddhist can enter it, I would suggest, only through the door of non-duality, where one lives, wisely and joyously, with the tension born from understanding that – on both Buddhist and postmodern grounds – the Dharma is both false and true, contingent and timeless, absurd and meaningful, empty and perfectly formed, ambiguous and fruitful, silent and full of poetry – and that it is found, in the end, only by those nimble enough to play both ends against the middle, and then play some more.

NOTES

1 The position I am taking here is influenced by, but distinct from, that of Clifford Geertz, who, in *Islam Observed*, argues that for modern people the question is not whether to be religious, but how (16–17).

2 This understanding has only belatedly begun to appear among Buddhologists; for works reflecting it, see, e.g., Eckel, Strong, Lopez.

3 For varying perspectives on this topic, see, e.g., Cassirer, Pepper, Wheelwright, Barbour, Lakoff and Johnson, and Reynolds and Tracy.

4 Briefly: by "aesthetic," used as both a noun and adjective, I have in mind more than just "the appreciation of beauty," or "a theory of art and beauty." Rather, hearkening back to the word's Greek roots, in the verb *aesthanesthai*, "to perceive," and the adjective *aesthētikos*, "relating to sense perception," I construe the aesthetic as broadly referring to all human perceptions of the forms, patterns, structures, and events in the world and in our lives, whether experienced conceptually, sensuously, or emotionally. I choose the word deliberately in preference to such oft-used substitutes for "religion"

as "world-view," "paradigm," "conceptual scheme," or even "symbol system," in order to emphasize the affective element of the phenomenon; at the same time, the intellectual structures that often are crucial to "religion" are by no means excluded – I would not, as Stephen Beyer does, define Buddhism (or any other religion) simply as "a performing art" (vi). An aesthetic, in fact, involves a *complete* range of ideas, symbols, emotions, and acts, which may be perceived, either emically or etically, as forming a meaningful constellation. A religious aesthetic, then, would entail a constellation of ideas, symbols, emotions, and acts that provided a mode of interacting with and interpreting the world that is felt and affirmed to be the broadest and deepest such mode that is possible. This discussion, of course, begs many questions, but it suggests the lines along which I am thinking.

5 I was influenced far more deeply at the time by a book that is not primarily about Buddhism, Norman O. Brown's *Love's Body*. Despite its dated patriarchal language, it remains, especially in its latter chapters, a brilliant meditation on psychology and religion, language and metaphor, politics and society, eros and the body, Christianity and Buddhism; and both in its verbally playful style, and in its subversion of traditional philosophical constructs, it anticipates much of what has come to be called "postmodernism." What is more, working only from a few secondary sources, Brown manages to capture quite well something of the radical spirit of both Mahāyāna and tantric Buddhist thought.

6 Many *lam rim* works have been now been translated into English. In the early seventies, there were far fewer; the three that were accessible to me in Asia during that time were sGam-po-pa, Dhargyey, and Zopa Rinpoche.

7 For the dissertation itself, see Jackson 1983; for the book into which it evolved, see Jackson 1993.

8 For recent versions of this argument, see Griffiths 1991, Jackson 1993: 35–42. Readers familiar with my earlier stance may feel that I am weakening it here. However, my earlier arguments were primarily descriptive – an attempt to assess how most Buddhists traditionally have regarded truth; my purpose here, on the other hand, is more normative – I am attempting to prescribe an approach to truth that will serve critically-thinking Buddhists in the postmodern age.

9 For a fine exploration of metaphors in a Theravādin Buddhist context, see Collins; on the Christian side, see, e.g., Pelikan, McFague.

10 The best-known version of this text is that preserved in the Pāli canon, found at *Saṃyutta Nikāya* LVI: II, and translated many times, e.g., in Rahula: 92–94; for a translation from a Sanskrit version, see Strong: 32–34.

11 This Pāli text also has been translated in excerpted form many times; the major complete translation remains that of Rhys Davids.

12 A translation of the Pāli version of this text (=*Saṃyutta Nikāya* XXII:

90) is found at Warren: 165–166.

13 For a survey of Indian Buddhist philosophy that uses this premise, see Jackson 1997.

14 On the *Madhyāntavibhāga*, see , e.g., Friedmann, Warder: 439–440, Williams: 86 ff., Nagao, 53 ff.

15 Indeed, in the *Saṃdhinirmocana*, the first two turnings of the wheel of Dharma, the Hīnayāna and the Mādhyamika, are rejected as merely provisional (*neyārtha*) because they lead, respectively, to the extremes of eternalism and nihilism, while the third turning is upheld as definitive (*nītārtha*) because, implicitly, it locates the middle by discriminating properly between those dharmas that should be affirmed (the absolute nature as defined in Yogācāra) and those that should be denied (the imputed nature; the dependent nature may be either affirmed or denied, depending upon the way it is viewed.)

REFERENCES

Ambedkar, B. R. (1957). *The Buddha and His Dhamma*. [Bombay:] Siddharth College Publication.

Barbour, Ian (1974). *Myths, Models and Paradigms: A Comparative Study in Science and Religion*. New York: Harper & Row.

Batchelor, Stephen (1983). *Alone With Others: An Existential Approach to Buddhism*. New York: Grove Press

Batchelor, Stephen (1997). *Buddhism Without Beliefs: A Contemporary Guide to Awakening*. New York: Riverhead Books

Beyer, Stephan, trans. (1974). *The Buddhist Experience: Sources and Interpretations*. Encino and Belmont, CA: Dickenson.

Borges, Jorge Luis (1984). *Seven Nights*. Trans. Eliot Weinberger. New York: New Directions.

Brown, Norman O. (1966). *Love's Body*. New York: Random House.

Cassirer, Ernst (1946). *Language and Myth*. Trans. Susanne K. Langer. New York: Dover Publications.

Chan, Wing-tsit, ed. (1963). *A Source Book in Chinese Philosophy*. Princeton: Princeton University Press.

Collins, Steven (1982). *Selfless Persons: Imagery and Thought in* Theravāda *Buddhism*. Cambridge: Cambridge University Press.

Conze, Edward, trans. (1973). *The Perfection of Wisdom in Eight Thousand Lines and Its Verse Summary (Aṣṭasāhasrikāprajñāpāramitā)*. Bolinas: Four Seasons Foundation.

Dante Alighieri (1945). *La Divina Commedia, vol. I: Inferno*. Commento di Attilio Momigliano. Firenze: G. C. Sansoni.

Dhargyey, Geshe Ngagwang (1974). *Tibetan Tradition of Mental Development*. Dharamsala: Library of Tibetan Works and Archives.

Eckel, Malcolm David (1994). *To See the Buddha: A Buddhist Philosopher's Search for the Meaning of Emptiness*. Princeton:

Princeton University Press.

Eliot, T. S. (1980). *The Complete Poems and Plays, 1909-1950.* San Diego: Harcourt Brace Jovanovich.

Friedmann, David (1984). *Sthiramati Madhyāntavibhāgaṭīkā.* [reprint] Talent, OR: Canon Pubs.

Garfield, Jay L., trans. (1995). *The Fundamental Wisdom of the Middle Way: Nāgārjuna's* Mūlamadhyamakakārikā. New York: Oxford University Press.

Geertz, Clifford (1968). *Islam Observed: Religious Developments in Morocco and Indonesia.* Chicago: University of Chicago Press.

Glass, Newman Robert (1995). *Working Emptiness: Toward a Third Reading of Emptiness in Buddhism and Postmodern Thought.* Atlanta: Scholars Press.

Griffiths, Paul J. (1991). *An Apology for Apologetics.* Maryknoll, NY: Orbis Books.

Griffiths, Paul J. (1994). *On Being Buddha: The Classical Doctrine of Buddhahood.* Albany: State University of New York Press.

Guenther, Herbert V. (1976). *The Tantric View of Life.* Boulder: Shambhala Publications.

Gyamtso Rimpoche, Khenpo Tsultrim (1986). *Progressive Stages of Meditation on Emptiness.* Trans. Shenpen Hookham. Oxford: Longchen Foundation.

Hayward, Jeremy (1987). *Shifting Worlds, Changing Minds: Where the Sciences and Buddhism Meet.* Boston and London: Shambhala.

Hookham, Susan (1991). *The Buddha Within: Tathāgatagarbha Theory According to the Shentong Interpretation of the Ratnagotravibhaga.* Albany: State University of New York Press.

Inada, Kenneth K. (1970). *Nāgārjuna: A Translation of his Mūlamadhyamakakārikā with an Introductory Essay.* Tokyo: The Hokuseido Press.

Jackson, Roger R. (1983). *Is Enlightenment Possible? An Analysis of Some Arguments in the Buddhist Philosophical Tradition, with Special Attention to the* Pramāṇasiddhi *Chapter of Dharmakīrti's* Pramāṇavārttika. Unpublished Ph.D. dissertation, University of Wisconsin-Madison.

Jackson, Roger R. (1989). "Matching Concepts: Deconstructive and Foundationalist Tendencies in Buddhist Thought." *Journal of the American Academy of Religion* (LVII: 3) 561–589.

Jackson, Roger R. (1992). "Ambiguous Sexuality: Imagery and Interpretation in Tantric Buddhism." *Religion* (22) 85–100.

Jackson, Roger R. (1993). *Is Enlightenment Possible? Dharmakīrti and rGyal tshab rje on Knowledge, Rebirth, No-Self and Liberation.* Ithaca: Snow Lion.

Jackson, Roger R. (1997). "Buddhism in India." In Brian Carr and Indira Mahalingam, eds., *Companion Encyclopedia of Asian Philosophy,* 318–348. London: Routledge.

Kaufmann, Walter (1972). *Critique of Religion and Philosophy.* Princeton:

Princeton University Press.
Lakeland, Paul (1997). *Postmodernism*. Minneapolis: Fortress Press.
Lakoff, George and Mark Johnson (1980). *Metaphors We Live By*. Chicago: University of Chicago Press.
Lamotte, Étienne (1935). *Saṃdhinirmocana sūtra: L'explication des mystères*. Louvain: Université de Louvain.
Lopez, Jr., Donald S., ed. (1995). *Buddhism in Practice*. Princeton: Princeton University Press.
Loy, David (1988). *Nonduality*. New Haven: Yale University Press.
Lyotard, Jean-Francois, et al. (1993). *The Postmodern Explained: Correspondence 1982-1995*. Trans. Don Barry. Minneapolis: University of Minnesota Press.
McFague, Sallie (1987). *Models of God: Theology for an Ecological, Nuclear Age*. Philadelphia: Fortress Press.
Magliola, Robert (1984). *Derrida on the Mend*. West Lafayette, IN: Purdue University Press.
Makransky, John J. (1997). *Buddhahood Embodied: Sources of Controversy in India and Tibet*. Albany: State University of New York Press.
Nagao, Gadjin M. (1991). *Mādhyamika and Yogācāra: A Study of Mahāyāna Philosophies. Collected Papers of G. M. Nagao*. Ed. & trans. L. S. Kawamura. Albany: State University of New York Press
Pelikan, Jaroslav (1985). *Jesus Through the Centuries: His Place in the History of Culture*. New Haven: Yale University Press.
Pepper, Stephen C. (1961).*World Hypotheses: A Study in Evidence*. Berkeley: University of California Press.
Rahula, Walpola (1974).*What the Buddha Taught*. New York: Grove Press.
Reynolds, Frank E. and David Tracy, eds. (1990). *Myth and Philosophy*. Albany: State University of New York Press.
Rhys Davids, T. W., trans. (1963). *The Questions of King Milinda*. 2 vols. New York: Dover Publications.
sGam-po-pa (1970). *Jewel Ornament of Liberation*. Trans. Herbert V. Guenther. London: Rider & Co.
Spretnak, Charlene (1991). *States of Grace: The Recovery of Meaning in the Postmodern Age*. San Francisco: Harper SanFrancisco.
Strong, John S. (1995). *The Experience of Buddhism: Sources and Interpretations*. Belmont, CA: Wadsworth.
Suzuki, D. T., trans. (1978). *The Laṅkāvatāra Sūtra*. Boulder: Prajñā Press.
Thurman, Robert A. F., trans. (1976). *The Holy Teaching of Vimalakīrti*. University Park, PA: Pennsylvania State University Press.
Tracy, David (1987). *Plurality and Ambiguity: Hermeneutics, Religion, Hope*. San Francisco: Harper & Row.
Trungpa, Chögyam (1985). *Journey Without Goal: The Tantric Wisdom of the Buddha*. Boston & London: Shambhala.
Warder, A. K. (1980). *Indian Buddhism*. 2nd ed. Delhi: Motilal Banarsidass.
Warren, Henry Clarke, trans. (1970). *Buddhism in Translations*. New York: Atheneum.
Wheelwright, Philip (1962). *Metaphor & Reality*. Bloomington: Indiana

University Press.
Williams, Paul (1989). *Mahāyāna Buddhism: The Doctrinal Foundations.* London: Routledge.
Wolfe, David L. (1982). *Epistemology.* Downer's Grove, IL: Intervarsity Press.
Zopa Rinpoche, Lama Thubten (1974). *The Golden Wish-Fulfilling Sun of Mahayana Thought Training.* Kopan, Nepal: Kopan Monastery.

Twelve

Impermanence, Nowness, and Non-Judgment: A Personal Approach to Understanding Finitude in Buddhist Perspective

Rita M. Gross

Buddhism has a reputation among religions for going "against the grain," for analyses of the human situation that completely contradict the usual conventions and norms of religions. On no point are such religious surprises more striking than with Buddhism's teachings on impermanence and its corollary – finitude. I have long appreciated that what other religions mourn as the finitude of the human condition, which their faithful hope to transcend eventually, Buddhists acknowledge as impermanence, regarding it simply as the way things are, without praise or blame. This link between finitude and impermanence, as well as the differences between Western assessments of finitude and Buddhist assessments of impermanence have long intrigued me. And I have long felt that the most profound teachings of Buddhism circle around the Buddhist naming of reality and human experience as all pervasive impermanence.

In this essay, I will narrate how personal experiences with grieving made transparent to me the wisdom and comfort inherent in Buddhism's matter-of-fact, nonchalant statement that to be human is to be impermanent and finite. These experiences have transformed my life and made existential the teachings of Buddhism as has nothing else. But the wisdom that comes with accommodating finitude and impermanence is not limited to dealing with personal loss; once the reality of finitude and impermanence become clear, existentially as well as theoretically, the destructive effects of the ways in which some religious teachings and practices war against these realities becomes ever more obvious. At the end of this essay, I will briefly discuss how dis-ease with finitude and impermanence fuels wasteful attempts to defy and defeat death, and how this dis-ease is implicated in wanton and careless disregard for the finite matrix of life that is our planet and its ecology.

IMPERMANENCE, NOWNESS, AND NON-JUDGMENT: LEANING INTO GRIEF

For me, the topics of finitude and death are most immediate in my experiences with grief. I probably have more experience of grieving the loss by death of loved and valued immediate collegial consorts than most people my age. The single most life-giving experience I have ever had was a genuinely mutual relationship of collegial consortship. But that experience was framed by two experiences of intense grief over loss by death of a lover or consort. Both of these experiences of loss were literally life-shaping and life-changing. One of them brought me into Buddhist practice and the other matured my practice in ways that go well beyond what I had learned from thousands of hours of formal meditation. I have never learned as much from anything else as I have from these three experiences. It is not hard to understand that a "positive" experience, such as a relationship of mutuality and appreciation with a consort, would result in learning and growth. What is more counter-intuitive is that the anguish of grieving, which no one would ever choose, could be so productive. I want to explore why this is so by suggesting that through leaning into grief, I learned that finitude is impermanence, and that fighting impermanence only brings suffering, while dancing with impermanence launches one into the immediacy of nowness, beyond judgments about good or bad. But these rather theoretical statements need to be fleshed out in story, for understanding and expression flow out of experience, rather than the other way around.

In September 1973, I was walking across the parking lot towards my office on the kind of almost unbearably beautiful fall day that makes living so far north so pleasurable, thinking about how to teach the Four Noble Truths, which I didn't think I understood very well, in my upcoming Buddhism class. I was also quite miserable, for I had spent the previous year living with the grief and trauma of discovering that the young philosopher with whom I was in love had a terminal brain tumor. I had just moved to Eau Claire after my first teaching appointment, truly a "job from hell," and, though I knew no one in Eau Claire, it was already apparent to me that I was far too radical religiously to find much collegiality at UW-EC. I had spend the previous week-end visiting my friend for what I knew would be the last time. So there I was, experiencing at one and the same time both intense misery at my own situation and intense appreciation for the beauty in which I was immersed. Clearly, by conventional standards, one of these experiences was "desirable" and the other was "undesirable," but their co-emergence rather than their contrast impressed itself upon me. Something suddenly snapped in my mind and I said to myself in wonder, "The Four Noble Truths are true!" This experience was not superficial or short-lived, for it motivated me to seek out Buddhist meditation disciplines and sent my life onto a course that previously I had never deemed possible or appealing.

But what had I noticed that had eluded me before? Certainly not the First Noble Truth, that life lived conventionally is pervaded by suffering, for I had been more aware of my misery than I cared to be for quite some time, without any sudden insight as to the truth of the Four Noble Truths. Rather, the Second Noble Truth, that suffering derives from desire, and its connection with the First Noble Truth impressed itself upon me. I realized that my own desperate longing for things to be different was actually what made what seemed to be "inside" my mind so painful in contrast to what seemed to be "outside" my mind. This connection between suffering and one's own mental state is much more basic to Buddhism than acknowledging suffering but attributing it solely to external factors. The clarity of this insight brought some of the immediate relief to my anguish that the Third Noble Truth – the truth of the cessation of suffering – promises. Altogether, this experience convinced me that if the more philosophical teachings of Buddhism were true, then I should also heed Buddhism's practical advice, as conveyed in the Fourth Noble Truth regarding the path of moral development, meditation practice and the seeking of wisdom. Classic Buddhist texts suggest that the Four Noble Truths are not realized sequentially but simultaneously; for me, clearly, the experience that turned me toward Buddhist practice was an insight into the coherence of the vision provided by the Four Noble Truths, not a piecemeal deduction from one assertion to the next.

After this surprising fruit of grief, I had to wait a long time to experience again the creativity and renewal that come with a consort relationship of mutuality and collegiality, since I would not settle for long for the living death of a relationship based on conventional gender roles. Discussing why such a relationship is so vital for women's intellectual and spiritual creativity is not the topic of this paper, but is discussed instead in another paper, on the links between eros and intellectual or spiritual creativity in women. Nevertheless, my beliefs in the potential of such relationships were confirmed by my experience of such a relationship.

However, after a few years, I was again dealing with the loss by death of a consort with whom I had a mutual and collegial relationship – this time within the context of a relationship that had, in fact, been much more complete. The level of anguish was sometimes profoundly unbearable. But after more than fifteen years of Buddhist meditation, I was also much more familiar with the practice of neither leading nor following my thoughts and other mental activities.[1] When I worked with my mental processes as I had been trained to do in meditation, I discovered an overwhelming urge to indulge my memories of a lovely past and my fears of a lonely future. I discovered that what I wanted to believe was grief was simply a habitual pattern of discursive thought – fantasies and projections run wild. When I simply stayed in the immediate moment, something very different happened – pure feeling that was neither this nor that, neither grief nor happiness. And no matter how intense such feelings might be, they were bearable. They did not leak out into an intense desire to do something to change what I was feeling because it was too unbearable. That only happened when I was, in fact, not in the present but in the past and what I had lost or in the future and what I wouldn't have. Nevertheless, the temptation to indulge in memory or in dread was constant. So I learned to do better than I had ever done in thousands of hours of formal meditation practice the essential meditative technique of dropping thoughts, without judging them, and returning to nowness – the nowness of winter sunlight, of incense smoke, of cat's fur, of Gregorian chant . . . . Whatever the content of immediate nowness, the experience always had the same quality as that second of sunlight on the fall-colored trees in the parking lot on my way to my Buddhism class.

Due to having countless opportunities to practice returning to nowness, gradually the process became more self-existing in the fabric of my spirit. The results were quite astonishing. It became clear to me and to many of my friends that I was, in fact, in better shape psychologically and spiritually than I had ever been previously, including during the happy and creative years of collegial consortship. I frequently told people that, while I had benefited immensely from finally having a mutual relationship, I had learned as much from having to deal with losing it as I had from having it.

Why should that have happened? I certainly don't want to draw ridiculous conclusions from my experiences, such as that suffering is good for us and so we should not seek to alleviate it, or that some theistic entity is pulling strings to bless us in disguise. Rather, the whole key to understanding how such processes could occur is in the Buddhist insight into all pervasive impermanence, the fulcrum point of all Buddhist teaching, and the closely allied teaching that fighting impermanence is the root cause of suffering.

> The basic teaching of Buddhism is the teaching of transiency, or change. That everything changes is the basic truth for each existence. No one can deny this truth, and all the teaching of

> Buddhism is condensed within it. This is the teaching for all of us. Wherever we go, this teaching is true. (Suzuki: 102–103)

Impermanence is something so basic that we all can easily concede it intellectually. It is so obvious. Nevertheless, emotionally it is the most difficult teaching of all to integrate into one's being which is why it is the fulcrum point of all Buddhist teaching. From the Buddhist point of view, whole religions are built mainly on the denial of impermanence, which it understandable, given how difficult impermanence is to accept emotionally, though unfortunate, given how important acceptance of impermanence is to spiritual freedom. One could accurately state that Buddhist meditation is nothing more than a discipline that brings home again and again, ceaselessly, how impermanent everything is.

From an intellectual point of view, such teaching may seem to be cold comfort, but experientially, the results of really getting this teaching are astounding. Really accommodating impermanence, not merely as an intellectual doctrine, but emotionally as the most intimate fabric of our being, is nothing less than the cessation of suffering, the *nirvana* that so mystifies so many. To continue quoting Suzuki Roshi,

> This teaching is also understood as the teaching of selflessness. Because each existence is in constant change, there is no abiding self. In fact, the self-nature of each existence is nothing but change, the self-nature of all existence. . . . This is also called the teaching of Nirvana. When we realize the everlasting truth of "everything changes" and find our composure in it, we find ourselves in Nirvana. (Suzuki: 103)

Since *nirvāṇa* is always evaluated by Buddhists as a transformative and valuable experience, it is clear that experiencing impermanence fully brings freedom and joy, rather than sadness and grief, which is how most people evaluate impermanence when they analyze these issues intellectually.

Finding our composure in impermanence can also be discussed as the experience of staying in the present, of experiencing *now* rather than past or future. As is so commonly said by Buddhists, since everything is always changing, *now* is all we really have or are. Therefore, it could also be said that *nirvāṇa* or the cessation of suffering is a matter of riding the razor's edge of nowness. Most people, in fact probably would evaluate moments of nowness very positively. The vividness, intensity, and joy that come with being fully present to one's life and one's experiences are intensely appealing.

The problem is that it is very difficult to realize that nowness and impermanence are two names for the same thing, one of which people want and the other of which they don't want, conventionally. Suzuki Roshi continues his commentary: "Without accepting the fact that everything changes, we cannot find perfect composure" (Suzuki: 103). Thus all the positive states that we strive to cultivate, such as equanimity, joy, vividness, appreciation, and a sense of humor are, in fact, dependent on our ability to find our composure in impermanence. They cannot be experienced in any consistent way so long as we believe in and strive for permanence. It would be very nice to experience nowness without impermanence, but that does not seem possible. How can the exact razor of nowness be anything other than completely fleeting and impermanent? How can there be something else that lasts forever? The trick is simply to give up on achieving something other than impermanence and "find our composure in it," which are both the point and the result of Buddhist spiritual discipline.

Real experience of impermanence and nowness also involve non-judgment. When one is immediately focused in present experience, what is central is the experience itself, not some judgment about it. Judgment follows after rather than being one with experience and is less definitive than experience itself. Usually, indulging in judgment about an experience is a clue that one is not finding composure in impermanence, but has strayed from nowness into past and future, hope and fear. In fact, judgmentalism usually interferes with the vividness of experience itself, distancing one from its immediacy and raw power. This is why value judgments and determinations that something is absolutely good or bad are relatively unimportant to Buddhists. (Relative judgments, subject to change and not tightly held are much more appropriate.)

Finally, we can come full circle. Clearly, in many cases, suffering arises from the judgment or the view that I shouldn't have to experience this or that I don't want to experience this, rather than being inherent in the experience itself. In most cases, what one doesn't want to experience is simply impermanence. One is rebelling against impermanence, which brings grief rather than the permanence or the changes that one thinks one wants and needs. As Suzuki Roshi continues (after stating that only by accepting impermanence can we find composure),

> But unfortunately, although it is true, it is difficult for us to accept it. Because we cannot accept the truth of transiency, we suffer. So the cause of our suffering is the non-acceptance of this truth. The teaching of the cause of suffering and the

teaching that everything changes are two sides of one coin. (Suzuki: 103)

All these points are very clear in the autobiographical comments made earlier in this paper. The link between experiencing suffering and fighting impermanence is completely clear. What may still be less obvious is how these grief-filled experiences gave way to something else. But when I really gave in to impermanence and experienced the present, repeatedly, more than a hundred thousand times,[2] something else happened. I began to find composure in impermanence and needed less to try to be someone else experiencing something else. I needed the judgment that I couldn't or didn't want this experience less and less. Eventually, I found a way to enjoy my life in spite of grief and loneliness. However, let me make one point absolutely clear. I am *not* talking about not experiencing feelings, such as grief or anger or longing or disappointment, the usual misinterpretation of equanimity. I am talking about the *impermanence* of feelings, *all* feelings, no matter their content. Wallowing in feelings, seeking to prolonging them, accepting some and rejecting others – these are what promote suffering and what one no longer does when one finds some composure in impermanence. But *experiencing* feelings, the sheer raw power of feeling, is unavoidable. When one stays with the immediate impermanent, fleeting, evanescent, ever-changing feelings, they are *much more vivid and intense*, precisely the opposite of the dullness of feelings judged, analyzed, and clung to or pushed away.

To say that I found a way to enjoy my life as I became more proficient at staying in the present is not to say that things have gone smoothly. Many experiences have been quite frustrating, most especially seeking a collegial consort with whom mutuality is possible in a world is which even accomplished men usually practice a patriarchal politics of mate selection, preferring less accomplished women to more accomplished women. Nevertheless, I have been unconditionally cheerful for too long now to have manufactured that cheerfulness. I get frustrated, but I don't dwell on frustration as I used to. Instead, I notice my frustration and drop fixation on it – at least much of the time. I am more efficient and productive, rarely wasting time thinking about how busy I am or despairing that I can't get everything done.

Furthermore, I take as a deliberate practice not only leaning into every experience as much as possible while dwelling on none, but also contemplating, on a daily basis, my own impending and inevitable death. Such contemplations are a venerable and famous technique in the Buddhist repertoire of formal meditation exercises, going all the way back to the charnel ground meditations recommended in early Buddhism. But, though I have done such formal practices, the spontaneous contemplations that I now do, based on my own coming to terms with impermanence through grieving, have more pith and poignancy for me. Interestingly, I find my own death more regrettable now that I enjoy life more than I did when I fought impermanence all the time. But the regret is not a complaint; it is part of the appreciation of nowness that comes with accommodating impermanence.

STOP THE WORLD! SOME EXAMPLES OF DISSATISFACTION WITH IMPERMANENCE

I began this essay by suggesting that what Buddhism understands as finitude and impermanence, which simply names things as they are without praise or blame, other religions often regard as a problem that the faithful hope to transcend eventually. It is now time to turn to this contrasting belief system. It is well known that changeability and limitation are widely regarded as flaws, especially in the stream of Western religious thought that was most influenced by Greek thought. In classical expressions of theistic religions, the deity is perfect precisely because deity does not participate in flawed mutability and limitation. Ordinary human life is problematic, simply because the natural human condition involves uncompromising finitude and unceasing changeability leading to death. But the hope and the promise of many religions is that this "flawed" human condition can be transformed into a condition of permanence and infinite life by the proper relationship with some transcendent reality. This generic portrait of conventional religion is so familiar that many people, including most of my students, do not imagine that there could be any religious alternatives, which is why Buddhism often seems so odd, so against the grain, when it is first encountered.

At the most extreme, these alternatives present two radically different interpretations of the same basic experience. In any case, an embodied human being experiences ceaseless change and limitation throughout the life cycle and death follows. The Buddhist interpretation, which I have discussed elsewhere as "freedom within the world" (Gross: 146–151) is that finitude and impermanence are inevitable, but that does not have to be a problem. Another classical interpretation of these same facts of life, prominent in many streams of Western theistic religions, regards these facts as an immense problem, for which humans are to blame. (This is the most frequent interpretation of the myth of Adam, Eve, and the serpent in the Garden of Eden.) As many feminist scholars have pointed out, a common solution to this intolerable problem is to reject finitude, to abhor and fear it, as well as any reminders of finitude, such as the mortal body, the ever-changing realms of nature, and women, who seem, according to this analysis, to be more bodily and more natural.[3] In this same interpretation of bodily life, the classic proposed solution is salvation from impermanence and finitude, not by way of finding composure in impermanence, but by way of eventual abolition of impermanence effected by a deity who is infinite and eternal and who rescues some from the curse of finitude and impermanence. Even in a post-modern culture, in which believe in a transcendent deity has been severely eroded, denial of impermanence still persists, and other saviors, such as medical technology, function to allow denial of the reality of impermanence, finitude, and death.

Such wholesale rebellion against impermanence and finitude has many negative consequences which are rarely linked with their true cause – denial of impermanence and finitude. For example, once one accommodates impermanence, the enormous resources spent at the extremities of the life cycle become morally unacceptable. How can over a million dollars be spent on one premature infant in an overpopulated world in which millions of other basically healthy children lack even the most basic medical care, such as routine vaccinations? How can we tolerate the percentage of our total health care costs that go into the last few days of forced living for dying people who are not fortunate enough to die quickly, before the medical establishment can get them hooked up to tubes? It is clear that denial of impermanence drives most of the extraordinary measures that have become routine medical practice. Only the attitude that death is an insult to be avoided at all costs, rather than an unproblematic part of life, could fuel such practices. It seems that in the post-religious Western world, we have given up the other-worldliness and transcendence of classical religious beliefs, but not the hatred of the impermanence of this embodied earthly life that went with them.

After death, common funeral practices continue the denial of death, as has often been pointed out by cultural commentators. Professionals have taken over dealing with the body, so that friends and family do not confront the reality of a cold, stiff corpse. Formaldehyde is shot through the body to preserve it from the decay that is natural, making it like a pickled laboratory sample. Make-up disguises the pallor of death. Fancy, expensive coffins continue the waste and denial. Finally, the body is encased in a concrete box, prohibiting it from mingling with the earth that is its source, robbing the earth of its trace minerals forever. Thus, even in death, permanence is sought as much as possible.

Perhaps because Buddhist attitudes toward death are so different, so matter of fact, Buddhists have become experts in dealing with death in many cultures to which the Buddhist religion has traveled.[4] Here in the U.S., Buddhist practices surrounding dying and death are far different from the common cultural norm. Dying is viewed as an unavoidable process that offers great opportunities for the dying person and her family and friends to deepen their understanding of impermanence and to develop greater detachment and equanimity. Death itself is one the main experiences that are conducive to enlightenment if the dying person is detached and mindful. But there is no reason for useless medical extremes, particularly if they dull the mind and cloud awareness. After death, as before, the body is not given over to impersonal experts, but is prepared for cremation by family and friends, who meditate with the body non-stop until cremation. There is no embalming and no make-up or other cosmetic measures.

Outsiders sometime recoil from these descriptions, but I have found the practices to be anything but gruesome. Instead, they are grounding and energizing and one feels gratitude toward the dying/dead person for all the lessons they are imparting, even in such extreme circumstances. It seems so matter-of-fact and so same for the dead person to be in his bedroom or shrine room, surrounded by shrine objects and meditators. Chanting around the body while waiting for the crematorium to heat up is a final service and watching the body burn is a final teaching imparted by the dead person. The whole experience is very ordinary, very matter-of-fact, grounding and energizing at the same time.

Turning from the intimate concern of death practices that do not attempt to evade impermanence to the very large concern of the survival of our environment, we find a similar dis-ease with finitude and impermanence and preference for non-earthly transcendence at the heart of the matter. Beginning with Lynn White in 1967, many commentators have sought the root of the Western world's disregard for this finite earth that we know and on which we depend unconditionally. While his proposed explanation, locating the roots of environmental devastation in the permission to dominate the earth, given in the creation story in Genesis, has merit, I would claim that this permission is imbedded in a deeper set of values. In Western theistic religions, the transcendent creator of the world alone is of supreme worth; the world, seen as a dependent creation, is robbed of the sacredness many religions would attribute to it. Therefore, humans are to thank and honor the transcendent creator, not the earth on which they live.

The same feminist theologians who have articulated so clearly the dualistic, other-worldly world-view of much classical Western religion have pointed out that the classic other-worldly world view goes hand in hand with rejection of our world of ceaseless change and finite capabilities as our true home, to be treasured and cared for. Instead we are taught to long for a transcendent realm, which, unlike this earth, is immutable and eternal (and in which we also become immutable and eternal). In that process, this earth becomes something of a throw-away, to be used and then discarded for a superior alternative. No wonder people can plunder and pollute the earth with abandon; because it is finite and ever-changing, it is of limited value, to be replaced eventually by an infinite, unchanging realm. The fragile, finite, ever-changing earth is not good enough as it is; it is tamed, cleared, damned, mined and fertilized until it becomes toxic. It is regarded as a temporary dwelling place, of instrumental value only, and not quite up to par, certainly not by contrast with its imagined opposite, the realm of other-worldly transcendence.

By contrast, feminist theologians concerned with the environment have suggested that our only solution is to embrace and affirm finitude. In a provocative essay Carol Christ links reverence for life with an acceptance of finitude and death. She claims that rejecting finitude and death for transcendence and immortality is at odds with reverence for the only life we know – a life that is very finite and ends in death. She makes clear the connection between embracing finitude rather than transcendence and reverence for life.

> If we experience our connection to the finite and changing earth deeply, then we must find the thought of its destruction or mutilation intolerable. When we know this finite earth as our true home and accept our own inevitable death, then we must know as well that spirituality is the celebration of our immersion in all that is and is changing. (Christ: 226–227)

In a similar vein, Rosemary Ruether suggests that classical Christianity has misnamed finitude as sin, in the process encouraging humans to think that finitude and mortal life can be overcome through other-worldly salvation. She explains how this belief system fosters environmental degradation.

> The evaluation of mortal life as evil and the fruit of sin has lent itself to an earth-fleeing ethic and spirituality, which has

> undoubtedly contributed centrally to the neglect of the earth, to the denial of commonality with plants and animals, and to the despising of the work of sustaining the day-to-day processes of finite but renewable life. By evaluating such finite but renewable life as sin and death, by comparison with`immortal' life, we have reversed the realities of life and death. Death as deliverance from mortality is preferred to the only real life available to us. (Ruether 1992: 139–140)

CONCLUSION

"When we realize the everlasting truth of everything changes' and find our composure in it, we find ourselves in Nirvana" (Suzuki, 102-3). Everything always changes and everything is finite, including ourselves. But that basic fact has been assessed very differently by Buddhism and by classical Western religions. In this essay I have tried to indicate how the shock of dealing with impermanence in the form of death of loved consorts taught me to discover "the everlasting truth of everything changes'" and to find may own composure in that truth. I have also suggested that discussion of many current issues could benefit from a healthy dose of the wisdom that everything always changes and is finite and I have highlighted terminal care and dying, as well as concern for the viability of our supporting environment as two concerns that would be handled differently if impermanence and finitude were taken more seriously. Clearly, I would suggest that Buddhist teachings regarding impermanence and finitude have great merit and wisdom.

It strikes me that one of the points at which classical Buddhism and classical Christianity most differ from each other is in their evaluation of impermanence. It also strikes me that this is one of the points at which what I understand as the mainstream of Christian tradition could learn the most from the mainstream of the Buddhist tradition. I am not suggesting that Buddhism is free from tendencies to promise or threaten some kind of permanence, especially in certain strands of popular Buddhism. Nor am I suggesting that all versions of Christianity are so oriented to eternalism. Most especially, it is important to recognize that Buddhist and Christian people both grasp and cling to permanence, trying to make things last, or to push away the impermanence that is not wanted. That is the nature of saṃsāric or conventional human psychology. But a major difference is striking. Classical Buddhist thought does not encourage or promote such longing for permanence, whereas classical Christian thought, deriving from the

Hellenistic version of Christianity, seems to encourage people to believe that they can overcome impermanence. And the results of trying to overcome impermanence are devastating for everyone.

NOTES

1 The phrase "Don't lead, don't follow" is sometimes regarded as pith meditation instruction for relating with thoughts in meditation practice. Thoughts cannot be suppressed or repressed, but one does not encourage them to arise or linger with them once they do arise, but rather returns immediately to one's focal point for developing meditative awareness, usually the breath. Though it is always claimed that meditation instruction cannot really be learned from a book (and that is also my experience), several accurate published accounts of meditation instruction do exist. For the technique with which I am familiar, see Trungpa: 37–41.

2 Many Buddhist practices are done a hundred thousand times as a formal way of completing that practice before moving on to another formal practice.

3 The most famous discussion of this thesis is found in Ruether 1974.

4 While it is too soon to tell if a similar pattern will emerge with Western Buddhism, the enormous popularity of Sogyal Rinpoche's book, *The Tibetan Book of Living and Dying*, indicates that Westerners may be hungry for the Buddhist way of dealing with impermanence and death.

REFERENCES

Christ, Carol P. (1987). *Laughter of Aphrodite: Reflections on a Journey to the Goddess.* San Francisco: Harper and Row.

Gross, Rita M. (1993). *Buddhism After Patriarchy: A Feminist History, Analysis, and Reconstruction of Buddhism.* Albany, NY: State University of New York Press.

Ruether, Rosemary Radford (1974). "Misogynism and Virginal Feminism in the Fathers of the Church." In Rosemary Radford Ruether, ed., *Religion and Sexism: Images of Women in the Jewish and Christian Traditions*, pp. 150–183. New York: Simon and Schuster

Ruether, Rosemary Radford (1992). *Gaia and God: An Ecofeminist Theology of Earth Healing.* San Francisco: Harper and Row.

Sogyal Rinpoche (1992). *The Tibetan Book of Living and Dying.* San Francisco: Harper and Row.

Suzuki, Shunryu (1970). *Zen Mind, Beginner's Mind: Informal Talks on Zen Meditation*. New York and Tokyo: Weatherhill.
Trungpa, Chögyam (1988). *Shambhala: The Sacred Path of the Warrior*, Boston: Shambhala.
White, Lynn (1967). "The Historical Roots of our Ecological Crisis." *Science* (155) 1203–1207.

Thirteen

Gendered Bodies of Illusion: Finding a Somatic Method in the Ontic Madness of Emptiness

Sara McClintock

INTRODUCTION

The ontic madness of emptiness is the lack of fixed ontologies. A fixed ontology pins down the world with fixed identities. It sees essences in things and holds them to be ultimately real and independent entities that cannot change. Buddhists protest fixed ontologies as compulsions whose results are pain. Rather than clinging to identities, Buddhists seek an experience of identitylessness, or freedom from identity. From the perspective of the everyday world – where fixed ontologies are habitually embraced and defended without reflection – this approach to identity appears insane. But Buddhists revel in the perception that reality is fluid and not fixed.

Yet Buddhists, too, are and must be part of the everyday world. For Buddhists, as for others, it is challenging to confront the ontic fluidity that emptiness implies. While we argue intellectually that identities are not fixed, we still feel rooted in particular forms of life and experience. At times, we may even feel that it is possible for there to be *too much* emphasis on identitylessness, that some form of identity is necessary for our practice and our well-being. In recent times, Buddhist women in particular have voiced a feeling that too strong a focus on the emptiness of identity can work in favor of a patriarchal status quo by denying the realities of embodied existence with the message that ultimately womanhood is unreal.[1] In this case and others like it,[2] the question becomes how Buddhists can work toward a genuine experience of identitylessness without denying the realities of the fluid and embodied identities that we experience on the path. The question is how to find a somatic method within the ontic madness of emptiness.

Two assumptions underlie this question. This first is that we want to enter into the ontic madness of identitylessness. The second is that *we do not want* to ignore the relative realities of our shifting identities.

Both these assumptions have resonances with the currents of traditional Buddhist thought, and the question should therefore be understood as flowing within the Buddhist tradition itself. When couched in Buddhist terms, we can think of the question as a question about method, or skillful means. We can also think of it as a question about the relationship between the ultimate and relative realities. Finally, we can think of it as a question about the relationship between the body and the mind.

The aim of this essay is to offer some ways of thinking about this question and its implications through drawing on diverse streams within the Buddhist tradition. Like the mind, which Buddhists have frequently referred to as a stream (Sanskrit: *cittasaṃtāna*), the Buddhist tradition can be likened to a river comprised of innumerable, intersecting currents.[3] As Buddhists, we are part of this stream, carrying it forward and changing it as we do so. The most responsible attitude toward this situation is – to take a metaphor whose origins lie considerably upstream – to first develop the "wisdom that is comprised of listening" (*śrutamāyīprajñā*). Once we have listened to as many voices of the tradition as we can, we should then begin to develop the "wisdom that is comprised of contemplation" (*cintāmāyīprajñā*). I hope that this essay will contribute to our collective development of both these kinds of Buddhist wisdom.[4]

Given the question with which we are concerned – namely, the experience of gender identity and embodiment and its relationship to the experience of identitylessness – it would not be surprising if our listening were to begin with texts that deal specifically with gender. This, in fact, has been the approach of a number of feminist scholars, whose valuable works on gender and Buddhism have allowed us to more clearly discern a range of discordant voices within the tradition.[5] In this essay, however, rather than choosing texts and traditions that speak specifically about gender, I listen instead to discussions centering around the issues that I outlined above: namely, the question of skillful means, the relationship between the conventional and the ultimate, and the relationship between the body and the mind. The consideration of this last topic also leads me to eavesdrop a bit on some Buddhist conversations about the relationship between mind and matter more generally. Since time and space are limited, I can only report on a few snippets of conversations overheard; I hope that they will inspire others to further listening.

SKILLFUL MEANS AND CONVENTIONAL REALITY

Let's begin with the question of skillful means or method (*upāya*), which, as a concept, is inextricably connected with conventional reality.[6] When the term "skillful means" is used in relation to a buddha, it generally refers to the methods that the buddha uses to coax sentient beings toward an experience of emptiness. When used in relation to ordinary sentient beings, it refers to the techniques that they use to propel themselves toward such an experience. In the Mahāyāna tradition, these techniques consist mainly of the first five "perfections" (*pāramitās*), of giving, ethics, patience, heroic enthusiasm, and meditation.[7] All of these methods must be enacted at the level of conventional reality, whether the actor is a buddha or an ordinary person.[8] As Nāgārjuna said "without relying on the conventional (the buddhas) cannot teach the ultimate."[9] Likewise, Candrakīrti maintained, "Conventional reality is the method; ultimate reality is the goal."[10]

The act of claiming or experiencing an identity is also a part of the conventional reality. For this reason, it can also become part of our method or our skillful means. In the case of gender identity in particular, our sense of identity is closely connected with our experience of embodiment. That is, we identify ourselves as female, male, or some other gender in part because of the type of physical bodies and experiences that we have.[11] At the same time, the act of identification is located within the conventional reality. That is, we dissect and label the parts of our experiences as if they were fixed and truly real, but ultimately such identifications do not correspond to any fixed ontic reality. Concepts, language, and identification all fall under the purview of the conventional realm.

Understanding this, it is therefore possible to note that both gender identity and the categorization of the body can be considered part of method and the conventional reality. Does this resonate with what we have heard from the tradition? Nāgārjuna said that one attains the form body of a buddha through the collection of merit and the body of dharma through the collection of wisdom.[12] The collection of merit is gathered through the five "perfections" mentioned above; it therefore must be accumulated in the relative world of contingent identities. Thus Nāgārjuna, too, indicates a link between the conventional reality and physical form (the form body, or *rūpakāya*).[13]

At the same time, Nāgārjuna's statement also indicates a link between the realization of emptiness and the experience of the ultimate reality (the body of *dharma*, or *dharmakāya*).[14] In this formulation, it is hard to avoid a sense of dualism – of body and mind as existing on different tracks, heading off toward distinct destinations. From the ultimate perspective, of course, we can quickly dispel this notion with an oft-quoted phrase from the *Heart Sūtra*: "form is emptiness; emptiness is form."[15] Yet from a conventional, or everyday, perspective we experience that form is embodiment, form is matter. The appearances of form – our bodies, habitats, food, and so on – present themselves to us and seem to demand our attention. In the tradition of the *Heart Sūtra*, Nāgārjuna and other Madhyamaka thinkers demolish the dualism of body and mind with the realization that ultimately both body and mind are equally devoid of fixed identities. But such philosophers do not heal the bifurcation in conventional terms.

HEALING THE BODY-MIND BIFURCATION IN CONVENTIONAL TERMS

Why should we want to heal the breach in conventional terms? Why not simply accept that, on the level of the conventional reality, mind is mind and body is body? Several reasons prompt us to move beyond this dualism. First, such a stark body-mind dualism contradicts our experience. While it is obviously true that we are able to distinguish in some ways between the material and the mental, when it comes to our experience as embodied beings the lines are less clear. Unlike Robin Williams, the King of the Moon in Terry Gilliam's film, *The Adventures of Baron Munchausen*, our heads (read: minds) cannot fly off our bodies allowing us to become blissfully free from the physical. Neither can our bodies – freed from those annoying rationalists, our minds – proceed to engage in an orgy of sensation while our intellects are busy with less bestial matters. Given our own experience of the interconnection between body and mind, a strict dualism between them seems inappropriate.

A second reason for attempting to overcome the body-mind dualism is related to the above mentioned concern of many Buddhist women – namely, that too strong an emphasis on the realization of emptiness can serve as a factor in disregarding the situation "on the ground" such that long standing patriarchal biases may be allowed to stand. People who share this concern want to ensure that the statement "form is emptiness" is always clearly accompanied by its counterpart, "emptiness is form," so that the everyday world of experience is not forgotten in the void of emptiness. At the heart of this concern lies an impetus to reject the dualism of the ultimate and the conventional realities. But insofar as the Buddhist tradition has tacitly connected the body with the conventional reality, on the one hand, and the mind with the ultimate reality, on the other, the concern also involves a rejection of body-mind dualism.

Finally, a third reason for wishing to engage in a critique of mind-body dualism in Buddhism is related to the new historical context that has been formed by the transmission of Buddhism to the West. In recent decades, Western feminists have pointed to the existence of a body-mind dualism in many Euroamerican traditions. Sharing similarities with some Buddhist formulations, this Western dualism tends to associate the body with "immanence" and women; and the mind with "transcendence" and men.[16] These categories are then ranked hierarchically such that the complex *mind-transcendence-male* is valued over the complex *body-immanence-female.* In Elizabeth Spelman's words (126), this hierarchy results in the development in the West of "what might be called 'somatophobia' (fear of and disdain for the body)." It is understandable and reasonable that Buddhists who have been raised in contexts influenced by such somatophobia might be wary of any dualism that appears to devalue the body and the conventional realm. This historical situation thus presents us with a third reason for attempting to overcome a Buddhist body-mind dualism at the conventional level.

An old Buddhist saying tells us that "the mind is the forerunner of things."[17] Obviously, one could interpret this statement in various ways, and certain dualistic interpretations might well lead to some form of somatophobia. On the other hand, if one were to take a less dualistic approach to matter and mind, one might wish to consider the idea that matter is a manifestation, or perhaps an expression, of mind. The first idea – that matter is a manifestation of mind – has strong resonances with the Yogācāra stream of the Buddhist tradition, a tradition that many have called idealist. But the idea that matter is an expression of mind seems to leave open the possibility of a "middle way" approach to matter and mind which could not be strictly characterized as either materialist or idealist.

VOICES FROM THE ABHIDHARMA TRADITION

In thinking about this problem, I found myself turning to what might be considered one of the stronger currents within the river of Buddhist tradition: Abhidharma philosophy. In Abhidharma, the conventionally designated "personality" is described as a collection of five aggregates, or *skandhas*, one of which is material and four of which are mental.

Collectively, these five aggregates are designated as "name-and-form" (*nāmarūpa*), where "name" refers to the mental elements and "form" refers to the material. In Abhidharma sources, these five aggregates of the personality are equated with existence (*bhava*), suffering (*duḥkha*), and "the world" (*loka*).[18] Another way of saying this is that the five aggregates are synonymous with worldly existence, conventional reality, or saṃsāra. On this interpretation, one could also say that any state that can be characterized as existing in the world must be comprised of *all five aggregates*. In other words, conventional reality necessarily includes both a mental and a physical element.

The Abhidharma texts do not confirm this intuition. Instead, numerous passages demonstrate that for most Abhidharma thinkers it is *not* necessary for all five aggregates to be present in order for an experience to occur in *saṃsāra*. The majority of Abhidharma philosophers maintain that there are places within *saṃsāra*, such as the formless realm (*ārūpyadhātu*), where matter is completely absent.[19] Likewise, they also claim that there are meditative states (like the cessation absorption, or *nirodhasamāpatti*) that are completely devoid of mind.[20] In describing the relationship between matter and mind, Buddhaghosa said that "mentality and materiality are not mixed up together, the mentality is devoid of the materiality and the materiality is void of the mentality."[21] For such thinkers, the separability of mind and matter is paradigmatic, a position that seems to echo the dualism implicit in Nāgārjuna's statement about the buddha's bodies above. But the debates surrounding the question of matter and mind in the Abhidharma texts indicate that the tradition is not quite as univocal as it at first appears. In one discussion of the formless realm, for example, various reasons are put forth for why the realm must include form (*rūpa*), even if it is "just barely form" (*īṣadrūpa*). One of the arguments is that there must be form in the formless realm "since it is said that name and form are mutually dependent, like a bundle of reeds."[22] In response, Vasubandhu offers other arguments (consisting primarily of appeals to scripture), concluding finally that form does not exist in the formless realm. The material body of a person who is reborn into the form or desire realms from the formless realm is produced through the mind, which, however, "contains the cause for the ripening of that (form)."[23]

In the case of the cessation absorption (*nirodhasamāpatti*), we can likewise discern traces of alternative interpretations. In one interpretation, attributed to the Sautrāntikas, the mind is held to arise directly from the body with its faculties at the end of the cessation absorption. The reason is that these two, body and mind, are held to mutually contain the seeds of each other.[24] But in the same context we also hear about a scholar named Vasumitra, who apparently held that the attainment of cessation was accompanied by a mental element or mind (*sacittaka*).[25] The commentator Yaśomitra indicates that this mental element would be an "unmanifest mental consciousness."[26] The discussions preserved in the Abhidharma tradition point to the possibility of an interpretation of the five *skandha*s in which the categories "name" and "form" are simply convenient conventions for talking about an integrated body-mind system. In saying that this body-mind system is integrated, it is not necessary to also accept that there some fixed essence that we can identity as "the system." Instead, what we could assert is that – at least within the conventional realm of *saṃsāra* – the mind always appears as/in/with some form. Mind and matter together form a syzygy in which neither can be extracted without entailing the collapse of the entire edifice of conventional reality. One might wish to argue that matter and mind are "single in nature but conceptually distinct."[27]

A TANTRIC PERSPECTIVE

While the above view of the indivisibility of matter and mind does not accord with the majority opinion of Abhidharma thought, it does find resonance in another area of the Buddhist tradition, Tantra. There are several reasons why one might turn to Buddhist Tantra in contemplating our stated question concerning gender identity and embodiment. First, we have said that our question concerns method or skillful means, and tantra is frequently described as the *method vehicle* within the Mahāyāna.[28] This appellation refers to Tantra's assertion that the ultimate reality of identitylessness as taught in tantra is no different from that embraced by the rest of the Mahāyāna tradition. Instead, Tantra is distinguished by its faster, more skillful method for attaining the realization of that identitylessness. Second, we are concerned with embodiment, and Tantra places a special emphasis upon the body – both as a tool for transformation and as an essential component of the resultant state of freedom. Since gender identity seems so integrally related to the classifications we make about our bodies, Tantra may prove useful in allowing us to work with our shifting identities as we move away from any fixed identity.

Finally, Buddhist Tantra appears to have a special knack for turning identities topsy-turvy, a feature that might be useful in trying to find ways to overcome stark dualisms and hierarchies within the tradition. Figures who defy conventions with regard to caste and gender are fairly common in tantric literature. This may be related to the fact that Tantra is held to be a method for attaining the realization of identitylessness within a single lifetime, in a single body. Rather than envisioning buddhahood as a distant goal toward which one will move over the course of many lifetimes (and many bodies), Tantra sees buddhahood as a possible reality for each of us right now. The transformations that must occur in order for us to eliminate our addictions to fixed identities must take place within our present embodiment. It thus becomes even more imperative that one find ways to work with and acknowledge present identities, even while seeking to overcome them.

In a recent article on the body in Mahāyāna Buddhism, Paul Williams (222) refers to the Buddhist tantric theory of the body and mind, saying that "there is a direct link made in Tantric theory between consciousness and the physical." The subtle body of Buddhist Tantra, with its vital energies or winds (*prāṇa*) which the mind is said to "ride" or "mount," allows for a highly fluid conception of form. Even in the death process, when the subtle consciousness leaves the visible body, it still "rides" on the form of the clear light wind. The subtle body and the subtle mind are, in Geshe Yeshe Thabkhay's words (2), "essentially indivisible." According to this view, when one transforms one's mind, one necessarily also transforms one's body; and, likewise, when one transforms one's body one also necessarily transforms one's mind.

Tantra offers numerous tools for working with the subtle body. In the Guhyasamāja system associated with Nāgārjuna, the tantric path is presented as consisting of the generation and the completion stages. In the generation stage, one practices manipulating the subtle body, or winds, until one gains sufficient control over them to make them arise in a new form, called an "illusion body" (*māyādeha*) at the completion stage. One "arises" as the illusion body during meditation, and one can also arise as the new body after death – thus subverting the usual rebirth process. The illusion body is considered "impure" for as long as one has not eliminated all traces of the ignorance that imagines and clings to fixed identities. But whether the illusory body is impure or pure, it takes the form of "the body of a deity adorned with the marks and signs of an awakened being" (Thabkhay: 13). According to traditional Buddhist tantric theory, such a body can be male or female in gender, although, like all such designations, this classification is still conventional.

But there is something else that is extraordinary about the new body that one creates through the manipulation of the subtle winds. That is, as Yeshe Thabkhay explains, "when the pure or impure illusory body is created, it is not the case that just the body arises;

rather, the entire *maṇḍala* residence with all of its residents also arises" (13). This statement calls to mind other Buddhist traditions that speak of pure lands and buddha-fields – places that have in some sense been created or shaped through the mental power of a bodhisattva's vow (*praṇidhāna*).[29] The concepts of *maṇḍala*s, pure lands, and buddha-fields challenge us to expand our notion of body so as to include our environment and perhaps even our universe. Returning for a moment to the Abhidharma stream of the Buddhist tradition, one is reminded of the teaching that the form aggregate includes not only one's sense faculties, but also the objects of those faculties.[30] In speaking of the conventionally designated personality in terms of the five skandhas, then, it is appropriate to consider the objects that one sees, hears, smells, tastes, and touches as part of the form aggregate.

Tantric practitioners learn to manipulate the winds so as to arise in illusion bodies that have particular colors, shapes, genders, and *maṇḍala*s according to the teachings they have received from their preceptors. Although the variations in the forms are designed to correspond to the propensities of individual practitioners, it is also true that most of the forms have their origins long ago in India. Tenzin Gyatso, the present Dalai Lama, recently said that the appearance of the *sambhogakāya*, the celestial body of a buddha that is homologized to the illusion body, is culturally determined. While it is legitimate to maintain that it is "an utterly perfect and absolutely sublime body," one needs to remember that "it's not the case that there is some kind of intrinsic, autonomous form of this *sambhogakāya* totally independent from those whom the *sambhogakāya* is designed to help."[31] As people who are concerned with method, we need to inquire into the usefulness and benefit of our present forms of practice.

Not only do we as practitioners need to take a greater interest in re-imagining the shape of our future buddhahood, we must also take responsibility for shaping the world in which we live. The Buddhist tradition univocally maintains that the universe and all that we experience within it is not created by an omnipotent, transcendent being, but by the mental and physical actions of the sentient beings inhabiting it. If the universe is our collective creation, then we need to think about how to transform it, starting with our own bodies and minds. Through envisioning ourselves as awakened, compassionate beings, we can begin to plant the seeds for bringing about a more awakened and compassionate universe. Through developing and sustaining our own prayerful aspirations (*praṇidhāna*), we can begin to contribute to the creation of a universe where many of our present problems are eliminated. For example, we may aspire to create a world in which diversity of embodiment is a cause for celebration and not a source of suffering and oppression. We may aspire to create a world in which the mountains, rivers, oceans, and trees are understood as a part of our own form *skandha*, and are protected with the same tenacity with which we protect our physical bodies. And we may aspire to create a world in which identity is neither reified nor diminished, but is used compassionately – and playfully – for the benefit of all.

Clearly, the Buddhist tradition does not speak with a single voice on the questions of the relationship between the body and the mind. Even though some voices present themselves as authoritative and correct, others have survived as echoes, whispers, and traces. As we attempt to listen to as many voices as we can, we are bound to allow the full range of these voices to influence our contemplation – giving rise, perhaps, to new readings and interpretations of Buddhist philosophy. Once we have developed a certain degree of wisdom in the area of our contemplation, we can move on to the next stage: the development of the "wisdom that is comprised of cultivation" (*bhāvanāmāyīprajñā*). Such an approach should be viewed neither as disrespectful to nor as a radical departure from the tradition. Rather, as Buddhists we act with the greatest responsibility when we concern ourselves not only with what the Buddhist tradition has been and is, but also with what it can become.

NOTES

1 See, for example, Sallie Jiko Tisdale (1996). In the same volume of collected essays, Tsultrim Allione says, "It is often those who most adamantly insist that one should go beyond relative considerations about men and women who abuse and undervalue women practitioners the most" (109).

2 Similar concerns may be raised for other kinds of identities, including race identity, ethnic identity, and the identification of certain body types as "disabled."

3 The religionist W. C.. Smith pointed out (79) that religious traditions are more like rivers than mountains.

4 Although these tasks are conceived as sequential, with listening coming first and then contemplation, we actually engage continuously in both. The usefulness of ranking them, however, is that we are encouraged to delay taking the results of our contemplations too seriously until we have done a significant amount of listening.

5 Perhaps the best known example of this genre is the anthology of Buddhists texts about women compiled and commented upon by Diana Paul. For examples of feminist contemplations about gender in

Buddhism, see, among others, Gross; Klein; Shaw; and Wilson.

6 For an in-depth look at skillful means, see Pye, who argues (14) for the use of the English phrase "skilful means" as a translation for the technical term *upāya*.

7 The sixth perfection, wisdom, is also a part of method, or skillful means; likewise, method is ineffectual without wisdom. But since these two are often treated as separate yet necessary counterparts (i.e., in the formulation "method and wisdom"), I treat them separately here. See Geshe Lhundrup Sopa (48), who breaks down the six perfections slightly differently, with giving, ethics, patience, and meditation on the side of method, wisdom on the side of wisdom, and heroic enthusiasm common to both.

8 Although method is always seen to exist on the level of conventional reality, there is considerable disagreement among Buddhists concerning the mechanics of how an awakened buddha experiences the conventional. For discussions of this problem, see, e.g., Dunne; Eckel; Griffiths 1994; and Makransky.

9 *Mūlamadhyamakakārikā* (Nāgārjuna 1959) 24: 10ab: *vyāvaharam anāśritya paramārtho na deśyate* .

10 *Madhyamakāvatāra* (Candrakīrti n.d.) 6: 80ab: *upāyabhūtaṃ vyavahārasatyam upeyabhūtaṃ parmārthasatyam.*

11 In stating that gender identity has a relation to the experience of embodiment, I do not imply that gender identity is fixed. Rather, gender identity comes about through the imposition of socially and mentally constructed categories on bodies that are, in fact, unique. For more on the diversity of gender identification and its fluid relationship to biological sex, see Feinberg, among others.

12 *Ratnāvalī* (Nāgārjuna 1982) 3: 12: *sangs rgyas rnams kyi gzugs sku ni bsod nams tshogs las byung ba ste / chos kyi sku ni mdor bsdu na rgyal po ye shes tshogs las 'khrungs.*

13 Like most things about buddhas, the nature of their form bodies is a matter of controversy. Unfortunately, we do not have space to consider this problem here. For intriguing presentations of some aspects of the problem see Griffiths 1994; and Makransky.

14 My gloss of the term *dharmakāya* reflects the broad understanding of the Mahāyāna *sūtra* tradition, where the body of *dharma* indicates, in Makransky's words, "a Buddha's own nondual knowledge" of emptiness (61).

15 Conze: 81: *rūpam śūnyatā śūnyataiva rūpam.*

16 One of the earliest feminists explicitly to delineate this dualism was Simone de Beauvoir (1949).

17 *Dhammapada* 1: 1: *manoppaṅgama dhammā.*

18 See *Abhidharmakośa* (Vasubandhu) 1: 8: *ye sāsravā upādānaskandhās te saraṇā api / duḥkhaṃ samudayo loko dṛṣṭisthānaṃ bhavaś ca te.*

19 See, for example, *Abhidharmakośa* (Vasubandhu) 8: 3: *nārūpye rūpasadbhāvaḥ.*

20 The view that asserts matter without mind is more controversial than the claim for the existence of mind without matter – undoubtedly because of the general primacy accorded to mind in the Buddhist tradition. For an excellent analysis of *nirodhasamāpatti* in Buddhism, see Griffiths 1986.

21 *Visuddhimagga* 18: 33; trans. Buddhaghosa: 185.

22 See *Abhidharmakośabhāṣya* on 8: 3ab: *naḍakalāpīdvayavan nāmarūpayor anyaniśritavacanāt* (Vasubandhu: 1132).

23 See *Abhidharmakośabhāṣya* on 8: 3cd: *rūpasya cittād evotpattis tadvipākahetupaibhāvitāl labdhavṛttitaḥ* (Vasubandhu: 1137).

24 See *Abhidharmakośabhāṣya* on 2:44: *evaṃ cittam apy asmād eva sendritāt kāyāt jāyate na cittāt / anyonyabījakaṃ hy etad ubhayaṁ yad uta cittaṁ ca sendriyaś ca kāya iti pūrvācaryāḥ* (Vasubandhu: 246).

25 See *Abhidharmakośabhāṣya* on 2: 44: *bhadantavasumitras tv āha paripṛcchāyāṃ yasyācittakā nirodhasamāpattis tasyaiṣa doṣaḥ mama tu sacittakā samāpattir iti* (Vasubandhu: 246).

26 See *Abhidharmakośabhāṣyavṛtti* on 2: 44: *aparisphuṭamano-vijñānasacittakānīti sthaviravasumitrādayaḥ* (Vasubandhu: 247).

27 The phrase is taken from Buddhist logical discourse (*pramāṇavāda*), where all concepts and identifications are said to be *vyāvṛttibheda*, "distinct only by virtue of conceptually constructed exclusions."

28 Tsong kha pa, in his most famous treatise on Tantra, says: :Because the Vajra Vehicle has more skillful means than that of the Perfections, it is called the Method Vehicle" (Hopkins: 108).

29 For an example, see the *Avataṃsaka Sūtra* (91b-92a). Here, the bodhisattva Samantabhadra describes ten causes and conditions of the "oceans of the worlds" (*'jig rten gyi rgya mtsho*). Along with the "blessings of the tathāgatas" (*de bzhin gshegs pa'i byin gyi rlabs*) and the "karmic collections of sentient beings" (*sems can rnams kyi las kyi tshogs*), he includes the "special prayerful aspirations for the purification of [buddha-] fields on the part of bodhisattvas" (*byang chub sems dpa' rnams kyi zhing yongs su dag pa'i smon lam gyi khyad par*) and "that which is established through the prayerful aspirations that are produced through the bodhisattvas' activities" (*byang chub sems dpa' rnams kyi spyod pas rnam par bsgrubs pa'i smon lam gyis mngon par bsgrubs pa*).

30 See *Abhidharmakośa* (Vasubandhu) 1: 9ab: *rūpaṃ pañcendriāny arthāḥ pañcavijñaptir eva ca.*

31 As quoted in Varela (112).

REFERENCES

Allione, Tsultrim (1996). "The Feminine Principle in Tibetan Buddhism." In Marianne Dresser, ed., *Buddhist Women on the Edge: Contemporary*

Perspectives from the Western Frontier. Berkeley: North Atlantic Books.

Buddhaghosa (1975). *Visuddhimagga*. Trans. by Bhikkhu Ñāṇamoli. Kandy: Buddhist Publication Society.

de Beauvoir, Simone (1949). *Le Deuxieme Sexe*. Paris: Librairie Gallimard.

Candrakīrti (n.d.). *Madhyamakāvatāra*. Tibetan translation by Tilakakalaśa and Pha tshab nyi ma grags. In Derge, *dbu ma*, 'a: 201a–217a.

Conze, Edward (1958). *Buddhist Wisdom Books: Containing The Diamond Sutra and The Heart Sutra*. London: George Allen & Unwin.

Dunne, John (1996). "Thoughtless Buddha, Passionate Buddha." *Journal of the American Academy of Religion* (64: 3) 525-556.

Eckel, Malcolm David (1993). *To See the Buddha: A Philosopher's Quest for the Meaning of Emptiness*. San Francisco: HarperCollins.

Feinberg, Leslie (1996). *Transgender Warriors: Making History from Joan of Arc to Rupaul*. Boston: Beacon Press.

Griffiths, Paul J. (1986). *On Being Mindless: Buddhist Meditation and the Mind-Body Problem*. La Salle: IL: Open Court Publishing.

Griffiths, Paul J. (1994). *On Being Buddha: The Classical Doctrine of Buddhahood*. Albany: State University of New York Press.

Gross, Rita (1993). *Buddhism After Patriarchy: A Feminist History, Analysis, and Reconstruction of Buddhism*. Albany: State University of New York Press.

Hopkins, Jeffrey (1977). *Tantra in Tibet: The Great Exposition of Secret Mantra, vol. 1*. London: George Allen & Unwin.

Klein, Anne Carolyn (1995). *Meeting the Great Bliss Queen: Buddhists, Feminists, and the Art of the Self*. Boston: Beacon Press.

Makransky, John (1997). *Buddhahood Embodied: Sources of Controversy in India and Tibet*. Albany: State University of New York Press.

Nāgārjuna (1959). *Madhyamakaśāstra of Nāgārjuna with the Commentary Prasannapadā by Candrakīrti* [*Mūlamadhyamakakārikā*]. Ed. P. L.. Vaidya. Darbhanga: Mithila Institute.

Nāgārjuna (1982). *Nāgārjuna's Ratnāvalī: the Basic Texts (Sanskrit, Tibetan, Chinese)* [*Ratnāvalī*]. Ed. Michael Hahn. Bonn: Indica et Tibetic Verlag.

Pye, Michael (1978). *Skilful Means: A Concept in Mahayana Buddhism*. London: Gerald Duckword & Co. Ltd.

Paul, Diana (1979). *Women in Buddhism: Images of the Feminine in the Mahayana Tradition*. Berkeley: Asian Humanities Press.

Shaw, Miranda (1994). *Passionate Enlightenment: Women in Tantric Buddhism*. Princeton: Princeton University Press.

Smith, Wilfred Cantwell (1967). *Questions of Religious Truth*. New York: Charles Scribner's Sons.

Sopa, Geshe Lhundrup (1983). "An Excursus on the Subtle Body in Tantric Buddhism (Notes Contextualizing the Kālacakra)." *Journal of the International Association of Buddhist Studies* (6: 2) 48-66.

Spelman, Elizabeth V. (1988). *Inessential Woman: Problems of Exclusion in Feminist Thought*. Boston: Beacon Press.

Thabkhay, Geshe Yeshe (1995). "The Three Bodies as the Path." Unpublished article presented at the International Symposium on Indo-Tibetan Tantric Buddhism at the Central Institute for Higher Tibetan Studies, Sarnath, India. Trans. by John Dunne.

Tisdale, Sallie Jiko (1996). "Form, Emptiness; Emptiness, Form." In Marianne Dresser, ed., *Buddhist Women on the Edge: Contemporary Perspectives from the Western Frontier*. Berkeley: North Atlantic Books.

Varela, Francisco J. (1996). *Sleeping, Dreaming, and Dying: An Exploration of Consciousness with the Dalai Lama*. Boston: Wisdom Publications.

Vasubandhu (1987). *Abhidharmakośa and Bhāṣya of Ācārya Vasubandhu with Sphuṭārthā Commentary of Ācārya Yaśomitra* [*Abhidharmakośa*]. Ed. Swami Dwarikadas Shastri. Varanasi: Bauddha Bharati.

Vasubandhu (1987). *Abhidharmakośabhāṣya*. For publication information see entry above.

Williams, Paul (1997). "Some Mahāyāna Buddhist Perspectives on the Body." In Sarah Coakley, ed., *Religion and the Body*. Cambridge: Cambridge University Press.

Wilson, Liz (1996). *Charming Cadavers: Horrific Figurations of the Feminine in Indian Buddhist Hagiographical Literature*. Chicago: University of Chicago Press.

Yaśomitra. *Abhidharmakośabhāṣyavṛtti* or *Sphuṭārthā-vyākhyā*. Published together with the *Abhidharmakośa* of Vasubandhu (see above).

Fourteen

On Essences, Goals and Social Justice: An Exercise in Buddhist Theology

John D. Dunne

When I was invited to present a paper on the panel from which this volume is derived, I originally intended to spend most of my time engaging in a bit of applied Buddhist theology, so to speak. Specifically, I intended to discuss certain categories relevant to the pursuit of social justice. But as I thought more deeply about how best to proceed, the need to examine the term "Buddhist theology" and to discuss in some detail the "theological" principles I intended to apply became apparent. As a result, the applied aspect of this exercise – the attempt to address issues within the realm of social justice – remains somewhat truncated. This is not to say, however, that an examination of "Buddhist theology" itself is merely an annoyance that I am obliged to endure. Rather, the way we envision Buddhist theology is crucial, for the vision we choose to accept corresponds to limits on the possibilities that appear to us when we formulate theological principles and apply them in practice. Our examination of Buddhist theology, however, is complicated by the question of where to begin: do we start with a metatheory of Buddhist theology, then move on to the principles implied by that theory and the praxis that stems from those principles? Do we begin with some praxis, then derive principles and hence a metatheory? Or do we begin with some principles that imply both a metatheory and a particular praxis?

I do not raise the question of beginnings so as to offer a direct answer; instead, I merely ask the reader to note that these three theological moments – metatheory, principles, and praxis – are inextricably interrelated. Hence, if my remarks on application or praxis are necessarily somewhat brief, by dwelling on metatheory (or "metatheology") and a set of related principles, I hope to spark some interest among Buddhist activists and others in a further exploration of the practical or applied theology that I will touch upon.

As is suggested by the three theological moments that I have highlighted, my presentation falls into three parts: in the first, I will discuss some difficulties of "Buddhist theology" and explain the approach I favor. In the second part, I formulate the Buddhist principles that I will apply to the question of social justice. And in the third, I present a brief application of those principles.

BUDDHIST THEOLOGY

The night before presenting the original version of this article, I told a senior colleague that I was to give a paper on Buddhist theology. In response, he burst out, "Isn't that kind of kinky?!" He contended that since Buddhism lacked *theos*, Buddhist Theology could only be an oxymoron. To rejoin, one might note that there are some Buddhist notions that function like a *theos*, but another tack is simply to say that there are other interpretations of Buddhist theology to which the question of a *theos* is irrelevant. On one such interpretation, the term Buddhist theology draws a parallel between the self-consciously Christian thinking that Christian theologians engage in, even within an academic context, and a kind of self-consciously Buddhist thinking that a Buddhist might engage in, even in an academic context. Essaying a definition of this approach, wc might say:

> Buddhist theology is the self-conscious attempt to present reasoned arguments from within the tradition on issues of importance to Buddhists in order to correct, critique, clarify or expand upon the tradition.

Now, although this definition does not seem all that problematic, this is in part due to the vague nature of the terms employed. For the sake of argument, we might assume that one can specify without great controversy what it means to be "self-conscious" in this context. But other aspects of the definition raise more persistent problems that are rather hard to ignore. The first and most obvious of these is simply the question of how we understand the *Buddhist tradition*, and the second is the related problem of what constitutes *presenting reasoned arguments from within the tradition.*

Contemporary Buddhists are certainly not the first to confront these problems. Consider, for example, the Tibetan doxographical enterprise. In order to assess the tremendously diverse philosophies of Indian Buddhists and fit them into a hierarchical schema, Tibetan doxographers are faced with the problem of defining what constitutes Buddhist thought. As always, such problems become most clear with liminal cases, such as the Vātsīputrīyas. These misguided fellows were rather sloppy about the notion of Selflessness, and as a result, they have been vilified ever since the time of Vasubandhu (some fifteen hundred years ago) as the paragons of bad Buddhist philosophers.[1] But for Tibetans such as the eighteenth century philosopher lCang kya rol pa'i rdo rje, these wayward Indians pose a special problem. That is, according Tibetan philosophers such as lCang kya, to be truly Buddhist, a philosopher must assent to four basic points: all things are impermanent; all contaminated things are or produce suffering; all things are devoid of any ultimately real Self; and *nirvāṇa* is peace.[2] On his view, then, a Buddhist philosopher cannot admit any ultimately real Self and still be a Buddhist. And since the Vātsīputrīyas allegedly admit an ultimately real Self, they cannot be Buddhists. In institutional terms, however, they are (or more precisely, were) Buddhists because they had taken refuge in the Buddha, Dharma and Saṅgha and ran around claiming to be *bhikṣus* – indeed, they were *bhikṣus*, for their monastic rules were not vilified in the way their philosophy was.

lCang kya solves this problem by allowing it to stand: the Vātsīputrīyas are at once Buddhist – because of their faith in the three jewels and their adherence to Buddhist vows – and not Buddhist – because their philosophy includes views that lCang kya has defined as non-Buddhist (55-58).

Certainly, on the definition given earlier, lCang kya's doxography is an instance of Buddhist theology: it speaks from within the tradition about a central issue – the proper way of thinking so as to become a Buddha; it critiques that which fails to be Buddhist; it corrects those Buddhists who are stuck at the "lower" philosophical levels; it clarifies the nature of the tradition; and by its very nature it enlarges on the tradition, in that doxography is only possible after the philosophies it purports to analyze have been formulated. But while lCang kya's doxography clearly meets our first definition of Buddhist theology, we should note with considerable interest that his Buddhist theologizing has created an insurmountable tension for itself: the Vātsīputrīyas must be both Buddhists and not Buddhists.

On my view, this tension is unavoidable because it is created precisely by the way this form of Buddhist theology proceeds. That is, this form of Buddhist theology necessarily involves, on the one hand, an all-encompassing definition of the tradition and, on the other, a definition of what it means to reason from within that tradition. On lCang kya's fairly typical view, to reason from within the tradition one must shun excluded middles and pay proper homage to the law of contradiction.[3] The problem, however, is that a truly all-encompassing definition of any living tradition would almost certainly be bursting at the seams with excluded middles, and it would most likely trample all over the law of contradiction.

My point in saying all this is really quite straightforward. If Buddhist theology must locate itself within the tradition as a whole, and if it is to say something coherent about the tradition, then it must essay some systematic and over-arching definition of the tradition. But in the process of formulating anything more than a trivial definition, one inevitably excludes some who would claim to be Buddhist. In other words, by attempting to speak for the whole tradition, one inevitably fragments it – one of the five worst deeds for a Buddhist to commit. And a sojourn in hell is a heavy price to pay for a bit of Buddhist theology!

Of course, any good bodhisattva is willing to plunge into hell for others' sake, so the threat of karmic retribution need not dissuade us from accepting the vision of Buddhist theology suggested by works such as lCang kya's. One can, however, find far more compelling reasons for rejecting the approach typified by lCang kya. These reasons are derived from a hypothesis that I would like to introduce at this point: when we attempt an exhaustive definition of, for example, a "Buddhist," we must proceed either from an *essentialist* perspective or a *teleological* one. To be *essentialist* is to construct one's definition on the basis of an essence, construed as a property or set of properties, that is purported to be truly present in every instance – every "true" Buddhist assents, for example, to certain beliefs while rejecting other beliefs. To be *teleological* is to construct one's definition in terms of some *telos* or goal – in our case, either a goal that all Buddhists are alleged to seek, or a goal that the definition itself is meant to fulfill.

These two options – to be essentialist, or to be teleological – are at the heart of what I wish to raise in this article, and I will discuss them in greater detail below. But at this point, in anticipation of that discussion, I will make this claim: an essentialist definition is actually a teleological one in which the *telos* has not been made explicit, and to the extent that the *telos* in question is imposed by the concept of an essence, rather then derived through consensus, it may harm those who have had no voice in the formulation of that essence. With this in mind, I would argue that the definition of a monolithic tradition required by the approach exemplified by lCang kya slips all too easily into essentialism, for it attempts to define what is "Buddhist" by appealing to some universalized properties – whether a set of beliefs or vows – that are meant to characterize all Buddhists. Tending toward essentialism, such definitions do not present explicit goals, and one is therefore left wondering what those goals might be – what, in particular, requires lCang kya to offer what amount to two competing definitions? What is being preserved? What is being rejected and excluded? Who benefits and who is harmed thereby?

Answering questions such as these would require an extensive examination of lCang kya's own historical milieu. In any case, the answers are less important than the queries, for the mere plausibility of these questions justifies our suspicions about the motives behind the essentialism nascent in this approach. It is not so much that we should be suspicious of lCang kya himself – perhaps his motives were entirely benign. Instead, we should be suspicious of the hidden goals themselves, for it is entirely possible that some later interpreter could employ lCang kya's definitions to justify the suppression of those who are not "true" Buddhists. This inchoate harm would be true of any essentialization of the tradition, and since our first definition of Buddhist theology requires just such an essentialist view, we must find some other approach if we wish to avoid such harm.

In an effort to avoid the essentialism implicit in the approach I have discussed so far, one might propose any number of other approaches to Buddhist theology. The one I prefer can be stated in an almost embarrassingly simple fashion: to do Buddhist theology is to think like a Buddhist (or, perhaps, some specific Buddhists). In saying this, I do not mean to suggest that to do Buddhist theology one must think like a Buddhist in general; rather, one must think like a *particular* Buddhist (or Buddhists). Likewise, in suggesting that one think like a Buddhist, what I mean is that one adduce certain principles from the works and words of some Buddhist(s), and that one then attempt to think in accord with those principles about the issue at hand.

What is immediately obvious here is that this version of Buddhist theology must begin with an act of interpretation. But this act does not attempt to be normative, in that it does not make any claims about the way in which all Buddhists should think. Rather, this interpretive act is of quite limited scope, for it claims merely to be formulating principles on the basis of the explicit statements of a particular Buddhist (or Buddhists) in such a way that they would or do elicit the agreement of that Buddhist (or those Buddhists). In the case of living figures, this would be a dialogic process; in the case of philosophers to whom one has no access, it would be a process that involves the construction of an interpretive context and authorial persona for what might be called an imaginary dialogue. Of course, the interpretive issues at stake here range far beyond the scope of this article. Suffice it to say that I presume no statement or text can have only a single possible interpretation, but that at the same time there are definite limits on interpretation.[4] The result, in any case, is that this approach is explicitly teleological from the beginning, for it is oriented toward the straightforward goal of arriving at an interpretation that is acceptable to one's interlocutor, whether actual or imaginary.

Of course, one might claim that this approach is somewhat trivial if its *telos* consists solely in arriving at a consensual understanding of some principles. But I envision an approach that also applies what might be called a "teleological analysis" of those principles themselves. That is, when one examines these principles in terms of the mode of rationality through which they are presented,[5] what are the expected results of these principles, and do those results conform to the *telos* that one seeks? This analysis requires that some choice of *telos* has been made, and it implies a self-conscious sharing of that *telos* with the Buddhist(s) in question. In the course of such an analysis, it would be important to note that one need not agree on all principles, but rather only on those whose efficacy is essential to the shared *telos*. Likewise, the self-conscious identification of oneself and one's interlocutor as Buddhist need not enter into the analysis. In other words, unless one's goals have something to do with preserving Buddhist institutions or identities, one can relinquish the debate about who is "Buddhist" as irrelevant to the pursuit of one's goals.

One might argue that, thus far, this form of Buddhist theology is simply careful, primarily emic scholarship: it is an attempt to understand a person's spoken or written words in the clearest possible fashion and to formulate that understanding in a set of manageable principles. Indeed, the interpretive approach I would favor might prove unfamiliar or even objectionable to some who identify themselves as Buddhist, in as much as it relies on motifs – such as notions of historical consciousness and a nuanced approach to authorial intent – that are unfamiliar or challenging to them. Moreover, since anyone with some training should be able to engage in the same manner with a text or oral testimony, this interpretive aspect of Buddhist theology is not really all that Buddhist. One might respond that the interpretation becomes Buddhist when the interpreter affirms the philosophical principles derived thereby, but this would raise an amusing corollary to lCang kya's theory (one that underscores the difficulties of his enterprise) – namely, that one might well be philosophically a Buddhist, but a Christian, for example, in terms of faith and practice.

Be that as it may, the point here is that there is something that the Buddhist theologian and the academic should share, if any attempt at interpretation is to be possible: namely, a belief[6] that languages, cultures and time do not constitute insurmountable barriers to understanding; a belief that one can speak with other human beings or read their words (even if, in the latter case, those persons be long dead) and be able to come to understand them. And if Buddhist theology is to be more than an interpretation, but also an attempt to apply the principles derived thereby, an additional belief is necessary: the belief that what is understood in interpretation is not entirely restricted to a particular time or place, but that it is somehow applicable now in one's own context.

The justification of these first two beliefs – the belief in the penetrability of cultural, linguistic and historical barriers and the belief in the possibility of genuine understanding – is no mean task. Suffice it to say that if these beliefs are not justified, then you would not be able to understand any of the words written on this page. The justification of the third belief – that the principles adduced from interpreting a Buddhist text or testimony are applicable to our own situation – is in the pudding, so to speak; that is, it is only by actually attempting to apply some principles to some contemporary issue that the viability of such a project will become evident. Without further ado then, I will now gather the ingredients for the pudding.

SOME PRINCIPLES: ESSENTIALISM AND PURPOSE

I have already mentioned a certain choice: a choice between focusing on essences, or focusing on purposes or goals. These two possibilities, I would maintain, pertain to any use of language or concepts. In other words, when I say or think, "This is a chair," I can either be doing so on the basis of a belief in real essences, or I can do so with the awareness that that statement or determination is meaningful only in terms of the expectations that arise in relation to a particular goal. These two are mutually exclusive, and they are exhaustive: one must either believe that one is trafficking in real essences, or that one is organizing one's perceptions in relation to some goal; one cannot believe that one is doing both. I will maintain that the first option – to accept the reality of essences – would constitute a mistaken belief. Hence, it is the second option – the recognition of the regulative function of our goals – that we must accept; not because it is preferable, but because it is in fact what we do.

This, then, is the principle with which I would like to do my thinking (or theologizing, if you prefer) about social justice: that the belief in essences is mistaken, and that it must be supplanted by a full awareness of one's telos.

This is an extremely concise way of stating the gist of a very lengthy and detailed series of arguments from the philosophy of Dharmakīrti, a seventh century Indian philosopher. At this point, it may all seem a bit opaque, so perhaps I should step back a bit and explain in greater detail just what I am getting at. I will begin with Dharmakīrti's view of essences, then I will consider how and why he rejects essentialism. Finally, I will consider how he supplants essences with the notion of goals.

ESSENCES

I use the term essence to capture the nuances of Dharmakīrti's usage of the term *sāmānya* (or *jāti*), a "sameness" or universal. For Dharmakīrti, the notion of an essence arises most obviously in the context of language, although conceptual awareness, which he understands to operate much in the same way as language, is equally relevant in this regard. If we restrict ourselves to a discussion of language, however, we can say the following: by *essence* (*sāmānya*) Dharmakīrti means an entity that is instantiated in multiple points of time and space such that all the spatio-temporal loci in which it is instantiated are the objects of the same expression (understood as a type, not a token). Consider, for example, the expression person. We would understand that expression to take each of us panelists as an object. Now, we can ask ourselves, "Why is it that this expression can refer to each of these individuals? Why does it not also refer to chairs?" On the essentialist account, the answer is that there is something the same about all of these individuals; present in all of us is an entity – call it *personhood* – and it is by virtue of this entity's presence that each of us can be called a *person*. Moreover, since this entity is not present in chairs, they cannot be called *persons*; only things that instantiate *personhood* can be called *persons*, and chairs lack *personhood*.

At first glance, this does not seem all that implausible. Certainly, our intuition would tell us that if some things are the objects of a certain expression while others are not, there must be something identical about those things that differentiates them from the other things.[7] But although this may seem plausible, Dharmakīrti points out that it makes no sense at all.

Dharmakīrti offers numerous arguments against essentialism, but perhaps his favorite motif is an identity/difference analysis, especially with regard to two basic criteria for the success of any semantic theory: those criteria are continuity or repeatability (*anvaya*) and action (*pravṛtti*). Continuity is similar to the notion of sameness. That is, each use of the expression person, for example, is picking out something that is the same in each case – the same essence, personhood, is continuous across all persons. In Western philosophical terms, this amounts to the notion that essence is repeated in each instance, or that it is distributed over all its instances.

The criterion of *action* rests on the notion that any expression is successful in its semantic function if and only if it directs the interpreter of the expression toward only the intended referent and not something else. For example, if I say to you, the reader, "Please point to the paper on which these words are printed," that expression must give you some information that directs you toward this paper. And if you were to abide by that injunction, you would extend a finger and point to this paper; you could not abide by that injunction by, say, standing on your head and wiggling your legs in the air.

Dharmakīrti employs these two criteria – *repeatability* and *action* – as part of an identity/difference argument. Basically, he asks: Is the essence *personhood*, for example, different from its instances – the individuals in question – or the same as those instances? If *personhood* is identical to its instances, then it could not be repeated in all persons, because if it were repeated in all of its instances, then all persons would be exactly identical. That is, if *personhood* were exactly the same as a particular person (such as my friend John), then, in order for *personhood* to be repeated or instantiated in all persons John would have to be repeated or instantiated in all persons. Amusing as this might be, it is clearly not the case. And if *personhood* it is not repeated in all persons but is instantiated only in John, then only John is a person. Thus, the essentialist theory fails the test of continuity.

The criterion of *action* becomes an issue when one considers the essence to be distinct from its instances. Consider again the injunction, "Please point to this paper." On the essentialist theory, the expression *paper* picks out some *paperness* that is instantiated in every piece of paper. But if this *paperness* is distinct from any individual paper, and if it is in fact what the expression *paper* picks out, then that injunction would not direct one toward any actual paper; it would direct one toward the essence. Thus, since the essence *paperness* is distinct from the paper – which is thc same as saying that it is something other than the paper – in order to act on that injunction, you would have to ignore the paper. You would be obliged to ignore the paper because my injunction directs you toward something other than the paper, namely, the essence. Hence, if you were to follow my injunction, you would seek to point to the essence, but since the essence is necessarily not an instance, you could not point to anything at all.

As refutations of essentialism, I find these arguments quite convincing, and I would agree that essentialism is a flawed theory. But more than being merely philosophically flawed, on Dharmakīrti's view, essentialism is practically flawed. In fact, he maintains that essentialism about one's personal identity is the primary cause of all suffering.[8] Certainly, some of the ways that this might be true are obvious. That is, while we habitually assume essences to be real entities in the world, there are in fact no such entities; hence, we must be supplying them. And if in the process of supplying essences, I wish, for example, to claim that a particular individual or group of individuals are not persons because they lack *personhood*, or that a particular place is part of "the Motherland," because *Motherland-hood* is instantiated in it, the only thing that will stop me will be other, competing attempts at supplying other essences. That such attempts can come to blows is obviously the case. In this regard, I am reminded of quip I heard from the late A. K.. Ramanujan: "A language is a dialect with an army." Here, we should say, "An essence is an assertion with an army."

I am, however, anticipating my discussion of social justice, and before doing so, one more issue must be dealt with. I mentioned above that the principles I wish to employ are that the belief in essences is mistaken, and that it must be supplanted by a full awareness of one's *telos*. I must now explain how it is that the question of one's goal or *telos* becomes an issue here.

To discuss this point, we should begin by recognizing that the critique of essences appears to make language and conceptual thought impossible. That is, if there is in fact no real *personhood*, for example, that is the same in all that we call *persons*, then how is it that we are able to use that expression for all of them? Dharmakīrti responds to these objections by noting that the absence of some real, hypostasized essence does not mean that one cannot *construct* or supply some unreal, imaginary essence or sameness for things.

The construction of unreal essences begins with the claim that, if there are no real essences, then no two things can be identical; ontologically, this means that all things are entirely and completely unique. However, despite the uniqueness of all things, it is obviously the case that expressions such as *person* still manage to make sense. If then, there is in fact no real entity that is the same in any two persons, and if the expression *person* can still be used for those persons, then there must be some way of accounting for their sameness without positing some positive entity. Dharmakīrti claims that their sameness consists of a negation: namely, their *difference* – but not their difference from each other; rather, their sameness is their difference from all *non-persons*. Thus, persons are the same in that they are not *non-persons*.[9]

On Dharmakīrti's ontology, at least, this makes good sense. That is, since any thing is in fact entirely different from all other things, to base one's categories on difference is initially not problematic. The difficulty comes when one tries to move from the absolute difference of any given thing, such as the paper of this page, to the notion that it is *not* different from all other papers because it *is* different from all non-papers. What this requires, clearly, is that we have a way of ignoring or "filtering out" the difference between papers while focusing upon their difference from non-papers. This "filtering mechanism" consists of a set of expectations that arise from one's intended goal.

Consider, for example, the papers once again. We should note first that, if the papers were to have some *paperness*, they would present themselves as such in sense perception; that is, sense perception would be *determinate*; in perceiving them, we would necessarily perceive them as papers.[10] But if there is no *paperness* in the papers, our sense perceptions are necessarily indeterminate. To construe them as papers requires some act on our side – an act that attributes a constructed essence to them and determines them as papers. One can ask at this point: Why do we bother to make determinations? Dharmakīrti's contention is that we do so because we have some purpose in mind: we need the papers to fulfill some goal, or to avoid some undesirable outcome. This need for a means to a goal amounts to a set of expectations about causal functions – there are things that can perform the functions we need, and those that cannot. But again, these expectations must be stated negatively, because there is no positive entity – no essential causal potentiality – to which they could refer. The upshot, then, is that one's goals require a certain kind of causal functionality, but since that causal functionality cannot be pinpointed affirmatively, it is approximated negatively by excluding those things which do not have the desired effects or functions.[11]

Hence, when I ask you to point to this paper, the term *paper* is really a marker for a certain disposition that I have – a desire to achieve a goal whose accomplishment requires a kind of causal functionality that *non-paper* things (chairs, tables, etc.) cannot perform. And both you and I can see all the papers as the same (i.e., as "papers") on this basis – namely, that they are all different from those things that cannot perform the desired causal function.

Now, there is obviously quite a lot more that could be said here, especially about how conventions are constructed such that persons using language can share a set of expectations, but the key issue I wish to raise is how goals are regulative. As I have noted, the determination of these things as papers has to do with their function or causal capacity – they produce effects that other things do not produce. Obviously, the papers, as with all real things (*bhāva*, *vastu*), always present the effect of interaction with one's senses. If this is all we had to go on, we could not say very much. All we could say is that these things are perceptible, but since we can say this of any real thing, we cannot differentiate the papers from other things on this basis. Hence, if we want to identify them as *papers*, then we must have something more in mind. That "something more" is precisely a goal that guides our inquiry into these things – it establishes a set of expectations about function by which additional determinations can be made – flat, thin, combustible, capable of bearing ink, and so on. Again, it is important to note that these distinctions are made by ignoring the differences among combustible things, for example, in favor of excluding what is not combustible. And in order for me to make those determinations, I must have some *interest* – something that makes me focus not on the difference among the papers, but the papers' difference from everything else. This *interest* amounts to a desire to attain a goal. In other words, it is all a matter of what one chooses to focus on, and these choices are regulated by one's goals. In a certain sense, one might even claim that to choose a goal is to choose a reality.

SOCIAL JUSTICE

With all this in mind, allow me now to finally suggest how the principles adduced above might be applied to questions of social justice. This is where the largely interpretive enterprise above becomes Buddhist theology, at least as I understand it.

In accord with the usage of the term in the United States, I will briefly define the pursuit of social justice as the attempt to ameliorate (or more optimistically, eliminate) oppression and inequities in society. This, of course, is not much of a definition at all, since the difficult issues concern questions about what constitutes oppression and inequities. These include issues about resource distribution, quality of life, expectations and so on.

While clarifying these issues is clearly crucial to the effective pursuit of social justice, I will restrict myself to another issue – one that has received more attention of late, but still remains an extremely difficult issue for many activists. I am referring to the question of what I shall call *communal identity*. By this I mean the way in which a person is identified as a member of a particular community; and when I use the term *community* here, I mean it in its broadest sense. Hence, religious identity, racial identity, ethnic identity, class identity and the like are all species of communal identity. My purpose in throwing all these different forms of identity into the same barrel is to show how they all tend to generate certain assumptions about the persons so identified.

The first and most obvious of these assumptions has to do with the notion of essences. Let us consider, for example, the notion of "racial" or "ethnic" identity. Almost inevitably, to identify an individual as the member of a some "ethnic group" or "race" is to assume that that individual is somehow the same as all other individuals of that ethnicity or race. In this regard, it is crucial to note that Dharmakīrti's theory of essentialism includes the notion that an essence necessarily implies other properties. That is, when one believes that some person or thing has some particular essence, one assumes that that person or thing also necessarily has some other essential qualities; these latter qualities are assumed to be necessitated by the presence of the aforementioned essence.[12] That which has "paperness," for example, necessarily has the essential quality of being combustible, capable of bearing ink and so on. What is interesting about this process of associating certain qualities with a given essence is that one can associate qualities that have absolutely no sensory evidence for them, or even qualities that are contradicted by sensory evidence. For Dharmakīrti, a standard example is the notion of something "being one's own" (*ātmīya*), where anything that has that essence, anything that is one's own, is assumed to have qualities such as desirability and so on.[13]

If we now return to the question of ethnic or racial identity, when an essentialist says that all persons of a particular "ethnicity" or "race" necessarily have the same essence – such as "*whiteness*" – s/he is at the same time saying that all the persons with that essence also have certain essential qualities which are necessarily present with that essence; these latter qualities function as the definition, in a loose sense, of that essence. On a Eurocentric world-view, for example, *whiteness* might be necessarily present with *superiority*.

It is quite easy to find instances of this kind of ethnocentric essentialism, but what is even more common is to *deny* that certain essential qualities are present with some essence. For a long period during the Euroamerican slave trade, for example, it was commonly claimed that Africans were not fully human. Interestingly, a similar claim was made in the Eighteenth century by some English with regard to the Irish, who were considered to be little better than beasts.[14] The point behind these examples is that, by essentializing the identity of Africans or Irishmen, one can assume that they all have the same traits, and that these traits necessarily exclude the trait of being truly human.

The Buddhist response I offer here is simply that, as has been shown above, essences are unreal; they cannot possibly exist. And ontologically, this necessarily means that there is nothing whatsoever that is actually the same about any two Africans or any two Irishmen. Of course, reflectively, many of us know this to be true: even our popular notions about biology – such as the notion that no two persons have exactly the same gene sequence – tell us that no two persons can be physically identical. Likewise, one cannot even identify any particular physical structure or pattern that every single member of a particular ethnic group has. If we branch away from mere physicalism, it becomes even more obvious that, on the mental level, persons must be unique due to the uniqueness of their sensory experiences. Yet even though, at this level of particularity, the differences among individuals are undeniable, the essentialists attempt to obscure the trees with the forest – to claim that there is some macro level at which sameness persists. Again, the Buddhist response is simply: there is no macro level, except in one's imagination.

Clearly, then, a critique of essences can be employed as a tool to counter racism and ethnocentrism (in which I include, for example, Orientalism). For to be racist or ethnocentrist is certainly to be essentialist: it is the presumption that the essence that is allegedly instantiated in each individual of the ethnic group in question is necessarily co-instantiated with (*sāmānyādhikāraṇya*) other essential qualities such as "intellectual inferiority," "dishonesty," "lack of cleanliness" and so on. If one critiques the essentialist world-view and points out that any such sameness is fabricated, one has at least removed the rationale for racism and ethnocentrism.

This application of a critique of essentialism, however, is not as straightforward as it appears. For in an ironic twist, these anti-essentialist arguments could be easily used to hinder attempts at social justice. Here, I am thinking particularly of the repeal of affirmative action policies in California and the conservative politics with which it has been associated. Many of the voices against affirmative action claimed that affirmative action is a racist policy because it perpetuates divisions among ethnic groups. And although this largely conservative response was not extended to a full critique of essentialism, an official anti-essentialism might serve some oppressive purposes quite nicely. On the other side, we find that the California issue put those working for social justice in the odd position of defending the kind of essentialism that allows oppression in the first place.[15]

Indeed, essentialism on the part of communities seeking social justice is a persistent issue; in some ways, the perception of diversity as mere "political correctness" points to the essentialist manner in which those seeking social justice sometimes conceive their communal identities. Some persons from within these communities have pointed out the problematic nature of the essentialization of their identities (and I am not thinking here only of conservatives), and if we take the principles adduced earlier seriously, this essentialism must be uprooted, since it contains the seeds of oppression.[16] As Dharmakīrti might have put it, just as essentialism about one's self perpetuates suffering, essentialism about one's community perpetuates oppression.

Despite, however, the need to critique the essentialization of oppressed communities from within those communities themselves, it has thus far been difficult to conceive of a way to eliminate essentialism without also eliminating those communities themselves. How, in other words, does one eliminate communal essentialism without also robbing historically oppressed communities of their voices and their identity?

This is where the notion of *telos* becomes crucial, for on the analysis I presented above, even when one *purports* to just be pointing out essences, one is *in fact* constructing an essence on the basis of some *telos*, although one may not be aware of this fact. Hence, in the explicit essentialism of the *Hindutva* or "Hindu-ness" movement in India, one can argue that this alleged essence actually stands for a series of goals concerning social conservatism, Indian nationalism and (perhaps most of all) political power in India. Affirming the reality of the essence merely serves to obscure the sometimes unsavory goals hidden within an essentialist enterprise.

For the purposes of social justice, the key is to make these goals explicit. In terms of responding to oppression, one begins by pointing out that essences are unreal; one then demonstrates the implicit goals of the essentialism in question, and one shows that other goals are more desirable. In terms of one's communal identity, one takes control of the construction of its essence by explicitly formulating its goals – the most obvious and straightforward such goal being the elimination of oppression itself. The point, in any case, is to stop playing the *essence*-game, for one will inevitably lose.

Obviously, there are many more issues that need to be considered here, not the least of which being the way in which one can (in practical terms) formulate goals in a consensual manner. So too, questions of resource distribution are crucial, in as much as scarcity, inequity and notions about proportional need are certainly products not just of essentialism, but of the goals which are currently in place. Despite the difficulties of such issues, I would maintain that one cannot think clearly about them without first critiquing essentialism, and if there is any hope for solutions, it can only come through the consensual construction of goals – the vision of a common *telos*.

NOTES

1 See Vasubandhu's presentation refutation and refutation of the Vātsīputrīya position (1189ff).

2 lCang kya (58) follows the opinion of mKhas grub dge legs dpal bzang, an earlier philosopher in his tradition, in identifying a Buddhist view by appealing to these four points. For a specific enumeration of these points, known as "the four seals that authenticate a philosophical view (*lta ba bkar btags kyi phyag rgya bzhi)*," see the work of lCang kya's student, dKon mchog 'jigs med dbang po (76).

3 As with most Buddhist philosophers, lCang kya is not explicit in his views on the excluded middle or the law of contradiction. Nevertheless, throughout his work he clearly follows what the Euroamerican tradition would consider a nondeviant approach to these issues. In the section of his work under consideration here, see, for example, his treatment of the relationship between person (*gang zag*) and aggregates (*phung po*) (55–56).

4 It is worth noting here that a naive view concerning the recoverability of some unitary and unique authorial intent can itself be considered a form of essentialism.

5 For more on the notion of different "modes of rationality," see the collection of essays entitled *Rationality and Relativism*, edited by Hollis and Lukes.

6 I use the term belief in its philosophical sense, where it means to entertain some proposition to be true.

7 An important point to note here is that, when this kind of intuition about language is played out, we find that not only must be the same essence be instantiated in all the objects of an expression, but that essence must *always* remain the same. It must be immutable, for if the essence *person*hood, say, were to change when I snapped my fingers, what were persons before I snapped my fingers would now be something other than persons afterward. That is, if the expression *person* still applies to all of us, yet *person*hood has changed, then either we were not persons a few moments ago, or we are not persons now. Either before or after, we would be non-persons, like chairs. For a related passage in Dharmakīrti's works, see, for example, *Pramāṇavārttikasvavṛtti* on *Pramāṇavārttika* 1: 144a. On all Dharmakīrti references, see both Dharmakīrti 1960 and Dharmakīrti 1989.

8 This is the basic point of *Pramāṇavārttikasvavṛtti* on *Pramāṇavārttika* 1: 221-223. On my interpretation of Dharmakīrti, what I have called "essentialism" lies at the core of *satkāyadṛṣṭi*, inasmuch as it is a form of ignorance (*avidyā*), which Dharmakīrti explicitly identifies with conceptuality and language (*Pramāṇavārttikasvavṛtti* on *Pramāṇavārttika* 1: 98-99ab).

9 Dharmakīrti discusses this important notion throughout his

Pramāṇavārttikasvavṛtti; perhaps the most concise statement occurs at *Pramāṇavārttikasvavṛtti* on *Pramāṇavārttika* 1: 68-69.

10 For simplicity's sake, I have only discussed the model according to which essences, if real, would be directly intuited through the senses. For Dharmakīrti's discussion of more nuanced positions, as when the universal is somehow "manifested" (*vyakta*) by its instances, see *Pramāṇavārttikasvavṛtti* on *Pramāṇavārttika* 1: 146-156.

11 See especially *Pramāṇavārttikasvavṛtti* on *Pramāṇavārttika* 1: 92-95ab.

12 The most often cited source for these views is *Pramāṇavārttikasvavṛtti* on *Pramāṇavārttika* 1: 40-42. One might argue that this necessary association of "essential properties" amounts to a "complex" notion of essence, where an essence is a set of properties, rather than a single property. For our purposes, however, it is far more useful to see how a single property – an "atomic" essence – becomes associated with other essential properties. As for Dharmakīrti himself, his discussion of "essential properties" (*svabhāva*) remains at the level where these properties are understood to be mere constructions; he thus avoids falling into the essentialism that he criticizes.

13 See, for example, Dharmakīrti's definition of "desire" in *Pramāṇavārttikasvavṛtti* on *Pramāṇavārttika* 1: 12.

14 As Poliakov points out, perhaps the most influential figure to have seen Africans as non-human animals was Voltaire (55–56, also cited by Smedley: 169). Smedley, in her brilliant study, discusses several other such instances (see especially 181–185) with regard to Africans. As for the Irish, Smedley (52–70) is one of many scholars who see the roots of contemporary Euroamerican racism in early English attitudes toward the Irish.

15 Not long after the events in question, the journal *Social Justice* (22: 3, 1995) devoted an entire issue to the attack on affirmative action in California. The issue is well worth reading, for it contains the full gamut of approaches – both essentialist and non-essentialist – to communal identity as expressed by persons who identify with minority communities.

16 Among the more influential voices against essentialism is that of Cornel West. On my reading, West's "The Pitfalls of Racial Reasoning" in his *Race Matters* is an eloquent critique of the essentialization of the African-American identity. He seeks to replace essentialism with a "prophetic framework," which, with its emphasis on "vision," is teleological in tenor. Another outstanding example of a critique of essentialism in this context is Elizabeth Spelman's *Inessential Woman.*

REFERENCES

Dharmakīrti (1960). *Pramāṇavārttikam: The First Chapter with the Autocommentary*. Ed. Raniero Gnoli. Serie Orientale Roma, 23. Rome: Istituto Italiano per il Medio ed Estremo Oriente.

Dharmakīrti (1989). *The Pramāṇavārttikam of Ācārya Dharmakīrti: with the Commentaries "Svopajñavṛtti" of the Author and "Pramāṇavārttikavṛtti" of Manorathanandin*. Ed. Ram Chandra Pandeya. Delhi: Motilal Banarsidass

dKon mchog 'jigs med dbang po (1977). *Le Grub mtha' rnam bzhag rin chen phreng ba de dKon mchog 'jigs med dbang po*. Ed. Katsumi Mimaki. *Zinbun: Memoirs of the Research Institute for Humanistic Studies, Kyoto University* (14) 55–111.

Hollis, Martin and Steven Lukes, eds. (1989). *Rationality and Relativism*. Cambridge, MA: MIT Press.

lCang skya rol pa'i rdo rje (1989). *Grub mtha' thub bstan lhun po'i mdzes rgyan*. Lhasa, Tibet: Krung go'i bod kyi shes rig dpe skrun khang.

Poliakov, Leon (1982). "Racism from the Enlightenment to the Age of Imperialism." In R. Ross, ed., *Racism and Colonialism*. The Hague: Martinus Nijhoff.

Smedley, Audrey (1993). *Race in North America: Origin and Evolution of a Worldview*. Boulder, Colorado: Westview Press.

Spelman, Elizabeth V. (1988). *Inessential Woman: Problems of Exclusion in Feminist Thought*. Boston: Beacon Press.

Vasubandhu (1970). *Abhidharmakośa and Bhāṣya of Ācārya Vasubandhu with Sphuṭārthā Commentary of Ācārya Yaśomitra*. Bauddhabhāratī Series, 5–9. Vārāṇasī: Bauddhabhāratī.

West, Cornel (1994). *Race Matters*. New York: Vintage Books.

Fifteen

Human Rights in Contemporary Engaged Buddhism

Sallie B. King

(I)

Scholars have often assumed that there could be no place for human rights in Buddhism; the very concept of "rights" seems to presuppose individualism and self-assertion, values incompatible with Buddhism. Nevertheless, contemporary Engaged Buddhists readily use "human rights" language. The conceptual world which Buddhist "human rights" language inhabits, however, differs from dominant Western concepts in important ways.

(1) In practice, Buddhist human rights are usually evoked on behalf of whole communities and less often (though sometimes) on behalf of individuals; (2) Buddhist human rights language avoids a rhetoric of self-assertion and speaks instead of the protection of the weak and the compassionate care of others; (3) Buddhist ethics are fundamentally non-adversarial and do not permit the trade-off of one person's "good" with harm to another; (4) while in Buddhism a person is not an "individual" in the Western sense, s/he nonetheless possesses great value as one who may attain Buddhahood; (5) Buddhist understanding of interconnectedness in the modern world yields an understanding of the importance of many social and political factors that support the possibility of spiritual liberation; (6) human "good" cannot justify harm to non-human beings or the matrix of life. Let us examine these points more carefully.[1]

(II)

I will draw broadly on Buddhist sources as might a Vietnamese Buddhist. Vietnam is the only traditional Buddhist country in which both Theravāda and Mahāyāna forms of Buddhism flourished (of course, this condition is characteristic of contemporary Western Buddhism, as well). Consequently, a Vietnamese Buddhist, such as Thich Nhat Hanh, who has greatly influenced my thinking on the present subject, can and does draw broadly on both Theravāda and Mahāyāna sources and concepts, especially such central, key teachings as the Four Noble Truths and *pratītya-samutpāda* taught by Śākyamuni Buddha and the buddha-nature concept embraced by Mahāyāna Buddhism. In the end, of course, this is simply a Mahāyāna perspective, since Mahāyāna incorporates the early Buddhist material. I will also give myself license to perhaps say something slightly new but which I believe to be continuous with these venerable and well-established teachings.

(III)

It is well known that the notion of human rights originated in the West. Indeed, in the arena of international political relations, Western insistence upon the importance of human rights is sometimes rejected by non-Western countries as an unwelcome imposition of Western values upon cultures or nations which embrace other, and contradictory, values. Moreover, the development of the notion of human rights in the West can clearly be traced through Western liberal political thought, through Protestantism and the Renaissance, and ultimately back to the Biblical concept of human being. Thus, the notion of human rights is closely linked to Judeo-Christian thought and values. There is no reason necessarily to expect that these values will be duplicated in, or compatible with, the values of other religions and cultures. Given the great difference between Buddhist and Judeo-Christian conceptions of human being, it might in particular be reasonable to expect Buddhist rejection of the notion of human rights.

Such an expectation is well founded. As is well known, a number of Buddhists and Buddhist scholars have commented negatively about the very idea of rights from the point of view of Buddhist concepts and values. (See Unno; Santikaro). I sympathize very much with their concerns, though I think they can be satisfactorily addressed. What are those concerns? I think their object is well expressed in the following quotation. In 1956 William Ernest Hocking wrote, "free individuals, standing for their rights, are 'the best fruit of modernity'" (cited by Rouner: 1). Herein are two problems for a Buddhist.

(1) The notion of the autonomous individual, conceived as an isolated and free-standing island, does not fit anywhere within the Buddhist world-view. To a Buddhist, Western emphasis upon the individual is (a) a focus upon something that does not and cannot ever exist; and (b) an active aggravation of the core problem with human beings, namely our self-centeredness and tendency toward ego-mania. As Buddhadasa puts it,

> Liberal democracy is totally free and doesn't define clearly what freedom it means. This allows the defilements in people to take advantage of the situation to be free according to the power of defilement (quoted by Santikaro: 176).

(2) The notion of rights carries a larger contextual connotation of an adversarial stance: me vs. you, me vs. them, me vs. the state, me vs. the world! This is how the Western hero is imagined. Obviously, the first problem – excessive emphasis upon the self – is replicated here, but beyond that, the adversarial stance itself is problematic. Given that for Buddhists the basic reality of life is our mutual interdependence, our pervasive interconnectedness, it is unnatural and unproductive in the extreme to draw lines between individuals and groups, pit one against another, and expect anything good, anything workable in the long run, to emerge.

Now, how can we respond to these concerns?

Let us consider four relatively straightforward points before getting into the deeper philosophical issues involved here. (1) Most Buddhist thought, of course, was composed in the ancient and medieval worlds. Most Buddhist countries are still, for better or worse, in the process of modernization. As Buddhist thought modernizes, the core concept of interconnectedness takes on added dimensions. In the thought of many contemporary Buddhist leaders, interconnectedness refers not only to the classical connections between, for example, the twelve links on the chain of conditioned genesis driving us from birth to death and on to countless future lives. Modern understandings of inter-connectedness indicate a clear understanding that while, for most Buddhist teachers, the spiritual life with the goal of enlightenment remains the most important aspect of human life, this spiritual aspect of life cannot be separated from all the other aspects of life: economic, social, political, psychological, cultural, etc. Thus, Buddhists whose main concern remains the traditional goal of enlightenment are newly motivated to take with the utmost scriousness other aspects of human life that may directly impinge upon the fortunes of an individual's spiritual aspirations and efforts.

Thus, many contemporary Buddhist social activists (of whom I will say more later) recognize an implicit hierarchy of needs. Taking as their model the Buddha, who refused to lecture until a hungry man was fed, Buddhist social activists recognize in their actions a hierarchy of needs in which: (a) the protection and maintenance of life is most basic; (b) second come human physical necessities such as peace and reasonable security, an adequate material base to life, including food, shelter, etc.; (c) third come human psychological and social necessities such as education, the maintenance of dignity, a place in the community, etc.; and (d) finally is spiritual liberation. Spiritual liberation is most difficult to attain, and rests upon an essential base of social, economic, psychological and political requisites. No one attains enlightenment while war is raging all around. The Buddha himself gave up fasting, saying it was a hindrance in his effort to attain enlightenment. Thus Buddhists have a new-found investment in seeking particular human social, economic, and political goods which overlap considerably with the agenda pursued by human rights activists.

(2) It is simply a fact that those Buddhist leaders who have dealt most extensively with the international community (I am thinking in particular of the Dalai Lama, Thich Nhat Hanh and Sulak Sivaraksa) show no hesitation whatsoever in speaking of human rights; their speeches and writings frequently draw on this language. These men are spiritual leaders first, social-political leaders second. They clearly do not find "rights" language unusable. They have voted with their tongues and pens: Buddhists can find a way to work with the notion of human rights.

(3) Regarding the concern with the adversarial stance: it is true that the human rights agenda is, ineluctably, party to an adversarial stance; it is a matter of one group or individual against another group or individual. But let us look more closely. The human rights agenda is all about the protection of groups and individuals from more powerful groups and individuals. With its emphasis on compassion, from its beginnings to today, Buddhism does believe in its very foundation in active compassionate action to protect and help the poor and the weak. The *Metta Sutta* states, "Just as a mother would protect her only child even at the risk of her own life, even so let one cultivate a boundless heart towards all beings" (Rahula: 97). If human rights is about protecting and aiding those in need, Buddhism can have no objection to this intention.

(4) Human rights, as we discuss them today in the global arena, do not focus exclusively upon the individual. The human rights agenda is as concerned with whole societies and with component groups within society as it is with individuals. Thus an excessive focus upon the human individual should not be attributed to this discourse, even outside the Buddhist context.

(IV)

More deeply now, in order to resolve the issues regarding individualism and the adversarial posture that are implicit in this discussion, it is necessary to address some fundamental questions about Buddhist social ethics.

First let us consider the status of the individual in Buddhism. We may investigate this for our purposes by considering the relationship between the individual and society. The question here is: what relative weight does Buddhism give to the importance of the individual and to society as a whole? Is one regarded as of greater value than the other? Is one regarded as subordinate to the other?

For Buddhism, as for every system of philosophy, the answer to the social ethical question regarding the relative importance of individual and society will follow from its conceptual understanding of human being. For Buddhism, the most important concept for understanding human being is *anātman*, no-self. I hasten to state that the fact that Buddhism denies the existence of an individual, autonomous self does not mean, as some Western interpreters have surmised, that the human person is unimportant in Buddhism and therefore society and its demands must be dominant. On the contrary, as Thich Nhat Hanh characteristically puts it, *anātman* means that the "self" is constructed of non-self parts. In other words, a given person in the present moment is constructed not only of memories and dispositions built up from her past, but also of many physical parts incorporated into her body from the environment, and many dispositions, attitudes, etc. incorporated from society. Buddhadasa draws the obvious implication for social ethics from the facts of *anātman* and interdependence:

> Everyone is indebted to society and is bound by the social contract from the moment one was born from one's mother's womb, or even from the time one was in the womb (quoted by Santikaro: 167).

In Mahāyāna thought it is clear that society also is empty of selfhood and is constructed of non-society parts, i.e., human persons. Thus society and person are interactive; they are mutually constructive. From a Buddhist perspective, since society and the human person are interactive, it is fundamentally wrong to conceive them as adversarial.[2] Things that are not separate cannot be opposed. Similarly, since society and the individual are deeply interactive, the value of one cannot be finally separated from the value of the other.

This being the case, it is quite futile to attempt to see either the human person or society as bearing relatively greater importance in Buddhism than the other. Thus, in the end, in Buddhism neither the human person nor society may rightfully dominate, or negate in its behavior, the other. Consequently, it is best to see final importance resting on the values that Buddhism embraces: an end to suffering and the nurturance of awakening in all. Both society and the individual are equally answerable to, should serve and contribute to, these values. This view will have important consequences for Buddhist social ethics, as we shall see.

Now let us look more carefully at the view that "human rights" discourse must imply adversarial postures and therefore Buddhism, which as a rule rejects adversarialism, must have no place for "human rights" discourse.

The foundation of Buddhist social ethics can be located most firmly in the five lay precepts. Therein we see that Buddhists have never traditionally spoken of rights, but have emphasized responsibilities, or obligations, in a sense. Simply put, these state: I undertake to observe the precept (1) to abstain from the taking of life; (2) not to take that which is not given; (3) to abstain from misconduct in sensual actions; (4) to abstain from false speech; (5) to abstain from liquor that causes intoxication and indolence (Saddhatissa: 73). These may be understood as restraints that one willingly takes upon oneself for the sake of others *and* oneself. In this respect, they are an interesting nexus of the constructive interaction of person and society discussed above.

Let us illustrate this. One makes a decision and determines to undertake, for example, the first precept.[3] By not taking life, one not only avoids harming others, one avoids harming oneself by exerting oneself to restrain whatever habitual tendencies one may have to harm others (a habitual tendency established by one's having harmed others in the past and/or by the conditioning power of the violence of one's upbringing or of society), thus deconditioning that habitual tendency, thereby lessening its power to construct one's future, keeping one trapped in *saṃsāra*. Thus the precepts, while recognizing the great power of conditioning (including the power of society to construct the human person), emphasize in this very context one's power to decondition oneself, through decision and unrelenting effort.

Note that the precepts cut directly through the line between individual and society. It is clearly good for society to be made up of individuals who will not harm others, steal, lie, etc., but in the Buddhist view it is equally and inseparably true that it is good for oneself as well. Thus not only is there no conflict between the individual good and the social good, these goods are one and the same.

Buddhadasa's comments on *śīla*, morality, bear this out. He identifies *śīla* with *pakati*, which is glossed by his translator as meaning, "normal and natural." Buddhadasa says, "*Śīla* means '*pakati*.'" And, "The word *pakati* means not to collide with anyone and not to collide with oneself, that is, not to cause distress for oneself or for others" (quoted in Santikaro: 171).

Now, classically in Western thought, the language of both "rights" and "responsibilities" is framed in terms of at least potential conflict between the individual and society: "rights" are what society, or others, owe me and "responsibilities" are what I owe to society, or others. A society which does not respect my "rights" is not Good, and I may be morally justified in taking steps to ensure that my "rights" will become respected. Likewise, society may be morally justified in restraining or coercing me if I do not fulfill some of my essential "responsibilities" – such as to share the cost of government or to refrain from harming others in my society.

The Buddhist precepts, however, are formulated in the language of responsibility: I undertake not to harm you. The precepts don't say anything about you not harming me![4] But let us examine this matter philosophically.

Philosophically, the precepts imply that that society will be Good in which its members do not harm each other, steal from each other, lie to each other, etc. This in turn implies that a member of a Good society should have a reasonable expectation not to be harmed, stolen from, etc. Now one may or may not want to call such a thing a "right," but it is certainly closing in on that ground in a practical sense, if not in the full conceptual sense. This is especially true since, as we have seen, from a Buddhist point of view, society *should* contribute to the ending of suffering and the nurturance of awakening in all. Since the Good society brings into being conditions conducive to these ends, the individual is fully justified in claiming a kind of right to live in such a society. However, since society and individual are deeply interactive and mutually constructive, the individual likewise has a responsibility to contribute to the construction of such a society.

In short, if we choose to use the five lay precepts as our guides towards a Buddhist social ethic, they seem to imply a definition of a Good society as one in which we simultaneously have rights and responsibilities both not to harm others and not to be harmed, not to steal and not to be stolen from, not to lie and not to be lied to, etc.[5] However, the kind of "rights" we are talking about here are fundamentally unlike "rights" as conceived in Western political theory insofar as they are fundamentally *non-adversarial*. That is, they are non-adversarial insofar as my responsibility not to harm you is in my own interest as a karma-produced and karma-producing being; both my interest and your interest are fulfilled by my not harming you. Similarly, my "right," if we want to call it that, not to be harmed by you constitutes an opportunity for you to promote your own interest by practicing self-restraint. Thus understood, rights and responsibilities are interdependent to the point almost of fusion. Buddhadasa notes,

> . . . Buddhists . . . respect and accept the social contract, that is, the fact that everyone in the world has rights, duties, and obligations inseparably and unconsciously linked (quoted in Santikaro: 168).

In this light, from a Buddhist conceptual point of view, it might be best to drop the separate terms "rights" and "responsibilities" and speak in a unified way of a community of "mutual obligation" in which our individual Goods and the social Good co-inhere such that my obligation to you is also my obligation to myself.[6] While this would be philosophically more accurate from a Buddhist perspective, the Buddhist community will probably want to continue to speak with the larger world using "rights" language, since this is the language to which we have become accustomed in international discourse.

We have seen, then, that, in the Buddhist view, an interactive, non-adversarial relationship exists between individual and individual as well as between individual and society. Within this context, we now need to ask, what is the moral value of a given human being? I will argue that while in Buddhism a person is not an "individual" in the Western sense, s/he nonetheless possesses great value as one who may attain Buddhahood. I will try to show that this traditional Buddhist idea may be used by Buddhists to justify concern with human rights.

Of course, Buddhism's theory of human being evolved over time. Nevertheless, there is a continuous thread which evolves, namely the notion that human beings are beings with the potential of enlightenment. This notion was relatively implicit in early Buddhism and became explicit later. Some of the early teachings indicative of this idea are the following. (1) The Buddha taught all who would listen, without imposing restrictions by social class, gender, education, or other differentiating characteristics (this was, of course, highly unusual in his place and time). (2) Persons of all backgrounds were, in fact, confirmed as having attained the fruits of liberation during the Buddha's lifetime. (3) Most significantly, the Buddha's teachings strongly emphasized the rarity and preciousness of a human birth, urging everyone to take advantage of their human birth, to practice Buddhism and attain release, since release could not be had from any of the other five destinies.[7]

These early suggestions regarding the potential of humankind, of course, became fuel for later debates which directly raised the question whether all of humankind, without exception, was capable of ultimately achieving enlightenment, or not. Suffice it to say, that after considerable debate, the Mahāyāna wing of Buddhism explicitly affirmed the Buddha nature concept, according to which all members of humankind are capable of eventually attaining enlightenment and thus in the present should be regarded as embryonic buddhas, beings who carry the seed or germ of buddhahood within.[8] (There is considerably more to the buddha-nature concept than this, but as it is more controversial I propose that we limit our discussion to this part of the concept.)

This theory of human being, in its latent and its fully developed form, has important implications for ethics. I must note that these implications do not seem to have been noted in traditional forms of Asian Buddhism until relatively recently. It may be that it required the crises of modernity in order for these implications to come to the fore. Even now, they have scarcely been explicitly discussed, though they have been acted upon, as we shall see.

To see in what way Buddhism's theory of human being is important for its social ethic requires a brief excursus into the nature of the ethical theory that Buddhism sets forth.

As is often noted, the Four Noble Truths of Buddhism seem to express a teleological perspective. The First Noble Truth, *duḥkha*, or "suffering," names the inherently unsatisfactory nature of human existence as the problem. The Second Noble Truth analyzes the cause of the problem. The Third Noble Truth, the cessation of *duḥkha*, offers the hope that that problem can be resolved, and the Fourth Noble Truth maps out the way in which the cure of the problem may be realized. In short, suffering and unhappiness are the problem for which Buddhism is the cure. In other words, suffering and unhappiness are bad, while the elimination of suffering is good. Thus it would seem that any action which eliminated suffering would be good, while any action which produced suffering would be bad. Such a view would fit comfortably within the teleological family of ethical theory.

Note that both ethical egoism and utilitarianism seem to fit within Buddhist parameters. As we have seen, the five precepts are to be followed both for one's own sake and for the sake of others: self and other are both benefited when a person adheres to the precepts. (Of course, insofar as the aim of the Buddhist path is to eliminate ego, "egoism" would not do as a name for a Buddhist ethical theory! However, enlightened self-interest is widely recognized as a workable starting point for Buddhist practice, though in both Theravāda and Mahāyāna it is expected that the focus on oneself will be transformed as one progresses in the practice.) While enlightened self-interest has a place in Buddhism, concern for others has a far greater place insofar as Buddhist practice is designed to eliminate ego and the resulting selflessness is expected at all times to be demonstrated in behavior expressive of concern for the well-being of others.

But Buddhism fundamentally has two conceptions of the Good. The first, as we have seen, is the elimination of *duḥkha*. The second, which we will now consider, is the realization of *nirvāṇa*, or buddhahood. The elimination of *duḥkha* and the realization of *nirvāṇa* might appear upon first consideration to be two names for the same thing, and certainly in some respects they are. (Buddhahood *is* freedom from the production, and the suffering, of *duḥkha*.) However, in another respect they differ in a significant way. While the elimination of *duḥkha* is a Good that falls into the teleological camp of ethical theory, the realization of *nirvāṇa* is an absolute, or deontological, Good. To see why it is deontological, we need to return to Buddhism's theory of human being.

Whether one assumes with both Theravāda and Mahāyāna that a human birth is a rare and precious birth inasmuch as it provides an opportunity for realization, or one assumes with Mahāyāna that all human beings are embryonic buddhas carrying the nature of buddhahood within, either way we have the basis for a deontological form of ethics.[9] Buddhahood and/or the realization of buddhahood is an absolute Good in Buddhism.[10] Two ethical propositions follow from this affirmation. (1) Any action conducive to the enlightenment of any human being is a Good action, and any action inimical to the enlightenment of any human being is bad. (This is still teleological.) (2) Any action which partakes of the nature of buddhahood (wisdom and compassion) is a Good action; any action contrary to the nature of buddhahood is bad. This is deontological since it refers not to the consequences of an action but to the intrinsic nature of the action itself as measured against an absolute value in determining the moral value of that action.[11]

Let us return to the five lay precepts. It can now be seen that to violate the first precept, to harm life, is morally wrong not only because its consequences include the production of suffering for oneself and another, but also because the very nature of the action itself, harming life, is intrinsically incompatible with the nature of buddhahood. The same is true of the other lay precepts: to steal, to engage in sexual misconduct, to lie, or to intoxicate oneself all both produce suffering for oneself and another and violate the nature of buddhahood.

Our consideration of the Buddhist concept of human being and the deontological strain in Buddhist ethics also helps us to see how Buddhist ethics differs in important ways from Mill's utilitarianism. Mill defines a good act as one productive of greater happiness than unhappiness for all persons concerned. Thus an arithmetic calculation must be made in which one considers all the happiness produced for some against all the unhappiness produced for others, determine which is greater and consider ethically good that action which produces "the greatest good for the greatest number." There are two aspects of this approach with which Buddhism is incompatible.

First, there is an adversarial element involved in Mill's calculus; one person's happiness is in a competitive posture with another person's unhappiness. But Buddhist ethics are fundamentally non-adversarial. We have seen in our analysis of the five lay precepts that my good is conceived as your good and vice versa. Thus "the greatest good for the greatest number" is not the goal in Buddhism; the good of all is the goal.

Furthermore, suffering is simply an absolute bad in Buddhism. Nothing that produces unhappiness for any sentient being could be considered good. Thus nonviolence in Buddhism is an absolute, not a relative or situationally dependent value. To demonstrate the significance of this point, consider the theory of the "just war." Western just war theory presupposes an adversarial situation in which a greater good (say, freedom from tyranny) is presumed to arise out of the lesser evil of the morally justified war. But in Buddhism there are no just wars, whatever secular practice may have been in Buddhist countries. No matter how great the evil with which a society is confronted, Buddhism does not condone the use of violence – harm perhaps to a few in order to free many from severe suffering – to rectify that evil. Whereas Mill's moral theory would accept violence in such a case, Buddhism does not. This is not to say that as a matter of historical fact no Buddhists have ever violated this principle; I am simply trying to clarify the normative ethical principle itself.[12] Indeed, when a rare act of violence does appear in Engaged Buddhism, its immorality in Buddhist terms is recognized and implicitly acknowledged. Thus, for example, those who immolated themselves "for peace" during the Buddhist struggle to end the war in Vietnam, declared their willingness to accept the bad karma that would accrue to them as a result of their violent act.

Second, the deontological strain in Buddhist ethics allows it to resolve certain issues which Mill's ethics is incapable of resolving. The classic example here is slavery. On the basis of Mill's theory, it may be difficult to show why slavery is wrong if, for example, it is a minority which is enslaved and their suffering is not too intense, while the majority whom they serve are made very much happier by their service. It is necessary to have a deontological criterion in order to show why such a situation is morally wrong.

From a Buddhist perspective, slavery is wrong for two reasons. (1) Presumably the conditions under which the slaves live reduce their opportunity to learn and practice Buddhism and hence reduce the likelihood that they will be able to realize its fruits. (2) More importantly, to enslave another is an action inherently incompatible with the gentleness, the active compassion to relieve the suffering of others and the propensity to share sympathetic joy with the happiness of others characteristic of Buddhahood, as well as an active negation of the potential or embryonic Buddhahood of the slave, thus inherently the negation of absolute Good as recognized in Buddhism; while to be enslaved is to live in a condition expressive of the negation of one's potential or embryonic Buddhahood and thus again inherently the negation of Good.

(V)

Now let us shift our focus and reflect upon the actions of Buddhists in the modern world. It is simply a fact – a fact which we must recognize in our scholarly work – that Buddhist social activists in the modern world are already working for human rights by the millions. In this final component of the paper, I wish to briefly examine some contemporary forms of socially and politically Engaged Buddhism. My objective here is to consider whether, and in what ways, these movements live out in practice the ethical orientation I have sketched above.

Two essential, but unstated, premises of contemporary Buddhist social activism are: (1) every human being has the potential of Buddhahood and thus every human being is of great, perhaps absolute, value and should be so treated; and (2) it is good for human beings to express and nurture their emerging Buddhahood.

The first premise, that every human being is of great or absolute value and should be so treated, is rooted in the notion that a human birth is a rare and precious birth, the direct implication of which is that a human life is a rare and precious thing, a thing of great value. It is only common sense to protect, cherish and attend to the well-being of something that is rare and precious. This is the foundation of a good deal of Buddhist activist work for freedom from tyranny, for a politically open and democratic society, for freedom of religion, for economic justice, for social justice, and the like. This is the Buddhist foundation of much of what from a Western perspective is called "human rights work" pursued by Asian Buddhists, often at the risk of their life, liberty, or well-being. Let us consider some examples.

The most dramatic cases are in Vietnam, in Burma and in Tibet, where, even at the present moment – none of these struggles is over – Buddhists in vast numbers have risked everything to protect, cherish and attend to the well-being of precious human life. In each case, Buddhists have risked their lives in the attempt to repel or bring down brutal political regimes threatening and destroying human life and well-being. In all three cases a politically open society has been seen as essential to human well-being. In Burma, in 1988, Buddhist monks and students filled the streets calling for democracy and an end to the repressive rule of the military. Their leader, Aung San Suu Kyi, spent years in house arrest rather than abandon the cause. She and her followers continue, at this writing, daily risk of imprisonment or worse for their courageous challenge to the ruling regime. In the Tibetan case, of course, the Dalai Lama heads the Tibetan liberation movement with a tireless effort to gain the freedom of the Tibetan people in a nonviolent manner against seemingly hopeless odds. In Vietnam, during the war, Buddhist monks, nuns and lay people filled the streets to gain the freedom to practice their Buddhist religion, ultimately bringing down the Diem regime. In subsequent years, as the war ground on, they undertook every nonviolent act conceivable to bring the war to an end and protect the Vietnamese people. In Vietnam and in Tibet, the political struggles were and are inseparable from a struggle to preserve the opportunity to freely study and practice Buddhism. The fact that in all three cases Buddhists have risked and, especially in Vietnam and Tibet, often lost their lives in this struggle powerfully demonstrates just how deeply these values are held, how essential they are felt to be.

The ex-untouchable Ambedkarite Buddhists of India converted from Hinduism to Buddhism for expressly social reasons: in order to repudiate the Hindu caste system with its notions of more and less spiritually and socially acceptable people, and its labels of untouchability and outcaste. These Buddhists did not need the fully developed Buddha nature concept to tell them that Buddhism values every single human life as a rare and precious thing – to them the Buddha's repudiation of the caste system with its implicit embrace of human egalitarianism was sufficient to accomplish that. For them, Buddhism is the most important vehicle they know for egalitarianism, for social change based upon egalitarian values, for the enhancement of their own well-being, and for the nurturing of their own potential. The Buddhism they are constructing is, for the most part, a social way of life and a political challenge first, and a spirituality second.

Somewhat similar is Sarvodaya Sramadana of Sri Lanka, a vast Buddhist organization which works to "develop" the declining villages of Sri Lanka on the basis of Buddhist, rather than capitalist or Marxist, values. Its leader, Dr. A. T. Ariyaratne, recognizes spiritual liberation as the ultimate good, but believes that its attainment is facilitated among a population freed from grinding poverty with its associated social and psychological ills and is indeed enhanced by the nurturance of the individual's well-being in all its dimensions (within limits set by Buddhist middle path moderation, wisdom and compassion). Dr. Ariyaratne thus speaks of a right to food, to a clean and healthy environment, to full "engagement" (as opposed to full "employment"), etc.

In Thailand, Sulak Sivaraksa has initiated the development of numerous non-government activist organizations and publications on behalf of the poor, the oppressed and those whose human rights have been violated (as he himself puts it). A fearless critic of militarism, oppression and autocratic rule, Sulak has more than once stood trial for treason because of his speeches critical of the government.

Finally, in this highly selective list, I must mention the Buddhist nuns and quasi-nuns of East and West who have organized themselves to overcome millennia of institutional oppression from Buddhism itself – for the sake of the supreme Buddhist value, spiritual liberation – and are actively supported in this by the more progressive wing of Buddhism scattered throughout the world.

The actions of all these people fall within the purview of the human rights agenda, as justified by the first premise (every human being has the potential of Buddhahood and thus is of great, perhaps absolute, value and should be so treated). They are working for freedom of religion, a politically open society, minimum economic justice, human dignity, human equality, and the like. Millions upon millions of Buddhists have devoted themselves to these efforts, sometimes at the risk of their lives. Buddhism in the modern world is a force with the proven ability to inspire millions to risk everything in nonviolent efforts to gain human rights.

The second premise underlying contemporary Buddhist social activism is the belief that it is good for human beings to express and nurture their emerging Buddhahood. This premise is explicitly stated by some Japanese Buddhists (specifically Rissho Kosei-kai and Sōka Gakkai) and by Thich Nhat Hanh, but is often an unstated premise of Buddhist activism more broadly. It should be noted that this premise is a corollary of the deontological thesis in Buddhist ethics, namely the thesis that "any action which partakes of the nature of buddhahood (wisdom and compassion) is a Good action." Here the notion frequently found in Buddhist tradition that one first needs to free oneself of one's own delusion before one is in any condition to work for the welfare of others is either expressly repudiated or ignored and replaced with the notion that Buddhahood is not something one finds later, at the end of a long path, but instead is something one expresses now, in the present moment, to the best of one's ability, and in so doing one makes real the Buddha whom one is striving to be (in other words, means and end are collapsed).

Every conceivable kind of spiritual social activism, as long as it is an attempted expression of wisdom and compassion, becomes possible on the basis of this second premise. Indeed, the variety of actions found among Buddhist activists is virtually limitless and includes all the human rights work discussed above, plus: work to protect animals, work to protect our planet, anti-war and anti-nuclear work, work to develop respect and understanding between traditional foes, work with the dying, work with the homeless, work with AIDS patients, and much more. These kinds of activities, of course, are also an expression of such traditional Buddhist ethical values as compassion and *ahiṃsā*. Thus work to protect the planet is motivated by urgent concern to protect the matrix of all life, and work for gender equality and the protection of women is motivated by compassion for the oppression of women and the desire to open Buddhist practice more effectively to women. From a modern Buddhist perspective, such compassion and concern for the sake of others, if expressed and pursued calmly, mindfully, selflessly, etc., may well be seen as signs of a person in the process of making real the Buddha whom s/he is striving to be.

The second premise underlying Buddhist social activism, the belief that it is good for human beings to express and nurture their emerging Buddhahood, also shows why Buddhist human rights work finally is inseparable from other forms of social action. All Buddhist social activism is an expression of the compassion for suffering beings that develops more and more as one engages in the process of making real one's embryonic Buddhahood. Suffering beings are suffering beings; Buddhism makes no distinction in that regard between human beings, animals and, for many modern Buddhists, the planet. Human rights work does carry extra distinction due to the importance of a human birth, but on these other grounds it can be seen as fundamentally not different in kind from other forms of social action.

Furthermore, concern for human rights can never be a justification for harm to non-humans both because of the compassion which is as available to non-humans as it is to humans without distinction and because of the non-adversarial nature of Buddhist ethics. Thus, as the example of Sarvodaya Sramadana in Sri Lanka shows, human economic needs cannot justify harm to the environment. In Sarvodaya, human economic well-being and the well-being of the eco-system are neither conceived as trade-offs nor allowed in practice to compete; they are simply two goods, both of which must be protected from harm and nurtured.

(VI)

In conclusion, we have seen that Buddhists today throughout Asia and the West do speak of and work for human rights. Reflection upon this movement yields two points of particular philosophical importance. (1) This contemporary activism can be fully understood and justified in explicitly Buddhist terms, as I have tried to show in this paper. (2) The kind of ethics that may be seen as underlying this Buddhist activism constitutes a provocative conceptual alternative to the better established Western theories of social ethics. I hope that the philosophers among us may continue to attempt to articulate this Buddhist social ethic, prodded by the Buddhist activists who continue to demonstrate in action what Buddhist ethics means

NOTES

1 The present paper was given at the American Academy of Religion meeting in New Orleans on November 24, 1996. I am grateful for the comments given on that occasion by Sumner B. Twiss and June O'Connor. Thanks also to my colleague, Richard Lippke, for his helpful comments upon reading a draft of the paper. This paper draws heavily upon two previous papers by the same author. The first is King 1994, published as King 1995a. The second is King 1995b.

2 There is, however, in early and Theravāda Buddhism an adversarial element in the relationship between society and the person to the extent that society is seen as part of *saṃsāra*, part of the fetters that keep a person enmired in *duḥkha*. This is expressed in the monk's or nun's needing to "leave home" and society in order to seriously pursue the Buddhist Path. Moreover, in early Buddhism and

Theravāda the solo human person is the nexus capable of achieving freedom from conditioning and suffering. Thus, if either the human person or society should be regarded as of greater value in early Buddhism, it is clearly the human person. The balance between the two becomes more equal in Mahāyāna Buddhism in which *nirvāṇa* and *saṃsāra* are equated and the goal becomes conceived as the enlightenment of all.

3 Of course, I break into an infinite chain of conditioning at an arbitrary point here; many personal and societal influences have conditioned this decision.

4 Traditionally, as David Kalupahana points out, a universal monarch (*cakravartin*), if there were one, might have taken this language of moral abstention and transformed it into language of prohibition: you shall not harm another. Dr. Kalupahana was kind enough to show me an electronic version of his manuscript, now published as *Ethics in Early Buddhism*, in time for me to benefit from it in writing this paper. The present point is made in ch. 15, "Law, Justice and Morals."

5 Damien Keown makes a similar point in Keown: 5. It appears that he and I composed and delivered our remarks on human rights in Buddhism at approximately the same time, though without any communication between us. I commend his article to the reader.

6 David Kalupahana speaks of human society as based upon "mutual self-interest." Since my interest is your interest, and vice versa, "mutual self-interest" could be synonymous with "mutual obligation." See ch. 5, "Individual and Society."

7 Damien Keown also points to the human potential for enlightenment as the most significant basis for a Buddhist human rights doctrine. He cites L. P. N. Perera as his source for this idea. See Keown: 9.

8 Of course, Mahāyāna affirms that "all sentient beings" possess the buddha-nature, a category considerably more inclusive than that of humankind. However, since we are discussing ethics in human society, I limit my references to humankind.

9 I believe that the deontological aspect of the ethics follows from both the early and the Mahāyāna understandings of human beings as beings capable of enlightenment, though it follows more clearly from the stronger, Mahāyāna version.

10 Compare the Zen scholar Masao Abe, who proposes the following as a value criterion for Mahāyāna Buddhism: ". . . Sunyata is boundlessly open. . . . This is the dynamism of Sunyata, and the focal point of this dynamism . . . is the 'vow' to save one's self and all others and 'act' to actually pursue the vow. . . . The vow and act realized through the self-emptying of Sunyata provide not only the center of boundlessly open Sunyata but also the ultimate criterion of value judgment. This judgment is to be made in terms of whether or not a thing or action in question does accord with the vow and act to make one's self and all others awakened. If the thing or action accords with the vow and act realized in the dynamism of Sunyata it is regarded as valuable. . . ."

(58).

11 The deontological criterion to which I have referred might find its closest Western counterpart in an ethics of virtue perspective. Buddhism conceived in terms of virtue ethics would characterize the morally good as the state of being of buddhahood, and the two fundamental virtues of buddhahood as wisdom (understood as actualized selflessness) and compassion (active care for the suffering of others). James Whitehill advocates conceiving Buddhist ethics in terms of virtue ethics in "Buddhist Ethics in Western Context" (see Whitehill).

12 I must say that there may be cases in which Mill's calculus may be more helpful than the Buddhist approach. Certainly many would consider the Buddhist perspective in which my good is your good to be simply naive. And it must be asked whether Buddhist ethics can help us to make some of the complex and difficult decisions we face in the modern world. Can Buddhist ethics help us decide the best way to allocate scarce resources, for instance who will receive an organ transplant when the need is greater than the availability of organs? Or can Buddhist ethics help us to choose between competing goods, for example whether to use a pool of tax money for education, hospices, or child care? I am not prepared to debate these issues here and indeed I am very aware that Buddhism has greater ethical resources for addressing such issues than those to which I have confined myself here. However, I am not sanguine that an ethical posture which fundamentally turns away from the acknowledgment of adversarial or competing goods and bads will be in the best position to address these kinds of issues.

REFERENCES

Abe, Masao (1990). "Kenotic God and Dynamic Sunyata." In John B. Cobb, Jr. and Christopher Ives, eds., *The Emptying God: A Buddhist-Jewish-Christian Conversation*, 3–65. Maryknoll, NY: Orbis Books.

Hocking, William Ernest (1956). *The Coming World Civilization* . New York: Harper.

Kalupahana, David (1995). *Ethics in Early Buddhism.* Honolulu: University of Hawaii Press.

Keown, Damien (1995). "Are There 'Human Rights' in Buddhism?" *Journal of Buddhist Ethics* (2) Http://jbe.la.psu.edu/2/keown2.html.

King, Sallie B. (1994). "A Buddhist Perspective on a Global Ethic and Human Rights." Paper presented at a conference on "The United Nations and the World's Religions: Prospects for a Global Ethic," October 7, 1994, at Columbia University.

King, Sallie B. (1995a). "A Buddhist Perspective on a Global Ethic and Human Rights." Edited version in Nancy Hodes and Michael Hays, eds., *The United Nations and the World's Religions: Prospects for a Global Ethic*, 75–82. Boston: Boston Research Center for the 21st Century. Expanded version in *Journal of Dharma* (22: 2 [April-June]) 122–136.

King, Sallie B. (1995b). "Towards a Buddhist Theory of Social Ethics." Paper presented at the Seventh International Seminar on Buddhism and Leadership for Peace, June 3-8, 1995, at the University of Hawaii.

Perera, L. P. N. (1991) *Buddhism and Human Rights: A Buddhist Commentary on the Universal Declaration of Human Rights*. Colombo: Karunaratne and Sons.

Rahula, Walpola (1974). *What the Buddha Taught*. Revised and expanded edition. New York: Grove Press.

Rouner, Leroy S. (1988). "Introduction." In *Human Rights and the World's Religions*, 1–14. Boston University Studies in Philosophy and Religion, vol. 9. Notre Dame: University of Notre Dame Press.

Saddhatissa, Hammalawa (1987). *Buddhist Ethics*. Reprint, London: Wisdom Publications.

Santikaro Bhikkhu (1996). "Buddhadasa Bhikkhu: Life and Society Through the Natural Eyes of Voidness." In Christopher S. Queen and Sallie B. King, eds., *Engaged Buddhism: Buddhist Liberation Movements in Asia*, 147–193. Albany: State University of New York Press.

Unno, Taitetsu (1988). "Personal Rights and Contemporary Buddhism." In Leroy S. Rouner, ed., *Human Rights and the World's Religions*, 129–147. Boston University Studies in Philosophy and Religion, vol. 9. Notre Dame: University of Notre Dame Press.

Whitehill, James (1994). "Buddhist Ethics in Western Context." *Journal of Buddhist Ethics* (1) Http://jbe.la.psu.edu//1/whitehill.html.

Sixteen

Pluralism And Dialogue: A Contemplation on the Dialogue Relationship

Judith Simmer-Brown

In recent years I have read, somewhat dutifully, essays and books on pluralism with an attitude much like that of a spectator, appreciating that Christian theologians are finally getting to the root of their dialogue dilemma, the assumptions of superiority which prevail in Christian theology. It was only when I read Diana Eck's book, *Encountering God* (1993), that I began to see directly the relevance of this discussion for the non-Christian, and her chapter entitled "Is Our God Listening?" struck me like a freight train. Pluralism was a phenomena in modern life with effect on all people, whether religious or not, whether in dialogue or not. It was then that I began to deeply reflect on the implications of pluralism for contemporary Buddhism.

EXCLUSIVISM, INCLUSIVISM, AND PLURALISM IN BUDDHIST TRADITIONS

The foundations of an understanding of pluralism come from an understanding of the differences between exclusivism, inclusivism, and pluralism. These stances have been pointed out effectively in Christian theology by Paul Knitter and others,[1] but obviously, these positions can be found as well among Buddhist approaches. Exclusivism, or the conviction that my sect or practice has the exclusive understanding of truth or access to enlightenment could be found in some Nichiren traditions in Japan: until recently, the Soka Gakkai has been a prime example, but its recent divisions and developments have yielded an American movement very interested in commonalities with other traditions. It can also be found in a ritually-expressed context in Vajrayāna Buddhism when liturgical celebrations or tantric teachings and gatherings are open only to the initiated. Of course, institutionally, sectarianism of this sort is not uncommon, with rival monasteries and communities in neighboring valleys in Thailand, Tibet and China, but it rarely expressed itself as theologically-expressed exclusivism.

Inclusivism is much more common in Buddhism, an approach which suggests that all forms of Buddhism have partial truth, but the most complete truth is contained in one's own scriptures, practices, and lineages of teachers. The *Lotus Sūtra* presents the parable of the burning house, and three types of enticements the father uses to distract his children away from their games into safety.[2] The last of these, called the *ekayāna*, is the supreme message of the *Lotus Sūtra*, the teaching concerning skillful means and compassion, and this teaching was deemed superior to all others, the only complete path to awakening.

From this example in the *Lotus Sūtra* and elsewhere came the prevailing paradigm of the "three turnings of the wheel," or three phases in the Buddha's teachings. This paradigm described graded levels of evolving teachings, each surpassing the one before, which characterized and classified various schools of Buddhism. These views became popular in Tibet, China, and Japan to explain various contradictions and divergences in the Buddhist teachings. However, various schools gave different interpretations as to which teaching or which *sūtra* was considered the ultimate teaching. The Lotus schools of Japan, associated for example with Nichiren, considered the *Lotus* to be the most complete teaching. In Tibet, generally speaking,[3] the dGe lugs pa school considers the Prāsaṅgika-Madhyamaka (*rang stong*) school to be superior, while the bKa' brgyud and rNying ma schools consider the Great Madhyamaka (*gzhan stong*) school to express the ultimate teachings of the Buddha.

In my view, exclusivism, and probably inclusivism as well, are contrary to a Buddhist understanding of things as they really are. The Buddhist view of an absolute cannot be the exclusive property of any teacher, community, or lineage, for a radical understanding of *śūnyatā* carries with it an appreciation of the variety of forms and practices which arise. And it seems to me that no doctrine, ritual form, or practice can be superior in and of itself. Everything depends upon the moment of experience of the practitioner and the efficacy of the practice situation. Besides, in Buddhism the primary realms of dispute between schools have less to do with truths and more to do with efficacy or expediency.

Could there be a contribution to understanding religious pluralism from the perspective of the practice traditions of Buddhism? Let us define pluralism in this way: pluralism is the recognition that truth is not exclusively (or inclusively) the property of any one religious tradition, and that the myriad understandings of truth or the "ultimate" in religious traditions provide an opportunity for celebration and dialogue rather than providing obstacles to be overcome.[4] From this point of view, authentic interreligious dialogue flourishes best in an environment of pluralism rather than one of exclusivism or inclusivism, in which the dialogue partner's position is being appropriated or categorized. In this essay, we shall examine what foundation there might be in selected Buddhist traditions for understanding pluralism and its implications for the dialogue relationship.

TRUTH IS NOT THE PROPERTY OF ANY ONE TRADITION: AN ANATOMY OF DIALOGUE

As we begin to look for the ground of discussion of religious pluralism in Buddhist terms, we find the issues to be somewhat different than those found in Christianity. It seems that Christians have focused on the issue of the uniqueness of Christ, and the theological ramifications of this uniqueness, whether actual or mythical, have shaped Christian writing on pluralism. What shapes pluralism in Christianity as I understand it is the notion that truth could be understood to be broader than that expressed in the Incarnation, life, and Resurrection of Christ.[5]

From a Buddhist perspective, rather than beginning with a discussion of the hierarchies of religious truths, it is probably more characteristic of certain Buddhist discourse to examine the fundamental presuppositions of interreligious dialogue. From this perspective, the foundations for pluralism and interreligious dialogue can be found in notions of sameness and difference, especially regarding religious standpoints or truths. These notions of sameness and difference were of central concern for the philosophical school of Madhyamaka, founded by the great master Nāgārjuna in the second century CE. In the Madhyamaka (and general Mahāyāna Buddhist) context, "things as they are" (*yathābhūtam*) can never be directly expressed in words, and so all reasoning must ultimately fail to fully articulate the absolute. Reasoning and discourse in Madhyamaka have two related roles: they are used to show the pitfalls of a merely logical approach: and they demonstrate what one can constructively say about the nature of reality, such that realization can be evoked in the practitioner. The Madhyamakan enters the conversation in order to train the mind and to demonstrate that while the logical approach is inadequate to fully express the ultimate, that it develops the mind and powerfully points to non-conceptual experience.

The *Mūlamadhyamakakārikā* of Nāgārjuna speaks of the tendency toward extremes in conceptual formation, expressed as the four extremes or alternatives (*catuṣkoṭi*). (Garfield: 189–195). When we examine issues of pluralism in an actual dialogue setting, we can see the dynamic of dialogue from the view of Madhyamaka in this way. There are only four possible configurations of the dialogue relationship: no other positions are imaginable. Either the position of the dialogue partner is the same as one's own (A): or the position of the partner is different than one's own (not A): or the partner's position is the same in some ways and different in some ways (both A and not A): or the partner's position is neither the same nor different than one's own (neither A nor not A). To explore the validity of each of these positions is the Madhyamakan's training.

In this investigation, I would like to relate to the actual *praxis* of dialogue based on my own experience in dialogue with Christians, Jews, Hindus, Native Americans, and other Buddhists.[6] This will be a focus exercise in Madhyamaka logic, playfully executed, which does not follow strictly all the twists and turns of Madhyamaka logic: however, I hope it serves to give a Buddhist slant to the foundations of pluralism and dialogue, with practical application.

Alternative One: The Partner's Stance and My Own are the Same

There are notable moments in dialogue in which we find ourselves meeting the partner directly, and find no difference at all in our points of view. I have found myself in extended conversations with an Orthodox priest, or a Benedictine brother, or a Korean Zen nun, and have been shocked and delighted in a moment to find no distinguishable boundary between our views. I remember a stunning conversation fifteen years ago when a Carmelite mother superior confided in me that she felt more kinship with me than with many in her own Catholic communities, and having confessed this, she became embarrassed into deep, shocked silencc. These moments are rare and wonderful and, yes, unsettling.

Why was my Carmelite friend shocked? I was shocked as well. Are we the same or not? What does it mean to be the same in our perspectives? She had a different life, a different embodied experience, with specific liturgical, sacramental, and theological expressions different from mine. Is it possible to be identical in our views? Have any of us ever met another person, in dialogue or in our own communities, who have held positions truly identical to our own? If these other positions are truly identical, how can they be positions held by another person? The partner's position cannot be identical and yet remain the partner's position at the same moment – it is logically impossible.

How about the situation in which I experience my mind meeting the mind of my teacher? At that moment, I feel no boundary, no separation between the mind of my teacher and my own. Could this be an encounter with the same mind? But the Madhyamaka asks us to examine what we mean by mind. If I am to determine that my mind and my teacher's are the same, I must be sure what mind is and what it is not. How would I determine whether it is the same or different? Can I find my mind, or the mind of my teacher? This is a classic Buddhist question, and reminds me of the famous request Hui K'o made to his teacher, Bodhidharma:

> "My mind [*hsin*] has no peace as yet! I beg you, master, please pacify my mind!"
>
> "Bring your mind here and I will pacify it for you," replied Bodhidharma.
>
> "I have searched for my mind, and I cannot take hold of it." said [Hui K'o].
>
> "Now your mind is pacified!" (*Mumonkan* 41, in Sekida: 118)

If the minds are the same, no encounter is possible. If they are two, they will never meet. It is untenable to have a dialogue partner with whom one's own position is the same.

Alternative Two: The Partner's Stance and My Own are Different

A common view in the current literature on pluralism is that when we encounter the dialogue partner, we are encountering the Other. When we encounter the Other, our own biases and prejudices are reflected back to us in a very helpful way, and something transformative can happen. Raimon Panikkar observes that "what to do with the barbarian?" is the central question for the discipline of religious studies challenged by pluralism.

> How can we pretend to deal with the ultimate problems of Man [sic] if we insist on reducing the human being to only the American, or to only the Russian, or to the Christian, or to the black, or the male, or the exclusively heterosexual, or the healthy and "normal," or the so-called civilized? Obviously we

cannot. (Panikkar: 54)

But, often the Other sounds romantic or deified, as we can see from the capitalized "O" so prevalent in the literature. Who is the Other, and how Other is she or he? As Knitter writes,

> When I say "other" to describe my journey, I mean the *really different*, the unexpected, the unthought, the surprising, the jolting. I'm talking about people or events that didn't seem to fit into the world that I had experienced and understood. (Knitter: 3)

In dialogue situations there is tremendous excitement in meeting the Other in this way, in finding in the encounter the challenge to everything we hold dear. And when we go to meet the Other in her or his own land, we find our assumptions, our habits, our concepts challenged at every turn, and the effect is very powerful.

But, this is a sensitive subject for the non-Christian in dialogue with Christians. The Christian theologian challenged by pluralism is often seemingly looking for the partner who symbolizes the Other most dramatically. In dialogue situations, I have sometimes sensed disappointment in my Christian dialogue partners that I was not quite Other enough for them. I am "WASB", a white, tall and fair middle-class woman, married with children, educated,. . . and a Buddhist. If I am threatening or challenging in some way, it may be because I am not Other enough. The "real Buddhists" are those who are ethnically Asian, especially those without Western education, who are male, monastic, who may know not even one word of English. Is that where we have the real encounter with the Other?

Knitter writes of his friendship with Rahim, a Muslim student in Germany. Was he the Other? Knitter writes that Rahim was impressive in his commitment to practice, and that "ethically, he surpassed most Christians [I] knew" (7). When we are engaged in dialogue with the Other, it becomcs difficult consistently to sustain the Otherness. We find that our concepts about differences simply do not hold up when we have real contact.

What are the theological trappings involved in depicting the dialogue partner in the Rudolph Otto-like "Other?" When we view the dialogue partner in this way, we overlook the shared world so essential if dialogue is to occur, and the partner can never truly live up to the expectation of Otherness so anticipated. As the Madhyamaka would challenge us to examine, is it possible to have a dialogue with someone who is truly Other? What would the Other look like? Can any human, in communication, be Other? Is the truly Other even imaginable? And if we could imagine the complete Other, would there be any ability to have conversation, or any communication whatsoever? Dialogue presupposes a shared humanity, a sentient existence, bodily manifestation, language or communication of some kind, a common matrix of existence. If we had no such shared existence, it would have never occurred to us to ponder each other, much less communicate. From this point of view, dialogue could never be carried on with a partner who was an actual other. It would be a logical impossibility.

Perhaps this is why Knitter finally describes the relationship with Other as "incomprehensible."

> While similarities in religious experience and expression abound, the differences are even more abundant – and many of them are incommensurable. To describe who the religious Other has been for me and how it has affected me, I find Rudolf Otto's expression most fitting: it has been a *mysterium tremendum et fascinosum* – a mystery both frightening and fascinating. I have been unsettled, confused, often put off by what the religious Other makes known to me, but at the same time (or soon thereafter) I just as often find myself touched, lured, persuaded by the very strangeness that frightened me. (Knitter: 13)

When we seek the Other, we may not be prepared for the other we actually meet, as Knitter points out. And when we finally encounter the other, we find that she or he was perhaps not other at all.

Alternative Three: The Partner's Stance and My Own are the Same in Some Ways and Different in Others

Our most common assumptions in dialogue situations fall into alternative three, in which we are in dialogue with the partner whose position is the same as ours in some ways, and different from ours in some ways. In fact, most of my dialogue experiences have fallen into this category. In a dialogue at Gethsemani Abbey,[7] I found the liturgical life of the Trappist community provocative in its resonance with my own practice, and yet the differences in medium, language, and tenor of the liturgy were obvious. When I return to the Methodist Sunday services in which I was raised, there is great familiarity and yet enormous distance from my current experience as a Tibetan Buddhist practitioner.

Knitter speaks of these as joining pluralism (otherness) and liberation (sameness), or dialogue (otherness) and global responsibility (sameness). Eck speaks of engaging with religious pluralism (otherness) while identifying a world sense of community (sameness). Panikkar speaks of dialogical tension (otherness) and cosmic trust (sameness).

But this not a position at all: it is actually ambivalence and instability, which carries great peril in the area of pluralism. One moment we embrace the partner as the same, and yet (as we have explored in discussing the first alternative) we recognize the deceptiveness of the sameness of ourselves and the partner. The next moment we experience the Otherness of the partner, and the possibility of dialogue vanishes in the sheer terror of difference.

This ambivalence, I would submit, is not really pluralistic, for the instability of it gives rise alternately to two familiar positions. First, ambivalence gives rise to exclusivism, touched by the sameness and yet more afraid of the otherness. This solidifies its position of defense by deeming its own position as superior, and consciously excluding the other. Dialogue sometimes has the effect of threatening us so deeply in the power of recognition and intimacy that it drives us to exclusivism.

The other stronghold into which we fall in this ambivalence is that of inclusivism, in which the differences we recognize in the other are defended by calling them partial truths which are part of our own truth. Here sameness becomes a refuge from the threat of ambivalence, and yet it is a sameness which we own, control, and dole out to those partners to whom we might otherwise not know how to relate.

For the Madhyamakan, this third position is not really pluralism, because the ambivalence it expresses rests on the uncertainty about the relationship summarized in alternatives one and two, and in itself is not really a position. This approach combines the confusions of two previously demonstrated confused positions: hence it is no less confused than its constituent parts, and so it is also an untenable position. Even worse, this ambivalence becomes a position when it falls into expression as exclusivism or inclusivism, which are definitely not pluralism.

Alternative Four: The Partner's Stance and My Own are Neither the Same Nor Different

The fourth alternative is that of refusing to recognize either resonance with the partner on the one hand, or to resist the partner's differences on the other hand. This is a non-committal encounter which deems a relationship so incomprehensible that nothing could be said about it on the issue of sameness or otherness, or in any real context at all. This is an unlikely relationship in a dialogue situation, and may be more appropriate to the conventional encounters which arise briefly on an elevator, in neighboring cars at a stoplight, or passing in a grocery store aisle. From the Madhyamaka point of view this position, like the previous one, is untenable because it relies on the negations of two positions which have already been deemed untenable, and the negation of an untenable position does not make it tenable.[8]

PLURALISM AND ENCOUNTER IN BUDDHISM

Where does this discussion leave us? We have found through Madhyamaka analysis that the concepts of same or other (different) in dialogue relationships do not apply in the way that we assumed they did. This leaves us in a positionless position which has been given the label, *śūnyatā*.[9] We are left, in Buddhist terms, in open space, in a realm of emptiness in which we recognize that relative concepts cannot accurately describe the nature of our relationship with our dialogue partner. On an absolute level, we are joined by our mutual and distinct experiences of no reference point: on an relative level, we experience in that vast space the warmth and wildness of our mutual humanity, which Buddhists call compassion.

When we turn to classical examples of encounter and dialogue in Buddhism, we find these basic principles of the Madhyamaka dialectic illustrated. Encounter is a popular theme in selected Buddhist traditions, for it is the ordinary situations on the spiritual path which provide the most direct instruction for the practicing Buddhist. Whether these encounters occur between student and teacher, between teachers, or between the practitioner and a visionary being or obstructing spirit, the exchange often becomes significant for spiritual progress, and its details have been recorded in hagiographical literature. We shall examine two of these encounters, from the Zen and Tibetan traditions respectively, to identify the themes of sameness and otherness explored by the Madhyamakan.

What really happens when we encounter another person? In the context of our discussion, dialogue partners recognize that on a relative, conceptual level, there are no words which adequately describe the dialogue encounter. Notions of sameness and otherness have no precise referents in experience, and yet we are left in face-to-face encounter of some kind.

The Zen Mondō: Kyozān and Sanshō

For a first example, from the Japanese Zen tradition, the *Blue Cliff Record* describes an exchange between Zen masters Kyozān and Sanshō.[10] This encounter has been preserved in a collection of *mondōs*, which record ordinary encounters between great Zen masters and their contemporaries from the Chinese and Japanese traditions. These encounters, often beginning with mundane questions, express the deep Zen experiences responding to seemingly ordinary exchanges with students or other masters. In the Zen tradition, the records of these encounters have served, in lieu of scripture, as important pedagogical tools of Zen training. Many of the *mondō* became the source for the koans in the Japanese tradition.[11]

This *mondō* depicts the encounter between Kyōzan and Sanshō, who were Chinese masters living in ninth century. Kyōzan (whose given name was Ejaku) was born in Canton, and when he was a young adult, there was a fierce persecution of Buddhism. When his parents refused permission to allow Kyōzan to enter a Buddhist monastery, he cut off two fingers and bowed before them, supplicating them to change their minds. (Shaw: 123–4) He became one of the closest students of Isan, and many anecdotes are preserved in the record of their interchanges, in which Kyōzan demonstrates his true Zen spirit. Sanshō (whose given name was Enen) was from north China, the younger of the two. He studied with Rinzai, and succeeded him, compiling the *Rinzairoku.* His reputation as a penetrating Zen master was impeccable.

Since Kyōzan and Sanshō were spiritual successors of the same teacher, Hyakujō, they had long been known to each other, but this encounter occurred upon Sanshō's first formal visit to the elder master Kyōzan. The *mondō* in the *Blue Cliff Record* is recorded in this way:

> Kyōzan asked Sanshō, "What is your name?"
> Sanshō said, "Ejaku!"
> Kyōzan said, "Ejaku is my name!"
> Sanshō said, "My name is Enen!"
> Kyōzan laughed heartily. (Sekida: 328)

When Kyōzan inquired Sanshō's name, what was he asking, since he surely already knew Sanshō's name? In asking, is he declaring the otherness of Sanshō? This is no ordinary meeting: Kyōzan is challenging Sanshō to declare himself, to reveal his understanding in a direct, immediate manner. Here Kyōzan takes a threatening, absolute stance. No superficial answer will do. It is a challenge, but it is also a question of great honor and respect, potentially a meeting between two peers, depending upon Sanshō's response.

How is Sanshō to respond? When the elder Kyōzan pretends not to know his name, it could be construed a great insult. Engo in his commentary remarks: "He ignored both the name and the reality" (Sekida: 329). Sanshō responds in the most direct manner, using Kyōzan's private, personal name, Ejaku. He is saying, I am the most personal you! You have deprived me of my name and reality. I will deprive you of yours! It is the answer of a peer, returning the challenge, invoking their sameness. In this moment they are rivals, like *samurai*, facing each other with their hands on the hilts of their swords.

In surprise, Kyōzan responds immediately, "Ejaku is my name!" Both sameness and otherness are challenged, and Kyōzan steps out of threatening, absolute role, stepping into a relative world in which everyone has a name. In this moment, the encounter shifts from the atmosphere of two rival *samurai* facing. Kyōzan withdraws his hand from his sword in genuine surprise, and in that moment true intimacy and connection are possible.

Sanshō's response completes the exchange, as he declares, using his given, personal name, "My name is Enen!" Again Sanshō meets Kyōzan as a peer, confirming himself as a relative being as well. He too has withdrawn his hand from the sword, acknowledging that relationship is possible, and that the notions of sameness and otherness simply do not apply. He and Kyōzan are able to meet in the unconditioned ground, without parallel or reference point. Kyōzan acknowledges this as he closes with a roaring laugh, "Ha ha!"

The *mondō* ends with a celebration of pluralism, a celebration characteristic of the warrior traditions of Asia. In all direct encounter, there is an edge of potential enmity which comes from recognizing otherness. The warriors face each other with hands on their swords, great danger palpable. Truly meeting in this otherness, the warriors then recognize their sameness, with no discernible boundary, and they lift their hands from their swords in surprise. Then, understanding that this also does not fit the case, they join each other in laughter. They each appreciate the integrity and interconnectedness of the other, without attempts to appropriate, categorize, or subjugate. It is in this moment that the warriors share tea, or compose poetry, or drink together in the moonlight. They are each fully alone and fully with the other person at the same moment. They drink and revel in the full awareness of their swords at their sides, but warfare has become sport and companionship.

Setchō's verse, explaining the *mondō*, expresses the essence of the encounter.

> Both grasping, both releasing – what fellows!
> Riding the tiger – marvelous skill!
> The laughter ends, traceless they go.
> Infinite pathos, to think of them. (Sekida: 328)

Both Kyōzan and Sanshō hold fast, and the "whole universe vanishes." They both let go, release, and "the individual world appears, in which everyone asserts his existence." The splendor of the encounter is expressed as two masters riding tigers, and because they are so complete they depart without a trace. Sekida concludes his commentary on the last line: "In the sublime culmination of love, one wants above all to become one with the other person, but one knows the impossibility of such union – hence the pathos, which is infinite and eternal" (Sekida: 329–330).

Tibetan *rNam thar*: Nāropa and the *Ḍākinī*

In a second example from the Tibetan Buddhist tradition, let us look at a different kind of encounter described in the *rnam thar* or hagiography of the great yogin Nāropa. Typically, encounters in *rnam thar* are between guru and disciple or between the yogin and particular obstructing spirits or messengers, with exchanges between peers rare. Also, it is common in these interchanges for a particular obstacle or blind spot to be pointed out, either directly or indirectly. Given our discussion above, the *rnam thar* deal with how it is that the yogin has identified some aspect of experience as alien or "other," and failing to realize this, has inhibited his own spiritual development.

At the time of this encounter, Nāropa was an erudite professor and abbot of the great Indian Buddhist university, Nālandā, in the eleventh century, accomplished in scripture, debate, and commentary (see Guenther). He was a monk, renowned for purity and refinement, and a scholar with many accolades. In spite of his achievements, or perhaps because of them, he was arrogant, aloof, and finicky. One day, as Nāropa labored over his texts in the dim light of his monastic cell at Nālandā University, a terrifying shadow fell over his books. He turned to find a horrible old woman standing before him, displaying thirty-seven ugly features. It is significant that this was a vision of a decrepit old woman, the emblem of all that is counter to the monastic, scholarly life. She was as "other" as any being could be for Nāropa. Nālandā University was a male monastic institution, bound by explicit warnings about contact with women. The student body, which included laymen from all over Asia, had no place for women.

Unbeknownst to Nāropa, the hag was a wisdom-*ḍākinī*, an enlightened feminine visionary being who embodied intuitive wisdom, the sharp and penetrating quality of non-dual knowing which is beyond books and logic.[12] She was old, as Herbert Guenther writes, because her wisdom is much "older than the cold rationality of the intellect" (iii), representing the everyday world of life and death, childbearing and weaning, and emotions from anguish to ecstasy. And she was ugly, because through excluding her and her wisdom from his world, Nāropa had stunted and deformed that aspect of his own understanding.

In Tibetan Buddhism, there is a recurring motif of the erudite scholar or great teacher being confronted by a *ḍākinī* woman, who punctures his arrogance and points out the essence. She might be old, wrathful, and horrid: she might be a vision of graceful beauty: she might be ordinary looking, with unusual moles, features, or birthmarks. She might be initially perceived as "other," representing an alternative perspective or mode of being. But, when acknowledged and heard, she embodies the wisdom inherent in the practitioner, more "same" than "other." She had something to teach which the great Nāropa needed in order to progress on the spiritual path.

Nāropa the scholar regarded the old woman with horror and fascination, noting all thirty-seven of her decrepit features. To name a few, her deeply wrinkled and bearded face held deep, piercing, bloodshot eyes, and a crooked nose. Her gaping mouth held rotted teeth, and constantly chewed on its tongue. Her rough complexion was darkish-blue and her hair was "fox-colored and disheveled." Her body was deformed and twisted, and she leaned heavily on a stick. He felt deep revulsion, and reflected that these thirty-seven horrific features reflected the certainty of impermanence, egolessness, and unsatisfactoriness of cyclic existence.

Nevertheless, when she quizzed him about his studies, he responded immediately, eager to please.

> "What are you looking into?"
>
> "I study the books on grammar, epistemology, spiritual precepts, and logic," he replied.
>
> "Do you understand them?"
>
> "Yes."
>
> "Do you understand the words or the sense?"
>
> "The words."
>
> The old woman was delighted, rocked with laughter, and

began to dance, waving her stick in the air. Thinking that she might feel still happier, Nāropa added: "I also understand the sense." But then the woman began to weep and tremble and she threw her stick down. (Guenther: 24)

When Nāropa asked about her behavior, the *ḍākinī* explained that she had first been delighted that a great scholar such as Nāropa had been so honest as to admit that he only understood the words of that which he studied. But when he went on to say he understood the sense of these texts, she was deeply saddened to hear him lie so boldly.

"Words" (Sanskrit *neyārtha*, Tibetan *drang don*) refers to the literal, explicit meaning of the texts he studied. In the Tibetan tradition, this refers to a level of meaning which requires further explanation or commentary before it can be understood. "Sense" (*nītārtha, nges don*) refers to the deep, profound meaning which is complete, requiring no further explanation in order to be understood. Nāropa the scholar was prepared to understand the words, for he was well-trained in the definitions, etymologies, and logics necessary to interpret the literal meaning of the texts. But, lacking meditation and realization, he was unprepared to understand the profound inner sense of the texts. For the wisdom-*ḍākinī*, the tragedy was that he did not know his own limitations.

Initially in this encounter, the hag represented all that was "other" for Nāropa, and he was shocked and horrified by her. But when she responded to him in this way, he recognized her direct, penetrating insight which exposed him at the core of his being, and he knew at that moment that she was a wisdom-*ḍākinī*, a manifestation of his own wisdom mind, neither purely "same" nor "other." Realizing she spoke the truth, the chastened Nāropa then asked, "who, then, understands the sense?" and the old woman directed him to her brother, the great yogin Tilopa, saying, "go yourself, pay your respects to him, and beg him that you may come to grasp the sense." And instantly Nāropa gave up his books, belongings and position and set out to seek his teacher, Tilopa.

In the journey that followed, Nāropa repeatedly encountered additional visions and situations which continued to revolt him and challenge his basic patterns. He encountered a leprous woman; a dying dog, infested with vermin; men cheating or torturing their parents; several men disemboweling a corpse and a live man; a hunter with bow, arrow, and hounds; an old couple killing fish, frogs, and insects and devouring them; a beggar killing lice. In each case, he was invited to join in the activities, and in each case he was revolted and refused, recognizing their threat to his status as a monk and scholar. And each time the vision dissolved with the voice of Tilopa calling, "you have missed your opportunity again! Nāropa, you cannot meet the guru unless you open your mind, drop your habitual discriminations, and engage with the world."

Finally, deeply depressed, Nāropa resolved to commit suicide, and as he poised to draw the razor over his wrist veins, Tilopa again called,

> "If you have not found, how will you find
> the teacher if you kill the Buddha? . . . ."

> "Ever since you met me in the form of the leper woman, we were never apart, but were like a body and its shadow. The various visions you had were the defilements of your evil deeds and so you did not recognize me. . . ."

> Seize the wish-fulfilling gem, your true spirituality,
> The Ḍākinī's hidden home. (Guenther: 36–37)

With this instruction, Tilopa pointed out to Nāropa that all the revolting and challenging situations which he encountered were necessary teaching for his entering the yogic path. As a monk and scholar, he had developed great disdain for many aspects of his own mind and emotions and a great disdain for the gritty world around him. These aspects appeared to him in exaggerated fashion as horrific visions, beginning with the appearance of the old hag. But, as he rejected these visions, he also rejected the yogic path, and the true sense of the teachings was closed to him. To the extent that he found these visions to be "other," he had no ability to practice meditation.

It was only when he fell into deep despair and attempted suicide that his barriers to the "other" dissolved, and Tilopa appeared to him. Tilopa pointed out that his search for the teacher could only be resolved by finding the teacher, the Buddha, within. That is, the sheer "otherness" of these negative situations must be claimed as one's own. When he claimed all aspects of his experience in this way, the wish-fulfilling gem of buddhahood, could be realized, and the hidden home of the wisdom-*ḍākinī*, his own mind, could be discovered. Of course, this realization entailed more than his conceptual mind: this instruction awakened Nāropa's vast awareness, empty, non-referential and luminous, which was indistinguishable from the mind of his teacher.

This was a moment of genuine encounter between Tilopa and Nāropa, in which he was able to recognize his habit of rejecting what he considered other, and attempt to include all situations he encountered in his practice. Then he could be open to what his teacher, Tilopa, could impart. True openness of this kind is possible only when the fallacies of same and other are transcended and that which is perceived as other is included on one's spiritual path.[13]

Whether we speak from the tradition of the Zen *mondō* or of the Tibetan *rnam thar*, dialogues occur in the groundless environment in which we cannot say that our position is the same or different from that of our dialogue partner. Authentic exchanges dawn when the presuppositions concerning the relationship begin to break down. Of course, such encounters are exceedingly rare. Concepts abound in dialogue situations, and it takes great commitment, penetration, trust, and openness for us to give up our concepts in dialogue encounters. But, if we hold the view that this view of pluralism is the most conducive atmosphere in which to conduct dialogue, we then have an avenue along which to travel in order to open up the dialogue relationship.

CONCLUSION

Much has been written about interreligious dialogue concerning etiquette, language, composition, and theological stances. Much of that discourse certainly applies to dialogue, but the most radical assertion imaginable is one which suggests that dialogue take place in an environment of pluralism. In Buddhist language, pluralism is an expression of discovery of *śūnyatā*, the recognition that there is no way to grasp conceptually what the relationship is with the dialogue partner. Out of this positionless position, tremendous warmth and interest arises naturally. In environments such as these, attempts to appropriate, categorize, or subjugate the partner have been given up and genuine interest in communication has dawned. When we have this kind of interest, we appreciate that the truth of the other person is his or her own, and we might learn from the partner's truth. Engaging in dialogue with this view could radically transform interreligious communication, its conduct and its tenor. Rang 'byung rdo rje, the third Karmapa, was a renowned scholar and yogin who had extensive experience in dialogue with the various Tibetan Buddhist schools and the imperial court of China. In his most famous devotional prayer, he wrote:

> The play of overwhelming compassion being unobstructed,
> In the moment of love the empty essence nakedly dawns.

May we constantly practice, day and night,
This supreme path of unity, devoid of errors. (Kunsang: 15)

NOTES

1 An early rendering of these views can be found in Race; later books include Hick and Knitter; and D'Costa.

2 *Saddharmapuṇḍarīka Sūtra* III (Watson: 47–79).

3 There are exceptions even to this generalization: for example, the great bKa' brgyud master Mi bskyod rdo rje held the *rang stong* to be the superior approach.

4 Eck eloquently distinguishes pluralism from what might erroneously be taken as its analogs: diversity, tolerance, relativism (both nihilistic and uncommitted), and syncretism. As she clarifies, "religious pluralism requires active positive engagement with the claims of religion and the facts of religious diversity. It involves not the mere recognition of the different religious traditions and the insuring of their legitimate rights, but the active effort to understand difference and commonality through dialogue" (Eck: 192). Pluralists also respect difference, and yet commit to a particular religious tradition and community.

5 It has interested me that there are a range of opinions regarding what pluralism is for Christianity, specifically regarding Christianity's uniqueness, and the ramifications of that uniqueness for relationships with other religions. John Cobb, for example, takes issue (in a way that has overtones quite resonant with Madhyamaka – could it be his Buddhist-Christian dialogue experience showing? – with the notion of religions at all, asserting that if there is no such thing as "a religion," then it is difficult to establish a pluralism between religions. Cobb: 81–84.

6 For this experience, I refer to a variety of interreligious dialogues in which I have been involved since the early 1980's at The Naropa Institute, the Cobb-Abe Theological Encounter Group, the Society of Buddhist-Christian Studies, and the Monastic Interfaith Dialogue meetings.

7 Monastic Interreligious Dialogue conference, July 1996.

8 In the Madhyamaka dialectic, the kind of negation used is different from the kind used in conventional speech, for it is a "non-affirming negation," which negates without assuming that the negation implies that its opposite is valid. Hence, in this case, the dialogue stance described is based upon notions of neither sameness nor otherness. Since both sameness and otherness have been shown to be invalid, and since their opposites cannot be said to be valid in the context of non-affirming negation, this dialogue position is an untenable one.

9 I quake to introduce this in a "theological" paper, because of how this

topic has been so targeted and belabored in Buddhist-Christian dialogue. On the other hand, it is important that it is introduced in a way which is not merely the word, but the classical method which evokes the experience of the word itself. Hence, perhaps it is important to reintroduce this in a new way.

10 In an early essay on relationship in Buddhism, Keiji Nishitani examined this particular *mondō*, providing his own unique, intricate and somewhat involuted commentary. Rather than recapitulate that here, I have provided a somewhat simpler one from the *Hekigan-roku*, with influence from Nishitani's original essay (see Nishitani: 71–87).

11 The relationship between the koan tradition and Nāgārjuna's Madhyamaka logic is well-documented. In this case, Nishitani is drawing on the presentation of the two truths, relative and absolute, for his explanation of the *mondō.*

12 In the Tibetan tradition, the feminine principle is Prajñāpāramitā herself, the penetrating insight which is the basis of all enlightenment. See Simmer-Brown forthcoming.

13 The relationship between Tilopa and Nāropa continued over the next years in an intense student-teacher fashion, with many more trials and tribulations for Nāropa before he attained enlightenment. In this series of encounters, Tilopa and Nāropa emerged as peers only at the end of his journey, the descriptions of which are brief and lackluster. Much more emphasis is put characteristically on the difficulties along the way.

REFERENCES

Cobb, John (1990). "Beyond Pluralism." In Gavin D'Costa, ed., *Christian Uniqueness Reconsidered.* Maryknoll, NY: Orbis Books

D'Costa, Gavin, ed. (1990). *Christian Uniqueness Reconsidered.* Maryknoll, NY: Orbis Books.

Eck, Diana (1993). *Encountering God: A Spiritual Journey From Bozeman to Benares.* Boston: Beacon Press.

Garfield, Jay, trans. (1996). *Fundamentals of the Middle Way.* Oxford: Oxford University Press.

Guenther, Herbert, trans. (1963). *The Life and Teachings of Nāropa.* London: Oxford University Press.

Hick , John and Paul F. Knitter, eds. (1987). *The Myth of Christian Uniqueness* Maryknoll, NY: Orbis Books.

Knitter, Paul (1996). *Jesus and the Other Names.* Maryknoll, NY: Orbis Books.

Kunsang, Erik Pema, trans. (1992). *Song of Karmapa: The Aspiration of the Mahāmudrā of True Meaning by Lord Rangjung Dorje.* Kathmandu: Rangjung Yeshe Publications.

Nishitani, Keiji (1969). "On the I-Thou Relation in Zen Buddhism," *Eastern*

Buddhist (2: 2) 71-87.

Panikkar, Raimon (1995). "The Myth of Pluralism: The Tower of Babel" In *Invisible Harmony: Essays on Contemplation and Responsibility.* Minneapolis, MN: Augsburg Fortress Press.

Race, Alan (1983). *Christian and Religious Pluralism: Patterns in Christian Theology of Religions.* Maryknoll, NY: Orbis Books, .

Sekida, Katsuki, trans. (1977). *Two Zen Classics: Mumonkan and Hekiganroku.* New York: Weatherhill.

Shaw, R. D. M., trans. (1961).*The Blue Cliff Records: The Hekigan Roku.* London: Michael Joseph.

Simmer-Brown, Judith (forthcoming), *Dākinī's Breath: Feminine Principle in Tibetan Buddhism.*

Watson, Burton, trans. (1993). *The Lotus Sūtra.* New York: Columbia University Press.

Seventeen

From Buddhology To Buddhist Theology: An Orientation To Sinhala Buddhism

Mahinda Deegalle

"Saying 'I go for refuge to the Buddha,' virtuous people should go for refuge to the Buddha."
Vidyācakravartī (c. 1200-1293)

Most Theravāda scholars have been repugnant to notions of faith and devotion within Buddhism. They are hesitant to admit that Theravāda texts contain Buddhological concepts or Buddhist theological discussions. For most, a rational and creative work on Buddhist doctrines as a form of Buddhology[1] or Buddhist theology is inconceivable. In most Theravāda writings, one encounters an overwhelming emphasis on the scientific and rationalistic nature of the Buddha's teachings. These overt emphases do ignore Buddhological tendencies within Theravāda. In the development of Sri Lankan Theravāda with close contacts with Sinhala people, with their beliefs and practices, Sinhala Buddhism has inherited a vast corpus of Buddhological literature. In medieval Sinhala prose texts, Buddhist writers employed a kind of rationalism to justify the goodness of the Buddha and to argue for Buddha's greatness as a spiritual power sometimes consciously or unconsciously elevating him to a savior. With special focus on Vidyācakravartī's *Butsaraṇa*, a thirteenth century Sinhala text, I will examine some Buddhological and Buddhist theological orientations in Sri Lankan Theravāda.

VIDYĀCAKRAVARTĪ'S TREATISE ON *BUDDHABHAKTI*

Vidyācakravartī is believed to be a Buddhist layman. Vidyācakravartī's faith in the Buddha and his commitment to the generation of faith and devotion (*bhakti*) among Sinhala readers are well expressed in the text, in the form of summaries of Buddha's virtues. The *Butsaraṇa* ("Refuge in the Buddha") has four-hundred-seventy-eight paragraphs which end with the refrain "*satpuruṣayan visin 'Budun saraṇa yemi' yi Butsaraṇa yā yutu*" ("saying 'I go for refuge to the Buddha,' virtuous people should go for refuge to the Buddha").[2] Because Vidyācakravartī emphasizes the act of *taking refuge* (*saraṇa*) in the Buddha at the end of each paragraph, this *baṇapota* (preaching text) has come to be known as the *Butsaraṇa*. Because of its richness, it has been admired both as a literary masterpiece as well as a *baṇapota*. Puñci Bandara Sannasgala (d. 1997), an important literary critic, once remarked: "The *Butsaraṇa* is one of the three or four Sinhala prose texts which became most popular both as a literary work as well as a *baṇapota*" (136).

In his writings, Vidyācakravartī employed an unusual theological rhetoric. His use of an affective language in a theological rhetoric can be seen well in his unconventional approach to the explication of *kāma* (desire), a concept which was relatively ignored and downplayed by Buddhists (see Deegalle 1995: 122–129). In the opening paragraph of the *Butsaraṇa*, Vidyācakravartī used the non-religious concept of *kāma* to justify good actions and to show the importance of taking refuge in the Buddha. He structured the first introductory paragraph with the refrain of taking refuge in the Buddha:

> Knowing the sweetness in pleasure and hardness in pain and desiring to enjoy pleasures effortlessly in the six heavens (*sadev lova*), desiring to rest by entering into the city of *nirvāṇa* (*nivanpura*) which the Buddha, *paccekabuddha* (*pasē budu*) and arahants (*rahatun*) have enjoyed, desiring not to listen to the names of hell (*niraya*), . . . having affection (*seneha*) for oneself, desiring to ease one's heart with the taste of precious ambrosia (*amārasa*), that is not available at the time when there is no Buddha,[3] desiring to enjoy the taste of the consolation of heart (mind) while being a human being, which is not available for gods and *brahmas*, . . . desiring to make friends of enemies, . . . desiring to be settled in immortal *nirvāṇa* just by worshipping and making offerings to the Buddha, virtuous people (*satpuruṣayan*) should go for refuge to the Buddha saying 'I go for refuge to the Buddha.'" (Vidyācakravartī 1966, 1968: 1)

Though the Pāli commentaries of the fifth century CE contain some compounds such as *saddhammaṭṭhitakāma* (the desire for the endurance of good doctrine), the concept of *kāma* is often treated negatively. Vidyācakravartī's usage in this opening paragraph is distinct from such previous usages, not only because the term *kämäti* is frequently used, but also because it is employed in an innovative rhetorical construction. To convey his affective, religious sentiments, Vidyācakravartī has used the term '*kämäti*' twenty-one times in twenty-two lines.

This verbal noun derives from the root √*kam*, which means "desire."[4] In general, in the Theravāda Buddhist tradition, 'desire' is not considered as a positive quality; it is often seen as negative. *The Pali Text Society's Pali–English Dictionary* states that "[i]n all enumerations of obstacles of perfection, or of general divisions and definitions of mental conditions, kāma occupies the leading position....Under this aspect kāma is essentially an evil" (Rhys Davids and Stede: 203). Since desire is not a virtue, it can divert one from the path of *nirvāṇa* (*nibbāna*). In the Buddhist context, desire is a sign of craving and thus it is considered a defilement. It is against the religious path, since it causes the extension of the cycle of birth and death (*saṃsāra*). On the contrary to Theravāda Orthodoxy, Vidyācakravartī has employed a concept which theologically had a negative connotation in Theravāda in a novel way, in order to popularize the Theravāda theology of heaven and hell among the peasants of late medieval Sri Lanka. All kinds of traditional allusions and expectations are used to justify the importance of taking refuge in the Buddha.

In the first paragraph of the *Butsaraṇa*, Vidyācakravartī mentions several concepts which can be taken as aspects of Theravāda theology. The doctrine of heaven and hell has, from an early date, been an important part of popular Theravāda religiosity. Though notions of heaven and hell are found in earlier Pāli canonical texts, the way such notions were employed by Vidyācakravartī in the *Butsaraṇa*, in particular, in the first paragraph, is novel and creative. Vidyācakravartī does not give detailed expositions on central doctrines such as *dukkha* but just reminds such doctrines in a candid way by stating "knowing the sweetness in pleasure and hardness in pain" (1). This opening paragraph mentions explicitly the benefit of enjoying happiness in the six heavens and avoiding even listening to the names of hell (*niraya*). The aspiration to enjoy happiness in the divine world (*deva*) is very common among average Buddhists (Gombrich: 326); however, this idea is not distinctively medieval, and has a long history of its own. Vidyācakravartī seems to have appealed to average Buddhists by employing such a theology at the very beginning of the *Butsaraṇa*. The paragraph as a whole encourages Buddhist devotees to enjoy happiness in the heavens effortlessly. *The issue is not just going to hell, but rather avoiding even listening to names* of *niraya*. In this paragraph, fourfold unpleasant states[5] are presented, with the goal of pointing out the immense suffering they contain. In general, in Theravāda Buddhism, notions of hell are a driving force for the practice of virtues.[6] Diverse kinds of discourses on suffering in hell, which are important aspects of Theravāda theology, are intended to persuade ordinary Buddhists to be virtuous; to motivate them to avoid negative actions in daily life; and to encourage them to perform positive deeds with the aspiration of making life better in the future.[7]

To achieve all these mundane and worldly goals, Vidyācakravartī recommends relatively easy religious practices such as worshipping and making offerings (*pūjā*) for average lay people. For example, in the first paragraph of the *Butsaraṇa*, Vidyācakravartī motivates people as follows: "Desiring to be settled in immortal *nirvāṇa* just by worshipping and making offerings to the Buddha, virtuous people should go for refuge to the Buddha" (Vidyācakravartī 1996, 1968: 1). It seems that, like medieval Kamakura Buddhists, such as Hōnen (1133-1212 CE), Shinran (1173-1262 CE) and Nichiren (1222-1282 CE), Sinhala Buddhist preachers of late medieval Sri Lanka recommended relatively easy methods such as worshipping, *pūjā*s etc. In the medieval period, these devotional activities may have helped to protect Buddhist communities from external pressure of Śaivism which was felt more severely at that time than in any other period in the history of Sri Lanka.

THE RELIGIO-HISTORICAL CONTEXTS OF SINHALA DEVOTIONALISM

With the internal political instability which resumed during the tenth century with foreign invasions, Sri Lanka's role as a leading propagator of Buddhism dwindled and Sri Lanka became isolated from the international affairs of the time. In the twelfth and thirteenth centuries, to a certain extent, the "Buddhist world" and its "cosmopolitanism" had been disrupted by the fall of the Buddhist "homeland" and the destruction of the Indian center.[8] In particular, in Sinhala Buddhism, the thirteenth century was a turning point both in terms of doctrinal developments in theological lines and in the changing geographical shape of Buddhism. In the case of Sri Lanka, the thirteenth century marks a great revival of "vernacular" Buddhist literature (see Deegalle 1995: 103–104; 1997c). In the early years of the late medieval period (11th-13th centuries CE), Theravāda Buddhism in Sri Lanka extended its impact in Sri Lanka and became thoroughly embedded in village contexts throughout the island.

After the defeat of the Sinhalas by the Choḷa King Rājarāja (983-

1014 CE) in 993 CE and his rule from his capital in Polonnaruva resulted in the rapid development and spread of Hinduism in Sri Lanka. Hindu temples were constructed[9] and, by contrast, "no Buddhist sculptures" belonging to the Choḷa occupation between 993 and 1070 CE have been found (von Schroeder: 98). Even after the defeat of the Choḷas by Vijayabāhu I (1055-1110 CE), "many Tamils remained in Sri Lanka." According to von Schroeder, the "majority of the Choḷa residents in Sri Lanka were worshipping Hindu deities" (98) and "[t]he Buddhist orders of Sri Lanka suffered hardship at the hands of the Tamil occupants, who were traditional Hindus and propagated the worship of Śiva especially" (109).

Reflecting on devotional activities within the late medieval period, two Buddhologists commented:

> In Sri Lanka in the twelfth and thirteenth centuries . . . devotional religion also seems to have been influential in the Buddhist community, generating new genres of Buddhist literature that were written primarily in Sinhala rather than Pali . . . a whole new devotional component was incorporated into the Theravāda tradition and subsequently diffused to the Theravāda cultures in Southeast Asia. (Reynolds and Hallisey: 19)

Since devotion to Śiva and Viṣṇu was on the rise in Sri Lanka, due to strong South Indian influences, as an antidote to *devabhakti* (devotion to gods), some Sinhala writers began to compose texts to generate *Buddhabhakti* (devotion to the Buddha).

In understanding religious competition in matters of devotion in late medieval Sri Lankan Buddhism, Max Weber's (1864-1920) observation about religious communities is quite appropriate: "Once a religious community has become established it feels a need to set itself apart from alien competing doctrines and to maintain its superiority in propaganda, all of which tends to the emphasis upon differential doctrines" (Weber: 70). Dharmasēna Thera's *Saddharmaratnāvaliya* ("The Garland of Jewels of the Good Doctrine," c. 1220-1293) presents important textual evidence for such religious competition in thirteenth-century Sri Lanka: "Without *bhakti* towards [Hindu] gods such as Viṣṇu-Maheśvara but having *bhakti* only in the three refuges (*tunuruvanhi ma*), virtuous people should engage themselves in virtuous activities (*sucarita*) in order to realize *nirvāṇa*."[10] Dharmasēna Thera's explicit remark reveals the religious need for *Buddhabhakti*. In another place, he further advises that "one should obtain this–and–other–worldly benefits having *affection* (*ādara*) and *bhakti* in the Buddha, etc."[11] This textual evidence shows an orientation towards the generation of *Buddhabhakti*; this phenomenon can be taken as an important feature in the process of "localization" of Theravāda Buddhism in Sri Lanka. It was a *conscious* Buddhist response aimed at avoiding possible conversions to Hindu Brahmanic religious practices and reinforcing localization and "*local consciousness*" during the late medieval period.

VERNACULAR TEXTUAL STRATEGIES

Vidyācakravartī portrayed the life of the Buddha incorporating narratives from the Pāli canon and its commentaries. However, he did not recast those materials in exactly the same way; he reworked old materials, appropriating old narratives according to his needs, altering, changing, and recasting both characters and narrative descriptions. Vidyācakravartī aimed to describe the life of the Buddha, giving prominence to Buddhahood and employed a narrative framework to explicate the virtues of the Buddha. In so doing, he highlighted and affirmed the Buddha's ability as an "extraordinary person." He presented the Buddha's biography by showing that the Buddha was endowed with "maximal greatness."[12] In the *Butsaraṇa*, Vidyācakravartī presented ninefold virtues (*nava guṇa*) and devoted almost half the work (151 out of 360 pages),[13] to elaborate the Buddha as the "supreme trainer of persons difficult to discipline" (*anuttara purisadammasārathī*).

Though Vidyācakravartī used the Pāli canon and its commentaries in one way or another as the basis for his narratives, he employed different talents and skills in appropriating Pāli narratives into the text. In particular, in the *Butsaraṇa*, one can see that Vidyācakravartī subjects the Pāli narratives to serious editorial revisions. In so doing, Vidyācakravartī was able to appeal to pious Sinhala village Buddhists.

In the *Butsaraṇa*, the employment of the *Jātaka* stories, which illustrate the bravery of the Buddha in past lives, is an important narrative strategy. In the short account on Aṅgulimāla, Vidyācakravartī (61–66) draws readers' attention to several *Jātaka* stories which highlight the greatness of the Buddha. In particular, this *baṇakathā* (literally "preaching story") shows Vidyācakravartī's immense ability to utilize *Jātaka* stories in concrete situations. When he employs *Jātaka* stories to achieve his goals, he often summarizes them in one or two lines; these brief descriptions heighten the sense of the Buddha's "maximal greatness." However, as one notices, in the following example, there is an *irony*: it presents the *Buddha as exalting himself in his own mind.* In other words, Vidyācakravartī does not present these thoughts as they occurred in the minds of the observers who witnessed the Buddha's journey to the forest to meet Aṅgulimāla but rather as thoughts that arose in the Buddha's own mind. According to this story, the observers who were on either side of the road, saw that the Buddha was going to meet Aṅgulimāla, but did not recognize him as the Buddha, and consequently underestimated his ability. In this context, Vidyācakravartī reminds us that the Buddha himself reflected on *his own* brave deeds in the past:

> The Buddha heard the words of those who had *not recognized* him and thought himself: "In a previous life, as a swallow (*vaṭu*), I stopped the fire; as a rabbit, I turned fire into a bundle of white water lilies; as a banker, I made lotuses blossom in the fire; in various previous lives, as a deer, parrot, swan, and peacock I made the entire world free from the very chasers; as a Kähärala bird, I knew safe devices to be free from the throat of tigers once I entered in; as a beast, I healed those who fell from large rocks by accepting them on my back; when I had fallen into the ocean, I reposed in the bosom of the goddess Maṇimekhalā; as Mahauṣadha, I spread 18 septillion people in many directions *without shaking even as much blood as a fly drinks from one's body*; as king Kusa, I struck against the earth the fourfold armies of seven kings, by mounting on the elephant in rut, by shouting that 'I am the lion-voiced king Kusa,' and by spreading the sound of my clapping of hands for 10,000 leagues in Dambadiva; as a monkey, by drinking water from hot springs, I saved the rest from the devil who resided in the lake, turning his eyes round, to eat all of us; as paṇḍit Vidhura, I made our feet a garland on the top of the head of Pūrṇabhadra, the commander of the forces of devils, who waited, planning to break our heads striking on the sixty-league rock Kāla, to split our chests, and to take our hearts; as prince Pañcāyudha, I subdued the demon Śleṣarōma and made him a servant of our family; as king Sutasōma, I preached *baṇa* to the cannibal, who was ready to sacrifice all kings in Dambadiva for a demon by piercing their hands and hanging them on the banyan tree; by *preaching*, I made him a virtuous person (*hudī*) for his entire life. *In the past, I did all these (great) things when my wisdom was not ripened* and when my heroism and subjugative powers had not attained the greatest height. But *now I am the best among gods*, the best among *sakras*, and the best among *brahmas*. *I will show them my*

victorious return." Having thought thus, the Buddha crossed the stream and entered the forest path. (Vidyācakravartī 1966: 63–64)

This passage shows Vidyācakravartī's innovation in craft. He has been able to incorporate many *Jātaka* stories into the story of Aṅgulimāla without damaging the narration. In fact, his innovative inclusions reinforce the story; further, they give the reader/listener a clue that the Buddha will discipline Aṅgulimāla even though he is a fierce murderer; using the *Jātaka* stories, Vidyācakravartī forecasts what will happen later.

Vidyācakravartī's account of Buddha's encounter with Aṅgulimāla is very precise and to the point; he presents only the significant moments of Aṅgulimāla's life. He is able to incorporate all details to highlight his goal: to *affirm and justify his stock phrase* "saying 'I go to the Buddha for refuge,' virtuous people should go for refuge to the Buddha." Vidyācakravartī's account is a direct translation of neither the Pāli text – *Aṅgulimāla Sutta* – nor of its commentary, the *Papañcasūdanī* (Buddhaghosa: 328–344; Chalmers: 97–105; Horner: 284–292). It differs a great deal from the account in Guruḷugōmī's *Amāvatura* ("The Flood of Nectar"; 88–97; Reynolds: 57–66). Vidyācakravartī's portrayal is original; its precision attracts attention; it appropriates the Aṅgulimāla story to fit Sinhala culture very well, and in that way he is able to achieve his purpose of appealing to the piety of Sri Lankan village Buddhists.

Still another example of Vidyācakravartī's originality is the way he captures the moment of conversion in Aṅgulimāla, the highway robber:

> "I *know* you, lord. I *recognize* you. Are you the son of Queen Mahā Māyā? Are you the son of King Suddhodana? Lord, *have you seen* sins (*pav*) which your *servant* (*gättā*) has committed? Have you come so far *alone* out of compassion (*karunā*) for your *servant*? *With all my life, I take your refuge* (*saraṇa*). My eyes are cooled. My heart is calm. My sins (*pav*) are extinct. May I, your *servant*, have your compassion (*karunā*)! Please, ordain me!" (Vidyācakravartī 1966: 65)

These words which Vidyācakravartī puts into the mouth of Aṅgulimāla express very well the moment of *realization* that Aṅgulimāla had achieved through the Buddha's encounter with him. A few moments before the Buddha's visit, Aṅgulimāla was *the most fearful* murderer, who wore a necklace of 999 human fingers. But now after the Buddha's guidance, Aṅgulimāla has become one of *the most realized*, disciplined, civilized, and grateful persons imaginable. Aṅgulimāla's verbal expressions capture the attention of Sinhala audiences who listen to this *baṇakathā*. It is a confession of Aṅgulimāla's own bad deeds as well as an expression of his *dependence* on the Buddha and his *willingness to take refuge* in the Buddha as a result of his "spiritual *regret*." This kind of verbal expression seems quite appropriate for a text like the *Butsaraṇa*, which elaborates on the idea of *taking refuge* in the Buddha.

RELEVANCE OF VIDYĀCAKRAVARTĪ FOR UNDERSTANDING BUDDHISM

Buddhist Studies has to be modern. As a discipline, it has to be tuned to new categories and methods that can be profitably used to explicate Buddhist teachings and varieties of Buddhists expressions. No doubt Theravāda Buddhists cannot use the term 'theology' in the same way or sense as other traditions employ it. In the absence of a strong concept of "God," Theravādins still maintain a very limited and inferior notion of deities – deities who depend entirely on good deeds of human beings. But this apparent absence of a notion of *theos* within Theravāda does not limit Buddhists entering into serious theological discussions on issues that are central to Buddhism.

In general, "theology" is broadly defined as a "secondary form of praxis and culture consisting in more or less critical reflection on a particular religion" (Ogden: 174). Buddhist theology as a secondary form of praxis and as a critical reflection on Buddhist thought is a valid academic enterprise. A culture-specific engagement with Buddhist practices and a critical reflection on them from doctrinal, philosophical and analytical perspectives becomes a Buddhist theology. In the Theravāda case, Buddhist theology is more broadly thought out as an academic discourse secondary to original or Pāli canonical texts but inclusive of critical reflections on Buddhist ideas, texts, practices and institutions. The relative scarcity of theological discourse within Theravāda can be attributed to the kind of Buddhism that developed in Sri Lanka. At best, Sri Lankan Theravāda attempted to be authentic to the words of the historical Buddha and as a result, doctrinal innovations in theological tone received no significant place.

In this socio-religious context of Pāli orthodoxy, the contemporary relevance of devotional literature of Vidyācakravartī becomes more and more important for (a) the study of Sinhala Buddhism and for (b) the understanding Sinhala Buddhist thought and practices.

In evaluating devotional dimensions in late medieval Sinhala literature, modern scholarship, however, has been very negative. For example, in Sinhala literary criticism, Vidyācakravartī's innovative religious rhetoric has been attacked. Viewed from a puritan Buddhist perspective, the imitation of the Pāli texts by Guruḷugōmī (c. 1187-1225), a contemporaneous lay Buddhist writer, has been seen as a "virtue," rather than as a weakness. Martin Wickramasinghe, one of the most renowned literary critics and writers of this century, wrote:

> If Vidyācakravartī...had followed his [Guruḷugōmī's] example and moulded the language of Guruḷugōmī to suit the temper of his own writings, we should have been able to boast today of a simple language not second to any modern language in its fitness for expressing poetic thought.... Vidyācakravartī deserves our praise for having employed a language that was intelligible to a wider circle of readers and listeners, though he would have done a service for all time if he had re-moulded the language of Guruḷugōmī instead of following the model of ornate Sanskrit prose." (Wickramasinghe: 66–67)

Vidyācakravartī's innovative religious rhetoric has been attacked as an inferior religious tactic appealing to "pious old women":

> Guruḷugōmī did not use the sentimental epithets and the hyperbolic descriptions...His was the truly intellectual attitude of the Buddhist to the world and the Buddha. It was this rational mind of his that influenced his selection of material, his *ruthless rejection of tales [of] credulous faith and blind adoration, his indifference to the sob-stuff dear to the hearts of pious upāsikas.*" (Wickramasinghe: 80; emphasis added)

Wickramasinghe further stated that Vidyācakravartī's "work overflows with the sentimental faith" and his "sonorous compounds and alliterative epithets lull the devoted listener into a state of drugged *bhakti*" (81). According to Wickramasinghe's judgment, "[t]he luxurious overflow of religious sentiment and feeling" is "the strength as well as the weakness of Vidyācakravartī's genius" (89).

Objections could be raised to this puritan, purely intellectual and biased confession of Wickramasinghe. Furthermore, it is obvious that such unfair criticisms on the works of Vidyācakravartī do ignore the real daily practices of Sinhala Buddhists today. When one takes into account recent anthropological field works on Sri Lankan religiosity (for example, the publications of Richard Gombrich and Gananath

Obeyesekere), it seems that there is a continuation from the late medieval Buddhist religiosity at the time when Vidyācakravartī was composing the *Butsaraṇa* to the popular mass religiosity in the modern period. This continuity, however, would not be an apparent, straightforward one but rather a continuity through phases of discontinuity. The apparent continuity from religious texts to devotional practices emerges as a consequence of using Sinhala prose texts such as *Saddharmaratnāvaliya* in more didactic ways of preaching practiced in late medieval Sri Lanka (Deegalle 1995). Seen from this socio-historical religious perspective, Vidyācakravartī's work stands as a landmark in bridging the gap between the views expressed in the Pāli canonical literature and non-canonical popular Buddhist practices with strong devotional tendencies that are found in the twentieth century Sri Lanka. I believe that historically the literary tendencies towards devotionalism represented in texts like the *Butsaraṇa* in Sinhala Buddhism attempt to explain two things: the way Sinhala Buddhism became very syncretistic and the way the atmosphere of competitive religious environment created within Theravāda against devotional tendencies from Śaivaist Hinduism and pietistic Mahāyāna cults.

CONCLUSION

I have introduced here some Sinhala Buddhist orientations to a devotional form of Theravāda. Late medieval Buddhists, for example, Vidyācakravartī, may have composed such theologically charged texts like the *Butsaraṇa* with or without the knowledge of the impact such creative works would have for future generations of Buddhists and scholars. Whatever may have been Vidyācakravartī's authorial intentions, at present Buddhologists are in an advantageous position in analyzing, interpreting and studying because they have access to a rich resource of vernacular Buddhist works for Buddhist theological discourse. More than Vidyācakravartī, Buddhologists and Buddhist theologians are in a position to judge the relevance, importance, and creativity of such materials; they are equipped with many resources for the study of Buddhist theology and devotional tendencies in Theravāda more than any late medieval Sinhala Buddhists like Vidyācakravartī ever were. My engagement with Vidyācakravartī here has been solely for the purpose of arousing intellectual and theological curiosity by pointing to a literature which has not been so far adequately explored in Buddhist theological discourse. I hope that Buddhist theologians will exploit these resources in building theories on Theravāda and will use them for general purposes of hermeneutics in creating intellectual categories, structures, and theories for the study of Sinhala Buddhism in Theravāda Sri Lanka.

NOTES

1 Note the existence of two different usages – "Buddhology" and "Buddhalogy." Western scholars who were researching on Buddhist traditions invented the term "Buddhology." In its German form, *Buddhologie* designated a discipline parallel to *Theologie* but it was conceived as much broader and vaguer in its connotations than "theology." In general, it was accepted as a scientific discipline on the study of Buddhism and hence came to be known as Buddhist Studies. However, those who invented the term "Buddhology" seem to have neglected to define it and reflect upon the implications of such a new term for the study of Buddhism and the practices of Buddhists. Though most previous scholars used "Buddhology" very vaguely to refer to, designate, and encompass any studies on Buddhism, "Buddhalogy" has been self-consciously invented recently to designate particular academic "discourse just about Buddha" (Griffiths: xvii-xviii).

2 See Laṅkānanda's edition of Vidyācakravartī's *Butsaraṇa* (1968) for clear separation of paragraphs with this refrain.

3 Compare this *Butsaraṇa* statement with that of the *Purāṇa Sinhala Baṇapota* (Śrī Ratnapala: 15–16) which states that at the time when the buddhas are not born (*abuddhotpādakāla*) one cannot listen to *saddhamma*.

4 *Kāma* is often defined as "pleasantness, pleasure–giving, an object of sensual enjoyment and sense–desire" (Rhys Davids and Stede: 203). This term is not analyzed or discussed much until its appearance in "later books of the Canon" (*ibid.*: 203), for example, the *Niddesa* which divides *kāma* into two types as (i) *vatthukāmā* (desires relating to external/physical objects) and (ii) *kilesakāmā* (desires relating to defilements).

5 The four-fold unpleasant states which Vidyācakravartī mentions are hell (*niraya*), the realms of animals (*tirisan*), spirits (*preta*), and titans (*asurakāya*). According to Theravāda Buddhism, sentient beings are born in five realms. They are broadly divided into two as *sugati* (realm of bliss) and *dugati* (realm of misery). They are hell (*niraya*), the realm of animals (*tirisan*; Pāli *tiracchānayoni*), the realm of spirits (*preta*; Pāli *pittivisaya*), the human world (Pāli *manussaloka*), and the world of gods (Pāli *devaloka*). While the first three are realms of misery, the last two are realms of bliss. These five *gatis* increased to six later (see next footnote).

6 Frank and Mani Reynolds draw our attention to a contemporary (14th century) Thai text called the *Three Worlds According to King Ruang* which has graphic descriptions of miserable (*dugati*) states. It

mentions six *gatis* – the realm of the hell beings, animals, suffering ghosts, *asura*, human, and *devatā* – and presents a detailed and graphic outline of hells such as Lohasimbali (Reynolds and Reynolds: 66–84).

7 In this respect, it is important to keep in mind the popularity of the cult of Maitreya, the future Buddha, in late medieval Sinhala Buddhism. The account of future Buddha Maitreya became the culminating ritual performance in the Two-pulpit preaching tradition (see Deegalle 1997b: 5–6).

8 Note the gradual disappearance of Buddhism from India, its birth place, at the end of twelfth century. While the attacks of the troops of the Turk Muḥammad Ghūrī on two major Buddhist universities – Nālandā (1197 CE) and Vikramaśīlā (1203 CE) – may have been one major factor for the decline and subsequent disappearance of Buddhism from India, recently scholars have also emphasized internal forces such as the gradual assimilation of Buddhism into Hinduism (Gómez:94-95).

9 In Polonnaruva, the Choḷas built Hindu temples for the worship of Śiva and Viṣṇu and one such important religious place is the Śiva Dēvālē No. 2. For more information on several sculptures of Hindu deities such as Śiva Naṭarāja, Pārvatī and Gaṇeśa that were discovered in Polonnaruva belonging to the eleventh and twelfth centuries see von Schroeder (109–133).

10 *e heyin sujanayan visin viṣṇu-maheśvarā dī bhakti nätiva tunuruvanhi ma bhakti ätiva sucarita purā nivan daham pasak kaṭa yutu*" (Dharmasēna Thera: 604).

11 *Buddhādīn kerehi ādara bhakti ätiva aihalaukika vūt pāralaukika vūt prayōjana sādhā gata yutu*" (Dharmasēna Thera:661).

12 Here I am reminded of Paul Griffiths's notion of "maximal greatness." According to Griffiths, for Buddhists the "Buddha is maximally great, that whatever great-making properties there are, Buddha has them maximally" (182). The relevance of the notion of "maximal greatness" for Sinhala Buddhist theological discourse will be further clear in the following discussion on Vidyācakravartī's use of *Jātaka* stories in narrating the Buddha's encounter with Aṅgulimāla.

13 See Laṅkānanda's 1968 edition of the *Butsaraṇa*.

REFERENCES

Buddhaghosa (1976). *Papañcasūdanī Majjhimanikāyā-ṭṭhakathā* [3: 328–344]. Ed. I. B. Horner. London: Pali Text Society.

Chalmers, R., ed. (1898). The *Majjhimanikāya* [2: 97–105]. London: Pali Text Society.

Deegalle, Mahinda (1995). *Baṇa: Buddhist Preaching in Sri Lanka* (*Special Focus on the Two-pulpit Tradition*). Ph.D. Dissertation, University of

Chicago.

Deegalle, Mahinda (1997a). "Buddhist Preaching and Sinhala Religious Rhetoric: Medieval Buddhist Methods to Popularize Theravāda." *Numen* (44) 180–210.

Deegalle, Mahinda (1997b). "Innovations in Theravāda Buddhist Rituals." *Journal of Indian and Tibetan Studies* (46: 1) 1–7 [520-514]

Deegalle, Mahinda (1997c). "Vernacular Buddhism: Neglected Sources in the Study of Sri Lankan Theravāda." *Japanese Journal of South Asian Studies* (9) 69–101.

Dharmasēna Thera (1971). *Saddharmaratnāvaliya*. Ed. Kiriälle Ñāṇavimala. Colombo: M. D. Gunasena.

Gombrich, R. F. (1971). *Precept and Practice: Traditional Buddhism in the Rural Highlands of Ceylon*. Oxford: The Clarendon Press.

Gombrich, R. F. and Gananath Obeyesekere (1988). *Buddhism Transformed: Religious Change in Sri Lanka*. Princeton, NJ: Princeton University Press.

Gómez, Luis O. (1989). "Buddhism in India." In Joseph M. Kitagawa and Mark D. Cummings, eds., *Buddhism and Asian History*. New York: Macmillan.

Griffiths, Paul J. (1994). *On Being Buddha: The Classical Doctrine of Buddhahood*. Albany, NY: State University of New York Press.

Guruḷugōmī (1972). *Amāvatura*. Ed. Väliviṭiyē Sorata. Mt. Lavinia: Abhaya Prakāṣakayō.

Hallisey, C. (1988). *Devotion in the Buddhist Literature of Medieval Sri Lanka*. Ph.D. Dissertation, University of Chicago.

Horner, I. B., trans. (1957). *The Middle Length Sayings* [2:284–292]. London: Pali Text Society.

Ogden, Schubert M. (1996). "Theology and Biblical Interpretation." *Journal of Religion* (76: 2) 172–188.

Rhys Davids, T. W. and William Stede, eds. (1972). *The Pali Text Society's Pali-English Dictionary*. London: Pali Text Society.

Reynolds, C. H. B., ed. (1970). *An Anthology of Sinhalese Literature up to 1815*. London: George Allen and Unwin.

Reynolds, Frank E. and Mani B. Reynolds (1982). *Three Worlds According to King Ruang: A Thai Buddhist Cosmology*. Berkeley: University of California Press.

Reynolds, Frank E. and C. Hallisey (1989). "Buddhist Religion, Culture and Civilization." In Joseph M. Kitagawa and Mark D. Cummings, eds., *Buddhism in Asian History*. New York: Macmillan.

Sannasgala, P. B. (1964). *Siṃhala Sāhitya Vaṃṣaya*. Colombo: Lake House.

von Schroeder, U. (1992). *The Golden Age of Sculpture in Sri Lanka: Masterpieces of Buddhist and Hindu Bronzes from Museums in Sri Lanka*. Hong Kong: Visual Dharma Publications.

Śrī Ratanapala, Jinavaradharmakīrti, ed. (1929). *Purāṇa Sinhala Baṇapota*. Colombo: Mahābodhi Yantrālaya.

Vidyācakravartī (1966). *Butsaraṇa*. Ed. Väliviṭa Sorata Nāyaka Thera. Mt.

Lavinia: Abhaya Prakāṣakayō.
Vidyācakravartī (1968). *Butsaraṇa*. Ed. by Labugama Laṅkānanda. Colombo: M. D. Gunasena.
Weber, Max (1966). *The Sociology of Religion*. London: Social Science Paperbacks.
Wickramasinghe, M. (1963). *Landmarks of Sinhalese Literature*. Trans. E. R. Sarachchandra. Colombo: M. D. Gunasena.

Eighteen

Concern for Others in Pure Land Soteriological and Ethical Considerations: The Case of *Jōgyō daihi* in Jōdo-Shinshū Buddhism[1]

Kenneth K. Tanaka

PREFACE

The classical Western view of Buddhism as "ahistorical," "passive," and "pessimistic" is well known. According to Thomas Tweed, a scholar of early Buddhism in America, these very qualities[2] contributed to the failure of Buddhism to make greater inroads into American culture in the late nineteenth and early twentieth century (Tweed: 133–156). Among the various Buddhist traditions, Pure Land doctrine is especially prone to this characterization on account of the otherworldly, transcendent qualities of its cardinal doctrines. Sukhāvatī Pure Land, for example, is said to exist far beyond our Sahā World, "billions of Buddha lands to the west" (*Taishō* 12: 270a, 346c). Similar separation characterizes later views on of the relationship between the spiritual and the secular realms. Rennyo (1415-1499), for example, urged his Jōdo-Shinshū followers to keep their faith private: "First of all, outwardly, take the laws of the state as fundamental. . . . Inwardly, rely single-heartedly and steadfastly on Amida Tathāgata for [birth in the Pure Land in] the afterlife" (Rogers: 215–16).[3]

Contemporary writers continue to subscribe to these views, especially concerning Jōdo-Shinshū, which has the largest following among the Pure Land traditions in Japan today. Christian theologian John Cobb, Jr., for example, states:

> Jodoshinshu has not yet worked through the crisis of the relation of history to faith. If this crisis must be faced, then in some respects its problems are more acute even than those faced by Christianity, for its basis is still further removed from the actual course of history. (Cobb: 139)

Similarly, Shin'ichi Hisamatsu, a Zen scholar and practitioner, note

> In Shinshū, even though we may have attained *shinjin*[4] in this life, we are incapable in our present existence of performing any actions associated with the aspect of returning.[5] (Hisamatsu: 376–377)

In the eyes of both of these writers who sit outside the tradition, Jōdo-Shinshū teaching and, by implication, its modern manifestation do not lead to an active involvement in the world. Cobb expresses this separation in classically Christian terms, "of the relation of history to faith," while Hisamatsu focuses on Jōdo-Shinshū's apparent belief in one's inability in this life to help others with spiritual as well as social and economic issues.

In a rebuttal to such critiques, Jōdo-Shinshū scholar Takamaro Shigaraki argued for the existence of a socially active dimension in the Jōdo-Shinshū teachings, based largely on the writings of the founder, Shinran (1173-1263) (Shigaraki: 219–249). While I find Shigaraki's arguments convincing, the rebuttal focused on the founder's views articulated some 750 years ago, and did not address the conditions of contemporary Jōdo-Shinshū institutions. Shigaraki, an outspoken critic of the Nishi-Hongwanji[6] establishment, would be the first to admit to the chasm that exists between the actual teachings of Shinran and the socially passive stance of contemporary institutions.

In recent years, however, we have witnessed some socially progressive initiatives within the Nishi-Hongwanji institution. A prime example is the antidiscrimination movement (*dōbō-undō*) which was initiated forty some years ago to eliminate discrimination against the Buraku-min ("hamlet people"),[7] many of whom are Jōdo-Shinshū Buddhists (Nakao: 195–251). Secondly, Jōdo-Shinshū priests and lay persons are at the forefront of a nationwide campaign to oppose what they regard as a constitutional breach of the separation of church and state. They are critical of the government's support of Yasukuni Shinto Shrine, evidenced in its public patronage by high government officials, including the prime minister[8] (Hishiki: 15). Further, there has been a growing self-criticism among certain segments within both Nishi and Higashi-Hongwanji institutions for their role in the doctrinal and political affirmation of the war efforts during World War II (*senji kyōgaku*) (Hishiki: 2–16).

These developments may indicate an evolution towards greater social engagement, but they are still limited to select groups. The majority of Jōdo-Shinshū temples show little evidence of active involvement in these issues. As one of the "established" Kamakura Period schools, the Jōdo-Shinshū institutions as a whole remain, relatively speaking, socially conservative. This becomes apparent when they are compared to Risshō Kōseikai and Sōka Gakkai, two of the largest schools that have attained prominence since World War II. The reluctance of most contemporary Nishi-Hongwanji members to become more active socially is reinforced by doctrinal explanations of the teachings. Nowhere is this seen more clearly than in the frequent citing of the following section from Chapter Four of the *Tannishō* ("An Essay Lamenting Deviations"):[9]

> Compassion in the Path of the Sages is to pity, sympathize with, and care for beings. . . . *Compassion in the Pure Land path lies in saying the Name, quickly attaining Buddhahood, and freely benefiting sentient beings with a heart of great love and great compassion.* In our present lives, it is hard to carry out the desire to aid others however much love and tenderness we may feel; hence such compassion always falls short of fulfillment. *Only the saying of the Name manifests the heart of great compassion (*daijihi-shin*) that is replete and thoroughgoing.* (Hirota 1982: 24)

Here we find a direct reference to a "heart of great compassion," which manifests completely only in recitation of the Name of Amida ("Namo Amida Butsu"). One is encouraged to recite the Name in this life and quickly become a Buddha in the next, wherein one is freely able to benefit others. However, recitation is carried out in the present life without any expressed or conscious concern for others. Any benefit to others is postponed until one realizes Buddhahood upon death. Therefore, in this life, the reciting of the Name is seen as the *only* way to do full justice in manifesting the mind of great compassion. The scope of one's spiritual activity is limited to oral recitation of the Name within the context of one's own realization of Buddhahood. The expression of compassion in this life is, therefore, limited to one form – recitation – and is noticeably introverted and lacking any clear sense of interconnection with others and their spiritual search.

I would here argue, as Professor Shigaraki did earlier, that this characterization is inadequate to the total body of Shinran's teachings, and go a step further in stating that it also does not agree with later Jōdo-Shinshū thinkers, some of whom lived during the extremely conservative Tokugawa Period. (1602-1867) This essay derives its cue from modern researchers who have shown that contemporary religious understandings are often neither as original nor authentic as the respective traditions would have us believe. According to these findings, received traditions are often the product of recent interpretations. As examples of recent publications, *Curators of the*

Buddha (Lopez) supports this argument concerning a number of traditions, and *The Rhetoric of Immediacy* (Faure) and *Dōgen's Manuals of Zen Tradition* (Bielefeldt) have accomplished the same for the Japanese Zen tradition. With regard to East Asian Pure Land Buddhism, *Visions of Sukhāvatī* followed a similar line of investigation, focusing on the role played by Shan-tao (613-681) (Pas). My own work, focusing on another Chinese Pure Land figure, Ching-ying Hui-yüan (523-592), questioned many of our assumptions about the development of Chinese Pure Land thought (Tanaka).

JŌGYŌ DAIHI AND ITS INTERPRETATIONS

Shinran's view of spiritual transformation in this life (known chiefly as *shinjin*) is that it automatically expresses itself in one's involvement with others. This is seen particularly in the doctrine of *jōgyō daihi* ("constantly practicing great compassion") that constitutes one of the "ten benefits in the present life" (*genshō jisshu no yaku*). These ten are found in the "Faith Chapter" of Shinran's *magnum opus*, the *Kyōgyōshinshō* ("Teachings, Practice, Faith and Realization"): (1) being protected and sustained by unseen powers, (2) being possessed of supreme virtues, (3) our karmic evil being transformed into good, (4) being protected and cared for by all the Buddhas, (5) being praised by all the Buddhas, (6) being constantly protected by the light of the Buddha's heart, (7) having great joy in our hearts, (8) being aware of Amida's benevolence and of responding in gratitude to his virtues, (9) constantly practicing great compassion, and 10) entering the Stage of the Truly Settled (*shojoju*) (Ueda, vol. II: 257–258).

Today, the precise meaning of *jōgyō daihi* has become, in my view, noticeably vague or generally not well understood. If there is any consensus among the general Shin Buddhist adherents today, this term is understood – and vaguely at that – to mean "to recite the Name" in a similar fashion as the *Tannishō* Chapter Four passage discussed above. However, since Shinran did not fully explain its meaning in the *Kyōgyōshinshō*, this common modern understanding could very well have evolved after Shinran's time, particularly in the doctrinally conservative environment resulting from the Sangōwakuran Controversy (described below) which concluded in 1806.

During the Tokugawa Period, the government used the Buddhist temples as government outposts where the people's official records were kept. All members of the same family were required to belong to the same school, and priests were discouraged from suggesting any new ideas that were not already in the tradition. Within this restrictive environment, the Buddhist schools were banned from preaching the Dharma to convert new followers.

A major doctrinal argument broke out among the scholars of Nishi-Hongwanji at the end of the 1700s. On one side stood the professors of the Academy (the highest center of sectarian learning) in Kyoto and on the other side were the scholar-priests in the Nishi-Hongwanji branch temples. The Academy professors emphasized the dynamic, active dimension of *shinjin* as manifested in one's daily activities. They valued the importance of expressing spiritual understanding through thought, speech, and actions. The technical name for this is "the three karmic actions" (*sangō*) of mind, body, and speech, from which the name of the controversy is derived.

On the other hand, the scholar-priests from temples in the outlying areas argued that the serene mind (*shingyō*) of *shinjin* is central to the life of the person of *shinjin*. In their view, the privileging of three karmic actions by their opponents came dangerously close to self-power (*jiriki*) practice, which Shinran categorically rejected. The clash between the two factions can be seen as that between a more active and outward interpretation versus a more passive and inward emphasis.

While arguments about doctrine were nothing new to the Shinshū scholarly community, this dispute is notable in the degree to which the government controlled and interfered in the affairs of religious institutions. Given the conservative tenor of Tokugawa society, it is not surprising, therefore, that the government courts finally brought an end to the argument in 1806 by deciding against what it perceived as change in the established doctrine. The courts ruled in favor of the more passive definition favored by the scholar-priests, a decision based largely on one simplistic rule: Accept the old and reject the new. Chido, the head professor of the Academy at the time, not only lost the case but faced exile to a distant island. Although Chido died in prison before this verdict was handed down, it is reported that his ashes were sent to the island in his place!

This dispute and the way it was solved had a strong impact on subsequent interpretations of the teachings, for today, the passive definition of *shinjin* is dominant in the Nishi-Hongwanji teachings. Emphasis is on the activities of Amida Buddha over those of the human seeker, the discussions of which are generally framed in such doctrinal categories as *hottoku* ("Dharmic virtues" of Amida) and *kisō* ("the characteristics of the capacity" of seekers), respectively. With the dominance of the *hottoku* position, there is less representation of the active definition of *shinjin*, whose advocates lost out in the government decision of 1806.

SUBSEQUENT SHIN COMMENTATORS

The passive modern understanding with regard to *jōgyō-daihi* is shown in a completely different light, however, when we look at the earliest Shin writings on the subject. Zonkaku (1290-1373), in his *Rokuyōshō,* the earliest extant commentary on Shinran's *Kyōgyōshinshō*, comments:

> The ninth benefit of *jōgyō daihi* is to be understood in accord with the meaning as explained in the passage from the *Great Compassion Sūtra* that is quoted in this scroll. (*SSZ* 2: 298)

That passage from the *Great Compassion Sūtra* is quoted in Shinran's *Kyōgyōshinshō* in the section on the "Buddha's true disciple" and as part of a long section cited from Tao-ch'o's *An-le-chi*:

> The *Sūtra of Great Compassion* states: What is "great compassion"? Those who continue solely in the recitation of the Name of the Buddha (*nembutsu*) without any interruption will thereby be born without fail in the land of happiness at the end of life. If these people *encourage each other and bring others to recite the Name*, they are all called "people who practice great compassion." (emphasis added) (*SSZ* 2: 306)

This *sūtra* passage advocates a range of activity that goes beyond mere recitation solely for one's own benefit. Followers are to mutually encourage oral recitation, and succeed in *getting others to recite the Name*. A mere recitation for oneself is insufficient, for only by encouraging others would followers qualify as "people who practice great compassion." This activity, furthermore, is to be actualized in this life, *prior* to both the realization of birth in the Pure Land and realization of Buddhahood.[10]

Zonkaku, then, comments on this sutra passage and, in my view, expands its meaning even further:

> In the latter passage, the statement "Those who continue solely . . ." reveals the benefit of birth [in the Pure Land] as benefit for oneself (*jiri*). The statement "If these people encourage . . ." reveals the benefit of the great compassion as benefiting others (*rita*). (*Sōsho* 2: 699–700)

By invoking the well-known Mahāyāna concept of benefiting others (Sanskrit *parārtha*; Japanese *rita*), Zonkaku significantly broadens the passage's meaning. The act of encouraging others to recite the Name constitutes an activity that benefits others in distinction to that which benefits oneself.

A similar view is expressed by Kaku'on (Senpū'in, 1821-1907). In his evaluation of the ten benefits mentioned earlier, Kaku'on includes the benefit of *jōgyō daihi* under the category of "the two benefits carried out by the practitioner" (*gyōja niri*). And of the two categories, he characterizes *jōgyō daihi* as benefiting others (*rita*), while the seventh and eighth benefits are seen as benefits for oneself (*jiri*). Kaku'on, therefore, clearly acknowledges *jōgyō daihi* as benefiting others as opposed to the self. Of particular interest to this discussion is the emphasis of this benefit as an attribute or activity of the seeker, not only that of Amida. Even though the source of compassion derives ultimately from Amida, Kaku'on sees this benefit as an explicit activity of the seeker, and one that is specifically directed to benefiting others.

Gizan (Gankai'in, 1824-1910) further expands Kaku'on's position:

> Next, *jōgyō daihi* is based on the *Great Compassion Sūtra* quoted in the *Anrakushū* which is cited below. The *Wasan* (*Shozōmatsu,* verse #97) states, "Without any repentance and shame," which addresses the point of view of Dharmic virtue (*hottoku)* as the object of faith and of recitation. However, Rōken'in maintains that if a practicer today were to give a Dharma talk to his wife and children it would constitute a dimension of *jōgyō daihi.* He has said that since the *Anrakushū* states, "If these people encourage each other and bring others to recite the Name, they are all called 'people who practice great compassion,'" *the activities of propagating great compassion should not be confined exclusively to the recitation of the Name.* (emphasis added) (*Sōsho* 2: 670-701)

Gizan explicitly acknowledges modes of exercising great compassion by means other than the recitation of the Name, for example, that of giving a Buddhist sermon to one's own spouse and children. While he gives no other examples, his view of exercising *jōgyō daihi* clearly includes benefiting others. I would further argue that, in the context of his commentary, Gizan went out of his way to make this point.

This broader perspective focused on human activity raises another interesting point in that Gizan expressly proposes his views in contradistinction to what he calls "Dharmic virtue" (*hottoku*), which as alluded to above refers to the point of view of the activity of Amida or the ultimate. The Dharmic virtue point of view was articulated by

En'getsu (Jōman'in, 1818-1902):

> The three benefits beginning with the seventh [benefit] constitute the manifestation (*sōhotsu*) of the practicer. . . . According to Jōshin'in, the benefit of *jōgyō daihi* derives from the fact that the Name is none other than the practice which is the transference of Tathāgata's great compassion, and that the recitation of the Name is none other than the practicing of Tathāgata's great compassion. The *Wasan*, "Without any repentance and shame, even though I lack any element of true mind, the virtues fill the ten directions of the universe with the Name that is transferred to us by Amida." How can this not be the practice of great compassion! (*Sōsho* 2: 670–671)

En'getsu's position emphasizes Dharmic virtue. Amida Tathāgata is herein given a prominent role as the ultimate source and agent of the great compassion. The *Wasan* that is quoted reinforces the greatly diminished capabilities of the practitioner (*kisō*) in contrast to the virtues of the Name that fills the universe. In contrast, Gizan's position as discussed earlier does not base itself on the perspective of Dharmic virtue but instead emphasizes the perspective of the practitioner. Gizan also makes it clear that his perspective is not informed by that of Dharmic virtue; accordingly, he does not appeal to the *Wasan* passage which En'getsu specifically cited in support of his Dharmic virtue perspective.

A representative exegete of the Ōtani or Higashi-Hongwanji Branch, Jinrei (Kōgatsu'in, 1749-1817) had earlier articulated a position similar to that of Gizan when he commented:

> The ninth benefit, the *jōgyō daihi* is based in the *Great Compassion Sūtra* as quoted in the *Anraku-shū* passage cited below. *Jōgyō daihi* refers to the practicers of Other Power *shinjin* who constantly engage in continuous recitation of the Name and mutually encourage others [to recite the Name] in the spirit of "*to realize* shinjin *and lead others to* shinjin" (*jishin kyōninshin*). The one moment (*ichinen)* of *shinjin* endowed by the Other Power is none other than the "*mind to save all beings*" (*do-shujō-shin).* Consequently, when one obtains this mind of saving others, one becomes a person who constantly practices the Buddha's great compassion that is expressed as "to realize *shinjin* and guide others to *shinjin.*"
>
> The eighth and the ninth benefits form a set. Being aware of Amida's benevolence and of responding in gratitude to his

> virtue (*chi'on hōtoku*) [the eighth benefit] constitutes the benefit to oneself expressed to the Buddha, *while the [ninth benefit] of* jōgyō daihi *is the benefit of converting others.* (emphasis added) (*Kōgi*: 470)

Jinrei, thus, promotes an even greater active involvement of the practitioner in sharing the teachings with others. He cites a well-known Pure Land Buddhist ideal "to realize *shinjin* and guide others to *shinjin*," a phrase attributed to a T'ang Period Chinese proponent of Pure Land teaching, Shan-tao. And this is also associated, if not identified, with the concept of "the mind of saving sentient beings." In effect, Jinrei regards the practitioner as embodying (*mi ni suru*) the mind of saving sentient beings which emanates from Amida. That Jinrei associated *jōgyō daihi* with the practitioner's act to reach out to or involve others is clearly evident in his usage of the term "benefit of converting others."

JŌGYŌ DAIHI AS A DIMENSION OF *HŌ'ONGYŌ*

This demonstration of the deeper meaning of *jōgyō daihi* should hardly be surprising, as it relates directly to the well-established Jōdo-Shinshū teaching of *hō'ongyō*, "action of responding in gratitude to the Buddha's benevolence." *Hō'ongyō*, a term known widely and intimately by many lay followers, is defined by former professor of Ryūkoku University Daien Fugen as "the propagation of great compassion" (*daihi denke*). (Fugen 1963: 296) In support of this view, Fugen cites the well-known passage from Shan-tao's commentary:

> To realize *shinjin* and to guide others to *shinjin* is among the difficult things yet even more difficult. To awaken beings everywhere to great compassion is truly to respond in gratitude to the Buddha's benevolence. (Fugen 1963: 296)

It would, thus, be safe to understand *jōgyō daihi* as a central element of *hō'ongyō*, or at the very least one of its expressions.

In Jōdo-Shinshū doctrinal development, theories and debates abound with regard to the range of activities that constitutes *hō'ongyō*. The Kūge doctrinal school, for example, maintained that *hō'ongyō* is expressed in the Five Contemplative Gates (*gonen-mon*).[11] The Seikisen school, in contrast, focused on the Five Correct Practices (*goshō-gyō*)[12] and stressed the recitation of the Name (*shōmyō*) as the primary action (*shōgō*), with the other four as supporting actions (*jogō*).

These discussions on the scope of *hō'ongyō* have generally been articulated within the categories of the Five Contemplative Gates and the Five Correct Practices. However, Daien Fugen has raised serious questions about limiting *hō'ongyō* to these categories. He cites the contributions of past teachers and lay practitioners who built temple halls, erected statues, and lit lanterns and burned incense. These actions, he argues, should be included as *hō'ongyō* so long as they are carried out in appreciation for the Other Power without the attitude of self-power.

Fugen, then, proceeds to include within the term *hō'ongyō* all actions in both the secular and religious arenas. To support this claim, Fugen notes that both Shinran and Rennyo (1415-1499)[13] prohibited the criticism of the teachings of other Buddhists and non-Buddhists, discouraged unethical actions, and encouraged the respect of secular authority and virtues. All of these, in Fugen's view, should be subsumed under supporting actions (*jogō*). To support this opinion, Fugen cites a passage from the *Wagotōroku* and underscores a section that stresses activities that are ordinarily not regarded as religious, "Actions related to the three activities of clothing, eating, and dwelling are the supporting actions of Nembutsu." These mundane activities qualify as proper *hō'ongyō* , enabling one to lead a truly religious life. Gizan articulated an enhanced scope of activities when he, as we saw earlier, cited preaching to his wife and children as a form of *jōgyō daihi* and concluded, "The activities of the propagation of great compassion should not be confined exclusively to the recitation of the Name" (*Sōsho* 2: 671).

Jōgyō daihi as one of the expressions of *hō'ongyō* particularly strengthens the element of reaching out horizontally to others. This was amply evident in many of the commentators such as Zonkaku, Kaku'on, and Jinrei who singled out *jōgyō daihi* among the ten benefits as one that specifically benefited others. Jinrei was particularly forceful in making this point as he contrasts *jōgyō daihi* with the eighth benefit, that of being aware of Amida's benevolence and of responding in gratitude to his virtue. Jinrei sees the eighth benefit as a self-benefit expressed to the Buddha, while *jōgyō daihi* constitutes a benefit of converting others. Jinrei further amplified this distinction when he invoked the concept of *jishin kyōninshin*, "to realize *shinjin* and to guide others to *shinjin*," as one of the primary features of *jōgyō daihi.*

In conclusion, our examination of several representative premodern and modern commentators shows that *jōgyō daihi* has not always been interpreted simply as one's act of oral recitation. Starting with Zonkaku, there has existed a strong tendency to regard this benefit in a broader context as: (1) encouraging others to engage in oral recitation, (2) manifesting the benefit in actions other than oral recitation, (3) regarding these actions as benefiting others in the classical Mahayana sense, (4) stressing the practitioner's role over that of Amida Tathāgata, and (5) concentrating on the activities of the present life.

In unearthing a broader meaning to *jōgyō daihi* as we have done, we find ourselves with a more solid doctrinal grounding for encouraging and justifying Jōdo-Shinshū involvement in the world. These interpretations further compel us to reevaluate the modern common understanding of *jōgyō daihi* as epitomized by the narrow reading of the *Tannishō* Chapter Four passage examined at the outset of this essay. In so doing, we became open to a more nuanced reading of that passage, inspired by another passage from the *Tannishō,* this time, in Chapter Five:

> For all living beings have been my parents and brothers and sisters in the course of countless lives in the many states of existences. (Hirota: 25)

JŌGYŌ DAIHI AS A MODERATING FORCE IN CONTEMPORARY ETHICS

In considering the implications of the above conclusions, I believe that *jōgyō daihi* reveals a paradigm for a basis of action that is (1) more spiritually-based and (2) more self-reflective[14] than the dominant forms of ethical models found in the West. As such, *jōgyō daihi* has the potential to add fresh insights to the field of contemporary ethics.

As demonstrated above, *jōgyō daihi* is not divorced from but an integral dimension of a spiritual or soteriological transformation referred to in Jōdo-Shinshū as *shinjin. Jōgyō daihi* is, thus, part of the paradigmatic Buddhist aim of realizing enlightenment by overcoming greed, hatred, and delusion, which are the root of one's spiritual pain (*duḥkha*) and, by extension, the suffering caused by social ills.

In this sense, *jōgyō daihi* can be seen in the context of Buddhist social and ethical actions which are regarded as inseparable from spiritual cultivation. Kenneth Kraft, for example, observes that modern Buddhist activists, especially Westerners, find a distinctive Buddhist perspective in that "social work entails inner work," and that while other religiously motivated activists share this view to some degree, it is the engaged Buddhists who apply this most consistently (Kraft: 12). The same integration of spiritual cultivation and social action is also well attested to in the life and writings of Thich Nhat Hanh, whose "engaged Buddhism" emerged from applying the insights gained in monastic practice to social relief and peace work done during the Vietnam War (Kraft: 17–23).

The above Buddhist perspective contends that, without the spiritual cultivation and transformation of the individual, society faces only temporary solutions. That is precisely the reason why ethical actions and social reforms based on socio-economic ideologies are believed to be ultimately inadequate.[15] Influencing these ideologies are the rationally-based, Kantian-inspired ethical models known generally in the West as deontological and teleological.[16] In both instances, one's motivation for action is not necessarily rooted in the spiritual dimension.[17]

In contrast to these categories, *jōgyō daihi* is similar to another category of Western ethics, generally known as "virtue ethics."[18] While "virtue ethics" and *jōgyō daihi* are not identical, they are similar in terms of the value placed on cultivating the self and the importance of one's virtue as the basis of ethical action.[19] A practitioner in this mode of ethics is, therefore, spontaneously motivated by compassionate concern for others arising from his or her personal virtues, and, in the case of *jōgyō daihi,* by the realization of an intimate interconnectedness with others in which he does not see himself as standing separate from and superior to others.

I wish now to turn to the second of two points, the self-reflective character of *jōgyō daihi.* This character can, ironically, be discerned in the very same *Tannishō* Chapter Four passage whose narrow modern interpretation I criticized in the first half of this paper. However, my criticism was directed at the passive and self-centered interpretation of human *actions*, as I personally agree with its evaluation of human *nature*. From the latter perspective, I find this excerpt from that passage particularly resonant:

> . . . it is hard to carry out the desire to aid others however much love and tenderness we may feel; hence such compassion always falls short of fulfillment. (Hirota: 24).

How often do we find ourselves falling miserably short of our idealistic aspirations to help others? Time and time again in my own life, I have been struck by the truth of Shinran's penetrating insight. I can see that my character is full of noble intentions, but in the final analysis unable to deliver even one-tenth of the initial inspiration. Not only am I not capable of giving fully to others but am actually taking a great deal from others. In fact, my very livelihood hinges on the sacrifices of other living beings. To be blunt, my salary depends on the sale of thousands of barbecued chickens at the temple bazaars, a major source of income of the Buddhist temples that support our educational institution. The Dharma encourages non-taking of life, but this Dharma "teacher" must depend on that very transgression. My profession, in a sense, is a dilemma, as is my very existence if I seek to fulfill Buddhism's highest ideal, which is refraining from taking life.

I have felt a similar sense of uneasiness and guilt about the Vietnam War. Over sixty thousand Americans of my generation paid the ultimate price, and many still continue to suffer from severe physical and psychological scars. My sorrow extends to the over two million Vietnamese who died and were maimed in the conflict as a result of weaponry bought with the taxes I paid. I did what I could to oppose the war, yet my efforts are no consolation for the victims. I did not condone the war, yet I was and continue to be a citizen of the U.S., which has become the most affluent and dominant nation in the world. As a member of this nation, I am partly responsible for its actions, no matter how insignificant my influence in this society. I am even more ashamed that these remorseful thoughts do not last long. Most of the time I am too busy and involved in my day to day life. As the Vietnam War slips further into the shadows of our history, it fades from my memory too easily.

These personal reflections lend credence to Shinran's self-appraisal in the Postscript of the *Tannishō*:

> I know nothing of what is good or evil. For if I could know thoroughly, as is known in the mind of Amida, that an act was good, then I would know the meaning of "good." If I could know thoroughly, as Amida knows, that an act was evil, than I would know "evil." But for a foolish being full of blind passions in this fleeting world – this burning house – all matters without exception are lies and gibberish, totally without truth and sincerity. The Nembutsu alone is true and real. (Hirota: 44).

The point of this statement is not moral relativism or anarchism, as Shinran clearly acknowledged the importance of conventional morality and ethics.[20] Instead, Shinran felt he lacked the ability to know good and evil in the ultimate sense, from an ultimate perspective as expressed in the phrase, "known in the mind of Amida."[21]

Shinran's reticence to be adamant and absolutist regarding the question of good and evil was due not only to his evaluation of human nature but also rooted in his assumption that Amida did not participate *directly* in his ethical decision-making. This issue was elaborated by later Jōdo-Shinshū commentators. For them, Amida as the ultimate truth does not manifest *directly* in human actions or deeds. The only exception is the spontaneous utterance of the Name, "Namo Amida Butsu." The Name is considered the only direct emanating action (*sōhotsu*) while other actions are carried out indirectly based on human reason (*risei*). Gizan of the Sekisen school describes this with a metaphor of a man who is under the influence of alcoholic beverage (*sake* in this case). The man begins to sing and dance. However, according to Gizan, his singing and dancing are the effects of being drunk, not the *direct* effect of the *sake*. Just as *sake* is not the direct source of this man's merry behavior, Amida is not the direct source of human ethical actions. Rather, the *realization* of *shinjin* results in compassionate and ethical actions. (Fugen: 286)

I have discussed at length the Jōdo-Shinshū evaluation of human nature in relation to ethical considerations in order to counteract the tendency in some ethical models to place excessive faith in human capability, without placing sufficient value on the need for serious spiritual cultivation. This tendency is evident in the deontological and, perhaps to a lesser extent, in the teleological models mentioned above.

Even within progressive Christian circles, considerable credence and faith is given to human ethical judgment, based on the strength of God's participation. Professor Cobb, for example, speaks of actions that are motivated by the "promptings of the Spirit":

> For Christians the goal is to decide in accordance with the promptings of the Spirit. In this way the blind will to live finds its true fulfillment in real life. (Cobb and Christopher: 98)

How do these promptings manifest themselves? And how does one know if these promptings are those of the Spirit/God or merely his own? Whatever the answer, the response will be ultimately be a *human* response. And given the above discussion of human nature, I find myself being extremely cautious of ethical actions that are based on divinely-sanctioned impulses. In the hands of a virtuous person within a supportive and self-reflective community as in the case of Dr. Martin Luther King, Jr., a divine prompting can unleash a powerful prophetic message. However, there is potential for immense abuse by psychologically deranged or emotionally unstable persons. Assassinations of well-known leaders from Gandhi to Yitzak Rabin have been inspired by divine impulses; the assassins are frequently members of the victim's ethnic or religious group.

In contrast, *jōgyō daihi* offers an approach that is more self-reflective, as well as tolerant of other differing positions. Some may find that it lacks the certitude of a divinely-inspired action. However, self-criticism, humility, and openness to others are crucial qualities in a world of nations and communities with widely divergent value systems. Perhaps *jōgyō daihi* can be included among other resources in the formulation of uncharted ethical considerations for healing old wounds and forging new cooperation.

NOTES

1 Some parts of this essay are based on an earlier essay. See Tanaka 1994.

2 Specifically, the late-Victorian Christian critics "agreed that Buddhism was passive and pessimistic." These features contrasted with activism and optimism. See Tweed: 133.

3 In fairness to Rennyo (the Eighth Monshu or Head of the Hongwanji branch), his admonition should be appreciated as a survival strategy, for his fledgling religious community existed in an unstable, warring political environment. However, his views became mainstream even after his school subsequently evolved into one of the most dominant and established Buddhist institutions.

4 The term literally means "trust or faith" (*shin*) and "mind-heart" (*jin*), and refers to a spiritual transformation that is realized in this life. Having attained the state of non-retrogression, a person of *shinjin* is assured of realizing Buddhahood in the Pure Land immediately upon death.

5 "Aspect of returning" (*gensō*) refers to the phase of returning from the Pure Land to a world of *saṃsāra* as an enlightened bodhisattva, when one is freely able to carry out actions to benefit others. This is in contrast to the "aspect of going" (*ōsō*) to the Pure Land, when one is still unenlightened and thus incapable of freely and completely benefiting others. Hence, Hisamatsu is arguing that since a person of *shinjin* is still in the aspect of going, he is not able to carry out thoroughgoing actions to help others completely.

6 Nishi-Hongwanji is one of the two largest branches of Jōdo-Shinshū, the other being Higashi-Hongwanji. They are also known as Honpa-Hongwanji and Ōtani, respectively. Prior to their split in 1580, they were of one school known as Hongwanji.

7 Buraku-min refers to an outcast segment of the Japanese population, whose ancestors in the medieval period were involved in reviled occupations such as butchering animals and working with hides. Despite their legal equality since World War II, their descendants

continue to be subjected to social discrimination, particularly in marriage. Their identity is traced through their family registries and addresses that are often identified with hamlets where the Burakumins were ghettoized.

8 Prime Minister Nakasone, for example, paid a visit to the shrine in 1985.

9 For example, Shigaraki cites this to point out the uniqueness of compassion in Pure Land Buddhism. (Shigaraki: 238) Further, I personally recall this passage being invoked by those who voted against a proposed human rights statement at a 1993 National Council meeting of the Buddhist Churches of America.

10 Departing radically from earlier Pure Land traditions, Shinran regards (1) birth in the Pure Land and (2) realizing Buddhahood as virtually a simultaneous process. One becomes a Buddha immediately upon birth in the Pure Land. The Pure Land is no longer a locus of spiritual practice.

11 The five are bowing, praise, aspiration for rebirth, visualization, and transfer of merit.

12 The five, according to traditional Jōdo-Shinshū understanding, are chanting of *sūtras*, visualization, bowing, recitation of the Name, and praise and offering.

13 The eighth Monshu of the Hongwanji Branch prior to the split into Nishi and Higashi.

14 I am using "self-reflective" to refer to an outlook that directs one's critical evaluation onto one's own assumptions, motivation, and behavior rather than onto others'.

15 One such example, though admittedly overly generalized, is the pervasive corruption among Communist Party leaders; its contribution to the disintegration of the Soviet system is now all too well known.

16 The deontological approach understands morality primarily in terms of duty, law or obligation. The concern in this approach focuses on right versus wrong. The teleological approach sees morality as a means for realizing what lies at the end as the ultimate goal (e.g., the union with the Ultimate or a birth in a paradise) and is concerned less with the question of right but more with relationship to the goal. See Eliade, vol. 3: 341a.

I would be remiss if I failed to note that Buddhist precepts contain elements of the teleological and deontological. For example, the Theravāda monks' adherence to the 227 *Pāṭimokkha* rules are motivated by their aim to reach their goal (teleological) of enlightenment and by the fact that they are required (deontological) to follow the rules as their monastic requirement.

17 This statement requires qualification, since there have been ethical thinkers who were spiritually inclined but who also subscribed to teleological or deontological approaches. My intent here is to focus on the rationally-based and spiritually-diminished nature of these models, largely rooted in the Kantian perspective on ethics.

18 Virtue ethics is often associated with the classical Greek philosophers, most notably within the Socratic-Platonic line. In both *jōgyō daihi* and virtue ethics, one's innate virtue (not one's sense of obligation or pragmatic considerations) informs and determines his or her handling of ethical issues.

19 One point of divergence can be seen in the manner in which virtue is cultivated: dialectic for Socrates and true entrusting for Shinran. There is a need for more comparative analysis of the two approaches beyond the essay by Lee and Leong.

20 Shinran severely reprimanded "licensed evil" (*zōaku-muge*), when some mistaken disciples advocated that they could intentionally commit evil since the Vow of Amida Buddha was unobstructed by evil deeds. He thus admonished, "Do no take a liking to poison just because there is an antidote." The antidote refers to Amida's Vow. (Hirota: 33–34)

21 It is important to remember that Shinran's evaluation was not forced upon him by the weight of his tradition, but emerged in a context. In the course of twenty years of spiritual cultivation as a Tendai monk accompanied by intense, uncompromising introspection, Shinran arrived at his evaluation of himself as a *bonnō guzoku no bombu*, "a foolish being full of blind passions." It must, however, be pointed out that this devastating but honest self-evaluation emerged within the context of his being affirmed unconditionally by the compassionate Vow of Amida, concretely expressed in the Nembutsu, or the oral recitation of the Name.

REFERENCES

Bielefeldt, Carl (1988). *Dōgen's Manuals of Zen Meditation.*. Berkeley, Los Angeles, London: University of California Press.

Cobb, John Jr. (1982). *Beyond Dialogue: Toward a Mutual Transformation of Christianity and Buddhism.* Philadelphia: Fortress Press.

Cobb, John Jr. and Christopher Ives (1990). *The Emptying God: A Buddhist-Jewish-Christian and Conversation.* Maryknoll, NY: Orbis Books.

Eliade, Mircea, ed. (1987). *Encyclopedia of Religion.* 16 vols. New York: Macmillan.

Faure, Bernard (1991). *The Rhetoric of Immediacy: A Cultural Critique of Chan/Zen Buddhism.* Princeton: Princeton University Press.

Fugen, Daien (1963). *Shinshū kyōgaku no hattatsu.* Kyoto: Nagata bunshodō.

Hisamatsu, Shin'ichi. "Jōdo-Shinshū Hihan." In *Zettai Shutaidō, Hisamatsu Shin'ichi Chosakushū.* Vol. 2.

Hishiki, Masaharu (1993). *Jōdo-Shinshū no Sensō Sekinin.* Tokyo: Iwanami Shoten.

Hirota, Dennis (1982). *Tannishō: A Primer: A Record of the words of Shinran set down in lamentation over departure from his teaching.*

Kyoto: Ryukoku University.

Kōgi (1975). *Kyōgyōshinshō kōgi shūjō*, vol. 6. Ed. Bukkyō taikei kanseikai. Kyoto: Hōzōkan.

Lee, David and Markus Leong (1994). "Jōdo Shinshū in Contemporary America: A Preliminary Comparative Study of Trans-Ethical Responsibility and Socratic Virtue-Ethics." *The Pure Land* n.s. (10-11) 288–302.

Lopez, Donald, ed. (1995). *Curators of the Buddha: The Study of Buddhism Under Colonialism*. Chicago and London: The University of Chicago Press.

Nakao, Shunpaku (1992). *Sabetsu to Shinshū*. Kyoto: Nagata Bunshodo.

Pas, Julian (1995).*Visions of Sukhāvatī: Shan-tao's Commentary on the Kuan Wu-Liang-Shou-Fo Ching*. Albany: State University of New York Press.

Rogers, Minor (1991). *Rennyo: The Second Founder of Shin Buddhism*. Berkeley: Asian Humanities.

SSZ (1941). *Shinshū Shōgyō Zensho*. Kyoto: Ōyagi kōbundō.

Shigaraki, Takamaro (1992). "*Shinjin* and Social Action in Shinran's Teachings." Trans. David Matsumoto. *The Pure Land*. n.s. (8-9) 219–249.

Sōsho (n.d.). *Shinshū Sōsho*. Kyoto: Hongwanji shuppan.

Tanaka, Kenneth (1990). *The Dawn of Chinese Pure Land Buddhist Doctrine: Ching-ying Hui-yüan's Commentary on the Visualization Sutra*. Albany: State University of New York Press.

Tanaka, Kenneth (1994). "*Jōgyō-daihi*: Constantly Practicing Great Compassion: Re-evaluation Based on Tokugawa Scholars for a Basis of Shin Involvement in the World. *The Pure Land*. n.s. (10-11) 93–104.

Tweed, Thomas (1992). *The American Encounter with Buddhism 1844-1912: Victorian Culture and the Limits of Dissent*. Bloomington and Indianapolis: Indiana University Press.

Ueda, Yoshifumi (1983-90). *The True Teaching, Practice and Realization of the Pure Land Way. A Translation of Shinran's Kyōgyōshinshō*. Volumes I-IV. Kyoto: Hongwanji International Center.

PART III

CRITICAL RESPONSES

Nineteen

Measuring the Immeasurable: Reflections on Unreasonable Reasoning

Luis O. Gómez

Within the limits of purpose and length set for the present essay I cannot comment on all the papers in this volume, much less develop a theological position in response to each one of them (whether to agree or disagree with the opinions expressed in the papers). I cannot summarize their positions – their assumptions, methods, arguments, and conclusions are too diverse. I have confined myself to a few remarks on selected themes from the papers, which I embed in a brief outline of what I believe the book as a whole has accomplished, a general discussion of some general problems and issues raised by the papers, and a few random thoughts on what remains to be done.

I cannot begin this essay without a series of statements that are necessarily problematic – certainly by virtue of their brevity, perhaps by virtue of their incongruity. These are statements that might help my readers understand some of the assumptions that I bring to my analysis of this book. They are not simple axioms or personal biases. I believe I have cogent arguments to defend most of these positions, although the exposition of such arguments is best left for a different forum. Furthermore, some of these assumptions straddle the dividing line between argued theses and life choices born from temperament and experience.

First, I believe the words "Buddhist" and "Buddhism" are ambiguous, and I believe they should stay that way for historical reasons (the two terms are always applied to a vast array of diverging phenomena and people, and with many different polemical aims) and for normative reasons (no human being should have the authority to decide how one should use any set of traditional beliefs or to rule on who can make a personal claim of allegiance to any part of that set of beliefs).

Second, I therefore do not hesitate to say I am a Buddhist in the sense that I find many, and diverse, aspects of Buddhist traditions (practices, ideas, and metaphors) inspiring and meaningful to a degree that makes me feel an intense and preferential degree of allegiance to, and commonality with those who have called themselves followers of "the teachings of the Buddhas." The inspiration I receive, and my interest and commitment vary, wax and wane, and coexist with despair as well as hope, doubt and suspicion as well as conviction.

Furthermore, I do not hesitate to add that within the definition of the respect I feel for the beliefs of all Buddhists I include the need to treat Buddhists as I treat other human beings: showing my respect with disagreement as well as with agreement.

What is more, in my view of Buddhism I must take seriously any evidence contrary to any statement among the myriad ideas and beliefs cherished by Buddhists throughout the history of the tradition – including evidence against statements attributed to "the Buddha." To take seriously such evidence means that if I am persuaded that the evidence is overwhelming, I will either modify or abandon the belief I had until then considered to be true. In practice, this may lead me, and often does lead me to find myself in greater agreement with certain ostensibly non-Buddhist positions and in disagreement with some who may have as much of a claim, if not a greater claim than I have on the epithet "Buddhist."

At least some of the contributors to this volume probably are willing to walk with me this far. However, I suspect most will begin to abandon me as I proceed to take a few additional steps. First, I do not believe any one of us can really know "what the Buddha taught," or what he most likely would accept, do, or prefer if he were alive today. And even if we could know this, I fail to see what such knowledge could do for us prior to a commitment to surrender our critical (theological) faculties. Second, I see no good reason to believe that there is such a thing as the Buddhist tradition "as a whole" (or if there were such a thing, that one can know what it is).

Third, I also believe that much of Buddhism (and religious practice generally) is not about truth, conviction, or authority, but about ways of imagining and rehearsing those aspects of life that are precisely not amenable to rational analysis. Much of what I mean when I say I am a Buddhist has a lot to do with my sense of what is suffering and what are the most effective metaphors to express this suffering, and what is the serene and compassionate breath I feel within me and how I can tap into this breath in spite of resentment, fear, arrogance, greed, and all the other forces that compete to capture the center stage of my sense of self.

Last, but by no means least, among the elements of Buddhism that cannot be reduced to notions of propositional truth and belief is the world of ritual. Being a Buddhist means to me that there are particular ways of "rehearsal," that is of ritualized behavior (worship, meditation) to which I conform in the hope that "conforming" will lead to "transforming" myself and others. These rehearsals are both means and end in my struggle with the sense of dissatisfaction that encompasses suffering, inadequacy, and helplessness.

Fourth, I regard as most relevant to a Buddhist theological reflection those teachings of the tradition that have to do with self-deception – the myriad moves I make daily in my attempt to protect this onion-like mass of phenomena I assume to be the me and the mine that bear my name. Therefore, I look at "systems" with suspicion – as organs that let us know in order not to know. In other words, the human capacity for self-deception and blindness is so strong that even our insights into this self-deception (especially when such insights are encased in doctrinal systems) are at best clouded by near-sightedness and self-deception, at worst tainted by subterfuge, cupidity and animosity.

Fifth, and last, my reverence for the Buddhist tradition leads not only to an ethics of agreement and disagreement, but also to an ethics of acceptance that makes me consider as desirable and good the capacity to restrain our impulse to turn disagreement into sectarian bias or into condemnation or disparagement. The question of which form or forms of Buddhism are preferable must remain open. Needless to say, this ethics of acceptance extends to non-Buddhists as much as it does to Buddhists.

This view of what it means to be a Buddhist and to do Buddhist theology I consider to be optimistic in the same sense that I consider the first Noble Truth to be optimistic: without recognizing suffering one cannot work towards its extinction, as long as one has not understood the fragility of one's own beliefs one cannot jettison attachment to theories and opinions.

Having already said this much, alas, I still must add additional caveats.

The editors of this volume have addressed some of the semantic and historical hurdles one must pass if one wishes to pair the words "Buddhist" and "theology." I will not repeat their arguments in defense of this problematic phrase – in fact, I feel that several papers in this collection spend too much time debating this minor point.[1] I also fail to see what is gained by some of the questionable arguments for pseudo-Sanskritic substitutes for theology.[2] For me the problems lie elsewhere – not in the question of the appropriateness of qualifying a putatively Christian word with the modifier "Buddhist." I am more concerned with two related issues, which I will use as my two guiding questions in the remainder of this paper.

(1) First, I am not sure I understand how an adjective denoting a religious ideology or a religious group affects any noun representing some form of rational, public discourse. Terms like "Buddhist psychology" or "Christian ecology" continue to baffle me (fortunately, we remain intelligent enough to avoid terms like "Christian chemistry"

or "Buddhist astrophysics"). Of course, "Christian theology" or "Buddhist theology" pass, though not easily. I still wonder: is the relationship between the two terms in each of these phrases different from that obtaining in phrases such as "Buddhist psychology" or "Christian cosmology"? Which brings me to a second criticism of several essays in the book. Several contributors protest too much trying to separate themselves from Christian theology. I would think that a greater commonality with Christian theological discourse would suggest that the discipline of theology, Christian or Buddhist, provides us with some of the necessary tools to go beyond apologetics into the terrain of dialogue and rational, truly public discourse.

(2) Second, I am also concerned with another, equally complex question. Is theology today at all possible? In fact, I have many times wondered whether it has ever been possible, or even desirable. But here I will focus on the contemporary question. What is the purpose and "sense" of theological reflection at the end of the twentieth century? This issue will be addressed below in light of what the papers tell us. In the end I will both review what I have learned from the papers and what I see as possible new directions, sidetracks, and dead ends in the contemporary rational examination of Buddhist doctrine and practice. At the outset, however, I want to raise the question of the impact of postmodernity on theology. This issue is discussed in particular in José Cabezón's "Truth in Buddhist Theology," and in Roger Jackson's "In Search of a Postmodern Middle." Other essays in this book for the most part appeared to me to be less aware of, if not oblivious of this important issue. I am not suggesting that they should all be written in the jargon *du jour.* But postmodernity broadly speaking is simply a cultural reality – not only a Franco-American fad already fading away. It is the cultural horizon within which Buddhist theology will have to exist and compete.

.oOo.

In response to the first of the above guiding questions one could argue that a Buddhist theology is a derivative rational discourse, a way of speaking rationally about a certain type of experience, the Buddhist experience. There is, of course, no *prima facie* reason for not arguing the exact opposite: that Buddhist theology and philosophy provide a rational grounding or foundation that limits or guides Buddhist experience – this is, after all, very much the position of Indian scholastics like Kamalaśīla. Most contemporary Western Buddhists, however, prefer the former view of the role of rational discourse about religious truth claims (that is, of theological discourse in one of its primary functions). The contributors to the present volume who have addressed this issue also concur in favoring the first conception of the position of rational discourse (perhaps of discourse generally): that rational discourse is derivative of or ancillary to a foundational, non-discursive experience.

Recently, Robert Sharf (1996) created pandemonium in some circles by daring to attack the notion of "experience."[3] His arguments are complex and he offers more than one thesis. I agree with some of these theses, and I disagree with others. But regardless of one's disagreements with Sharf, one must take it into account seriously. His critique is consistent with a number of perceptive, and in my view strong analyses that make it very difficult to continue appealing to self-evident experiences without, at the very least, explaining how doctrinal discourse can be derived from the foundational, ineffable experiences of Buddhism.[4]

The paper by B. Alan Wallace on "The Dialectic Between Religious Belief and Contemplative Knowledge" is a good example of an argument from experience that has not taken into account these criticisms (that is, the body of literature that precedes Sharf, as well as Sharf's own contribution). I happen to believe that pure, ineffable experiences are possible.[5] I also believe that one can bridge the gap between language and the ineffable. But I also believe that the separation of language from experience is itself part of the problem, and that the meaning of experiences of silence as well as the connection of language to such silences is neither trivial nor self-evident. Wallace is correct in pointing to the importance of "practice" (in the special, and in my view narrow sense of meditation practice). He is also leading us in the right path in noting that many of the critics of the rhetoric of Buddhism (e.g., Faure) do not address the question of the nature of meditation practice or the value of individual encounters with such practice. But Wallace still has to tell us how the experience leads to the language of a Buddhist theology or a Buddhist doctrinal choice.

His use of the term "empirical" is especially problematic, since it implicitly invokes the myth of scientific certainty, yet the type of experience he uses to ground the authority of his claims is far from the methods of hypothesis testing and falsification, uncertainty and probability, mathematical laws and predictability that one usually associates with empirical science. In other words, how do I test or challenge the certainty of this experience?

One could argue, however, that the role of theology in Buddhism is not to express, point to, or recover the foundational experience that gives the characteristic single taste to the waters of the ocean of the eighty-four thousand meanings of the Dharma. An alternative view would see rational discourse as a means of persuading or as a means of achieving certainty. Cabezón, for instance, argues that Buddhist theology is the attempt to bring order to the great diversity and complexity of Buddhist doctrine (to make it "systematic"). I believe he is correct on this point, and I support his defense of "scholasticism" (in both his essays – and also defended by Makransky in "Historical Consciousness"). It is not clear to me, however, how Cabezón would distinguish systematic from critical (most systematic effort, especially in the area of dogma, is anything but critical). In fact, many papers in the book seem to me too fearful of critical thought – as if "constructive" were always good, and "critical" were always bad.

One could, of course, argue with Cabezón that "constructive" theology is not necessarily a strategy for avoiding criticism. And I will agree on this point – albeit only from an ideal viewpoint. I would also defend Cabezón's drive for coherence, except that I would add the caveat that traditions live for many reasons other than coherence (or, if you prefer: coherence works in mysterious ways). I therefore find Pannenberg's defense of coherence (quoted in Cabezón's "Buddhist Theology in the Academy," note 23) less than helpful. Systematic presentation is not necessarily a test of truth claims, but is certainly proof of thoroughness, neatness, and consideration.

On the negative side, the production of ordered systems is a poor substitute for critical examination of ideologies and arguments. On the positive side, coherence and systematic elegance are requisites of proper hypothesis and theory formulation, and they are dimensions of the ethics of public discourse. That is to say, systematic presentations allow potential objectors to review and critique one's arguments or one's evidence. But a presentation could be perfectly coherent, and yet "wrong." And a presentation could be incoherent and "messy" according to certain scholastic standards, and yet be extremely insightful.[6]

I advocate, therefore, a concept of theology that centers on public discourse and dialogue, rather than truth or doctrinal certainty (I believe, if I have understood them correctly, Makransky and Jackson both are struggling with the same issue). In this view, "wrong" and "right" as well as "systematic" have more to do with the ethics of truth than with truth itself – or rather, there can be no truth without the observation of certain rules of the protocol of public discourse.[7] Three important elements of this protocol are essential to sound and honest theology: (1) accounting for evidence from outside the system (in the case of science, this is empirical evidence, in the case of theology this is history, facticity, and life itself), (2) testing and application of theories (in the case of science, replication, in the case of theology, a capacity to generate new understandings and meanings), and (3) the capacity to speak to the guild – that is, either respond to the needs and questions of the experts, or show a radically new way to generate critical reflection. In the sciences the break occurs during so-called scientific revolutions. In the case of theology, a break can occur when a new interpretation of the tradition is radically distinct from the past, yet productive because a community sees a tie to earlier understandings.[8]

If one stays honest, and if all of the above rules of the protocol are fulfilled, the mythical tapestry of "Buddhism" will begin to unravel. Personally, I have no problem with this – in my view, this tapestry is like Laertes's shroud, except that Penelope will never meet her Odysseus. However, since so many of the papers in this volume invoke the mythical tapestry (not the shroud!), I will review some of the difficulties we encounter when we assume that the term Buddhism is somehow univocal.

Most trained Buddhologists are well aware of the complexities of Buddhist history. Hence, most contemporary scholars (Buddhist and non-Buddhist) at least pay lip service to the notion of many Buddhists and many Buddhist traditions. Nevertheless, it is not easy to speak about a tradition without sliding back into notions of origin, essence, core, or whole. One does not have to be a Buddhist to fall into this trap. However, the absence of origins and essences creates problems for Buddhists especially, because they tend to privilege particular aspects of the Buddhist tradition as the point towards which they wish to displace their own sense of authority and conviction. Jackson and Makransky are well aware of this danger; other contributors are not so clear or do not engage the issue at all (not that they have to). Makransky eventually reverts to the notion of a core or limited set of beliefs that Śākyamuni must have held, and even speaks of attitudinal attributes of the person Śākyamuni. I wonder if there might not be some other way of making use of the tradition without attributing words, thoughts, or attitudes to an elusive founder. What if Śākyamuni was in fact closed-minded and sexist, but he founded a community that eventually developed values that *today* we can use as a religious foundation for more open-minded and tolerant views? This is a scenario just as likely as that of an original teacher who was ahead of his times. And this scenario is no less compelling, if by theology we understand the exploration of a rich and diverse pool of tradition.[9]

Of course, new problems arise the moment we open up tradition by calling into question the myth of the single and consistent authoritative voice, and accept the possibility that the founder(s) could have held positions unacceptable to us today. By removing the single locus of authority or the single source, the "Buddhist" of Buddhist theology becomes contested territory to a degree contemplated in this volume only perhaps in Jackson's paper.

If one intends to claim that the theology one advocates derives its authority from some formal or material characteristics of the theology itself (conceived as a discipline of rational inquiry), then one must believe that what makes for good theology, not-so-good theology, and bad theology is something other than that which is added to the general concept "theology" when one attaches before it denominational or confessional modifiers – such as "Buddhist."

I have already summarized some of the reasons why one cannot avoid this difficulty by arguing that in the particular case of Buddhist theology the adjective does not designate a confessional preference or a denominational commitment, but rather an empirical foundation. It is not possible to appeal to experience in this way (even if we choose to posit a foundational experience at the root of our theology – a choice that is neither necessary nor sufficient as a point of departure for Buddhist practice and commitment). It is not possible to argue that the adjective "Buddhist" only means "derived from the experience of a Buddha," because we do not have agreement among Buddhists as to the exact content of that primal experience. In fact, one of the tasks of theology is to lead us in the direction of such an agreement.

And even if there were some sort of agreement, or if we could legitimately exclude all doctrinal preferences except one (our own, I predict), the putatively self-validating experience would be private, beyond the reach of theological reason and barely touching the outer boundaries of theological imagination.

I happen to believe that there are luminous, confirmatory moments of clear consciousness and that such moments or experiences have contributed to the development of Buddhism. I simply cannot accept the idea that these experiences are somehow disembodied, not mediated by culture and discursive consideration. Be that as it may, the problem with a "Buddhist theology" is precisely in the implied privileging of a particular use of dialectal or rhetorical parameters (e.g. experience as non-duality vs. experience as understanding of causality), or, what is even more problematic, the lumping together of a complex web of arguments and beliefs under the rubric of "pure experience."

Theology is about making religious practices and aspirations "thinkable" in the full extent of the word. Hence, it is about concepts and reasons, and it is about naming the unnamable, thinking the unthinkable. Furthermore, theology is about issues that can hardly be reduced to silence or inner experience. Some of the most interesting papers in this volume bear witness to this simple fact.

For instance, Mahinda Deegalle's "From Buddhology to Buddhist Theology" (arguably the crowning jewel of the volume) offers a cautionary tale from Buddhist history. Unpretentious and scholarly, the paper raises a crucial issue parallel to the one raised in Tanaka's paper: that is, the extent to which non-systematic, non-scholastic forms of belief an rhetoric can play the same authoritative role played elsewhere by the putatively more formal forms of theology. Even if the dichotomies popular/monastic and devotional/meditational are historically and ethnographically problematic, they have some basis in the tradition's conception of itself. Deegalle shows how traditional Sinhala scholarship dealt with these dichotomies, and demonstrates elegantly how one may change one's readings of these issues. Tanaka makes a similar point, ingeniously arguing for a theology that derives its force from a particular understanding of faith and practice.

Sallie King's "Human Rights in Contemporary Engaged Buddhism," in spite of some idealization of Buddhism and Buddhists, brings us back to the question of practice and its position within theology. Although she speaks of social justice generally, she raises the question of how Buddhism can discover a theology of justice – something that is rare, if not non-existent in classical sources. Arguing from a more abstract perspective, John Dunne ("On Essences, Goals and Social Justice") raises the same issues. In his paper, however, I see a problem that I find in some of the other papers in the volume (and in much theological discourse): an unbridged gap between abstract metaphysics and the concrete human issues that are supposedly illuminated by theology. Where King lacks in systematic insight, Dunne lacks in concrete application of abstract systematics.

The difficulty these two authors encounter trying to tie practice to principle is found in other papers and may be indicative of one of the great hurdles that lie ahead of us. These are difficulties inherent to the theological imagination generally, and Buddhism cannot escape them. I would argue that apart from the technical sphere of meditation, Buddhism has been traditionally rich in abstractions, poor in practical applications – *upāya* notwithstanding. We are still suffering from too much enthusiasm for the abstract notion of *upāya and* too little thought of how it should translate into action.

Sara McClintock's "Gendered Bodies of Illusion" struggles creatively with an old issue: how to retain the specificity and individuality of a gendered self while arguing for *some sort* of no-self (I choose the words "some sort" advisedly, since the question of what may be the exact meaning of this "no-self" is not a trivial issue). In some ways her paper epitomizes the problem of using the ineffable and the unthinkable as a basis for telling us what we should think, say, and do. Rita Gross's "Impermanence, Nowness and Non-Judgment" deals with parallel issues in a veritable tour de force raising issues of embodiment. I am not convinced that the author has succeeded in transcending the predictable appeal to doctrinal shibboleths (in this case impermanence and non-judgment). Yet Gross's paper gives us enough insight into a personal struggle to allow us to see a gap between theological speculation and the confusion of life.

Judith Simmer-Brown, in "Pluralism, Dialogue, and the Academic Study of Religion," raises a very different set of issues. Again, the issues are well chosen and indeed vital for theology, if not for human action generally; but the author will need tighter arguments if she is to connect the issues to Buddhism. Could we have made the same point without an appeal to Buddhism? I am not persuaded that we cannot.

Of all the abstractions that may be profound, but are not transparent, those we associate with the ineffable and the non-dual are the most problematic. King, Deegalle, and Tanaka avoid the pitfalls of the common, and predictable, appeal to the "non-dual." Deegalle's and Tanaka's papers are excellent examples of how one can speak about central issues from a Buddhist perspective without appealing to the ineffable non-dual. King's paper raises the important question, barely mentioned elsewhere in the book, of the connection between theology and the actual behavior of Buddhists in the world. This last element is in my view a central issue for any theology worth its salt (we can go hoarse defending Buddhist ideals, but if they do not somehow survive in the world, our efforts will have been in vain).

But, how can we move in the opposite direction? How can we turn general or abstract principles into tools for addressing concrete issues of ethics, truth, religious practice? We can make Buddhism thinkable in the abstract, but we must seek to make Buddhism doable. Our theological thinking has to create, as it were, a tool-box that will include the inspirational and the practical, the ethical and the confessional.

Viewed in this way, "to make Buddhism thinkable" has many meanings, and nothing can assure us that in the end these many meanings will lead to some harmonious or integral whole. For instance, I may propose that "Buddhism should be understood as "the active and compassionate manifestation of no self."[10] Such a statement is probably intelligible, if not transparent, to many Buddhists of a particular type (Western Buddhists more or less educated in the scriptural traditions of Mahāyāna). Nevertheless, the statement is far from being transparent to a non-Buddhist – and, what is even more problematic, each one of its terms will elicit variant, if not conflicting, interpretations and behaviors from different Buddhists. The statement, moreover, does not yield easily explanations for a vast range of "Buddhist behaviors." Nor is the statement in itself an answer to any concrete human situation.

Take, for instance, the worship of a Buddha image. There is no self-evident reason, no necessary inference to lead from the practice of no self to a prostration before a Buddha image. This does not mean that a reasonable connection cannot be made, but rather that whatever connections we make will not compel anyone to prostrate before a Buddha image.

Or take again the practice of meditation. Nothing in the primary statement suggests a need for meditation--much less a need for any particular form of meditation. Nothing in the concepts of "no self," "compassion," "practice," etc. implies that we should prefer *kōan* practice over *sādhana*. In fact, nothing entails the need to sit, and whichever position one's own tradition may prefer makes no difference.

This is then the first problem with the theory and practice of Buddhist theology in a time and country in which there is no tradition, very little community, and the need constantly to question our claims to authority: the connection between foundation and practice is much more unstable than it is at other times. Needless to say, I regard this "problem" as potentially a blessing.

The intellectual climate of the times leads to another weakness in our project. Although Buddhism appears eminently endowed to face an age of disillusionment, it is not prepared to do so – neither in theory nor in practice.

It is fair to say that, *in theory*, Buddhism is not fazed by the death of God, the end of the subject, the end of solid objects, realities and truths. But this is a peculiar use of the term "theory," for it means what we today, in this day and age, think about Buddhism, in other words what we believe follows from a select subset of Buddhist beliefs. If, on the other hand, theory meant what Buddhists themselves consider or have considered to be their theory, then there is much in Buddhism that is likely to be threatened by our age, and there are many Buddhists who will be shocked and embarrassed by the postmodern consciousness. For all the rhetoric of groundlessness, Buddhist emptiness does not always lead to an unconditional acceptance of a bottomless ground and a beginningless beginning. Buddhism retains presence and truth even as it denies substance and foundation. In Buddhism, the dissolution of the subject does not lead (as it has in this century that is almost over) to the disillusion of the person, truth, and order (a veritable *a-dharma* that would be repugnant to most Buddhists).

Many of the essays in this book attempt to take postmodernity seriously, but most end up telling us that Buddhism should not or will not be shocked by the loss of ground. The claim is made either by asserting that the ground has not vanished or that it can be recovered (e.g., Cabezón) or by asserting that Buddhists already knew about this groundlessness long before it became a historical cultural event. Only Jackson appears to understand fully both the limitations of classical

Buddhist "deconstruction," and the destructive impact of the cultural changes that have culminated not simply in a philosophical fad but in the culture of the simulacrum and the trivial, the virtual image and immediate gratification.

In fact, most Buddhists have yet to absorb and accept modernity, and most would never recognize themselves in the mirror of post-modernity. At a symposium some years ago, a distinguished lama argued that even if modern historical research showed that the Mahāyāna *sūtras* could not have been spoken by the Buddha, we must accept them as the word of the Buddha, and that historical research was simply wrong and irrelevant. In this volume, Makransky argues against this view with passion and clarity.

At another conference a leading Theravādin monk argued that the Buddha himself taught that the sexual drive led to negative rebirth, hence contemporary notions of sexuality as normal and sexual drive as healthy had to be wrong. Gross and McClintock hint at possible Buddhist objections to this view. Still, shifts in Buddhist views of human sexuality will need a careful examination in the future. I am not too sure that one can dispose of or ignore the ascetic vein that runs through much of Buddhism, or that one can choose and privilege those forms of Buddhism that appear to be non-ascetic. Even those forms of Buddhism that show some acceptance or validation of the sexual drive are far from contemporary secular notions of the importance of sexuality, let alone the importance of intimacy, and the life of the householder.

In spite of this resistance to rethink Buddhism in light of contemporary secular views of the world, or at the very least take these views into account in constructing Buddhist theology, Buddhists still insist that Buddhism is scientific. In doing so, many make no effort to recognize the obvious conceptual gap that separate ancient Indian cosmology and atomic theory from contemporary astrophysics, physics, and chemistry, or abhidharmic doctrines of the mind from contemporary philosophy, cognitive science, and neuropsychology, to say nothing of the historical gap that separates traditional Buddhist doctrines of the world and the mind from our own contemporary views.

Some of the papers in this volume are not only shy towards postmodern thought, but seem fearful of some of the ideas and methods of modernity. Philology and the hermeneutics of suspicion are criticized for their putative socio-political agendas – I sense that some of the contributors believe the hermeneutics of suspicion is motivated by some sort of bad faith. Perhaps it is (I believe it often serves the interest of particular social groups, very much like traditional theology); and the methodological suspicion itself can be applied as a very crude *argumentum ad hominem*. But one cannot simply dismiss suspicion with a countering *argumentum ad hominem*: regardless of the motivation, an attitude of suspicion is central to critical thought. The hermeneutics of suspicion has grown with, contributed to, and become essential to contemporary conceptions of individual psychology, culture, and sociology. It is the hermeneutical face of the realization that human individuals and communities are complex, and that "truth" and "meaning" function at many levels (whether we call one of these levels true and the other false, is not as critical as recognizing the differences and conflicts between these levels).

It is no longer possible to assume, as our ancestors did, that all human beings are always free agents in control of their behavior, or that there is no deception other than the one effected by conscious lying. It is not only that we learned from Freud that we can never fully fathom the conflicts within us. Modern insights into the brain and human development also suggest to us that we are conditioned and motivated by forces that shape, and can easily overwhelm, our spiritual aspirations.

Similarly, one need not assume that all social philosophies are ideologies of power, one need not follow Marx or Foucault sheepishly, to see that the noblest of human institutions are riddled by contradictions. If we cannot see this, then we may be blissfully ignorant, but blind nonetheless. And yet, if we do understand this, but fail to apply the same suspicion to the institutions that we favor and protect, we may be guilty of a naiveté that is far from a harmless and innocent.

These are but two examples of the many ways in which suspicion is necessary and "constructive." As a methodological assumption, it is properly applied to the historical study of institutions and ideologies. Among the contributors to this volume, Vesna Wallace is correct in raising objections against the application of suspicion (in the *technical sense* of the word) to religious ideals and the practices of individuals. Nevertheless, a critical questioning of doctrine and practice, and especially of religious institutions, is necessary and proper, as long as one does not use a critique of motives as a critique of validity.

Conversely, a critical challenge to doctrine and practice has to be suspicious of authority claims (they are powerful, and hence tempting and dangerous), but the challenge must argue not from motive, but from validity (*pace* Faure). For instance, a claim that meditation makes meditators more altruistic than non-meditators cannot be challenged by showing that advocates of the method used their advocacy as a means to secure influence, prestige, and power. But an attitude of suspicion is in order nonetheless. Buddhist and non-Buddhist alike need suspicion as the point of departure for a valid test of the claim. The Buddhist who practices and advocates the practice of meditation, must approach such claims with suspicion as a guard against self-deception.

Similarly, the reading of texts must be approached with the utmost care and constant re-examination. Although the methods of philology cannot be like those of philosophy, and the critical consideration of a text is not exactly the same as the critical reading of a doctrinal statement, scriptural texts must be read with suspicion, too. Some of the contributors express their criticism of traditional Western philology and historical criticism in a way that feels like a rejection of everything we have gained since the Enlightenment (the European Enlightenment, that is). I have criticized elsewhere (1993) the poverty of philology and historical criticism. I share some of the suspicion expressed in the present volume with respect to a certain "eagerness to debunk" that represents the psychological equivalent of fundamentalism (though it masquerades as its exact opposite). But this is a criticism meant to be a corrective, not an argument for substituting the critical methods of philology and history with the authoritative voice of living religious masters.

One must study Buddhism in all of its contexts, and nothing makes a contemporary Buddhist less authoritative than an ancient Master, much less a contemporary reading of an ancient Master. But one cannot use the living Buddhist as the last word on all of Buddhism, much less on the history of Buddhism.

Modernity gave us the freedom and the urge to seek our own answers, it gave us the obsession with texts and history. There is much to be learned from this legacy. Nothing is gained by fearing the consequences.

Postmodernity has increased our sense of doubt and suspicion. Text and author vanish. But one is able to practice this magician's trick in good measure because of what we know of the history of the text. Ignoring the cacophony of history will not take the confusion of the age away.

Most non-Western Buddhists share some of this fear of modernity and postmodernity, and fail to move out from traditional positions that are hardly tenable at the end of this turbulent century. A productive and successful theology needs individuals capable of shedding this fear and facing a confused age with the courage to change, as well as a desire to learn from multiple pasts – Buddhist and non-Buddhist alike.

The task of Buddhist theology is therefore formidable, and to make matters worse the challenge appears at a time when Buddhism could face extinction if it does not adapt quickly. Needless to say, a successful adaptation does not depend primarily on any intellectual maneuvers however nimble or any philosophical triumphs however brilliant, such as one would expect from the work of shrewd theologians. Nevertheless, theology may stimulate debates that will prove crucial to the social adaptability of Buddhism as a practice.

But the greatest limitation to theological reflection is the stricture that confines all attempts to rationalize human life: one may be able to create order and one may have to create order, but this order is always a veneer, under which, or beyond which, life itself flows. No amount of reflection on suffering can truly capture the subjective intensities and modalities, or the meanings of suffering itself.

The new theology, Buddhist or non-Buddhist, must in many ways be an antitheology, one that recognizes the fragility of theological reflection and its dogmatic edifices. The task of theology is in part the task of dislodging itself (that is reason and system) from its putative privileged position.

What are some of the ways in which theology can dislodge itself? It must, of course raise issues of class and gender, as some of the essays in this volume have done. We have to wonder what impact, if any such reflections will have on Asian Buddhists, who are only now beginning to struggle with these issues. But I also wonder why Western advocates of a social critique on Buddhist grounds have not explored other unfair presentations of humanity within the Buddhist doctrinal edifice. Serfs, servants, and slaves come easily to mind. A disturbing silence in traditional Buddhist literature regarding ethnic and cultural prejudice also come to mind. And, on a topic even more dear to me, where have all the children gone? The historical or sociological explanation for so much negative or absent presentation of children in the literature is not what interests us here, but rather the question of how one constructs a Buddhist theology of the child – of human development and of childhood wisdom, joy, and sorrow.

The essays in this book have only begun the task of the new theology. They are a beginning in the direction of dislodging the social center of Buddhist theology as well as its thematic and formal limits. They suggest new directions, but the volume cannot be comprehensive. What are some of the remaining issues and approaches that need to be explored if Buddhist theological reflection is to be revitalized?

First, there is the matter of genre. We can no longer expect to write in the style of the *śāstra*s, naturally. But we need not think only of scholastic alternatives. The Asian tradition itself presents us with a variety of genres – poetry, fiction, autobiography, drama – as vehicles that can help to shape the theological domain.[11]

Second, as already suggested above, there is the matter of moral theology. "Morality" alas has become a four-letter word, but unless we learn to reflect courageously on Buddhist moralism and asceticism, we will not be able to understand its meaning and value. A revaluation of Buddhism in light of modern conceptions of sexual intimacy, or a reconsideration of mores in light of our understanding of cultural diversity cannot take place without an understanding of the place and significance of monastic regulations and lay moral codes. Several papers in this collection raise the ethical issues but ignore traditional moral reflection.

Of course, I mean morality and ethics in the broadest sense of the terms, and hence include an examination of the psychology of moral decisions, moral habits and moral sentiments. For instance, how are we to understand the contemporary thirst for immediate gratification, or contemporary narcissism for that matter? Beyond a simplistic "no-self' argument, how are these characteristics of our culture best understood and countered, how do they creep back into our theology and our practice? How is the world of the virtual and the simulacrum a lesson in the nature of delusive and illusionistic thinking?

Third, taking a cue from Tanaka, I would propose that we reconsider notions of faith and hope, broadly understood. Is there a Buddhist answer to Job that is something better than the reduction of the question to karma or serene detachment? Is there something more to be said to the terminally ill patient or the mother of the schizophrenic adolescent than simply "all compounded things are impermanent"?

Although the list can easily continue to expand, I will close with only one more point. Fourth, how can theological reflection help us accept or understand suffering in its complexity beyond philosophical order, suffering in its randomness and absurdity? Contemporary scientific and secular thinking has undermined the neat edifice of karmic retribution. Cabezón, for instance, confesses to rejecting the doctrine of rebirth. In my more rational moments I reject it as well. Although I must confess to secretly harboring the hope that there is something like rebirth and karma, I still think that the mysteries of heredity, freak accidents and random killings, the suffering of innocent children, are not removed or dissolved in any way by a mythology of rebirth or karma. The solution is illusory. Is there then another solution, or another way of approaching the inherent fragility of all things, and the pain that that fragility brings – not to me as the observer of suffering, but to those who are innocent or unable to appreciate any deep significance in all this pain (children, the retarded and the mentally ill, persons trapped in moments of fear and despair that leave no room for serene reflection)? What happens when things fall apart . . . and the hurt overwhelms body and mind? What happens when all efforts at calm, insight, or self-transformation fail?

This brings me full-circle to the qualifications that began this essay, for, the above list of desiderata is in fact a critique, not only a critique of contemporary Buddhist theological speculation, but a critique of much of traditional Buddhist theology. Traditional Buddhists, like their contemporary counterparts, sought certainty – a truth that could be necessary, universal, and compelling. This is certainly very human, but not the only way to look at truth, and, not the only way to appreciate the Buddhist tradition and receive inspiration from it. We may fear a truth that is breakable or broken, uncertain and "local" (not universal, personal, culture-bound, etc.), but this fear is justified only if we assume that a limited truth can only lead to a defense of private whimsy, arrogant self-complacency, or solipsism. There is, however, another way of looking at the possible value of truth as limitation. It can be a recognition of history as change, diversity in the past, and the certainty that the future will also bring diversity. I can accept truth as a limited cultural artifact (and, as I have argued above, so are the criteria for truth), and truth as the fruit of personal preferences – personality and unconscious forces shaping our preferences, our choices of truth, and our choices of the brethren we will commune with in a quest for truth. My acceptance is not a surrender to personal whim, but a critique of my own limitations. It is also a confession of the fact that I cannot possibly know all beliefs, consider all arguments, and I cannot possibly know what my choices will be in the future.

To express this in terms that echo traditional Buddhist categories: I am the momentary joining of a vast array of causes and conditions. I am neither a single thing, nor a permanent arrangement of diverse elements, but a limited conjunction. Someone else made me what I am – a "someone else" that is many people and things, including, of course, the person I have willed to be, but including also what I have done in spite of myself or against my better judgment, including my parents, and my ancestors (as cultural and genetic agents), and whatever all of these may have been in past and future lives. These many "I's" can neither stand on nor possess an ultimate truth. I am not omniscient, and even if the Buddhist tradition contains somewhere the words of an omniscient being (a doctrine I personally cannot accept), I have no way of knowing which words are the words of this omniscient person and no way of knowing whether or not I have understood them.

And this, as I said earlier, is an optimistic view of myself; because it makes me want to strive (not that I always succeed) to struggle against the delusion that I am free from limitations, and the illusion of speaking with an authoritative voice. If I am to open up to others, I must begin by struggling against the idea that I am something more than this limited self. . . . This is, of course, the opposite of all the sound and fury about truth that concerns many theologians, but it may be a more reasonable way of looking at what Buddhist doctrines may tell us about being reasonable.

All of this I would summarize in a few sentences as follows. Buddhists, like their Christian counterparts, still suffer from the fever of certainty. Whenever we suffer an attack of this fever, we close ourselves to suffering, to the reality of human fragility, and to the dreams of others, and thereby undermine and betray one important reason (to me, the most important reason) for wanting to draw from the well-spring of Buddhism: the alleviation of suffering.

NOTES

1 If anything, the book suffers from a certain redundancy in the treatment of this question. The editors and at least four other contributors (Cabezón, Gross, Wallace, Corless) address the issues explicitly.

2 Dharmalogy" and "Buddhalogy," by the way, are poor Greco-Latin derivations. If we followed this false internal *sandhi*, we would have in English "psychelogy," "asternomy" and "asterlogy," "funi(s)ambulist," "physi(s)logy," etc.

3 Sharf continues the same line of argument in a forthcoming article for the volume, *Critical Terms for Religious Studies*, edited by Mark C. Taylor (University of Chicago Press).

4 These include the papers in Katz 1978, 1983, and 1992, and Proudfoot 1985. Needless to say, this reference should not be construed as a blanket statement of agreement or approval.

5 This is very different from saying that these experiences are privileged, authoritative or necessary, or that they are universal, or that all human beings should strive to attain them.

6 I was surprised to find a critique of the notion of truth in a book on Buddhist theology. After all, the concept of truth is itself problematic from some Buddhist philosophical perspectives, and at least intuitively closely tied to the human needs for authority, control, and a secure self-image.

7 Note the important, and meaningful use of the term "protocol" in experimental science and computer science, where the meaning of plan or ordered presentation overlaps with that of understandable communication.

8 The analogy with science is not meant to make theology into an empirical science, but simply to show the sense in which empirical science and the human sciences share a similar ethics of evidence. It should be clear by now that I have problems with the many loose senses given to the word "empirical" used in Buddhist Studies.

9 An increase in the population of Western conservative Buddhists is not the solution, because they too would want to make Śākyamuni in their own socio-political image.

10 The phrase "can be understood as" has a soft meaning (= Buddhism can be thought of if we assume that it is"), and a strong reading (= Buddhism should be understood as, and any other way of understanding it would be

wrong). Here, of course, I follow the soft reading.

11 See, for instance, Janet Gyatso's (1998) recent work on Tibetan autobiography as an example of traditional alternatives to the scholastic treatise. In this volume, Jackson and Gross rely on autobiographic accounts as a dimension of theological discourse.

REFERENCES

Faure, Bernard (1991). *The Rhetoric of Immediacy: A Cultural Critique of Chan/Zen Buddhism*. Princeton: Princeton University Press.

Faure, Bernard (1992). "Fair and Unfair Language Games in Chan/Zen." In Steven T. Katz, ed., *Mysticism and Language*, 158–180. Oxford: Oxford University Press.

Faure, Bernard (1995). *Chan Insights and Oversights: An Epistemological Critique of the Chan Tradition*. Princeton: Princeton University Press.

Gómez, Luis O. (1993). "Sources of Authority in Buddhism and Buddhist Scholarship." *Ōtanigakuhō* (72: 1) 1–37.

Gómez, Luis O. (1995). "The Authority of Compassion and Skillful Means." *Ōtanigakuhō* (74: 3) 1–35.

Gyatso, Janet (1998). *Apparitions of the Self: The Secret Autobiographies of a Tibetan Visionary. A Translation and Study of Jigme Lingpa's* Dancing Moon in the Water *and* Ḍākki's Grand Secret-Talk. Princeton: Princeton University Press.

Katz, Steven T., ed. (1978a). *Mysticism and Philosophical Analysis*. Oxford: Oxford University Press.

Katz, Steven T. (1978b). "Language, Epistemology, and Mysticism." In Steven T. Katz, , ed., *Mysticism and Philosophical Analysis*, 22–74. Oxford: Oxford University Press.

Katz, Steven T. (1983a). *Mysticism and Religious Traditions*. Oxford: Oxford University Press.

Katz, Steven T. (1983b). "The 'Conservative' Character of Mystical Experience." In Steven T. Katz, , ed., *Mysticism and Religious Traditions*, 3–60. Oxford: Oxford University Press.

Katz, Steven T. (1992). *Mysticism and Language*. Oxford: Oxford University Press.

Proudfoot, Wayne (1985). *Religious Experience*. Berkeley: University of California Press.

Sharf, Robert H. (1994). "Zen and the Art of Deconstruction." [Review of Bernard Faure, *The Rhetoric of Immediacy*]. *History of Religions* (33) 287–296.

Sharf, Robert H. (1995). "Buddhist Modernism and the Rhetoric of Meditative Experience." *Numen* (42) 228–283.

Sharf, Robert H. (1998). "Experience." In Mark C. Taylor, ed., *Critical terms for Religious Studies*. Chicago: University of Chicago Press.

Twenty

Constructive Buddhist Theology: A Response

Taitetsu Unno

While the term Buddhist "theology" may pose multiple problems, as noted by almost all the contributors to this volume,[1] the intent of the editors, Roger Jackson and John Makransky, to undertake a constructive reappraisal of Buddhist thought in a new direction is to be welcomed. Buddhist Studies in the West is maturing and may enter a new stage, a stage marked by self-critical awareness among practicing scholars who propose to address critical issues of universal concern from the Buddhist standpoint. The collected essays cluster around a "double movement," described by the editors as follows:

> Buddhist theology involves two types of critical reflection: 1) As contemporary Buddhist scholars trained in the Western academy, to reflect upon implications for Buddhist self-understanding, of the academy's historical, cultural, and critical findings. 2) At the same time, standing within the Buddhist tradition, and thus recognizing a trans-historical and trans-cultural significance of Buddhism which speaks to every place and time (as Christian theologians recognize for their tradition), to reflect critically upon the contemporary world from the perspective of Buddhist tradition, and thereby to offer something important to contemporary understanding.[2]

Unlike Christian theology, however, the Buddhist enterprise faces major hurdles, the two significant ones being that as a tradition it confronts the challenges of modernity for the first time in its history, and it involves a cross-cultural dimension of enormous complexity. The Buddhist tradition in Asia, including that of Japan which has adapted Western methods of Buddhist scholarship, has yet to develop the equivalent of Christian theology that has dealt with the contradictions of modernity and continues to seriously cope with pressing social issues of contemporary life (the claim of Buddhism being postmodern is of little consequence in this regard). And for the first time in its history Buddhism truly confronts a time-honored Western value system with its own religious and ethical views, defining anew its place in a world of religious pluralism and multiculturalism. Buddhist theology has much to learn from Christian theology, as well as from psychology, philosophy, the social and natural sciences, as it ventures forth to meet new challenges.

My task is to respond to the contributions to this volume, each of which adds to the project of Buddhist theology, and to share my major concern, which is the maintenance of its integrity. I will do so from the perspective of East Asian Buddhism, citing examples from Mahāyāna expressions with which I am most familiar – Hua-yen and Pure Land Buddhism.

To set the stage for our discussion, I suggest that there are three important areas to consider for Buddhist theology. First, it must respond to the deepest existential and spiritual yearnings of people who seek but cannot find answers to the perennial questions of life and death. All religions address these questions, but what will be the unique contribution of Buddhism towards this end – not something simply different or exotic but providing real answers to nourish the spirit? Second, it must respond to the intellectual, social, and cultural challenges of postmodernity without losing its critical perspective. How does Buddhism find its place in this new world? How does it translate spiritual practice into social praxis? And third, it must offer alternative solutions to concrete problems, ranging from conflict situations in everyday life to global concerns for the survival of the planet. Again all serious thinking people are grappling with these issues, but what does Buddhism have to offer?

Although it may sound far-fetched, I wish to take the example of Japanese gardens being built in North America to highlight some questions about the rapidly growing Buddhist interest in the West. The authenticity of Japanese gardens has been questioned by some concerned landscape designers; a similar question, although immensely more complex, can be raised about Buddhism as it is embraced and practiced in a new cultural and historical milieu.

According to landscape designers, almost all horticultural gardens and arboretums in North America seek to have a Japanese garden. The question of their authenticity was first raised by David Slawson[3] in October 1996 at the Symposium of the International Association of Japanese Gardens, held in Portland, Oregon. In his paper, "Authenticity in Japanese Landscape Design," he discusses two types of authenticity: lower and higher.

According to Slawson, the lower path to authenticity is said to follow

> a literal, precedent-driven interpretation of the tradition. . . . Here, creativity is rigidly constrained by external norms which favor the status quo. The primary recourse is to precedent (for the designer, existing types of stereotypes) rather than to universal principles and the intrinsic nature of the situation. (1996: 2)

As an example of this lower path, he cites the City of Miami's *San-An-Ai* Garden. In the 1960's, a wealthy Japanese businessman donated all the material necessary for the garden – 500 orchid bushes, a 300-year old lantern, an eight-ton eight-foot high statue of Hotei, a 15-foot stone pagoda, six smaller stone lanterns, three bridges, a tea hut, and an arbor. He also sent a landscape architect, six carpenters, and three gardeners. This garden is authentic in one sense, for it reproduces the past, but it might be described, more or less, as the Disneyland approach to Japanese gardens.

In contrast, the higher path of authenticity responds to the reality of the American landscape, while following the basic ideals of Japanese garden design. In Slawson's own words,

> [It] follows a metaphorical, principle- and situation-driven interpretation of the tradition. Here, the authority comes from within – from the desires and culture of those who will use the garden, from the site and surroundings, and from locally available material. . . . When the designer is attuned to the situation, intuition may, and often does, lead to a breaking with precedent. Such attunement is enhanced by a deepening knowledge of the tradition. (1996: 3)

Three points are important here. First, the garden should satisfy what Slawson calls the Accord Triangle – it must respond to the desires of the client, to the given environment, and to local material for its construction – in order to make it not just an exotic transplant but a natural part of the scenery. Second, this may mean breaking with precedent in garden design, a fact that occurred several times in the evolution of Japanese gardens, such as Daisen-in at Daitokuji and the tea gardens. And third, success is insured only in so far as one achieves deep knowledge and critical understanding of the tradition. Quoting Chögyam Trungpa, the author states that "[The artist who] firmly roots himself in the traditions . . . is not afraid to take a new step, but the reason he is stepping out of the tradition is because he knows it so well. His inspiration to step out comes from that tradition" (Slawson 1996: 3).

Applying the two types of authenticity to the Buddhist case, the lower type would continue to look to Asia for guidance, argue for the strict adherence to the tradition, whether it be doctrines, rituals, lineages, cultic practices, material accouterments, or religious customs. To receive a given tradition *in toto* into a new socio- historical context would be maintaining a form of authenticity, but whether it meets the real needs of the people would be open to question. Regardless, lacking roots in the new environment, it cannot hope to produce new growth and shoots.

The higher path to authenticity, where Buddhist theology would be located, fulfills its own version of the Accord Triangle – respond to local spiritual yearnings, to the intellectual and cultural ethos, and to material available for its use. This, of course, does not mean discarding the past; in fact, it will require a more accurate and thorough knowledge of Buddhist history, its past and present, as well as its basic scriptures and doctrines. Critical, objective scholarship is not only welcomed but required for developing Buddhist theology. The entire spectrum of Buddhist thought should be explored as much as possible, not just those that are fashionable or intriguing for the Western psyche. The integrity of a dynamic Buddhist theology requires it to remain open to the past and free to engage in creative encounters in the future. Our questions then become: What are the distinctive features that characterize Buddhist thought that will form the basis of its theology? What are some of the fundamental questions that it must address? What are the prospective contributions that it might make to society?

(I)

In pursuing the higher path of authenticity we are, first of all, reminded of the fact that religious doctrines, whether Buddhist or otherwise, are products of a historically conditioned world-view. Nietzsche's perspectivism which shattered any notion of absolute truth is inherited and underscored by the sociology of knowledge. According to Peter Berger,

> Religion implies the farthest reach of man's self-externalization, of his infusion of reality with its own meaning. Religion implies that human order is projected into the totality of being. Put differently, religion is the audacious attempt to conceive of the entire universe as being humanly significant. (Berger: 27)

The three-stage evolution in the social construction of knowledge – externalization, objectification, and internalization – is descriptive of the formation of basic Buddhist doctrines. The doctrine of non-self, for example, was an experience expressed in language (externalization) that took on a reality of its own (objectification) and people who followed sought to comprehend it (internalization). In this process was born the great variety of Buddhist schools and denominations.

This, however, does not nullify the transcendent in human life. In fact, after Berger's *Sacred Canopy: Elements of a Sociological Theory of Religion* (1968) was hailed as the curtain call for religion, especially among Eastern Europeans, when it first appeared, he immediately undertook to counter his sociological study to affirm the transcendent. The result was his *Rumors of Angels: Modern Society and the Rediscovery of the Transcendent* (1970) and *The Other Side of God: A Polarity in World Religions* (1980).[4]

In the case of Buddhism the multiple teachings understood as variations of skillful means should deter any reification or absolutization. As stated by Vesna Wallace, "From one perspective, all notions of emptiness, *tathāgatagarbha*, *nirvāṇa*, etc. are nothing more than the didactic devices aimed at leading the contemplatives to the direct experience of the ultimate, the unconditioned. But to reduce *tathāgatagarbha* to a mere pedagogical device may be to fall to the extreme of nihilism" (85). The deconstruction does not mean nihilism, for the transhistorical is fundamental to the Buddhist tradition, that "vast mystery through which authentic Mahāyāna experience has been made possible across diverse cultures through so many centuries." (118). This transhistorical is *dharmakāya* – "embodiment (*kāya*) of the real nature of things (*dharmatā*) in direct, non-conceptual knowledge." (115)

In accordance with this basic approach, José Cabezón's recourse to pragmatism, not as a general theory of truth but as a useful critical tool, seems most appropriate. On this particular point the words of William James resonate with basic Buddhist philosophy: "Pragmatism turns away from abstraction and inefficiency, from verbal solutions, from bad *a priori* reasons, from fixed principles, closed systems, and pretended absolutes and origins. . . . It means the open air and possibilities of nature, as against dogma, artificiality, and pretense of finality in truth" (James 1955: 21).

This use of a limited form of pragmatism would help us test the validity of time-honored doctrines developed in another time and place. Again, according to James,

> True ideas are those that we can assimilate, validate, corroborate, and verify. False idea are those we cannot. That is the practical difference........The truth of an idea is not a stagnant property inherent in it. Truth *happens* to an idea. It *becomes* true, is made true by events. Its verity is in fact an event, a process: the process namely of its verificating itself, its veri-*fication*. Its vitality is the process of its valid-*ation*. (James 1955: 160–161)

Although he himself did not subscribe to any formal religion, James leaves open the room for the transcendent, showing sympathy for "not a deity *in concreto*, not a superhuman person, but the immanent divinity in things the essentially spiritual structure of the universe." (James 1990: 36).

Some form of pragmatic testing might be applied to John Dunne's exercise in Buddhist theology, using Dharmakīrti's distinction between essentialist and teleological approaches to reality to formulate a new approach to the problems of race, oppression and injustice. In his words, "I would maintain that one cannot think clearly about (racism) without first critiquing essentialism, and if there is any room for solutions, it can come only through the consensual construction of goals – the vision of a common *telos*" (289). Here is a good example of Buddhist theology in the working, but his thesis needs to be tried out in actual practice.

In Buddhism what I call the pragmatic appears in the form of orthopraxy. Religious practice (*caraṇa*, *adhigama*, *prayoga*, *hsing*, *shugyō*) is not just a means to an end but the end itself, for reality is manifested in and through practice.[5] That is, the value of practice is not so much about form but content, not performance but embodiment, such that the teaching is concretely manifested in daily life. From this perspective "thinking" is not simply a rational or cognitive activity but a way of knowing that is not dependent on conceptuality. Orthopraxy in this sense has significant implications for two reasons: it liberates us from clinging to abstract concepts and becoming entangled with reified doctrines; and it helps us deal with the immediate realities of daily living, always in constant flux, with something more than discursive consciousness. Such is the driving force, in my view, that is the principle of middle way (*madhyama pratipad*) that Roger Jackson identifies as the common thread found among the diverse expressions of the Buddhist tradition:

> We cannot predict *what* middles will emerge in the course of postmodern Buddhist reflection – only that it will be a guiding

> metaphor in the future as it has been in the past, and that it will be at least one important way in which Buddhists will mark themselves off from proponents and practitioners of other religions or ideologies. . . . [T]hen Buddhism cannot so easily be regarded as a religion focused on specific doctrinal content. Rather it is the forms followed by Buddhists, from invoking he Buddha, to building stapes, to sitting in mediation, to seeking the middle way, that define it. (237)

His interpretation of the Buddhist path as an approach to life that is "aesthetic" is important, because it helps us break through our mental and linguistic projections, our subjective profile of the world couched in doctrinal terms. By aesthetic, Jackson means "a way of employing myths, symbols, metaphors, and rituals to reform habitual patterns of thought and behavior, conform to reality as it truly may be, perform our lives in the most meaningful possible way, and, perhaps, transform ourselves from 'bound' to 'liberated' beings" (237).

That the focus on practice, based on the somatic, fills a spiritual void is evident in the proliferation of Buddhist meditation centers – Vipassanā, Tibetan, Chan or Zen, and their American variants, such as the Insight Meditation Centers – and the range of practitioners, including Buddhist aspirants, Catholic monks and lay, Jews, atheists, agnostics, and psychotherapists. While people are entitled to their own reasons for pursuing meditative practices, even those off-center, the ultimate purpose of orthopraxy must be made clear by Buddhist theologians: realization of a decentered self liberated from any conceptualized notions of self and non-self, form and emptiness, *saṃsāra* and *nirvāṇa*, such that wisdom and compassion may be manifested in one's life.

The centering on the body, as Sara McClintock states, may help us avoid confusing the awakening to ultimate reality as the nullifying of all relative realities, including gender, class, and race, which has insidious consequences. In fact, the opposite is true, for relative realities are ultimately to be affirmed in their distinctiveness. It also helps us see through all forms of arbitrary distinctions, such as the mind-body duality which is a "mythology" (Staal: 62), undermining, for example, the hierarchical division into mind-transcendence-male and body-immanence-women. The aim of religious practice is for the whole person, mental and physical, to achieve tonus – a supple, pliant body supporting a gentle, open mind. This is the promise fulfilled in the thirty-third vow of the *Larger Sukhāvatūvyuha Sūtra*.

McClintock's extension of the body beyond its traditional boundaries is suggestive, especially in our age of heightened ecological concerns. She believes that the five *skandhas* of Abhidharma may be expanded "to create a world where mountains, rivers, oceans, trees, and even other sentient beings, are understood to be part of our form *skandha*, and are protected with the same tenacity with which we protect the physical bodies that we presently count as our own" (270). In the same vein the transformation experienced in Tantra may have far-reaching implications: "When the pure or impure illusory body is created, it is not the case that just the body arises; rather the entire mandala residence with all its residents also arises" (268–269).

This interpretation accords with traditional Buddhist thought, but its possibilities were never fully developed. If this is so, we discover another major agenda for Buddhist theology: to work out in detail the implications of form *skandha* and the Tantric body as fundamental to the web of life. How this is related to the creative endeavors of the ecofeminism of Rosemary Ruether (cosmic Christology) and Sallie McFague (universe as God's body) also requires clarification. An increasing number of Christian theologians are moving away from the duality, hierarchy, and mind-body bifurcation that has been part of the their legacy (see Ruether; McFague).

Related to the somatic and the experiential is the tension that exists between theory and practice, doctrine and contemplative knowledge. In so-called Buddhology this tension is non-existent for obvious reasons, but in Buddhist theology it plays a major role, both in our scholarship and in our teaching.[6] Historically this tension has existed in the various schools of Buddhism. B. Alan Wallace describes one such case in his article on religious belief and contemplative knowledge. He informs us that in the case of Tibetan Buddhism, the tension exits between the rationally-oriented dGe lugs order and the empirically-oriented rNying ma order. Both, however, according to the author, ultimately agree to "unmediated realization of ultimate reality as the goal of contemplative practice" (207–208). We can cite other examples, but for Buddhist theology this tension will be at the heart of the professional life – the challenge to balance reason and experience, critical analysis and faith commitment.

This tension appears as a real hermeneutical problem when working with texts on meditative practices. Although objective studies of Buddhist meditation is the accepted norm in academia, it is hard to conceive of research on this subject without some recourse to experiential knowledge. Careful textual and philological studies are indispensable for Buddhist theology, but so are critical reflections on meditative experiences. Even the social sciences are now moving from representational knowledge to relational knowledge and even in some cases to reflective knowledge (see Park).

Here we might turn to a classic example in East Asian Buddhism which balances practice and theory, experiential knowledge and doctrinal understanding. According to Chih-i of the T'ien-t'ai school,

> Although religious practice implies progressive movement, there is no advancing without *prajñā*. The guidance of *prajñā* would not be authentic unless it is based on true reality. The eyes of true wisdom together with the feet of true practice lead to the realm of coolness and serenity. Thus, understanding is the basis of practice, and practice completes *prajñā*. (*Fa-hua-hsüan-i*, Taishō Tripiṭaka 33: 715b17–18)

Religious practice must be guided by the teaching of *prajñā* wisdom; this is equivalent to the first of the three stages of Yogācāra awakening, *prayogika-nirvikalpa-jñāna*. One has yet to attain *prajñā*, but practice eventually leads to the awakening to true reality, *mūla-jñāna*, and to manifesting *prajñā* in the relative world, the third stage called *tat-pṛṣṭha-labdha-jñāna* (wisdom acquired after awakening to true reality). Thus, "understanding is the basis of *practice*, and *practice* completes *prajñā*."

In East Asian Buddhism the analogy of the spear, with its shaft and spearhead, is used to explain the relationship between experiential knowledge and doctrinal understanding. If one possesses the shaft (doctrine) with the spearhead missing (experience), it is useless. If, on the other hand, one plays only with the spearhead but has no shaft, it can be lethal. Likewise, the emphasis on scripture, doctrine, reason, and analysis alone, disregarding the experiential will not lead to productive results; but at the same time personal experience, insight, and embodiment without some knowledge of the different levels and potential dangers in meditative practice can prove to be counterproductive.

Scholars who do research on Buddhism without any experience are like people who embrace only the shaft and consider it sufficient to know how the spear works. Their studies would be advanced by considering some first-hand experiences which enrich, provide context, and enhance the research. On the other hand, Buddhist practitioners who know only the experiential and downplay the rational are like children playing only with the spearhead whose sharp point can cause injury to oneself and others. They can learn much from the scholars to avoid delusory experiences and critically evaluate their accomplishments.

The balance between theory and experience is especially

important for historical-critical research. Even if Buddhologists will not seriously consider this problem, Buddhist theologians must demonstrate its significance. By so doing, it may eventually influence scholars of Buddhist Studies who have personal investment and, in some cases, considerable monastic experiences, to include the experiential dimension as part of their "objective" approach. Buddhist scholarship in the true sense requires the inclusion of religious practice and its implications for historical understanding. Contemporary Biblical scholarship, according to Vesna Wallace, study Christian texts in relation to the reader or the receiving community. Although this may not have always been true, this approach places religious texts in their proper context. The exclusive reliance on texts, open to the hermeneutics of suspicion, is inadequate to fully appreciate them. In order to minimize misinterpretations and errors in historical-critical studies, the texts must be studied together with those who live by it.

Where such a community cannot be easily identified, whether in the past or present, as in the case of the *prajñāpāramitā sūtra*s, we must recognize it for what it is, that it is a guidebook to meditative practice and not a philosophical treatise. In this case we need to adopt the practitioner's stance by using the hermeneutical method suggested by Gadamer: "The understanding of a text has not begun at all as long as the text remains mute. . . . When it does begin to speak, however, it does not simply speak its word, always the same, in lifeless rigidity, but gives ever new answers to the person who questions it and poses ever new questions to him who answers it. To understand a text is to come to understand oneself in a kind of dialogue" (Gadamer: 57).

(II)

For the first time in world history the rich variety of Buddhist schools and denominations together with their foundational scriptures, as well as national expressions of Buddhist life, beliefs, customs, practices and world-views, are converging in the West, especially in North America. One of the tasks of the Buddhist theologian is to remain open to all of them, while probing deeply into the singular path of personal commitment and speaking out from within its center.

Unlike in Religions of the Book – Judaism, Christianity, and Islam – scripture in Buddhism does not have the same kind of sacrosanct authority. This is because of the centrality of religious practice whose purpose is to embody the teaching contained in scripture.[7] Since Mahāyāna scriptures encode experiences of enlightened beings or Buddhas, the practitioner's responsibility is to decode, internalize, and manifest the teaching in their own being. This, of course, is the ideal for practitioners. For others in the receiving community, for example, of the *Lotus Sūtra*, the five basic practices can be undertaken by anyone: upholding the scripture, reading, reciting, interpreting and copying it. Here, too, the bodily appropriation of the teaching is the goal.[8]

When Buddhist scriptures from India were translated into Chinese, the problem of understanding them was particularly acute, since the reader was confronted not only with strange, fantastic imageries and countless foreign names of buddhas and bodhisattvas but with a vocabulary rich in Sanskrit allusions. Even more confusing was the chaotic array of Buddhist scriptures, both Hīnayāna and Mahāyāna, introduced at random, disregarding the order of their appearance in the homeland. How to interpret the *sūtras* became a challenge for Buddhist practitioners from the earliest beginnings of Chinese Buddhism.

Just to take one example, the voluminous *Avataṃsaka Sūtra*, first translated into Chinese by Buddhabhadra between 418-420 CE, made little sense to the people until Tu-shun (557-640) composed a guidebook to meditative practice based on the contents of the scripture.[9] The result was a slim work, *Fa-chieh-kuan-men* ("Contemplation of *Dharmadhātu*"),[10] which outlines the stages of insight and provides an indigenous vocabulary for Buddhism, such as, *shih* for *rūpa* and *li* for *śūnyatā*. As Yuki Reimon first pointed out, his accomplishment was threefold: first, it was a native Chinese approach to enlightenment; second, it was equal, if not superior, to the Indian path; and third, it was in accord with the basic teaching of the Buddha.

Thus, while being almost unknown in history and leaving only one slim work, Tu-shun is considered to be the founder of the Hua-yen school, in spite of the fact that illustrious monk-scholars and translators, such as Buddhabhadra, were connected with this tradition before him. A comparable case can be made for the founders of other Chinese Buddhist schools, but the primary fact is that religious practice was the decisive factor. The focus on orthopraxy also laid the foundation for the *p'an-chiao*, the classification of doctrines, which was initially not a simple catalogue of schools but organized with progressive stages of practice in mind.

The efficacy of practice also is one of the turning points in Japanese Buddhism which undergoes transformation in the medieval period. Unlike the complex disciplines of Tendai and Shingon esotericism, the singularity of *nembutsu* practice first advocated by Hōnen (1133-1212) assured a simple but effective method to attaining enlightenment for anyone, including women and men of all classes, defrocked monks and nuns, and people considered "bad" – the illiterate, the unsophisticated, the violators of precepts – in the eyes of privileged society. The single-minded nembutsu penetrated the heart of Buddhist experience that had been obscured by the magico-religious practices of the existing orders. Utterly simple but supremely effective, because recitative nembutsu was not a human activity but the enlightened working of Amida Buddha in one's life. Hōnen's disciple, Shinran (1173-1263), clarified the internal dynamics of this practice, demonstrating the breadth and depth of Mahāyāna Buddhism compressed into it. This forms the basis of his classification of doctrine which distinguishes the multiple paths of Buddhism according to the efficacy of a given path.

The complexity that challenges us in the West is not only the great variety of Mahāyāna scriptures but the range of religious paths based upon them – Theravāda, Vajrayāna, Tendai, Shingon, Zen, Pure Land, Nichiren, Nichiren Shōshu, Risshō Kōseikai, Western Buddhist Order, and so on – as well as the broad spectrum of ethnic and cultural variations – Chinese, Korean, Japanese, Tibetan, Sinhalese, Vietnamese, Thai, Cambodian, Laotian, Burmese, etc.

This great variety should be welcomed and celebrated. While some may choose to follow the lower path to authenticity, making exclusive claims to orthodoxy and truth, it is the higher path that engages Buddhist theology. Without absolutizing any single path, we need to remain open to what is normative until Buddhist roots sink deeply into the Western soil and produce its own shoots. The task is summed up by John Makransky:

> The purpose of this critique, then, is to argue for a new appreciation of the tremendous wealth of methods for and perspectives upon awakening bequeathed to us from diverse, culturally specific communities of practice experience, as Buddhism and our culture enter a process of mutual transformation. . . . Another purpose is to demonstrate the inevitability of new authentic embodiments and expressions of Dharma in our culture, emergent now and in the future, as a phenomena in long continuity with the ancient process of ongoing (never closable) Mahāyāna revelation that has always been specific to time and space. (113)

He proposes that liberation from all systematic schemata, not only sectarian assumptions, but the contemporary rhetoric of critical method. This openness will enable Buddhism in the West to also embrace and develop significant trends not found in past Asian Buddhism – feminist issues, environmental concerns, interreligious dialogue, and the psychotherapeutic. Buddhist theology has the tremendous responsibility to insure that this be something more than just putting new wine into old wineskins.

(III)

The culmination of religious practice is the embodiment of non-self and emptiness, manifested as the vast web of interdependence and interconnectedness. This is not a static world but a universe of dynamic becoming; another challenge for Buddhist theology is to formulate its application to the basic issues confronting humanity today. The following takes up selected topics found in the contributions to this volume which offer a preliminary agenda for Buddhists theology to consider.

David Loy points to one possible direction for Buddhist theology to explore and to grow which he calls "Western Buddhist psychology." His analysis of *lack* leads ultimately to the world of interdependence. He writes,

> According to Buddhism, letting-go of myself and merging with that no-thing-ness leads to something else: when consciousness stops trying to catch its own tail, I become no-thing and discover that I am everything – or, more precisely, that I can be anything. . . . If each link of *pratītya-samutpāda* is conditioned by all others, then to become completely groundless is also to become completely grounded, not in some particular but in the whole network of interdependent relations that constitute the world. (164)

The potential to develop the implications of interdependent relations is endless, but one of its immediate application might be the question of human rights.

Sallie King's careful analysis of human rights from the Buddhist perspective is thought provoking. Rather than talking about rights from the traditional, adversarial position, she proposes the Buddhist alternative of an inter-active, non-adversarial approach to human rights. Instead of talking about rights or obligations, she chooses "mutual obligation" based on interdependence. And she concludes: "Given that for Buddhists the basic reality of life is our mutual interdependence, our pervasive interconnectedness, it is unnatural and unproductive in the extreme to draw a line between individuals and groups" (295). The question, however, that needs an answer is: how does one deal with the self-interest that drives people in all cultures?

Interdependence is also the philosophical basis of a mutually productive dialogue that Judith Simmer-Brown discusses. She critically examines four possible dialogical models and gives two ideal examples. First is the famous Zen *mondō* between Kyōzan and Sanshō, where the latter first claims the former's name for himself, and when challenged, voices his own name. Here we find interchangeability based on a true interdependent relationship; that is, when one negates the self for the sake of another, one comes alive in the other; simultaneously, when one negates the other, the other is brought to life within the self. Here again the problem of self-interest surfaces, when one actually begins to put this into practice.

Nevertheless, this interrelationship forms the field of compassion, as classically enunciated in the *Bodhicaryāvatāra*: the exchange of self for other. This is also elemental for the practice of compassion in Jōdo-shinshū or Shin Buddhism, as Kenneth Tanaka explains in his article. He expands on one of the ten benefits of Shin life, "constant practice of compassion" (*jōgyō-daihi*), but as Galen Amstutz points out in his recent work, compassion in Shin Buddhism has been the driving force behind its immense social and political influence in Japanese history. Beginning with the founder, Shinran, Shin Buddhism has sided with the oppressed classes during most of its history of 700 years.[11] Here, however, is a question for Shin Buddhists: What happened to its prophetic stance in the modern period? Can its positive contribution to society be given new life again?

Simmer-Brown's second example of dialogical encounter is the story of Tilopa and Nāropa. This is an encounter with the Other at a deeper level, touching on spiritual transformation. The Other in the case of Nāropa was the neglected, overshadowed, and suppressed darkness within, appearing in the form of an old hag. Nāropa's liberation came when he claimed this negative Other as his very own. He was now open to his guru Tilopa to accept his teaching.

A similar insight is offered by Mark Unno in the context of non-duality, relative and absolute truth, and karmic limitations. He gives us a summary of three cases of Western virtue theorists and their respective strategies to coping with postmodernity: Alasdair MacIntyre (conservative retreat), Charles Taylor (progressive reform), and Jeffrey Stout (constructive bricolage). They manifest tendencies which might also be identified in two Buddhist thinkers of medieval Japan, Dōgen (1200-1253) and Myōe Kōben (1173-1232), who also contended with the changing times and multiple demands of their age. As they did so as Mahāyāna Buddhists, they saw the diverse intellectual currents as "streams within the critical synergy where knowledge of the other in emptiness enlarges one's world and refines one's understanding." (188)

As an example, Unno cites Dōgen's famous line, "Flowers fall amid our grudging and weeds flourish in our chagrin," not as a sign of delusory attachment obstructing one's path but as a moment of deepening awareness of emptiness:

> There is a complementary relationship between attachment and awakening; without the former, the latter does not take place. Becoming one with attachment to the flower in the present is inseparable from the illumination of emptiness that brings that attachment into focus, simultaneously resolving and dissolving the experience of the flower in the field of emptiness. (188)

Myōe Kōben of the Kegon School, one of the most highly esteemed figures in Japanese Buddhist history, responded to the demands of the period by devising bold, imaginative forms of practices. But he also confronted the limits of his own discursive consciousness which prompted further spiritual transformations.

> The recognition of his own karmic limitations comes out of his attempts to meet the needs of the people of his time, and one senses in his voice the critical synergy of his bodhisattva-like creativity and his flawed humanity, a synthesis that renders him more fully human in a positive sense. (196)

In that moment of awareness of his karmic limitations, the non-duality of emptiness transformed karmic bondage to karmic freedom.

Buddhist theology here becomes not simply another academic exercise but a kind of religious practice unto itself. I wonder how does this would mesh with Christian theology, quoted by Mahinda Deegalle, as a "secondary form of praxis and culture consisting in more or less critical reflection on a particular religion" (339)?

Another aspect of religious life in a world of interdependence is also found in the personal account given by Rita Gross, who embraces finitude, sin, and evil as ultimately liberating. She tells us that in contrast to Western religions which heretofore has stressed transcendence of the body and the earth, the Buddhist tradition has affirmed this world which in personal terms mean finitude, sin, and evil. The affirmation is made within the world in which one discovers significance in the Other, the very opposite of one's ideal. Gross notes that the theologians Carol Christ and Rosemary Ruether are also critical of the one-sided emphasis on transcendence in traditional Christianity and affirm finitude which is none other than embracing our earth, the only way to create a responsible environmental ethics. Here is another area of Buddhist theology that might be developed in concert with Christian theologians. The question that requires clarification is what is the ultimate status of finitude and evil as experienced by the faithful in Buddhism and in Christianity?

We have touched on various possible agenda for Buddhist theology, but we need to turn to some basic question concerning interdependence or interconnectedness. The question is the validity of transferring a Buddhist concept, *pratītya-samutpāda*, and applying it to the multiple possibilities in the postmodern world – religious, philosophical, social, scientific, and so on. I raise this question by turning to a basic problem facing American society today, excessive individualism. It should be noted that excessive individualism is not only American but is endemic in all societies where self-interest is the only value upheld. In the famous study by Robert Bellah and his colleagues, *Habits of the Heart*, they state:

> The question is whether individualism in which the self has become the main form of reality can really be sustained. What is at issue is not simply whether self-contained individuals might withdraw from the public sphere to pursue private ends, but whether such individuals are capable of sustaining either a public or private life. If this is the danger, perhaps only the civic and biblical forms of individualism – forms that see the individual in relation to a larger whole, a community and a tradition – are capable of sustaining genuine individuality and nurturing both public and private life. (Bellah: 143).

The authors seek to revive a genuine individuality in relation to a greater whole, either a community (civic) or a tradition (biblical), that would respect and nurture both public and private life. What would be the Buddhist alternative to establishing such and individuality?

One possible starting point might be to consider the contrasting views of self described by Kawai Hayao, the pioneer Jungian analyst in Japan. In his work, *Buddhism and the Art of Psychotherapy*, he writes:

> The premise of modern individuality is to establish the ego first. In the young adult stage, ego will be the existence which is independent of others and equipped with initiative and integration. Reaching adulthood means that you have established your own identity. Ego which is established in such a manner will develop one's individuality. . . . Human beings

> in Buddhism, as so well clarified by Hua-yen thought, exists in relationship. When taken out of relationship, a person loses "self-nature" and thus cease to exist. . . . Accordingly, if one tries to respect one's own eachness, one has to be aware of others before contemplating her-his own independence. (Kawai: 108)

The author coins a new word, "eachness," to denote the self arising from the nexus of interconnectedness; it is synonymous with "suchness" (*tattva, tathatā*) in Buddhist vocabulary. Can we apply Hua-yen thought to address the issue of excessive individualism addressed by Bellah? The contrast between modern Western individuality and the Buddhist view of self may be valid in a sense, but questions must be raised for three reasons.

The first is the undeniable fact that a vast and profound world view not found in the West lies behind Hua-yen interdependence. By this I mean not only the complex evolution of Buddhist doctrines of non-self, emptiness and dependent co-origination leading to Hua-yen thought (which have yet to be fully analyzed) but the organismic conception of Chinese life from which it emerges. Roger Ames spells out its basic parameters:

> The separateness implicit in dualistic explanations of relationships conduces to an essentialistic interpretation of the world, a world of "things" characterized by discreteness, finality, closedness, determinateness, independence, a world in which one thing is related to the "other" extrinsically. By contrast, a polar explanation of relationships gives rise to an organismic interpretation of the world, a world of "processes" characterized as interconnectedness, interdependence, openness, mutuality, indeterminateness, complementarity, correlativity, coextensiveness, a world in which continuous processes are related to the other intrinsically. (Ames: 160)

How can such an organismic view of life be transmitted simply by recourse to using the term interdependence? How can we give it greater depth, scope and resilience to meet our needs today?

The second is the fact that the notion of self in the Western world is constantly undergoing change. Recent trends, for example, in the social sciences, including system thinking, seem to be approaching something similar to the interdependence of Hua-yen. To cite just one instant, Kenneth Gergen observes in his *Saturated Self*:

> As the self as a serious reality is laid to rest and the self is constructed and reconstructed in multiple contexts, one enters finally the stage of the relational self. One's sense of individual autonomy gives way to a reality of immersed interdependence, in which it is relationship that constructs the self. (Gergen: 147)

How different is this from what Kawai has said about Hua-yen interdependence and the formation of selfhood?

The third and most problematic is how Hua-yen, basically a soteriological system, can be transformed directly into concrete ethical action to implement real changes in the world. Constant references are made to the Hua-yen metaphor of Indra's net in environmental literature (e.g., in Tucker and Williams), and I find no problems with it, but my question is: Can it be translated immediately into an effective social policy? Being a soteriological system, the crucial factor in interdependence is the negation of the ego-self. We finds this negation implicit in each *adhigama-dharma* – "form is emptiness, emptiness is form" – but in Hua-yen the negation occurs between countless phenomenal *dharmas*.

I have also raised this question about the contemporary appropriation of Hua-yen elsewhere (Unno 1997), but it is not to disparage the efforts of conscientious Buddhist thinkers to develop an ecological ethics based on Hua-yen thought. Rather, it is to alert Buddhist theologians to one of many challenges that await them – making viable a pre-modern system of thought in a postmodern world – and hope that they can respond effectively to meet the needs of people everywhere. The first steps in that direction appear in this volume, and hopefully it will stimulate more thinking and reflection, so that Buddhist theology becomes a significant enterprise that might contribute to the well-being of all sentient existence.

NOTES

1 See especially the discussions on the term "theology" by Roger Jackson ("Editors' Introduction"), José Cabezón ("Buddhist Theology in the Academy"), Rita Gross ("Buddhist Theology?"), and Roger Corless.

2 From the original proposal for this volume, "The Need and Purpose of Buddhist 'Theology,'" p. 2.

3 Slawson's Ph.D. dissertation has been published (1987). He trained under Nakane Kinsaku of Kyoto and has built Japanese gardens at Carleton, Smith, Murray State and Hanover Colleges, as well as sites

in Aspen, Cleveland, etc.

4 The latter book grew out of our monthly religion seminar, sponsored by Radius Institute and chaired by Peter Berger, in New York City from 1978-1980. The purpose was to find the relationship to the transcendent in religions originating in India and in the Near East.

5 The broad range of Buddhist practice includes the Pure Land tradition which seeks to embody and manifest the Buddha Dharma in everyday life. The difference between Christian faith and Pure Land Buddhism has been accurately pointed out by Roger Corless (101–102). This becomes obvious, when we contrast the parable of the prodigal son in Luke 15: 11-32 and the parallel story in Chapter 4 of the *Lotus Sūtra*. The latter involves progressive stages of awakening, whereas the former is a matter of forgiveness. For the process involved in Shin experience, see Unno 1990: 41–49.

6 The tension would be greater for a scholar at a major research university and less so for a teacher at an undergraduate institution, such as Smith College. The Ada Howe Kent Program at Smith is funded solely for bringing to campus practitioners of world religions, especially Buddhism, to add to the educational experience of the students.

7 According to José Ignacio Cabezón, "The Buddhists, not concerned as much with the origins of scripture as with the transmission and internalization of the doctrine it contains, pose the question in pragmatic and dynamic terms: how can the soteriologically valid experiences of an enlightened individual, experiences that – by virtue of being mental states – are non-material, be coded into a material medium, language, and then decoded as the mental states of the adept" (1994: 32).

8 Copying, for example, involves quiet sitting, rhythmical rubbing of ink stone to ink slab, production of ink with right texture, proper posture, arms raised in mid-air, swift movement of brush with *ki* flowing out of its tip.

9 Two other translations followed: the 80-fascicle *Avataṃsaka Sūtra* translated by Śikṣānanda between 695 and 699 and the *Gaṇḍavyūha* section by Prajñā between 795 and 798.

10 There are some controversies regarding the authorship of this text; nevertheless, its historical impact on the Hua-yen school cannot be denied. For details, see Gregory: 10–15.

11 In all East Asian culture Shin Buddhism probably provides the strongest potential point of contact via its politics of egalitarianism, its rationalism and its universalism (not to mention the resemblances between Mahāyāna epistemology and modern Western theories of knowledge). So far the orientalist interests of the Western intelligentsia in exotic, nonsectarian, and individualistic ideas of religion have outweighed their appreciation of the social and political effectiveness of Shin" (Amstutz: 121).

REFERENCES

Ames, Roger (1993). "The Meaning of Body in Classical Chinese Philosophy." In Thomas Kasulis et al., eds., *Self as Body in Asian Thought and Practice.* Albany: State University of New York Press.

Amstutz, Galen (1997). *Interpreting Amida: History and Orientalism in the Study of Pure Land Buddhism.* (Albany: State University of New York Press.

Bellah, Robert et al. (1988). *Habits of the Heart: Individualism and Commitment in American Life.* New York: Harper and Row.

Berger, Peter (1967). *Sacred Canopy: Elements of a Sociological Theory of Religion.* New York: Doubleday.

Cabezón, José Ignacio (1994). *Buddhism and Language.* Albany: State University of New York Press,

Gadamer, Hans Georg (1976). *Philosophical Hermeneutics.* Berkeley: University of California Press.

Gergen, Kenneth (1991). *The Saturated Self.* New York: Basic Books.

Gregory, Peter (1991). *Tsung-mi and the Sinification of Buddhism.* Princeton: Princeton University Press.

James, William (1955). *Essays in Pragmatism.* New York: Hafner Publishing Co.

James, William (1990). *Varieties of Religious Experience.* New York: Vintage Books Edition.

Kawai, Hayao (1996). *Buddhism and the Art of Psychotherapy.* College Station: Texas A & M University Press.

McFague, Sallie (1993). *The Body of God: An Ecological Theology.* Minneapolis: Fortress Press.

Park, Peter et al., eds. (1993). *Voices of Change: Participatory Research in the United States and Canada.* Westport, CT: Bergen and Garvey.

Ruether, Rosemary Radford (1992). *Gaia and God: An Ecofeminist Theology of Earth Healing.* San Francisco: Harper SanFrancisco.

Slawson, David (1987). *The Secret Teachings of the Art of Japanese Gardens.* New York: Kodansha International.

Slawson, David (1996). "Authenticity in Japanese Landscape Design." Unpublished paper.

Staal, Frits (1993). "Indian Bodies." In Thomas Kasulis et al., eds., *Self as Body in Asian Theory and Practice.* Albany, State University of New York Press.

Tucker, Mary Evelyn and Duncan Ryuken Williams (1997). *Buddhism and Ecology.* Cambridge: Harvard Center for the Study of World Religions.

Unno Taitetsu (1990). "Interior Practice in Shin Buddhism," *The Pacific World,* n.s, (6; Fall 1990) 41–49.

Unno, Taitetsu (1997). "Hua-yen Vision of Interdependence: A Cross-Cultural Perspective." In *Kegon-gaku ronshū: Festschrift in Honor of Kamata Shigeo.* Tokyo: Daizō Shuppan.

Contributors

José Ignacio Cabezón teaches philosophy at the Iliff School of Theology in Denver. His most recent book is *Scholasticism: Cross-Cultural Perspectives.* He was a monk in the Tibetan tradition from 1977 to 1985, during which time he was affiliated principally with the Byes College of Se ra in South India. At present, his main religious affiliation is the Buddhist-Christian Contemplative Group, which he co-founded with the Rev. Toni Cook in Denver in 1996.

Roger Corless teaches in the Department of Religion at Duke University. His specialty is the Pure Land tradition. He has published four books and more than fifty articles on Buddhism, Christian spirituality, and Buddhist-Christian dialogue. He is a co-founder of the Society for Buddhist-Christian Studies.

Mahinda Deegalle is a Research Fellow at the Japan Society for the Promotion of Science and Aichi Gakuin University, Aichi, Japan. His current research focuses on Mahāyāna Buddhism in Sri Lanka and New Religions in Japan. His previous research was on Buddhist preaching (*baṇa*) traditions in Sri Lanka.

John D. Dunne, who has recently received his Ph.D. from Harvard University, is currently a research fellow at the University of Lausanne, Switzerland. Much of his current work focuses on Buddhist attempts to develop a nonessentialist philosophy of language. Although he has had the pleasure of studying Buddhism under numerous traditional teachers, he recalcitrantly practices Buddhism in his own haphazard way.

Luis O. Gómez teaches Buddhist Studies at the University of Michigan, in the Department of Asian Languages and Cultures and in the Program on Studies in Religion; he also is Adjunct Professor of Psychology. His publications focus primarily on Buddhism in India, early Chan in China and Tibet, and issues of method in the study of religion. He is co-editor of *Borobudur: History and Significance of a*

Monument, and author of *The Land of Bliss*, a translation of the *Sukhāvatīvyūha Sūtras*.

Rita M. Gross teaches comparative religion in the Department of Philosophy and Religious studies at the University of Wisconsin-Eau Claire. She is the author of *Buddhism After Patriarchy: A Feminist History, Analysis, and Reconstruction of Buddhism.* Currently, she is doing research for a major book on goddesses in historical, comparative, and theological perspectives, and writing a popular book, *Why Buddhism is Good for Women and Other Living Beings.* She is affiliated with Shambhala Meditation Centers, founded by Chögyam Trungpa, Rinpoche, and is a senior teacher in that denomination of Buddhism.

Roger R. Jackson teaches South Asian religions in the Department of Religion at Carleton College, Northfield, MN. He is the author of *Is Enlightenment Possible?* and co-editor of *Tibetan Literature: Studies in Genre.* His current research focuses on Mahāmudrā in Indian and Tibetan Buddhism, and on the works of the *mahāsiddha* Saraha. He has studied and practiced primarily in the dGe lugs tradition of Tibetan Buddhism.

Sallie B. King teaches in the Department of Philosophy and Religion at James Madison University in Harrisonburg, VA. Her books include *Journey in Search of the Way* and (with Christopher Queen) *Engaged Buddhism.* Her current research interests include the translation of Zen awakening stories of Japanese women, and analysis of the social ethics of Engaged Buddhism. She has studied primarily in the East Asian Zen tradition.

David R. Loy teaches in the Faculty of International Studies, Bunkyo University, Chigasaki, Japan. His main research interest is comparative philosophy and religion, especially comparing Buddhism with modern Western thought. He is author of *Nonduality* and *Lack and Transcendence.* He has practiced Zen in the Sanbō Kyōdan tradition, and is qualified as a Zen sensei.

John J. Makransky teaches Buddhism and Comparative Theology at Boston College. He is the author of *Buddhahood Embodied: Sources of Controversy in India and Tibet.* His current research focuses on the influence of diverse Mahāyāna practices upon developing doctrines of Buddhahood. He practices within the rNying ma, dGe lugs, and bKa' rgyud traditions of Tibetan Buddhism.

Sara McClintock is a doctoral candidate in the Study of Religion at Harvard University. Her research interests include Buddhist epistemology and the limits of knowledge. She has studied with a number of Japanese, Indian, Tibetan, and American teachers of Buddhism.

Judith Simmer-Brown teaches in the Religious Studies department at The Naropa Institute, in Boulder, Colorado. Her scholarly work has been in Tibetan Tantra and Buddhist-Christian dialogue, and her Buddhist training has been in the bKa' brgyud and rNying ma schools of Tibetan Buddhism.

Kenneth K. Tanaka teaches at Musashino Women's University, Hoya-shi, Tokyo. He is author of *The Dawn of Chinese Pure Land Buddhist Doctrine.* His current research is focused on Jōdo Shinshū Buddhist "theology" and Pure Land Buddhism. He belongs to the Jōdo Shinshū tradition.

Mark T. Unno teaches in the Department of Religion at Carleton College, Northfield, MN. His current research focuses on the Kōmyō Shingon, or Mantra of Light, as presented and practiced by the Kegon and Shingon monk Myōe Kōben. He has studied primarily in the Pure Land and Zen traditions of Japanese Buddhism.

Taitetsu Unno teaches in the departments of Religion and East Asian Studies at Smith College. He is currently writing a sequel to *River Of Fire, River Of Water: An Introduction To The Pure Land Tradition Of Shin Buddhism,* and preparing a translation of *Hua-Yen Wu-Chiao-Chang* for publication. He belongs to the Nishi Hongwanji Branch of Shin Buddhism.

B. Alan Wallace teaches in the Department of Religious Studies at the University of California, Santa Barbara. He is author or translator of numerous books, most recently *The Bridge of Quiescence*. His current research focuses on the rDzogs chen tradition of Tibetan Buddhism and on the interface between Tibetan Buddhism and the natural sciences. He has formal training in the dGe lugs and rNying ma traditions of Tibetan Buddhism and in physics and the philosophy of science.

Vesna A. Wallace teaches in the Department of Religious Studies at the University of California, Santa Barbara. Her current research is in the area of Indian tantric Buddhism; she has focused in particular on the Kālacakra Tantra. She has also studied the Tibetan dGe lugs and rNying ma traditions.